CRYPTOLOGY
Yesterday, Today, and Tomorrow

I. B. Friderici CRYPTOGRAPHIA

oder

Kunst geheime Schrifften zu machen und auffzulösen;

wie auch durch allerhand Zeichen, nah und fern, gewissen Personen seine Meinung verborgener weise zu entdecken.

CRYPTOLOGY
Yesterday, Today, and Tomorrow

Artech House

Cipher A. Deavours
David Kahn
Louis Kruh
Greg Mellen
Brian Winkel

Library of Congress Cataloging-in-Publication Data

Cryptology yesterday, today, and tomorrow.

1. Cryptography. 2. Ciphers. I. Deavours, Cipher A.
Z103.C76 1987 652'.8 87-14396
ISBN 0-89006-253-6

Copyright © 1987

ARTECH HOUSE, INC.
685 Canton Street
Norwood, MA 02062

International Standard Book Number: 0-89006-253-6
Library of Congress Catalog Card Number: 87-14396

10 9 8 7 6 5 4 3 2 1

Contents

Introduction
by David Kahn

Late in the afternoon of June 9, 1975, I arrived at the beautifully furnished art déco apartment of Cipher and Angela Deavours on Manhattan's Central Park West. Cipher and I were to go to a get-together of cryptologists in New York for the sessions on data encryption at the National Computer Conference. Brian Winkel, a mathematician interested in cryptology, whom I had just met the day before, was present. As he and Cipher chatted, they referred to a magazine on cryptology that they were planning to publish. Cipher had come up with the idea and written about it to Brian, whose name he had seen in *The Cryptogram*, the organ of the American Cryptogram Association.

My ears perked up because I had long been frustrated by the meager opportunities to publish serious historical articles on cryptology. *The Cryptogram* had neither the space nor the interest; it focused on "how-to-solve-it" articles, cryptogram-solving being the primary interest of its readers. The scholarly journals seemed unwelcoming, if not disdainful; they had not yet awakened to the importance of intelligence. Cipher's letter to Brian showed that the situation was the same for mathematicians and other cryptologists, who wanted to take the science beyond the puzzle level of *The Cryptogram*.

For years, I had thoughts—no doubt like many others—of editing a magazine on cryptology that would correct these faults, fill these gaps, but—also like the others—I had not gone beyond daydreams. Now, Ci and Brian were actually going to do something. I longed to join them in their venture, but I was hesitant. It was their idea, and I did not want to butt in on their venture. Finally, however, the desire to participate in something I had long wanted overcame my diffidence, and I asked whether I might join them. To my delight, they seemed pleased, and said they would be happy to have me. At the same time, they asked Lou Kruh to join.

So we began. Articles came in, were edited, and were sent to California to be assembled into a magazine that was printed and distributed. After a couple of years, we became our own publisher, changing the magazine's format, and the brunt of the work fell on Brian, who has borne it capably ever since. Several years later, Greg Mellen also became a co-editor.

Cryptologia's goal has been to publish the best it could in historical and scientific articles. The magazine's survival and success testifies to its fulfilling a need. Cryptology continues to grow and to advance, and *Cryptologia* has kept pace. In its first decade, it has printed many pathbreaking articles. The better ones are assembled here.

In an anthology more unified than most, these articles carry the science from the past to the future. This collection, *Cryptology Yesterday, Today and Tomorrow*, has three parts. Simply, they may be regarded as the historical, the mechanical, and the mathematical. Each part contributes to the understanding of what cryptology is today and where it may be going tomorrow. Among the highlights of each part are these:

Part I, "History, Literature, and Personalities," opens with Louis Kruh's persuasive conclusion that the invention of the multiplex cipher at the beginning of the 19th century by Thomas Jefferson and its reinvention at the end of that century by Etienne Bazeries were both inspired by a cylindrical combination lock using letters devised by Edmé Regnier. Kruh reveals that someone other than Herbert O. Yardley wrote the book of cryptogram puzzles called *Yardleygrams*, but concludes that Yardley wrote *The American Black Chamber*. This writer amplifies and corrects many of the statements in that classic of cryptology. John Lundstrom provides a valuable corrective to all the writings that proclaim the usefulness of codebreaking intelligence by telling of a case in which it did not help.

In Part II, "Machines and their Solutions," Robert Morris tells how to establish the lug and pin settings of a Hagelin machine, given a portion of the plaintext for a ciphertext. Elliot Fischer proposes a way of defending against Morris' attack. Ronald Rivest uses a formula proposed by Wayne Barker to estimate the quantity of ciphertext needed for solution of an M-209 cryptogram, and Barker solves a later Hagelin device with the help of a crib and a cryptogram overlap. Rotor machines are discussed extensively. James Reeds proposes an algebraic notation for their analysis. Deavours details a solution of a Hebern cryptogram, describes the widely used rod ("*batons*") method of solution, and explains the workings of the British Enigma-solving "*bombes*". The chief German teletypewriter cipher machine of World War II is exposed mechanically, cryptographically, and historically in four articles. Frank Rubin, on the basis of 15 known plaintext characters, solves a cryptogram produced by eight linear feedback shift registers.

Part III, "Mathematics and Cryptanalysis," begins with Deavours' valuable analysis and listing of the lengths of ciphertext in different cipher systems needed for a valid solution. In his two articles, Fischer discusses the complexity of cipher systems, and then proposes that the complexity of a sequence serve as a measure of cryptographic performance. Rivest discusses two pseudorandom sequences as keys. Carl Hammer, with tongue only partly in cheek, wonders whether the mysterious Beale cipher, which might reveal the location of a buried treasure, is of a certain type. Mellen analyzes algebraic digraphic and trigraphic ciphers, while Bruce Schatz and John Carroll and Steve Martin model computer cryptanalysis. In the article that has long been the most requested by readers of *Cryptologia*, Reeds solves a linear congruential random number generator in an analysis applicable to other such generators.

The entire collection, in the humble, if not impartial, opinion of the editors, is a feast of a very high order for the cryptologist. It exceeds by far whatever hopes I may have entertained on that June evening so long ago.

Part I

History, Literature, and Personalities

The Genesis of the Jefferson/Bazeries Cipher Device*
by Louis Kruh

ABSTRACT. Cipher Device M-94 was adopted by the United States Army in 1922, the same year papers found in the Library of Congress revealed that Thomas Jefferson had invented the same device about 125 years earlier.

Almost 100 years after Jefferson, Commandant Etienne Bazeries, a French army cryptologist, independently developed a similar device.

Both inventions, which ultimately formed the basis for the most widely used cryptosystems in the 20th century, apparently had a common antecedent in the letter lock, which was popularized in France by Edme Regnier during the late 18th and early 19th centuries.

DESCRIPTION AND BACKGROUND

The concept behind the cylindrical cipher device adopted by the United States Army under the designation M-94 (Figure 1), and the subsequent flat strip cipher board, M-138-A (Figure 2), which evolved from it, became "one of the most widely used systems in the history of American cryptography."[1] The two devices utilized the identical cryptographic principle; the simultaneous use of a number of different, sliding, mixed alphabets.[2]

The M-94, made of aluminum alloy, consists of a central shaft on which is mounted a set of 25 rotatable alphabet disks. On the rim of each disk is stamped a different, completely disarranged alphabet. Lugs and slots on each side of the disks enable them to be held together side by

From *Cryptologia*, Vol. 5, No. 4, Oct. 1981.
*A version of this article appeared in *The Army Communicator*, Winter 1980, pp. 48–54.

4

FIGURE 1. U.S. ARMY CIPHER DEVICE M-94.

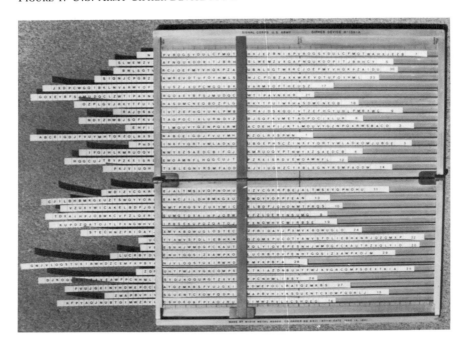

FIGURE 2. CIPHER DEVICE M-138-A (SIMULATED STRIPS).

side in any desired position by tightening the knurled thumb nut at the end of the shaft. Both sender and receiver must have a device.

Each disk has its own identifying symbols, a letter and number on its side. The numbers run from 1–25 and the letters from B–Z. These symbols are used to designate the sequence in which the disks are to be assembled on the shaft. This order constitutes the key which both the encipherer and decipherer must know.

After the encipherer places the disks on the shaft in the prearranged order, he revolves one disk after another to align the first 25 letters of the message in a horizontal row. Then he selects at random any one of the other rows, which will form 25 letters of gibberish, as the ciphertext. He repeats this process in groups of 25 letters to the end of the message.[3]

The decipherer begins the same way. He assembles the disks on the shaft in the order given by the key and then rotates each disk individually until the first 25 letters of ciphertext stand in a row. Then he scans the other rows for the one which will read intelligibly.[4]

The M-138-A works in a similar fashion. The device consists of a hinged aluminum board into which are milled 30 grooved channels. These channels are designed to hold removable paper strips containing randomly mixed alphabets. Each strip has its own mixed alphabet repeated twice and printed in a horizontal row.[5]

The strips, inserted in the channels in a particular order designated by a key, slide from side to side. The encipherer aligns the plaintext letters to read vertically alongside a guide rule which is part of the device. Then he chooses a ciphertext column at random and slides the guide rule adjacent to it for easier copying. This procedure is repeated for the entire message.[6]

The decipherer simply reverses the process after assembling the strips according to the key.[7]

Because the system underlying these devices employs several cipher alphabets, it is a polyalphabetic one. But because they are employed simultaneously and not serially, as in most polyalphabetics, the system is usually termed a "multiplex" one.

The system played an important role in secret communications, both prior to and during World War II.

The cylindrical version was first officially adopted as a United States cryptosystem by the Army in 1921.[8] In 1927, it was issued to the Navy under the designation CSP 488 for joint communications with the Army. Military attachés began using it in 1929, naval attachés in 1930, and in 1939 it went to the Coast Guard under the title CSP 493.[9]

The cipher device M-94 was used extensively between World War I and World War II and a total of 9,432 were eventually produced. When tests were started on the use of converter M-209, a more complicated mechanical printing device, plans were made for the discontinuance of the M-94. On August 9, 1943, when sufficient M-209's were available for replacement purposes, Cipher Device M-94 was declared obsolete.[10]

In 1933, the Army turned to the flat version. It wanted to provide an easy method for changing the random alphabets while still using the basic principle of the M-94.[11] Several experimental models were built and evaluated before one was officially adopted in 1934 as the M-138. In 1938, an improved model, the M-138-A, was adopted. Included in the improvements was an increase, from 25 to 30, in the number of mixed alphabets that could be used.[12]

The Navy had participated in the development of this strip device, designating it CSP 845. When a shortage of aluminum forced both services to seek substitute material, the Navy developed the CSP 845 (plastic). The Army ordered 5,000 of the plastic versions from the Navy in October, 1942, and distributed them widely around the world. The plastic strip boards, however, did not prove satisfactory, particularly in tropical climates where the hot, moist weather caused them to warp.[13]

The Army had developed a wooden board made of Honduras mahogany, Cipher Device M-138-A (wood) or SIGWOWO. Two thousand were ordered in February, 1943, but they also proved unsatisfactory in the field due to the friction of the paper strips on the wood and warping of the board.[14] In September, 1943, aluminum became available again and the Army ordered 8,000 aluminum cipher devices CSP 845 from the Navy because it was more expedient than renegotiating with the manufacturer for the aluminum M-138-A.[15]

All together, 17,872 flat strip cipher devices in all versions were ordered from 1935 through 1943.[16] In addition to the Army and the Navy, strip cipher devices were used by almost a dozen different government agencies during the war.[17] Strip cipher systems were also distributed to at least six foreign governments including France, Italy, and Russia so they would maintain secure communications with United States Army personnel.[18]

Even after cipher machines were introduced during World War II, strip cipher systems continued in use by individuals such as military attachés, or units not authorized to use cipher machines, and as standby equipment for machine users.[19]

They were also used after the war. A 1948 Army document said, "Strip systems . . . at the present time are a very important means of communication . . ."[20] Another author, in 1967, wrote that the Navy was using it at that time.[21]

This is an amazing longevity for a cryptosystem in a technological era that [makes] complex mechanisms [obsolete] almost overnight.

JEFFERSON, BAZERIES AND OTHER INVENTORS

The device was invented, or apparently so, a number of times. Charles Babbage, the eminent mathematician, scientist and precursor of the modern computer, hinted in the *Journal of the Society of Arts* in 1854 at a cylindrical type cipher device. His letter said that a cipher system proposed by a reader in a previous issue was not new and that Babbage had made, " . common centre, each circle having on its circumference the twenty-six letters of the alphabet."[22] He then wrote, "The best form is, perhaps, ring of box-wood placed side by side on a cylinder, and having the twenty-six letters on the circumference of each."[23] But this reference, precise and early as it was, faded into obscurity.

Apparently independently, for he never mentions Babbage, whose work seems not to have been known to cryptographers of the time, Major Etienne Bazeries, a French cryptologist, developed a 20-disk mechanism (Figure 3). On September 19, 1891, he described it in Marseilles at the convention of the French Association for the Advancement of Science.[24] And, after it was rejected by the French army, he pictured and wrote about it in his book, *Les Chiffres Secrets Devoiles*.[25] Probably because this work stood in the mainstream of cryptologic literature, Bazeries' invention influenced cryptography more than all the similar inventions.

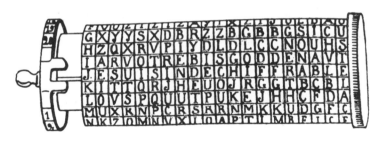

FIGURE 3. BAZERIES' DRAWING OF HIS "CYLINDRICAL CRYPTOGRAPH."

A contemporary, one Arthur J. Hermann, a member of the French Mathematical Society, proposed, apparently for the first time, a flat strip format of Bazeries' cylinder with 18 wooden or cardboard strips in his article, "Nouveau Cryptographe Construit d'apres le Systeme Bazeries," in the September 2, 1893 issue of *Revue Scientifique*.[26]

In 1900, an article in *Rivista Militare Italiana* by Gioppi di Turkheim, a writer on cryptology [27], described the Ducros Scotograph, invented that year by Colonel Oliver Ducros of the Italian army.[28] It was a 13-disk device similar to the Bazeries cylinder which had possibly inspired it, but with some added embellishments (Figure 4).

During the summer of 1913, Captain Parker Hitt, an instructor at the United States Army Signal School, Fort Leavenworth, Kansas, cre-

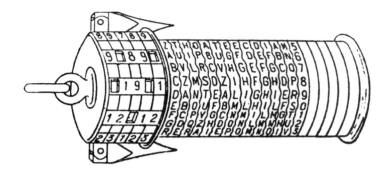

FIGURE 4. DUCROS' SCOTOGRAPH.

ated a 10-disk device.[29] He acknowledged that this work was influenced by the ideas of Bazeries.[30]

He then reinvented the strip cipher—he gives no evidence of having read Hermann's article.[31] Since Hitt preferred the flat form because of its "compactness, simplicity of operation, and ease with which alphabet strips could be reproduced if lost,"[32] he abandoned his work on the cylindrical device.[33] His first flat device had twenty alphabet strips, possibly because Bazeries' cylinder had twenty disks. But, by 1916, it had expanded to twenty-five [34] (Figure 5).

His friend, Major Joseph O. Mauborgne, Assistant Commandant of the Signal School at Fort Leavenworth, examined Hitt's alphabets and decided that they were not scrambled enough to assure sufficient crypto security. So he constructed mixed alphabets that would repeat as few pairs of letters among them as possible.[35] He then had two 25-disk devices using these alphabets made in the Army Signal School shop in early 1917 [36] (Figure 6). Mauborgne's work led directly to the M-94, Hitt's led to the M-138-A.

But the most remarkable inventor, discovered by chance in 1922 from his papers in the Library of Congress, was Thomas Jefferson. The discovery, by Dr. John M. Manly, a Chaucer scholar and cryptanalyst in World War I, revealed that before Babbage and Bazeries, Jefferson had invented a cipher device based on the same principle but using 36 disks [37] which he called his "wheel cypher."[38] Despite its precocity, however, it seems never to have been used and so was lost to the world of cryptography until Manly found it.

But where did Bazeries and Jefferson get the ideas for their systems? One was a professional cryptologist and the other a mere dilettante in an esoteric art. Did one evolve the concept from a deep-seated knowledge of the science, and did the other get a flash of inspiration? Or was there some mechanism that triggered their thinking along similar paths?

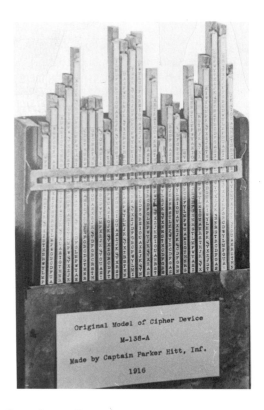

FIGURE 5. HITT'S STRIP CIPHER DEVICE.

FIGURE 6. ONE OF MAUBORGNE'S ORIGINAL MODELS OF HIS 25 DISK DEVICE.

LETTER LOCKS AND EDME REGNIER

Up to now no one has suggested a source for these virtually identical but almost certainly independently conceived ideas.

I believe I have found it.

One summer day I visited a lock museum and suddenly found myself in front of a letter lock. It contained six disks or wheels with a complete alphabet engraved on each one. When six particular letters—and only those six—are lined up with notched benchmarks at the edges of the lock, the lock opens. As an amateur cryptologist with a particular interest in cipher devices, I recognized at once that the lock resembled a six-disk M-94. It struck me that the letter lock might well be the forerunner of the Jefferson/Bazeries cylinder.

As I began to investigate this possibility, I reread General Luigi Sacco's *Manual of Cryptography* [39] and the following sentence, not noted in previous readings, almost leaped out of the page. "The Bazeries device resembles very much one of those word padlocks which are used for locking some secret box."[40] In the next paragraph, Sacco described the operation of the Bazeries device this way, ". . . to encipher we simply rotate the successive disks . . . in the same way we form the word in the word padlocks."[41]

Gioppi, too, said the similar Ducros device ". . . has no little analogy with the so-called word padlock (combination lock based on a word instead of numbers)."[42] Obviously, cryptologists other than just myself have seen the relationship between the wheel cipher and the letter lock. But how was the connection made?

Letter locks, the ancestors of modern combination locks, appeared about 1,000 years ago in China. They consisted of a group of rings engraved with symbols, letters or numbers revolving around their bolt, opening only when the rings were moved to spell out a prearranged set of letters or symbols.[43]

In the West, the letter lock dates back to at least the early 1400's [44] (Figure 7). Knowledge of it seems never to have been lost. In the mid-1500's, Girolamo Cardano, famed Milanese physician, mathematician and scholar who touched on cryptology in his writings, suggested a cipher lock with alphabet wheels that would open only when the wheels were correctly aligned to form a particular word.[45] Silvestro Pietrasantra's *De Symbolis Heroicis,* published in Antwerp in 1643, depicts letter locks on pages 3 and 254. The motto above the first lock says, "It opens to a word," and above the second lock the motto is, "By luck or hard work."[46]

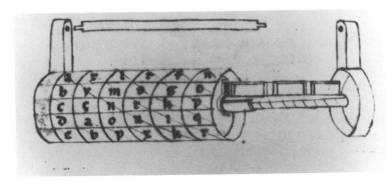

Figure 7. Letter Lock *circa* 1420.

Later, the letter lock seems to have become well enough known for writers of the 17th century to allude to it. The poet, Thomas Carew, used this verse in his poem, *To my honoured Friend, Master Thomas May, upon his comedy, The Heir.*

> The whole plot doth alike itself disclose
> Through the five acts, as doth the lock that goes
> With letters, for, till every one be known,
> The lock's as fast as if you had found none.[47]

In their play, *Noble Gentlemen,* Beaumont and Fletcher have a character say:

> A cap-case for your linens and your plate,
> With a strange lock that opens with AMEN.[48]

The Museum le Secq des Tournelles in Rouen has letter locks in its collection that predate the French Revolution.[49]

The device increased greatly in popularity during the last decade of the 18th century and the first part of the 19th century, due largely to the efforts of a Frenchman who claimed to have invented it, but, in fact, merely improved it. This improvement made it possible to change the combination of a lock when necessary. Previously, the combination of a lock was fixed and if it became known to others the lock had to be discarded.

The Frenchman was Edme Regnier (1751–1825), a prolific inventor with over 70 inventions to his credit.[50] He planned and organized the Artillery Museum in Paris and became its first director in 1796.[51] In 1777, he won first prize from the Societe libre d'Emulation de Paris for his invention of a combination lock.[52] Some years later he developed the letter lock or word padlock [53] possibly because a combination in the form of a word is easier to memorize than a string of numbers.

A description of his lock, important for this paper, appeared in 1790 in Volume VII, *Arts et Metiers Mecaniques,* of *L'Encyclopedie Methodique* [54], whose 194 volumes were published between 1782 and 1832. The encyclopedia's article pointed out that a picture was unavailable and, instead, furnished a thorough description of Regnier's invention. It said the lock had nine disks, each divided into eleven parts, containing the numbers 0 through 9 and a star.[55] It also described the combination lock that Regnier had improved upon. That one is illustrated in Volume IV of the encyclopedia's plates series, published in 1785, and is an 11-disk combination lock.[56] Although its description says that figures and characters distributed on the circumference of the disks must be properly aligned for the lock to open [57], the drawing shows blank disks (Figure 8). Still, if the shackle or U-shaped section is omitted, it clearly resembles a letterless version of Jefferson's wheel cypher.

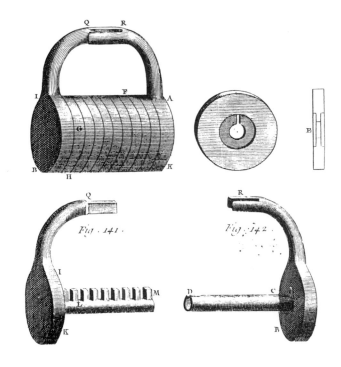

FIGURE 8. COMBINATION LOCK IN THE ENCYCLOPEDIE METHODIQUE.

Other papers and articles about Regnier's lock inventions also appeared around the turn of the century. Regnier himself prepared a three-page pamphlet which described and pictured his letter locks (Figure 9).[58]

One Regnier lock, similar to those in his pamphlet, is today in the Musée National des Techniques in Paris (Figure 10).[59]

Vanhagen von Ense, a German writer who spent some time in Paris around 1810, wrote in his memoirs that "Regnier was a man of some invention and had taken out a patent for a sort of lock,"[60] which he described:

> These consisted of broad steel rings, four, five or eight deep, upon each of which the alphabet was engraved; these turned round on a cylinder of steel, and only separated where the letters, forming a particular word, were in a straight line with one another. The word was selected from among a thousand and the choice was the secret of the purchaser. Anyone not knowing the word might turn the rings around for years without succeeding in finding the right one.[61]

Ense further said that the lock "made some noise at the time everybody praised his invention and bought his locks."[62] A lock collector specializing in letter locks confirms that they "were rather popular from 1750 to early 1900's."[63]

Could Jefferson have known of Regnier's lock?

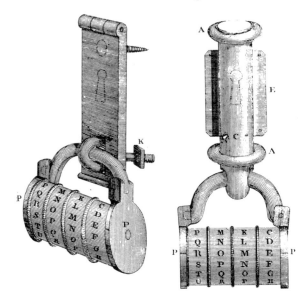

Figure 9. Illustration from Regnier's Pamphlet.

FIGURE 10. A REGNIER LETTERLOCK IN THE MUSÉE NATIONAL DES TECHNIQUES, PARIS, FRANCE.

CONNECTIONS

Chronology, first of all, permits [that Jefferson knew]. Regnier arrived in Paris in 1778 [64] and apparently spent the remainder of his life there. Jefferson went to France in 1784 and stayed for five years.[65] According to Dr. Julius Boyd, editor of *The Jefferson Papers,* Jefferson wrote the description of his wheel cypher in the period 1790–1793 or 1797–1800—or after he returned from France.[66]

Circumstances further make the connection likely. Jefferson considered himself ". . . one of the original subscribers . . ."[67] of the *Encyclopedie Methodique,* which had first published a description of Regnier's lock. His library included 136 of its volumes.[68] He thought so highly of it that in 1786 he began taking subscriptions for many of his friends back in the United States, including Benjamin Franklin and James Monroe.[69]

He corresponded with authors of articles, contributed his own material for use in at least one of the volumes, and mentioned the encyclopedia frequently in his correspondence.[70] Jefferson's intense and lengthy interest in the *Encyclopedie Methodique* is most important because it suggests with high probability that he was familiar with the secret combination locks described and pictured in its volumes.

Furthermore, an earlier edition of the *Encyclopedie Methodique*, the 39-volume *Encyclopedie Ancienne,* was also in Jefferson's library.[71] Volume II, published in 1751, carried a description of a "secret padlock"[72] and its picture in Volume IX, published in 1771 [73], shows that it is the same combination lock illustrated in the *Encyclopedie Methodique* (Figure 8). The publishers used the same drawings and virtually identical descriptions in both encyclopedias, doubling the possibility of Jefferson being exposed to it.

Finally, Jefferson's personality further makes his knowledge of Regnier likely. He was mechanically inclined and had "himself invented or adapted to personal uses numerous ingenious devices, the best known of which is his polygraph."[74] When he became Secretary of State in 1789 he was in effect the country's first Superintendent of Patents [75] and ". . . he scrupulously . . . investigated every claim to satisfy the statutory test of originality."[76]

A knowledgeable cryptologist, Rosario Candela, questioning in Bazeries' defense whether Jefferson was the originator of the wheel cypher, pointed out that ". . . Jefferson was a prolific writer who had the excellent habit of jotting down almost everything that struck him as being unusual. An insatiably curious man, he travelled widely."[77] Therefore, asks Candela, "Is it not possible that in his European peregrinations he had come across the device . . . ?"[78] Though in a narrow sense this seems improbable, in the broad sense of a general stimulus it appears not unlikely.

It thus seems highly probable that Jefferson knew of Regnier's letter locks which perhaps inspired his wheel cypher. But how about Bazeries?

He was born in 1846 [79], only 12 years after a biographical sketch of Regnier said his locks were in wide use.[80] Therefore, Bazeries may well have had many opportunities to become familiar with Regnier's combination locks. Their mutual association with the French Army may have also contributed to this possibility. The evidence, although circumstantial, makes it likely that Bazeries too got the idea for his cylindrical cipher device from the type of letter locks developed by Edme Regnier.

It is perhaps significant that Charles Babbage included a chapter in his autobiography on "Picking Locks and Deciphering," in which he said, "These two subjects are in truth more allied than might appear upon a superficial view of them."[81]

CONCLUSIONS

A careful review of the information available to Jefferson leads one to conclude that he almost certainly knew about Regnier's locks, or other combination locks, or perhaps both, and that his wheel cypher was consciously or unconsciously derived from one of those sources. The same apparently was true of Bazeries.

It therefore seems likely that the independent inventions of Bazeries and Jefferson had a common antecedent, the letter locks of Edme Regnier. And others, like Babbage, may have also gotten the ideas for their similar devices from the letter lock. This does not detract from the inventiveness of these individuals because their devices were not a simple adaptation of the letter lock, but required the addition of two new concepts: the variable arrangements of the disks and the idea of a key, which enables any user to place them on a shaft in the order agreed upon by themselves and by someone else. But the letter lock, of course, provided the initial idea.

So, to Regnier, to the unknown ancient technician who devised the first such mechanism, and to those ingenious individuals who borrowed that technology, cryptology owes one of the most widespread of its 20th century cryptosystems.

FOOTNOTES AND REFERENCES

1. David Kahn, *The Codebreakers* (New York: Macmillan, 1967), p. 325.
2. U.S. War Department, Army Security Agency, *The History of Army Strip Cipher Devices* (n. p.: n.n., 1948), p. 2.
3. U. S. War Department, Office of the Chief Signal Officer, *Instructions for Using the Cipher Device Type M-94* (Washington: Government Printing Office, 1922), pp. 9–10.
4. *Ibid.*, p. 10.
5. *The History of Army Strip Cipher Devices, op. cit.*, Tab. 26.
6.. *Ibid.*
7. *Ibid.*
8. *Ibid.*, p. 19.
9. *Ibid.*, pp. 22–23.
10. *Ibid.*, pp. 22–26.
11. *Ibid.*, p. 30.
12. *Ibid.*, Chapters IV, V and VI *passim*.
13. *Ibid.*, pp. 44, 56, 58–59.

14. *Ibid.*, pp. 61–62.
15. *Ibid.*, pp. 6, 62.
16. *Ibid.*, Tab. 33.
17. *Ibid.*, p. 111.
18. *Ibid.*, pp. 112–121.
19. *Ibid.*, p. 70.
20. *Ibid.*, p. 72.
21. Kahn, *op. cit.*, p. 195.
22. Home Correspondence, *Journal of the Society of Arts,* Vol. II, No. 93 (September 1, 1854) 707.
23. *Ibid.*, pp. 707–708.
24. Etienne Bazeries (Capitaine), "Cryptographe A 20 Rondelles-Alphabets (25 Lettres Par Alphabet)," *Compte rendu de la 20 e session de l'Association Francaise pour l'Avancement des Sciences* (Paris: Au Secretariat de l'Association, 1892), 160.
25. Etienne Bazeries (Commandant), *Les Chiffres Secrets Devoiles* (Paris: Librarie Charpentier et Fasquelle, 1901).
26. Arthur J. Hermann, "Nouveau Cryptographe Construit d'apres le Systeme Bazeries," *Revue Scientifique,* Tome LIII, No. 10 (September 2, 1893) 306–307.
27. L. Gioppi di Turkheim, "La Crittografia," *Rivista Militare Italiana,* Vol. 45, No. 12 (December 16, 1900) 2202–2235.
28. J. Bres (trans.), *Manuel de Cryptographie* by Luigi Sacco, (Paris: Payot, 1951), p. 58.
29. *The History of Army Strip Cipher Devices, op. cit.*, p. 14.
30. Kahn, *op. cit.*, p. 325.
31. *The History of Army Strip Cipher Devices, op. cit.*, p. 15.
32. Parker Hitt Cipher Papers, David Kahn Collection, Letter, December 19, 1914.
33. *The History of Army Strip Cipher Devices, loc. cit.*
34. Parker Hitt Cipher Papers, Letters, December 19, 1914, September 10, 1943.
35. *The History of Army Strip Cipher Devices, op. cit.*, p. 16.
36. *Ibid.*, p. 17.
37. William F. Friedman, "Edgar Allan Poe, Cryptographer (Addendum)," *Articles on Cryptography and Cryptanalysis Reprinted from the Signal Corps Bulletin,* U. S. War Department, Office of the Chief Signal Officer (Washington: Government Printing Office, 1942), pp. 181–182.
38. Kahn, *op. cit.*, p. 192.
39. Howell C. Brown (trans.), *Manual of Cryptography* by Luigi Sacco. U. S. War Department, Office of the Chief Signal Officer (Washington: Government Printing Office, 1941).

40. *Ibid.*, p. 34.

41. *Ibid.*

42. Gioppi, *op. cit.*, p. 2220.

43. "Lock and Key," *MD*, Vol. 8, No. 10 (October 1964) 248.

44. F. M. Feldhaus, *Die Technik der Vorzeit, der geschichtlichen zeit und der Naturvolker* (Leipzig: Verlag von Wilheim Engelman, 1914), pp. 969–970.

45. Girolamo Cardano, *De Subtilitate Libri XXI* (Basiliae: apud J. Petreium, 1560), pp. 1074–1076.

46. Silvestro Pietrasanta, *De Symbolis Heroicis* (Antwerp: Ex Officina Plantiniana Balthasaris Moreti, 1634), pp. 3, 254.

47. Arthur Vincent (ed.), *The Poems of Thomas Care* (New York: Charles Scribner's Sons, 1889), p. 128.

48. Alexander Dyce (Rev.), *The Works of Beaumont and Fletcher,* Vol. 1, (London: Edward Moxon, 1846), p. 183.

49. C. Vaudour, Conservateur-Adjoint, Musées De Rouen, Letter to author, February 17, 1976.

50. Pierre Larousse, *Grand Dictionnaire Universel Du XIX Siecle,* Vol. 13, (Paris: Libraire Classique Larousse et Boyer, 1873), p. 864.

51. Colonel Martel, Conservateur, Musée de L'Armée, Letter to author, January 20, 1975.

52. "Rapport sur le cadenas à combinaisons du C. Regnier, garde des archives de l'artillerie," *Bulletin de la Societe d'Encouragement pour l'industrie Nationale,* Premiere Annee, VII (Ventose An XI) 127.

53. *Ibid.*, pp. 125–127.

54. *Encyclopedie Methodique*, Tome Septieme, Arts et Metiers Mecaniques (Paris: Chez Panckoucke, 1790), pp. 471–473.

55. *Ibid.*, p. 472.

56. *Encyclopedie Methodique*, Tome Quatrieme, Recueil de Planches de L'Encyclopedie, Par ordre de Matieres (Paris: Chez Panckouke, 1785), p. 99.

57. *Encyclopedie Methodique*, Tome Septieme, *op. cit.*, pp. 496–497.

58. Edme Regnier, *Description et Usage Du Cadenas De Surete à Combinaisons* (Paris: De l'Imprimerie de Madame Huzard, n.d.).

59. Claudine Fontanon, Chef de travaus, Centre De Documentation D'Histoire Des Techniques, Letter to author, January 20, 1976.

60. Sir Alexander Duff Gordon (trans.), *Sketches of German Life* by Vanhagen von Ense (London: John Murray, 1847), pp. 141–142.

61. *Ibid.*

62. *Ibid.*

63. Linton Knight, Rincon Key Company, Letter to author, February 5, 1975.

64. M. Jomard, "Notice sur la vie et les Traveaux de feu M. Regnier, membre de Conseil d'administration de la Societe d'Encouragement," *Bulletin de la Societe d'Encouragement pour l'industrie Nationale,* CCLXV (July, 1826) 237.

65. Dumas Malone, *Jefferson and His Time,* Vol. Two (Boston: Little, Brown and Co., 1951), pp. 1, 243.

66. Kahn, *op. cit.,* p. 192.

67. E. Millicent Sowerby (comp.), *Catalogue of the Library of Thomas Jefferson,* Vol. V (Washington: Government Printing Office, 1959), p. 149.

68. *Ibid.,* p. 143.

69. *Ibid.,* p. 147.

70. *Ibid.,* pp. 143–147, 150.

71. *Ibid.,* p. 150.

72. *Encyclopedie Ancienne,* Vol. II (Paris: M. Diderot, 1751), p. 512.

73. *Encyclopedie Ancienne,* Vol. IX, Recueil De Planches (Paris: M. Diderot, 1771), plate XXX.

74. Dumas Malone (ed.), *Dictionary of American Biography,* Vol. V, Part 2 (New York: Charles Scribner's Sons, 1961), p. 33.

75. *Ibid.*

76. Merrill D. Peterson, *Thomas Jefferson and The New Nation* (New York: Oxford University Press, 1970), p. 450.

77. Rosario Candela, *The Military Cipher of Commandant Bazeries* (New York: Cardanus Press, 1938), p. 69.

78. *Ibid.,* p. 70.

79. Kahn, *op. cit.,* p. 244.

80. *Biographie Universelle et Portative Des Contemporaines,* Tome Quatrieme (Paris: Chez F. G. Levrault, 1834), p. 1072.

81. Charles Babbage, *Passages from the Life of a Philosopher* (London: Longman, Green, Longman, Roberts and Green, 1864), p. 233.

The Search for the Key Book to Nicholas Trist's Book Ciphers
by Albert C. Leighton and Stephen M. Matyas

The name of Nicholas Philip Trist is known to few Americans even though he negotiated a treaty which brought to the United States one of its greatest territorial accessions—the entire Southwest—after the 1848 victory over Mexico. Furthermore, he did this after having been disavowed and recalled from his position as special envoy to Mexico by the President of the United States. Sent to Mexico without secure means of communication, he was forced to devise methods of encipherment which he could use to inform Washington of his actions. This article will explain the bases of his ciphers and reveal hitherto unknown information about them.

The life of Nicholas Trist can be briefly sketched. He was born in Charlottesville, Virginia, in 1800. His grandmother had been an old flame of Thomas Jefferson. As a consequence, the families were friendly and Nicholas spent time at Monticello where he eventually married Jefferson's favorite granddaughter, Virginia Randolph, uncharitably described by Trist's mother as a tall girl of "not great personal charms."[1] Trist himself was a slender, unhealthy six feet weighing only 120 pounds (Figure 1). At Monticello he became the favorite companion of the aging ex-president and was present at Jefferson's deathbed in 1826, informing him that he had achieved his goal of surviving until the Fourth of July. As executor of Jefferson's will, he had the difficult task of dealing with Jefferson's confused finances and administering Monticello. After unsuccessful attempts at practicing law and running a newspaper, he eventually obtained a position as clerk in the State Department by political patronage, primarily because of his Jeffersonian connections. His position was continued into the administration of Andrew Jackson, where, once more

From *Cryptologia*, Vol. 7, No. 4, Oct. 1983.

FIGURE 1. NICHOLAS P. TRIST AT AN EARLY AGE.
(Photograph from the collection of Mrs. Gordon Trist Burke.)

because of personal relationships, he also acted as private secretary to the president.[2] Later made consul at Havana, for which he seemed well suited because of his knowledge of Spanish, he irritated many and had a difficult time. His reports and letters were characterized by extreme verbosity. It was said "Of wit he had none, if brevity be its measure" and his "written explanations from Havana were too prolix for comprehension."[3] By 1845 Trist was back in the State Department as chief clerk (which, under the conditions of the time, meant that he was next in authority to his friend James Buchanan, the new Secretary of State and the future president).

When the Mexican War came, Generals Zachary Taylor ("Old Rough and Ready") and Winfield Scott ("Old Fuss and Feathers") were both successful and both Whigs. The president, James K. Polk, was a Democrat and not eager for them to achieve great fame and become his potential political rivals. Not wanting these commanders in the field to gather additional laurels by negotiating the peace treaty, he selected Nicholas Trist as his personal representative to go secretly to Mexico with instructions and a draft treaty to present to the Mexican government.

A hint was even given of a "possible nomination to the presidency in the event of his success."[4] Trist attempted to travel incognito but his cover was soon blown and accounts of his "secret" mission were published in the newspapers. So were the seeds of distrust planted. Infuriated, Polk blamed both Trist and Secretary of State Buchanan for the leak.

Trist's arrival in Mexico was no more auspicious. Through ineptness, he quarreled with Scott, but after Scott later sent a gift of guava jelly to the sick Trist, they became fast, life-long friends. In the chaotic situation in Mexico, Trist had difficulty in finding any effectual Mexican government with which to negotiate.

TRIST'S CIPHERS

Trist soon realized he had no secure means of communication with Washington. Consequently, he devised two ciphers which he described in two letters to Buchanan.[5] The first system is described in his letter of June 3, 1847, pertinent parts of which are here excerpted:

Puebla, June 3, 1847

James Buchanan
Secretary of State

. . . I have been occupying part of my time here in making a cipher, which I shall probably have frequent occasion for. A duplicate and key can be made at the Department by sending to my daughter for a copy of the smallest of the books (there are several at my house) which she packed up for me: The work of our old instructor, who was sent to Spain as Consul. Let the letters of the prefatory address "To the British Nation" (excluding this title) be numbered, from one onward until every letter of the alphabet is reached, except Z (which I represent by zero). Each of the letters, with a few exceptions has three numbers corresponding to it.

Nicholas P. Trist

In a postscript to his dispatch No. 9 of July 23, 1847, he repeats the description of the first type of cipher and adds a description of his second encipherment method. He later called this "treble numbered" and planned to use it for particularly important passages. The pertinent parts of the P.S. are here excerpted:

Puebla, July 23, 1847

Hon: James Buchanan
Secretary of State

. . .

P.S. July 25
I have already given the Key to the cypher here used. Lest, however, my letter may have miscarried, I will here repeat it. Send to
my house for a copy (there are several) of the smallest of the books
which my daughter packed in my trunk—the work of our old instructor at Washington. Number the letters of the address "To the
British Nation" (omitting this title) and you have the key.

In future, I will, for passages of special consequences vary the
cypher as follows. Three numbers between brackets will indicate
the page, the line and the letter. The same book "Part Second," to
be used. If there be more than three numbers within the same
brackets, all after the third will indicate letters in the same line. For
example: (33,4,5) will indicate the letter g.

Nicholas P. Trist

The principle of the first method is that used by Charles William
Frederic Dumas and Benjamin Franklin in 1776 [6] and by the originator
of the Beale ciphers in 1822, where the letters of a selected text are
numbered serially, thereby furnishing several equivalents for each letter
of the alphabet.[7] Such a system is difficult to decipher without the key
text. Trist's second method of encipherment is similar to that used by
Benedict Arnold and British Major John André in their treasonous correspondence in 1779 [8] and to the Thurn-Taxis cipher used in Bavaria
in the early 1800's.[9] Such ciphers were described and may have been
popularized by Johann Ludwig Klüber in his book *Kryptographik* published in 1809 in Tübingen.

Several scholars have written of Trist, but most of them have had
little interest in his ciphers.[10] (Robert Arthur Brent's 1950 Ph.D. dissertation "Nicholas Philip Trist: Biography of a Disobedient Diplomat"
at the University of Virginia does not mention Trist's ciphers.) However,
Ralph E. Weber, professor of history at Marquette University and author
of *United States Diplomatic Codes and Ciphers*, was able to reconstruct
much of the key to Trist's first method by consulting official State Department decipherments.[11] From these decipherments, Weber determined that Trist's key text began with the words "The study of foreign
languages after . . ." (Figure 2). But Weber did not identify Trist's key
book, which would have been necessary to complete the key and unlock
those dispatches which used Trist's second method.

0 z	14 c,e	28 f	45 n	114 p
1 t	15 i	29 t	50 r	115 y
2 h	16 g	30 e	52 w	121 m
3 e	17 n	31 r	58 d	133 p
4 s	18 l	33 h	59 i	147 t
5 t	19 a	34 i	61 b	167 w
6 u	20 n	35 m	64 d	183 p
7 d	21 g	36 c	65 l	196 m
8 y	22 u	37 q	73 h	200 v,l
9 o	23 a	38 u	99 b	215 b
10 f	24 g	39 i	100 l	300 x
11 f	25 e	40 s	102 w	409 k
12 o	26 s	41 i	105 c	448 v
13 r	27 a	44 o	110 f	

FIGURE 2. TRIST'S CIPHER KEY RECOVERED FROM STATE DEPARTMENT DISPATCHES.

In Trist's slow and tortuous negotiations with the almost nonexistent Mexican government, he was considerably aided by the British diplomats in Mexico, particularly Edward Thornton (later to be Sir Edward Thornton, British ambassador in Washington for many years). In fact, it appears from a private letter to Buchanan attached to Trist's dispatch No. 10 of July 31, 1847, that Thornton was the originator of Trist's treble numbered cipher:[12]

Puebla, July 31, '47

Private.
Hon: James Buchanan
Secretary of State.
Sir,

To my No. 10 of this date I will here add, that my engagements are becoming quite laborious—such as would be so, even if I were in vigorous health and in a different climate. Yesterday, for instance, I was closely engaged from 12 o'clock till dusk, in what ought to have been the employment of a confidential assistant: putting in cypher (a treble numbered cypher selected by him) a short note to 121,13,1,2,17,5,9,20. It was to be ready by three o'clock, but this proved impracticable. Fortunately, however, the courier-spy (as these men may be called) was accidentally delayed, so that I did not miss the opportunity. Everybody—generals and lieutenants—

expresses great surprise at my not having "a secretary"; and independently of any interest I might have had in the question, I think it unfortunate, in more important respects than that of my being a little overworked, that this mission was not made a full one, as all seem to take for granted that it is. Genl. Scott has offered me assistance from the army; and although I have not yet, for various reasons, availed myself of it, I shall do so, to keep up appearances with the Mexican Commn., should there be a meeting.

I am, Sir, very respectfully
Yr observt
N. P. Trist

His identity is revealed by applying Weber's reconstructed key to the cipher text above:

```
 m   r  t h  n t o   n
121 ,13, 1,2,17,5,9,20
```

Despite his mistakes in enciphering, it is apparent that Trist intended to write "Mr. Th[or]nton."

Communications between Washington and Trist were extremely slow. For example, Trist's dispatch No. 9, sent on 23 July 1847, was only received in Washington on 15 September. Important events in Mexico were occurring without Washington's knowledge. Trist had finally made contact with Mexican peace commissioners on 27 August, but real progress only occurred after Scott's capture of Mexico City on 14 September and the fall of the Santa Anna government. A new government was organized in November which was willing to negotiate. However, authorities in Washington, unaware of the fall of the Mexican capitol and unhappy with what seemed to them long delays and no progress, sent a letter of recall to Trist on 6 October. The letter was only received by Trist on 16 November at a crucial stage in the negotiations.

Once the fall of Mexico City was known in Washington, many (including Buchanan) began to think that the instructions given to Trist were too liberal and that the whole of Mexico should be annexed. Trist, realizing that Washington was unaware of the true situation in Mexico, after considerable soul searching decided to ignore his recall and seized what he saw as a last opportunity to end the war by negotiating a treaty in accordance with his original instructions. Consequently, in a letter to his wife he asked her to inform Buchanan. The pertinent extract follows:[13]

Mexico, Dec. 4, '47

. . .
P.S.
In my last (28th ulto) I desired you to say to Mr. B. that I have had
a final irrevocable farewell to all official employment, and to give
him my very best regards and most heartfelt regret at parting with
him. Procure the key to this cypher (your sagacity will tell you
where) and decipher the following to be read to him most secretly.
This determination, I came to this day, at 12 o'clock. It is altogether
my own.

Knowing it to be the very last chance, and impressed with the
dreadful consequences to our country which cannot fail to attend
the loss of that chance 15, 52, 39, 18, 65, 19, 1, 13, 3, 23, 58, 41,
10, 39, 29, 14, 27, 20, 61, 30, 7, 12, 45, 30, 9, 17, 29, 2, 3, 99, 23,
4, 41, 40 of 6, 114, 5, 73, 3, 215, 50, 27, 200, 44 and across 61, 115,
32°, 21, 41, 200, 41, 20, 24, 15, 75, 26, besides the 3, 121, 4, 36, 23,
26, 73.

Mrs. Trist's sagacity was up to the challenge. She deciphered the
message as follows: "I will [make] a treaty if it can be done on the basis
of up the Bravo and across by 32° giving 15 m[illion]s besides the 3
m[illion]s cash." This uses Weber's key in Figure 2. Trist intended to
follow Polk's original orders by defining the boundary between the United
States and Mexico as running from the Gulf of Mexico up the Rio Grande
(known to the Mexicans as the Bravo) to 32 degrees north latitude and
then west to the Pacific.

Trist was eventually successful and the resulting treaty took its
name from the little village of Guadalupe Hidalgo where it was signed
on 2 February 1848. Although Polk was unhappy, he could hardly dis-
avow the draft instructions he had furnished Trist at the start of his
mission. Against the advice of Buchanan, he sent the treaty to the Senate,
which approved it on 10 March 1848 after much argument. Ratification
by the Mexican Congress followed on 25 May 1848 and, as a result, the
United States acquired California, New Mexico, Arizona, Nevada, Utah,
and parts of Colorado and Wyoming. Edward Thornton wittily observed
that Trist became the father of a healthy treaty nine months after his first
interview with the Mexicans.[14] Trist had shown outstanding skill, tact,
and patience in dealing with the chaotic diplomatic situation in Mexico
and had achieved a surprisingly just settlement which has endured with
relatively little friction to the present day.

Instead of the praise he merited, Trist was put under arrest, brought back to Washington in disgrace, removed from his State Department job, and not even paid for his expenses in Mexico after the date of his recall.[15] Trist found life very difficult after his return to Washington. Treated as an outcast, unable at first to find work, he eventually became a clerk on the Wilmington and Baltimore Railroad. His wife tried unsuccessfully to run a school for young ladies. Despite strong support from his friend Scott, who wrote in 1861 to Secretary of the Treasury Salmon P. Chase that Trist had been wronged by President Polk and neglected by Presidents Taylor, Fillmore, Pierce, and even Buchanan, nothing was done for him. In 1869 his always delicate health forced him to give up his railroad job. His cause was taken up by Senator Charles Sumner and the new administration of President Grant. In 1870 he was appointed postmaster at Alexandria, Virginia, and finally, in 1871 he was paid $14,559.90 for his salary and expenses in Mexico 23 years before, thus enabling him to spend his last few years in relative comfort. He died, several months after suffering a stroke, on 11 February 1874.[16]

THE SEARCH FOR TRIST'S KEY BOOK

Only the first type of Trist's cipher can be read with the partial key reconstructed by Weber. To complete Weber's key and to decipher passages using Trist's second type of cipher it would be necessary to recover the key book which Trist used. Other investigators faced with similar problems have successfully identified such key books. For example, William F. Friedman recovered portions of a key text in the trial of Hindu conspirators in 1915. Later investigators found the book from which the key was drawn.[17]

One of the present authors (Matyas) decided to try to find the book used by Trist as a key. He observed that in his letters of 3 June and 23 July 1847 to Buchanan, Trist described his key book—a small volume, with a prefatory address "To the British Nation," divided into at least two parts, and written by their old instructor in Washington, who was sent to Spain as consul. Weber's work had shown that the key text began with the words "The study of foreign languages . . ." With these slim clues Matyas set out to find the key book.

After some few preliminaries, including a search of the papers of James Buchanan that yielded no useful information about the key book, lists of all American diplomats in Spain and Spanish dependencies before 1847 were compiled from such sources as Congressional Directories and the 24 reels of microfilm containing correspondence from American consuls in Spain. The final list contained approximately 50 names. Consul-

FIGURE 3. NICHOLAS P. TRIST FROM A PHOTOGRAPH TAKEN IN HIS OLD AGE (LIBRARY OF CONGRESS).

tation of the Library of Congress card catalog revealed that many of them were prolific authors. Their books included Washington Irving's *Tales of the Alhambra* and *Legends of the Conquest of Spain,* John Henry Eaton's *Candid Appeal to the American,* John Forsyth's *Territorial Relations,* Edward Church's *Notice on the Beet Sugar,* William Kirkpatrick's *A Vocabulary, Persian, Arabic, and English,* and even a small book entitled *A Treatise on Milch Cows* by Francis Guenon, translated for the Farmers' Library from the French, by none other than Nicholas Philip Trist himself. Examination of many of these books failed to uncover the key book.

Finally, the name of Joseph Borras, consul at Barcelona from 1836, was suspected as being perhaps the Don Jose Borras who had published a small book entitled *Verdaderos principios de la lengua castellana; or, True Principles of the Spanish Language* (Figure 4). The entry in the National Union Catalog indicated that this was a small book in English and that one of the few extant copies was located in the Newberry Library in Chicago. A member of their staff was kind enough to read the prefatory address from the book over the telephone to Matyas: "The study of foreign languages . . ." (Figure 5). His feelings were indescribable. Eureka! A year's tedious research had paid off. The key book had been found. But more important to Matyas, his painstakingly thorough research had proven fruitful.

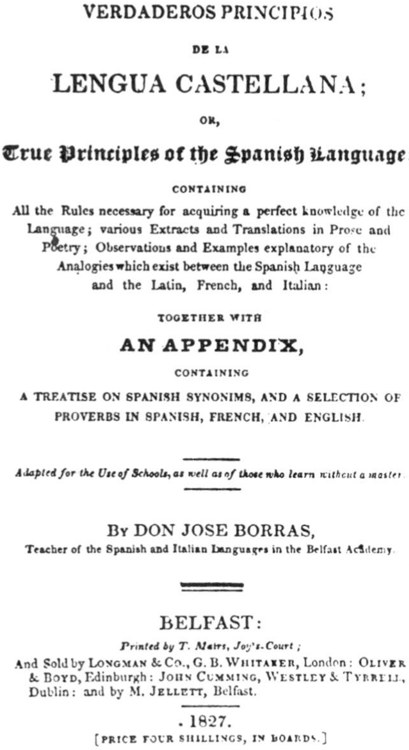

VERDADEROS PRINCIPIOS

DE LA

LENGUA CASTELLANA;

OR,

True Principles of the Spanish Language:

CONTAINING

All the Rules necessary for acquiring a perfect knowledge of the
Language; various Extracts and Translations in Prose and
Poetry; Observations and Examples explanatory of the
Analogies which exist between the Spanish Language
and the Latin, French, and Italian:

TOGETHER WITH

AN APPENDIX,

CONTAINING

A TREATISE ON SPANISH SYNONIMS, AND A SELECTION OF
PROVERBS IN SPANISH, FRENCH, AND ENGLISH.

Adapted for the Use of Schools, as well as of those who learn without a master

---

By DON JOSE BORRAS,
Teacher of the Spanish and Italian Languages in the Belfast Academy.

BELFAST:

Printed by T. Mairs, Joy's-Court;
And Sold by LONGMAN & Co., G. B. WHITAKER, London: OLIVER
& BOYD, Edinburgh: JOHN CUMMING, WESTLEY & TYRRELL,
Dublin: and by M. JELLETT, Belfast.

. 1827.
[PRICE FOUR SHILLINGS, IN BOARDS.]

FIGURE 4. TITLE PAGE FROM TRIST'S KEY BOOK.
(Courtesy of the Louis-Lucien Bonaparte Collection, The Newberry Library, Chicago.)

The *Verdaderos principios . . .* was a very logical book for Trist to
take on his Mexican mission. It was a small, handy compendium containing (as its title page stated) "all the Rules necessary for acquiring a
perfect knowledge of the Language."

It was now possible to complete Weber's key for the first type of
Trist's ciphers and also to decipher passages never before seen by his-
torians that were written in his more secure second type of cipher. As
Trist had written in his letter of 23 July, Part Second, page 33, line 4,
letter number 5 was the letter G.

An excerpt from Trist's dispatch No. 10 of 31 July 1847 (shown
below) illustrates the use of both his first and second forms of cipher.[18]

The first, based on numbering the letters in the key book's prefatory address, consists of a series of numbers separated by commas and dashes. (The dashes were used as fake word separators to confuse possible cryptanalysis.) The second form (or treble-numbered cipher), based on Part Second of the key book, consists of a series of numbers enclosed within slash marks: /......./. (Trist referred to them as brackets.) A series of three numbers within slash marks signifies the number of the page, the line, and the letter. When more than three numbers appear within the slash marks, all subsequent numbers signify letters in the same line. When two or more lines are used in succession from the same page, a double comma is written instead of repeating the page number:

Puebla, July 31/47

Hon. James Buchanan, Secretary of State

Sir,

In my last I said, "I consider the probabilities of an early peace very strong." The enclosed will be found to corroborate this belief. 1,2,3,10–15,13,4,1–39,26,11,31–44,75,121,31–/47,1,6,16/ 7,3,15,20,24,27,28,29/,,8,1,9/,,9,1/,,2,5/,,1,1/,,1,16,29/69,2,1/,,6,7/ ,,2,3,2/,,6,4,6,10,8/ under date July 29: 5,33,25,4–30,105,44,45,58– from a foreign merchant to this correspondent here . . .

If the letters of the prefatory address of Trist's key book (Figure 5) are numbered consecutively to develop a key (Figure 6) and the key is then used to decipher the above numbers up to the first slash mark (written in the first, or simple, form of Trist's cipher), the text is recovered as:

the   f i rst i s   f r o m   m r
1,2,3, 10–15,13,4,1–39,26, 11,31–44,75 , 121 ,31–

The ciphertext using the second (or more complex cipher) is replete with errors and more difficult to decipher. Three mistakes must be corrected in the exerpt above for a proper decipherment. The number 46 must be inserted between the second and third slash marks: / 46,7,3,15,20,24,27,28,29/. (Trist had changed pages in the key book without making the proper indication.) Similarly, the number 47 must replace the double commas between the seventh and eighth slash marks: / 47,1,16,29/ (Trist does it again!), and the number 1 must be inserted between the ninth and tenth slash marks: /,,1,6,7/. (Trist has forgotten the line number.)

TO THE BRITISH NATION.

THE study of foreign languages, after the acquisition of our own, is undoubtedly one of the most interesting and agreeable, which can occupy the time of literary persons, or engage the attention of those who are desirous of presenting themselves in society, as objects of a polite and accomplished education.

The Spanish Language, which yields to none in elegance, expression, or strength, has now become, by reason of commercial treaties recently established with South America, as necessary and important to the British youth, as it is instructive and entertaining to the learned, by reason of the infinite number of works,* which in all times, and on all subjects, have been written (notwithstanding the trammels of the Inquisition) by men of genius, in that once eminent, but now unfortunate country.

The study of this language, which for almost a century was but little attended to in this country, has now began to be revived, and it is the duty of those who profess to teach it, to render its acquisition as easy, and as interesting as the dryness of grammatical rules will permit.

It is not my intention to censure the methods pursued by different authors in communicating a knowledge of the Spanish Language; but as it is my own opinion that languages are more easily learned by *practice* than by *Grammar*, and that the latter is only useful in proportion as its rules are expressed with simplicity and brevity, I have composed this Work, to which I have given the title—"VERDADEROS PRINCIPIOS DE LA LENGUA CASTELLANA."

In composing the following Work, I have departed from the system too generally followed, of multiplying rules and examples, for the most part contradictory and obscure, and which serve rather

* See A. Anaya's English Treatise on Spanish Literature; also another on the same subject, in Italian, by Saverio Lampillas.

FIGURE 5. PREFATORY ADDRESS FROM TRIST'S KEY BOOK.
(Courtesy of the Louis-Lucien Bonaparte Collection, The Newberry Library, Chicago.)

The lines of text from Part Second of the key book necessary to decipher the text corresponding to the second type of cipher are listed below in the order of their use by Trist:

Page, Line	Text
47,1	FABLE T̲WENTY-FIFT̲H —The Fly and the Bull.
46,7	me habla? pregunt o̲ el tor̲o, con̲ un t̲ o̲ n̲ o brutal.
46,8	S̲oy yo. Quien? Aqui estoy. Oh, senora mos-
46,9	c̲a! es vm. quien me habla? vm. no es tan pesada

thestudyof	(10)	esinsociet	(210)	saryandimp	(410)
foreignlan	(20)	yasobjects	(220)	ortanttoth	(420)
guagesafte	(30)	ofapolitea	(230)	ebritishyo	(430)
rtheacquis	(40)	ndaccompli	(240)	uthasitisi	(440)
itionofour	(50)	shededucat	(250)	nstructive	(450)
ownisundou	(60)	ionthespan	(260)	andenterta	(460)
btedlyoneo	(70)	ishlanguag	(270)	iningtothe	(470)
fthemostin	(80)	ewhichyiel	(280)	learnedbyr	(480)
terestinga	(90)	dstononein	(290)	easonofthe	(490)
ndagreeabl	(100)	eleganceex	(300)	infinitenu	(500)
ewhichcano	(110)	pressionor	(310)	mberofwork	(510)
ccupytheti	(120)	strengthha	(320)	swhichinal	(520)
meoflitera	(130)	snowbecome	(330)	ltimesando	(530)
rypersonso	(140)	byreasonof	(340)	nallsubjec	(540)
rengagethe	(150)	commercial	(350)		
attentiono	(160)	treatiesre	(360)		
fthosewhoa	(170)	centlyesta	(370)		
redesirous	(180)	blishedwit	(380)		
ofpresenti	(190)	hsouthamer	(390)		
ngthemselv	(200)	icaasnecs	(400)		

FIGURE 6. TRIST'S CIPHER KEY OBTAINED FROM PREFATORY ADDRESS IN KEY BOOK.

46,2
UNA m$\overset{5}{\text{o}}$sca se puso sobre el cuerno do un toro, y

46,1
$\overset{1}{\text{F}}$ABULA VEGESIMA QUINTA.—La Mosca y el Toro.

47,1
FABLE TWENTY-FIF$\overset{16}{\text{TH}}$—The Fly and the $\overset{29}{\text{B}}$ull

69,2
$\overset{1}{\text{m}}$agnificencia a los mas celebres del Imperio: y

69,1
consul $\overset{67}{\text{es}}$ no inferiories en valor, en prudencia, y en

69,2
m$\overset{23}{\text{ag}}$nificencia a los mas celebres del Imperio: y

69,6
del $\overset{4}{\text{t}}$ r$\overset{6}{\text{i}}$ un$\overset{8}{\text{f}}$o^{10} fueron tambien Espanoles; y finalmente

(Complete pages 46, 47, and 69 from Part Second of the key book are reproduced in Figures 7, 8, and 9, respectively.) The corrected ciphertext and the decipherment of the second type of Trist cipher is:

```
      t  h    h o r n t o n   s e    c    o
/47,1,6,16/46,7,3,15,20,24,27,28,29/,,8,1,9/,,9,1/,,2,5/
    f       h  b   m   l e   ga    t i o n
,,1,1/47,1,16,29/69,2,1 /,,1,6,7/,,2,3,2/,,6,4,6,10,8 /.
```

The remainder of the ciphertext is in the first form of Trist's cipher and presents no difficulties:

```
t h e s e c o n d
5,33,25, 4–30,105,44,45,58
```

So the complete decipherment of the 31 July 1847 excerpt reads thus: "the first is from Mr. Thornton sec[retary] of H[er] B[ritannic] M[ajesty's] legation under date July 29: the second from a foreign merchant to this correspondent here . . ."

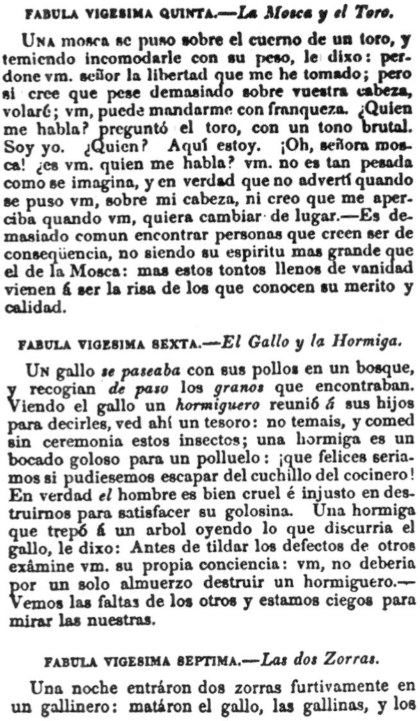

FABULA VIGESIMA QUINTA.—*La Mosca y el Toro.*

UNA mosca se puso sobre el cuerno de un toro, y temiendo incomodarle con su peso, le dixo: perdone vm. señor la libertad que me he tomado; pero si cree que pese demasiado sobre vuestra cabeza, volaré; vm. puede mandarme con franqueza. ¿Quien me habla? preguntó el toro, con un tono brutal. Soy yo. ¿Quien? Aquí estoy. ¡Oh, señora mosca! ¿es vm. quien me habla? vm. no es tan pesada como se imagina, y en verdad que no advertí quando se puso vm. sobre mi cabeza, ni creo que me aperciba quando vm. quiera cambiar de lugar.—Es demasiado comun encontrar personas que creen ser de conseqüencia, no siendo su espiritu mas grande que el de la Mosca: mas estos tontos llenos de vanidad vienen á ser la risa de los que conocen su merito y calidad.

FABULA VIGESIMA SEXTA.—*El Gallo y la Hormiga.*

UN gallo *se paseaba* con sus pollos en un bosque, y recogian *de paso* los *granos* que encontraban. Viendo el gallo un *hormiguero* reunió á sus hijos para decirles, ved ahí un tesoro: no temais, y comed sin ceremonia estos insectos; una hormiga es un bocado goloso para un polluelo: ¡que felices seriamos si pudiesemos escapar del cuchillo del cocinero! En verdad *el* hombre es bien cruel é injusto en destruirnos para satisfacer su golosina. Una hormiga que trepó á un arbol oyendo lo que discurria el gallo, le dixo: Antes de tildar los defectos de otros exâmine vm. su propia conciencia: vm, no deberia por un solo almuerzo destruir un hormiguero.—Vemos las faltas de los otros y estamos ciegos para mirar las nuestras.

FABULA VIGESIMA SEPTIMA.—*Las dos Zorras.*

Una noche entráron dos zorras furtivamente en un gallinero: matáron el gallo, las gallinas, y los

FIGURE 7. PAGE 46, PART SECOND, FROM TRIST'S KEY BOOK.
(Courtesy of the Louis-Lucien Bonaparte Collection, The Newberry Library, Chicago.)

One can only imagine the frustration and exasperation of the State Department cipher clerks trying to decipher Trist's dispatches and having constantly to make adjustments to correct his errors. Despite his clumsy, error-prone ciphers, Trist should be given considerable credit for his patience, perseverance, and diplomatic skill in bringing the Treaty of Guadalupe Hidalgo to a successful conclusion

AMUSING FABLES. 47

FABLE TWENTY-FIFTH.—*The Fly and the Bull.*

A FLY having seated himself on a bull's horn, and being afraid of incommoding him by his weight, said to him: pardon, sir, the liberty I have taken; but if you feel any inconvenience from my weight on your head, I shall fly away; you may freely command me. Who speaks? enquired the bull in a brutal tone. 'Tis I. Who? Here I am. Oh, madam fly! Is it you who were speaking to me? you are not so heavy as you imagine; indeed I did not feel you when you alighted on my head, nor do I think that I shall be sensible of the change when you fly off.—We too frequently meet with persons who think themselves of consequence, but whose spirit is as contracted as that of the fly: such vain fools, however, become the laughter of those who know their real merit.

FABLE TWENTY-SIXTH.—*The Cock and the Ant.*

A COCK *was taking a walk* in a wood with his chickens, who were gathering the *grains of corn* which they found *in passing.* The cock seeing an *ant's nest* collected his chickens and said: Behold a treasure; eat those little insects, and be not afraid; an ant is a dainty morsel for a young chicken: how happy should we be if we were only able to escape the cook's knife. Man is really very cruel and unjust to destroy us, for the purpose of satisfying his gluttony. An ant that was climbing a tree, hearing what the cock was discoursing of, said to him: Before censuring the errors of others, examine well your own conscience: you ought not for one single breakfast, to destroy a whole nest of ants.—We see the faults of others, but are blind to our own.

FABLE TWENTY-SEVENTH.—*The Two Foxes.*

ONE night two foxes entered by stealth into a hen-roost; they killed the cock, the hens, and the

FIGURE 8. PAGE 47, PART SECOND, FROM TRIST'S KEY BOOK.
(Courtesy of the Louis-Lucien Bonaparte Collection, The Newberry Library, Chicago.)

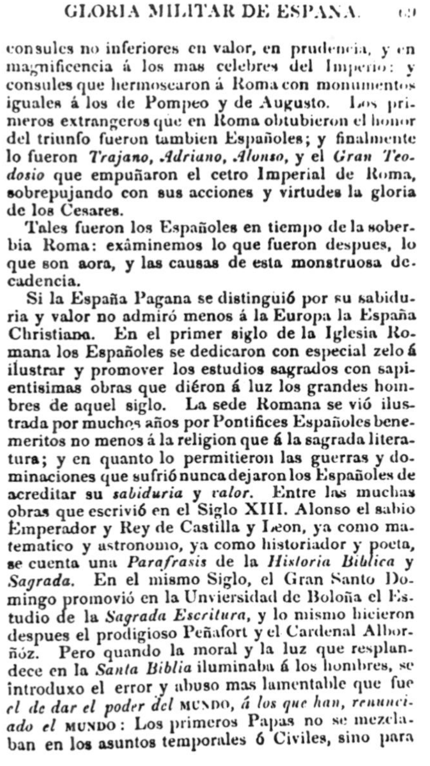

GLORIA MILITAR DE ESPAÑA.   69

consules no inferiores en valor, en prudencia, y en magnificencia á los mas celebres del Imperio: y consules que hermosearon á Roma con monumentos iguales á los de Pompeo y de Augusto. Los primeros extrangeros que en Roma obtubieron el honor del triunfo fueron tambien Españoles; y finalmente lo fueron *Trajano, Adriano, Alonso,* y el *Gran Teodosio* que empuñaron el cetro Imperial de Roma, sobrepujando con sus acciones y virtudes la gloria de los Cesares.

Tales fueron los Españoles en tiempo de la soberbia Roma: exâminemos lo que fueron despues, lo que son aora, y las causas de esta monstruosa decadencia.

Si la España Pagana se distinguió por su sabiduria y valor no admiró menos á la Europa la España Christiana. En el primer siglo de la Iglesia Romana los Españoles se dedicaron con especial zelo á ilustrar y promover los estudios sagrados con sapientisimas obras que diéron á luz los grandes hombres de aquel siglo. La sede Romana se vió ilustrada por muchos años por Pontifices Españoles benemeritos no menos á la religion que á la sagrada literatura; y en quanto lo permitieron las guerras y dominaciones que sufrió nunca dejaron los Españoles de acreditar su *sabiduria* y *valor.* Entre las muchas obras que escrivió en el Siglo XIII. Alonso el sabio Emperador y Rey de Castilla y León, ya como matematico y astronomo, ya como historiador y poeta, se cuenta una *Parafrasis* de la *Historia Biblica* y *Sagrada.* En el mismo Siglo, el Gran Santo Domingo promovió en la Unviersidad de Boloña el Estudio de la *Sagrada Escritura,* y lo mismo hicieron despues el prodigioso Peñafort y el Cardenal Alborñóz. Pero quando la moral y la luz que resplandece en la *Santa Biblia* iluminaba á los hombres, se introduxo el error y abuso mas lamentable que fue *el de dar el poder del* MUNDO, *á los que han, renunciado el* MUNDO: Los primeros Papas no se mezclaban en los asuntos temporales ó Civiles, sino para

FIGURE 9. PAGE 69, PART SECOND, FROM TRIST'S KEY BOOK.
(Courtesy of the Louis-Lucien Bonaparte Collection, The Newberry Library, Chicago.)

ACKNOWLEDGEMENTS

The authors wish to thank Professor Ralph E. Weber for initially acquainting them with Trist's ciphers. An earlier form of this article was presented at the Third Beale Cipher Symposium, Crystal City, Virginia, on 12 September 1981.

REFERENCES

1. Richard M. Ketchum, "The Thankless Task of Nicholas Trist," *American Heritage,* 21 (August 1970), 13.

2. *Ibid.,* 14.

3. Louis M. Sears, "Nicholas P. Trist, a Diplomat with Ideals," *Mississippi Valley Historical Review,* 11 (June 1924), 88–89.

4. *Ibid.,* 93.

5. General Records of the Department of State, Record Group 59, Despatches from United States Ministers to Mexico, 1823–1906, Microcopy 97, 197 rolls; National Archives, Washington, D.C., Microfilm Roll 15 (hereafter cited as General Records of the Department of State RG 59, M 97, Roll 15).

6. Ralph E. Weber, *United States Diplomatic Codes and Ciphers* (Chicago, 1979), 23–24.

7. James B. Ward, *The Beale Papers,* (Lynchburg, 1885), 20–22. Reprinted by the Beale Cypher Association, P.O. Box 216, Medfield, MA 02052.

8. Carl Van Doren, *Secret History of the American Revolution* (New York, 1969), 200.

9. Albert C. Leighton, "Secret Ciphers in Bavarian Archives," *Proceedings of the Second Beale Cipher Symposium* (1979), p. 79.

10. Examples are: Ketchum [1]; Sears [3]; Robert Arthur Brent, *Nicholas Philip Trist: Biography of a Disobedient Diplomat* (Ph.D. dissertation, University of Virginia, 1950); Eugene Keith Chamberlain, "Nicholas Trist and Baja California," *Pacific Historical Review,* 32 (1963), 49–63; Kenneth M. Johnson, "Baja California and the Treaty of Guadalupe Hidalgo," *Journal of the West,* 11 (April 1972), 328–347; Don Blevins, "The Forgotten Peacemaker, Nicholas Trist," *American History Illustrated,* 14 (June 1979), 4–8, 42–47.

11. Weber, 205–206.

12. General Records of the Department of State RG 59, M 97, Roll 15.

13. Papers of Nicholas Trist, Vol. 25, Library of Congress, Washington, D.C.

14. Sears, 96.

15. Ketchum, 89.

16. Ketchum, 89.

17. David Kahn, *The Codebreakers* (New York, Macmillan, 1967), 372–373.

18. General Records of the Department of State RG 59, M 97, Roll 15.

My Recollections of G.2 A.6
by J. Rives Childs

[On 31 October 1977, J. Rives Childs, one of the last if not the last surviving member of G.2 A.6, the cryptanalytic agency of the American Expeditionary Force in World War I, honored the New York Cipher Society with a talk on his memories of his experiences in America's first official combat codebreaking unit. He wrote out his talk, though he departed from this text slightly in speaking. The original is, with his kind permission, printed below. I have made some slight emendations, such as spelling out abbreviations, adding brief identifications or first names where needed, and trimming here and there.

After his World War I work in cryptology, Mr. Childs went on to a distinguished career in the State Department, rising to become ambassador to Saudi Arabia, Yemen, and Ethiopia. His career in letters is no less distinguished. He has written more than half a dozen books and is regarded today as one of the world's leading experts on Casanova, on whom he has published a biography and a bibliography, and on Restif de la Bretonne, a bawdy 19th-century French writer. *Cryptologia* regrets that its terms of reference exclude these juicy topics, but it is confident that its readers will enjoy these reminiscences of Mr. Childs, which it is proud to publish, quite as much.—D.K.]

My only interest in cryptography before World War I was a passing one stimulated by a reading of Poe's "The Gold-Bug." When we entered the war in the spring of 1917, I volunteered and applied for admission to one of the training camps for reserve officers. Shortly thereafter I was admitted to the First Officers' Training Camp at Fort Meyer. Discouraged at the prospect of reaching France, I decided to appeal to Senator Thomas S. Martin of Virginia for his support of my application for an assignment to Military Intelligence. This came through in orders to me in September,

From *Cryptologia,* Vol. 2, No. 3, July 1978.

1917, while serving as aide de camp to General Farnsworth, commanding officer of the 159th Brigade, 80th Division, at Camp Lee, to report to the Army War College in Washington for a course of instruction in Military Intelligence. This was one of only two efforts by me to use political preferment—the other having been exercised with Congressman Carter Glass in 1912 to obtain an assignment with the U.S. Geological Survey for the summer, which took me to Idaho and Wyoming. In 30 years with the State Department, from 1923 to 1953, in accordance with the traditions of the Foreign Service, I never once employed political influence for advancement.

On reporting for duty at the Army War College, I found myself in a first training session for work in Military Intelligence in a group comprising a dozen officers destined for appointment as military attachés at embassies and legations abroad and with three other junior officers with no particular duties in view. Among our lecturers was Captain Herbert Yardley who, while employed in the State Department as a code clerk before the war, had interested himself in cryptography, in which he was later to fill a brilliant career. His instruction was elementary owing to the very limited knowledge available to the armed forces. The most advanced work on the subject was a pamphlet known as "Hitt's Manual" [1] written by Captain Parker Hitt. A most useful addition was to be written and later published by Yardley entitled *The American Black Chamber* after his cryptographic bureau, established by the War Department [2] in the 1920s, had been dissolved by Secretary of State Henry L. Stimson with the naive explanation that gentlemen did not read others' correspondence. This was on a par with many other quixotic decisions which we embraced in our introduction to a new world into which we were destined to be ushered after 1914.

Yardley appeared before us one morning, holding in his hand a telegram received from General John J. Pershing's headquarters at Chaumont in France. It was a pressing request that four officers be given an urgent specialized course of instruction in cryptography and sent as speedily as possible to GHQ in France. Yardley asked for volunteers and four of us stepped forward including myself, Bob Gilmore, a Williams graduate and young lawyer practicing in New York City, Lee Sellers, a music critic on the staff of the *New York Sun* and John Graham, language instructor at Washington and Lee in Lexington. By a curious coincidence, Bob was later to turn up in Tangier as assistant naval attaché in 1943 while I was in charge of the American Legation there. Lee died of flu in Chaumont in 1918 after the Armistice; the next casualty was John in his prime, while Bob died in the '60s in Biarritz, where he had retired.

Before proceeding to France, we were assigned for a brief course of instruction by Bill Friedman and his fiancée, Elizabeth Smith, on the estate of a wealthy Chicagoan, George Fabyan, at Geneva, Illinois. Fabyan had instituted a number of esoteric projects, including a study of perpetual motion and one to establish that Bacon wrote Shakespeare by the presence of supposititious Baconian cipher in Shakespeare's plays. Nothing could have been more indicative of the elementary knowledge possessed by our armed forces of cryptography than the fact that our government had to resort to private enterprise for the instruction of its cryptographers.

There was such an atmosphere of mystery about "Riverbank," as the Fabyan estate was called, that, when we had unpacked in a comfortable private dwelling on arriving from Washington and were on the point of going to the dining room situated in another building for dinner and some observations were made by one of our number about the set-up, I placed a finger on my lips as a warning to my companions. On emerging in the open, I remarked that it was likely our quarters were bugged and that we would do well to limit our comments to exchanges outside our quarters. Years later, when I recounted this conversation to Friedman when we met at the Cosmos Club in Washington, while he was with the National Security Agency and I was on leave from a diplomatic post abroad, he laughed and remarked, "You guessed right!"

Friedman was to join us in G.2 A.6 at Chaumont a few months after our arrival there. Sellers and Graham were the first to leave on one ship and Gilmore and I on the *Andania* a few days after Christmas to join several hundred unattached officers proceeding to France for assignment. To avoid German submarines we navigated far north on a voyage which lasted almost a month. When we put in at Liverpool, after playing blackjack most of the time, we were almost as short of food as England itself was. Foodstocks were reported to be sufficient for a bare three weeks; we were given orders forbidding us to buy any to supplement the slender rations which had been doled out to us.

We entrained a few hours after arrival and after we had hustled our baggage ourselves for Southampton where we were to spend the night on the bare floors of a camp. It was January and it rained that night in a freezing temperature which made sleeping difficult. In the early dawn, Bob and I arose and determined to walk into town to restore our circulation and to forage for food notwithstanding the orders forbidding it. A walk of several miles brought us to the warm interior of a comfortable hotel. There we were greeted by the manager who regretted that he had orders not to serve any Americans, even in uniform, owing to England's depleted food supplies. Several British officers in the lobby protested at such treatment of the country's newly found allies. A senior officer ordered the manager peremptorily to conduct us upstairs to a private room and [be] served breakfast. Once we had filled our famished stomachs, we returned to camp to arrive in time for breakfast at camp—devoured by us with the same gusto as that in Southampton.

A little later we embarked by ferry for Le Havre, where we were to discover that neither there nor elsewhere in France was any shortage of food noticeable. The next day we went by train to Blois, where we learned to what extent the French were attached to creature comforts in the luxurious hotel where we were billeted. Unfortunately, we were hardly asleep when there was a thunderous knocking at our door.

It opened to disclose an American colonel who inquired our rank. When we sleepily announced, "Lieutenant, sir," the order was instantaneous: "Then get the hell out, it's too damned good for a shavetail." We had nothing to do but dress and, with our baggage, take to the street in search of other quarters. These we found in an American camp outside the town and after some further delays we proceeded via St. Aignan and Tours in the first days of February to our destination, Chaumont in northeast France, where Pershing had his headquarters and where we were to remain nine months until the Armistice.

I have told something of those days in an anonymous volume published in 1932 by Bobbs-Merrill entitled *Before The Curtain Falls*. It appeared during the dark days of the Depression in only 3,000 copies. It was extensively reviewed and generally most favorably. Today it is difficult to find and commands $20 or $30. I have the unfortunate fate of writing books which few read but which bring extravagant prices, sometimes as much as $60 or $70 when they can be found.

G.2 A.6 had been installed under the command of Major, later Colonel, Frank Moorman, who had risen from the ranks and whom we were to find possessed of his own peculiar ideas about reserve officers, as we were distinguished from regular officers making the army their career.

On arrival with Gilmore at the army barracks which housed offices of Pershing's staff, including Moorman's section, Sellers sidled up to me in the entry and whispered, "Don't be surprised by anything you hear and don't make any comments; I'll explain later."

With that introduction Gilmore and I were ushered into Moorman's presence.

Sellers' cautionary remarks served in good stead when Moorman welcomed us. With only casual attention to Gilmore he reserved his particular interest in me, remarking that I was to have charge of the cipher section of G.2 A.6.

I was dumbfounded until during the luncheon break Sellers disclosed that on arrival at Chaumont he had had access to the files where there was mention of a Childs, described as a "cipher expert." [3] It further appeared that GHQ had requested the War Department to run this Childs down and send him to France. Sellers was of the opinion that Moorman had mistaken me for the Childs in question. However neither on the occasion of my first interview with Moorman nor at any subsequent time had there ever been any reference to my double.

Very soon after our arrival, Parker Hitt came by to see Moorman, and after his departure Moorman sent for me. "I have just had the visit of Major Parker Hitt on his passage through Chaumont. He expressed himself as quite disturbed about the insecurity of our trench code and has so expressed himself to the section here who are compiling it. As they are unfamiliar with codebreaking, he came away with the impression that he had made very little impression on them on the subject. Hitt has proposed that I have some messages encoded and turned over to a member of our staff least familiar with their breaking. I have concluded that this would be you, so I want you to turn over for the time being your work on ciphers and devote yourself to solving the American code." The messages were set up for me and I went to work that same day with the aid of a clerical assistant. Within 24 hours, the code was solved [4] to the consternation of the officer having charge of its compilation. I analyzed the weaknesses of the system employed and recommended certain measures to adopt for its better protection against solution by the enemy.

One consequence of my achievement was a summons from Moorman to congratulate me. "Lieutenant, I am very pleased with your success, which has fully confirmed Major Hitt in his opinion of the dangerous weakness of the system. You have made an important contribution to safeguarding the future security of our trench code. I want you to know also that as you are a reserve officer and not in the regular army I am reserving all promotions for the professional officers under my command. What I can do is to appoint you liaison officer with the French and British War Offices on all aspects of Military Intelligence concerned with codes and ciphers. Captain Powell is coming from the War Department in a few days and you will accompany him on his visit to Paris and London to meet your opposite numbers at the French and British War Offices."

So it followed that a few days after Powell's appearance we set out for Paris where I was presented to the ace of aces among cryptographers, Georges Painvin, four or five years my senior. His masterly solutions of German ciphers caused him to become known some months later as "artisan of the victory" over the Germans when Paris might have fallen but for the knowledge gained of German intentions by Painvin of where they would strike. Then to London, where, among the shops of the Burlington Arcade, we were admitted, after our identities had been proven to the satisfaction of those in authority, to the section of British Military Intelligence devoted in secret rooms to the reading of enemy codes and ciphers under the direction of Major Ian Hay.[5]

When the British discovered how little I knew of the subject, they lost interest in my presence after turning over to me the keys to the so-called Fuer God ciphers. Messages in it were exchanged by wireless between Berlin and a German expedition dispatched to Misrate in Tripoli under the command of Captain of Cavalry von Todenwart to foment disaffection against the Allies among the Arabs of North Africa. The Fuer God [6] system of multiple alphabets had the longest life of any cipher employed by the Germans in World War I, used as it was from 1916 to 1918. It was also one of the few purely substitution ciphers employed by the German General Staff, most of their systems involving the use of intricate transposition methods or a combination of substitution and transposition. A more important accomplishment [7] of my initial mission was to agree upon a system of exchange of our respective code and cipher solutions which, however extraordinary it may seem, had never occurred to either of our intelligence departments to institute.

The American Expeditionary Forces had been established some eight months previous, GHQ at Chaumont a few months later. A high-powered radio receiving station had also been set up to intercept enemy radio communications and there had accumulated a great volume of intercepted code and cipher messages of the enemy; but not one cipher message had been read.

The instructions that had been given in cryptography in Washington had been necessarily rudimentary, confined as the knowledge of ciphers was to the simple systems employed by Mexico and Latin American countries; of the system employed by Germany and the other Central Powers, nothing was known to the United States Army when I arrived at Chaumont.

The first two weeks were spent by me in classifying the hundreds of cipher messages which were being received, in making elaborate tabulations and diagrams which filled huge sheets of paper and which gave evidence of an industriousness which helped to conceal my bewilderment and consciousness of my own shortcomings for the work to which I had been assigned.

The most fruitful means for my acquiring a knowledge of German ciphers was to be my periodic visits to London and Paris, and more particularly the great help given me by Captain Painvin. It was while I was in his office at the French War Office on March 5, 1918, that I acquired my first knowledge of the most important cipher introduced by the Germans on the western and eastern fronts. I was with him when I witnessed the arrival of the first messages in what became known as the famous ADFGX cipher. I remember so vividly when Captain Painvin brought over the first message in this cipher and exhibited it to me.

```
KR v ZS
CHI 82
AFADG  FXGFG  ACCFF  DADFX  FFGFD
GFXXA  DGAGA FFGGD  FADFA  AGZDG
AADAX  AFDAG DGAXG GDXGD  AZFAD
AFXGX  AX
```

The letters ZS obviously represented the German sending, and KR the German receiving, station, while the number "82" was a check on the number of letters contained in the message.

There had been widespread rumors for some time of a contemplated major offensive by the German Army in the spring and there was a nervous tension in every Allied headquarters, while redoubled energy was being put forth by the Allied cipher bureaus to gain every bit of information which might be revealed of the enemy's intention from a reading of German code and cipher messages.

The use of cipher on the western front by the Germans had been infrequent for some time past, principal reliance being placed upon the use of codes. Codes, however, while useful enough on inactive fronts, lack that essential element of security in times of activity on account of the danger of the code book falling into the hands of the enemy. On the other hand, a cipher, while more laborious to employ, requires no commitment to writing but may usually be memorized and, even if committed to writing, may be changed daily, while a code book is not so readily replaced.

The introduction of a new cipher system over the entire western front was plain warning of the imminent launching of the long heralded offensive. Such an offensive followed on March 21.

That the messages were cipher and not code was immediately apparent. If they had been code, the code groups, which are of an invariable number of letters [8] such as three, five or ten, would, when the number of letters in each message had been tallied, have been divisible by three, five or ten. But the messages in question had 82 letters, 50 letters, 66 letters and so forth, of which the only common factor was the number 2. Even a combination of 26 two-letter combinations would not suffice to give sufficient code groups to represent the 2,000 letters, words and phrases included in the ordinary German code book. Moreover, only five letters of the alphabet were used, namely, A, D, F, G and X.

Every message was characterized by two invariable factors: each message contained an even number of letters and in no case were any other than the letters A, D, F, G and X employed.

Here at least were two established facts on which deductions might safely be based, and to the trained and analytical mind of Painvin, they were suggestive of one positive and inescapable deduction. There was only one possible means by which five letters of the alphabet might be made to represent the normal 26 letters of the alphabet and that was by a square of five rows by five columns in which five letters were made to represent, in coefficients of two-letter groups, the 26 letters of the alphabet distributed among 25 squares, thus:

	A	D	F	G	X
A	A	B	C	D	E
D	F	G	H	IJ	K
F	L	M	N	O	P
G	Q	R	S	T	U
X	V	W	X	Y	Z

The letter A in the plaintext message would be enciphered by the letters AA, and the letter B by the letters DA, and so forth. A solution of the cipher should be easily possible, therefore, by separating the enciphered letters in groups of two and applying the test of frequency for the determination of the plaintext equivalents.

The frequency count of the groups thus broken up, however, was anything but encouraging; the conclusion was inevitable that either multiple alphabets had been employed or that, after a simple substitution, a transposition of the letters had been employed.

There was a sufficient volume of enciphered text to make the theory of the use of multiple alphabets untenable; accordingly, there was no doubt that after a substitution of the letters had been effected, the letters had been transposed and that a solution of the cipher would involve a solution, first, of the system of transposition, and thereafter, of the substitution alphabet employed.

This was a more formidable task than had ever been presented in a military cipher and seemed to defy the capacities of even that most brilliant of cryptographers, Painvin.

The German General Staff will no doubt be as incredulous as anyone else when it is stated that such a system, the keys of which were changed daily on the western front, was not only proved capable of solution but that three distinct methods of solution were in time developed by which messages enciphered in such a manner might be read, two of which Painvin contributed and one of which I was fortunate enough by long and patient endeavor to demonstrate.

That the German General Staff placed unreserved confidence in the security of this ADFGX cipher, which continued in uninterrupted use on the western front until the Armistice and was also introduced on the eastern front [9], was subsequently evidenced by cipher messages exchanged between the chief German intelligence officer in Berlin and General Kress von Kressenstein, a commander of German armies on the eastern front.

In August, 1918, a race had developed—of which the Allies knew nothing—between the allied Turkish and German armies for the possession of the rich oil district centering about Baku in the Russian Caucasus.

The first intimation of this conflict came to the Allies through a message sent by General von Kressenstein from Tiflis for the German Foreign Office through the German ambassador, Karl Helfferich, to defeated Russia, on August 3, 1918, reading as follows:

His Excellency Helfferich, Moscow.

For Foreign Office,

According to unconfirmed reports Baku has been taken by the Turks. German officers and soldiers have not taken part in either the earlier or present operations of the Turks in Azerbaidjan. Several days ago I visited Enver Pasha in Elizabethpol and received positive assurances that Baku would not be attacked without orders from his higher command, but for sanitary reasons he would improve his position. To make the Turkish advance more difficult I have placed obstacles in the way of every shipment of munitions from Baku via Tiflis up to the present time.

KRESS.

This message had been enciphered by means of a simple substitution system alphabet, a method so elementary and simple that I was able to determine the system employed and to reconstruct the alphabet within an hour after the text of the enciphered message, as it had been intercepted by our wireless receiving station at Chaumont, had been laid on my table.

A few days later I was working on a series of messages enciphered by the ADFGX system which were being sent from Berlin to Kressenstein. It required days of work before I succeeded in solving the keys employed. Although the messages were found to contain, after so many days of labor, no information of any strategic importance, I was fully recompensed for the time spent when in one of the messages sent on August 8 I read:

The cipher prepared by General von Kress was solved here at once. Its further use in operations is forbidden.

I, too, had solved the cipher of General von Kress without difficulty; moreover, I had solved the cipher of the chief of German intelligence in which such consummate faith had been placed and continued to be placed throughout the war.

In one respect an armistice existed between the Allies and the Central Powers from the moment of the declaration of war until its close. That was in the field of wireless communications.

By tacit agreement, no effort was ever made on either side to interfere with the sending or receiving wireless stations of the other, an agreement scrupulously observed and essential if uninterrupted communications, equally necessary to one side as to another, were to be assured.

The famous ADFGX cipher after a few weeks underwent the addition of the letter V, making possible 36 squares, or the use of 26 letters of the alphabet with the addition of the numerals 0 to 9. From the western front, its use became extended over the wide area of the eastern front, including Russia, the Balkans and Asia Minor.

During the last months of the war, on the eastern front, the same key was employed for three successive days, in contradistinction to the western front where the key underwent a vexatious change each day.

On November 2, 1918, I was enabled to reconstruct within one hour and a half the system of transposition and the alphabet employed for the encipherment of messages in the ADFGVX cipher on the eastern front by the German forces and to read, in consequence, all cipher messages which had been exchanged on the eastern front between German wireless stations on November 1 and 2.

This exceptional good fortune enabled the decipherment of the messages of November 3 as quickly as they were received from our wireless station. Among them there was included an enciphered message in thirteen parts from station UKS (Bucharest) to LP (Berlin) addressed by General August von Mackensen to the German High Command and sent at eight o'clock on the evening of the third. This message was undoubtedly the most important one deciphered during the war by us. It read as follows:

To the Higher Command:

Review of the situation. Up to date it has had to be reckoned with that the enemy will attempt a crossing of the Danube with the forces assembling at Lompalanka and vicinity of Rustchuk, with the object of cutting the railroad communication between Orsove and Craiova, and to strike forward on Bucharest. Since November 1st, 1918, however, it appears that the Serbian armies, together with three French divisions, are engaged in an advance toward Belgrade-Semendria, and the intended attack at Vidin and Lompalanka seems to have been abandoned.

(part missing)

It is therefore extremely probable that the Serbian armies, reinforced by the French, intend to cross the Danube at Belgrade-Semendria and march into Southern Hungary, while the French army marching up south of Svistov and Rustchuk retains the task of directing an offensive toward Bucharest. In conjunction with this operation it is not impossible that Rumanian forces from Moldavia will enter Transylvania through the Tolgyes, Gyimes and Oitos passes, thereby threatening the lines of communication in the rear of the army of occupation which have up to now as a result—

(part mising)

—is threatened with attack, and the further occupation of Wallachia, as laid down in order of Headquarters Staff 2 IA, N.R. 11161 OP [10], is useless, and in view of the stocks on hand of munitions, provisions and coal can not be carried out. In case a general armistice can not be expected in the immediate future, it is proposed that the army of occupation be withdrawn from Rumania at once and to start the march to Upper Silesia through Hungary, together with the German units of the 1 Army. Approval is requested.

(Signed) K.M.I. A GR-OP

By reason of its length, I was persuaded before the message had even been reduced to German plaintext, a long and tedious task, that it was likely to contain information of more than ordinary interest.

Every available German translator of the section was pressed into service, while I superintended the conversion of the ciphertext to German, of which language I was almost entirely ignorant save for that instinctive feel for the mechanics of it which any cryptographer acquires from such intimate daily contact with it as I had had.

So important was this message that I was instructed "to carry it over personally to the executive officer of the assistant chief of staff."[11]

When I did so and he had read it, he exclaimed: "This is so important it must be sent to Supreme War Council Headquarters by special plane." On glancing at my insignia of rank he remarked, "What on earth has happened that you have not been promoted?"

When I explained that Colonel Moorman did not believe in the promotion of reserve officers, he swore that he was going to see that this was corrected, and although I did not count on it, I was in fact promoted very soon thereafter.

REFERENCES

1. *Manual for the Solution of Military Ciphers* (Fort Leavenworth, 1916; reprinted 1977 by Aegean Park Press).

2. Actually the War and State departments.

3. The literature of cryptology gives no indication of whom this might be.

4. Actually just the monoalphabetic superencipherment proposed for the trench code. Childs was given the trench code and told to see whether he could recover and strip off the superencipherment. The story is told in David Kahn, *The Codebreakers* (New York, Macmillan, 1967), 327.

5. Actually Malcolm Vivian Hay of Seaton.

6. So called because it was for ("Fuer") a radio station with call sign GOD.

7. Childs neglects to say here that the first accomplishment was to solve the enciphered keys of the Fuer GOD. These were monoalphabetically enciphered German words, such as INSTRUMENTENMACHER. Childs' solution of them won him acceptance with the British and gave him confidence in his own cryptanalytic abilities. See *The Codebreakers,* 337.

8. Or are pronounceable, like TURBARIAS.

9. Except for the addition of a sixth letter, as Childs later says.

10. This is the serial number of a message. IA stands for the first general staff officer, the operations officer, in the headquarters staff; N.R. should be "Nr.," or "Nummer;" OP stands for "Operations." The same principles apply to the signature, but I do not know what K.M. means or why GR (probably "Gruppe") precedes OP.

11. It gave the Allies their first hint that the Germans would evacuate Rumania and a hope that the Rumanians would rise up against their occupiers—which they did. Childs also pointed out in his talk that the solution told the Allies of the significance of an intercept from the Austro-Hungarian front outlining the Austrian peace proposals, which included the right of free transit across Austro-Hungarian territory for the German army in Rumania.

Who Wrote "The American Black Chamber"?
by Louis Kruh

When Herbert O. Yardley exposed the cryptanalytic work of the United States in a series of articles in the *Saturday Evening Post* [5] early in 1931 and in his book, *The American Black Chamber* [6], published later that year, his former colleagues in the Army Signal Corps and Military Intelligence were outraged.

William F. Friedman circularized his associates in the American Expeditionary Forces for their opinions, and Colonel Frank Moorman, Colonel Parker Hitt, Lieutenant Edward Vogel, and Lieutenant Edwin Woelluer were unanimously critical of Yardley. Professor John Manly, however, defended Yardley. It should be noted that Manly had a close relationship with Yardley and was the only subordinate of Yardley to be mentioned by name in *The American Black Chamber*.[1,2]

Fifteen years after *The American Black Chamber* was published, an Army historian, writing about the 1917–1929 period [3,4] when Yardley was Chief of the Cipher Bureau (MI-8), described Yardley and his work in unflattering terms at almost every opportunity. It is obvious that most officials never forgave Yardley for what Friedman considered a most serious breach of ethics, if not a traitorous act.

A footnote in the official history [3] even alleges that the articles and book were not written by Yardley, but instead were ghost-written for $1000 by C---- K-----, an AT&T engineer.

This writer decided to attempt to ascertain the circumstances under which K----- cooperated with Yardley, and whether or not the allegation was correct.

According to the historical account, Lieutenant Colonel A. J. McGrail, a former member of the Cipher Bureau and specialist in "secret inks," was the source for the reference to K----- and mention was made

From *Cryptologia,* Vol. 2, No. 2, April 1978.

of a note on the flyleaf of the copy of *The American Black Chamber* owned by Friedman.

Assuming that Friedman's copy of *The American Black Chamber* was in the Friedman Collection now in the George C. Marshall Foundation (Library) in Lexington, Virginia, I wrote a letter to their archivist. He very graciously found the book and supplied the following text which was written on the title page:

> Sometime in 1942 McGrail told me that he had it on most excellent authority that this book was actually "ghost written" by an AT&T Company engineer named C---- K----- who received $1,000 for his work. I don't know K----- but feel sure Yardley had much help in writing, from somebody.
>
> W.F.F. 1945

In the meantime, I had located K----- living in retirement in Florida and wrote to him. His letter follows:

> Dear Mr. Kruh:
>
> This replies to your letter reporting that I helped Herb Yardley write the American Black Chamber.
>
> During the several years I intimately knew Herb and his wife at Jackson Heights, Long Island, he naturally never disclosed to me that he was director of the Chamber in New York City—which of course was a Federal top secret project. Therefore, I didn't in any way collaborate in writing his book. However, after its publication he sold a series titled "Yardleygrams" to Life Magazine which consisted of a couple-of-sentence squibs giving an encripted *(sic)*, intercepted enemy war message illustrating elementary cryptographic techniques such as Caesar Alphabets, Simple Substitutions, Transpositions, etc. After Herb got tied up collaborating with a professor in the English Department of Chicago U. on articles explaining historic developments in cryptography which he sold to the Saturday Evening Post, he asked me to ghost-write a book of short spy stories in which the intercepted encripted *(sic)* message was solved by simple, basic methods more or less similar to those involved in the Life "Yardleygrams."
>
> The book was published by Bobbs-Merrill *(sic)* under the same title. Apparently, this is the book which is <u>mistakenly</u> referred to as "The American Black Chamber" in your 3-volume report on the Signal

Security Agency. I have no background in cryptography other than reading a classified textbook used by the Navy for training in basic decripting *(sic)* methods.

Sincerely,
C---- K-----

The professor in the University of Chicago's English Department is obviously Manly, and although K----- has the sequence of events reversed, another minor mystery is created by his implication that Manly was Yardley's collaborator in the series of articles which preceded *The American Black Chamber* and became an integral part of the book.

The Army historian, who apparently never tried to contact K-----, wrote, "Whether the 'ghost-writer' or assistant was actually Mr. K----- or not is unimportant, but to judge from Yardley's official correspondence, there is good reason to believe that he did have assistance in writing *The American Black Chamber*. Literary analysis of his subsequent novels tend to confirm this belief. His mystery novel, *Crows are Black Everywhere* [Putnam's, 1945], was written in collaboration with Carl Grabow [on the title-page]."

Yardley, however, had described his writing of the book and articles in a letter to Manly in April 1931:

Well, it has been a unique experience. I hadn't done any real work for so long that I told Bye, my agent, and the Sat Eve Post that I would need some one else to write the stuff. I showed a few things to Bye and Costain, the latter editor of Post, and both told me to go to work myself. I sat for days before a typewriter, helpless. Oh, I pecked away a bit, and gradually under the encouragement of Bye I got a bit of confidence. Then Bobbs-Merrill advanced me $1,000 on outline. Then there was a call to rush the book. I began work in shifts, working a few hours, sleeping a few hours, going out of my room only to buy some eggs, bread, coffee and cans of tomato juice. Jesus, the stuff I turned out. Sometimes only a thousand words, but often as many as 10,000 a day. As the chapters appeared I took them to Bye who read them and offered criticism. Any way I completed the book and boiled down parts of it for the articles all in 7 weeks.

Except for K-----, all of the main people involved in this footnote to history have died, so that the disclosure of new information is unlikely.

This writer believes that the somewhat extravagant and ostentatious style of *The American Black Chamber* is reminiscent of Yardley's personality, and based on all evidence, Yardley apparently acted alone in writing the book.

REFERENCES

1.   Kahn, David, *The Codebreakers: The Story of Secret Writing* (New York: Macmillan, 1967).

2.   Turchen, Lesta V., Herbert Osborne Yardley and American Cryptography (Vermillion, SD: University of South Dakota, Master's Thesis, 1969).

3.   U.S. Army Security Agency, *Historical Background of the Signal Security Agency,* Volume Two: World War I 1917–1919 (n.p.: n.n., 1946).

4.   U.S. Army Security Agency, *Historical Background of the Signal Security Agency,* Volume Three: The Peace 1919–1939 (n.p.: n.n., 1946).

5.   Yardley, Herbert O., Secret Inks, *Saturday Evening Post,* April 4, 1931.

———, Codes, *Saturday Evening Post,* April 18, 1931.

———, Ciphers, *Saturday Evening Post,* May 9, 1931.

———. Cryptograms and Their Solution, *Saturday Evening Post,* November 21, 1931.

6.   Yardley, Herbert O., *The American Black Chamber* (Indianapolis: Bobbs-Merrill, 1931).

The Annotated "The American Black Chamber" by David Kahn

Herbert O. Yardley's *The American Black Chamber* is by far the best picture of the activities and personalities of a cryptanalytic bureau ever written. It provides more detail, more color, more specifics than any other book. But sometimes Yardley erred, sometimes exaggerated, even fictionalized. He omitted information. He changed some names. His publisher suppressed a few names that Yardley had in the typescript. Yardley assumes background information that would have been known to the reader of the 1930s but has been forgotten to a large degree by the 1980s.

All of this makes it worthwhile to annotate *The American Black Chamber*. My chief source for this was William F. Friedman's copy of this book, now in his collection in the George C. Marshall Library, Lexington, Virginia. In it, Friedman has put comments, corrections, and additions to Yardley's text, and has also had Charles J. Mendelsohn, an MI-8 cryptanalyst, and A. J. McGrail, an MI-8 chemist, write in their views. The animus of all these men against Yardley was evident, and this has been taken into account in using their annotations, which have been checked against outside sources whenever possible. In addition to this book, other sources include such standard ones as various volumes of the State Department *Biographical Register, The New York Times,* and various works on cryptology, and interviews with the second Mrs. Herbert O. Yardley, the former Edna Ramsaier.

The first page numbers refer to the original Bobbs-Merrill Company edition of 1931; those in brackets to the Ballantine Books paperback Espionage/Intelligence Library edition of 1981.

From *Cryptologia*, Vol. 9, No. 1, Jan. 1985.

* * *

Page 17 [1]: The State Department code room: "This spacious room with its high ceiling overlooked the southern White House grounds."

The old State, War and Navy Departments Building, in which the code room was located, is today the Old Executive Office Building, just west of the White House.

THE CIPHER CENTER OF THE REICH WAR MINISTRY.
Yardley dedicated his book "to the Personnel of MI-8 and the American Black Chamber and to Our Skilful Antagonists, the Foreign Cryptographers, Who still remain behind the Curtain of Secret Diplomacy." Here are some of those antagonists, out from behind their curtain. The photograph was taken in 1925 at the time of the transfer to another post of the founder of the post-World War I German army's cryptanalytic unit, Major Erich Buschenhagen, seated center with scroll and flowers. Among the others in the photograph are, in front row, second from left, Walther Seifert, later head of evaluation in Göring's Forschungsamt, and third from left, Dr. Novopaschenny, head of Russian cryptanalysis in the Cipher center; in the top row, fifth from left, Wachter, later head of English cryptanalysis in the Forschungsamt, and seventh from left, Max Bottger, one of the three founders of the Forschungsamt in 1933; at the extreme right, with bow tie and glasses, Wilhelm Flicke, later author of *War Secrets in the Ether.*

* * *

Page 19 [2]: After referring to most members of the U.S. diplomatic corps as "jolly, smartly dressed pigmies," he noted that "The Chief of the Latin American Division was an entirely different type . . . he preferred to hold the strings that made the armies, generals and presidents of South and Central America dance at his bidding . . . he was a strong man and the author of American 'dollar diplomacy.' Bryan, when he was appointed Secretary of State, kicked him out for this policy."

This man was probably William Tecumseh Sherman Doyle, who became chief of the Latin American division in 1911 and was replaced in 1913, a few months after William Jennings Bryan became secretary of state under Woodrow Wilson.

* * *

Page 20 [3]: "I quickly devoured all the books on cryptography that could be found in the Congressional Library."

In English, there were probably fewer than half a dozen, mostly concerned with cryptography and barely touching on cryptanalysis. A number of articles in widely scattered English and American magazines had dealt with the solutions of individual cipher systems, but it is questionable, in view of the lack of bibliographies on the subject at the time, whether Yardley saw any of these.

* * *

Page 21 [3]: "At last I found the American Army pamphlet on the solution of military ciphers . . . The book was full of methods for the solution of various types. The only trouble was that the types of cipher it explained were so simple that any bright schoolboy could solve them."

Not so. Parker Hitt's *Manual for the Solution of Military Ciphers* (Fort Leavenworth: Press of the Army Service Schools, 1916), 101 pages, is much better than Yardley suggests.

* * *

Pages 21–22 [4]: "One night . . . I heard the cable office in New York tell the White House telegraph operator (we used the same wire to New York) that he had 500 words from Colonel [Edward M.] House to the President [Wilson] . . . I made a copy . . . This would be a good material to work on, for surely the President and his trusted agent would be using a difficult code. Imagine my amazement when I was able to solve the message in less than two hours."

It is not possible to identify with certainty which of the several systems then used by Wilson and House [that] Yardley solved. He could have stripped the encipherment from what was probably a State Department code, or he could have ascertained the meanings of codewords for individuals that Wilson and House had agreed upon and that were inserted into the code messages, such as WHITE for British Foreign Minister Sir Edward Grey. If House and Wilson used their own specially constructed code of several thousand equivalents, no one could have reconstructed it in two hours.

* * *

Page 23 [5]: "For months now, I had been working on the solution of the American diplomatic code."

Since Yardley, working in the Code Room, almost certainly had access to the State Department codes, what he could have solved remains unknown.

* * *

Page 26 [7]: "All this time my work on the decipherment of the American diplomatic code was slowly progressing. At last I laid some one hundred pages of typewritten exposition before my immediate superior."

He was David A. Salmon, 34, chief of the Bureau of Indexes and Archives, who seems to have had no experience in codebreaking and therefore little insight into what makes codes strong.

* * *

Page 26 [7]: "'What's this?' he [Salmon] asked, 'of the Solution of American Diplomatic Codes,' I replied."

A cryptanalyst who has seen this says that it has little merit. The National Security Agency says it cannot find it in its files.

* * *

Page 30 [9]: "A month later my superior introduced a new method for encoding our secret dispatches."

This was almost certainly a new form of encipherment for the existing code—not a new code.

* * *

Page 30 [9]: "My fingers itched to tear it [the new method] apart . . . ways and means of attack on this new system crept through my brain. It was the first thing I thought of when I awakened, the last when I fell asleep."

This has come to be called "the Yardley symptom" in cryptology.

* * *

Page 32 [11]: Yardley was trying to get a release from the State Department to go to the army to set up a codebreaking unit. He went to see "Assistant Secretary Phillips" to request it.

This was William Phillips, who held many State Department and Foreign Service posts, including ambassador to Italy from 1938 to 1941.

THE OLD STATE, WAR, AND NAVY DEPARTMENTS BUILDING.
Yardley began his career as a code clerk in this Victorian pile, which stands just to the west of the White House and serves today as the Old Executive Office Building for members of the White House staff.

* * *

Pages 33–34 [11]: "I must make myself appear so indispensable to the War Department that it would demand my release . . . Inquiries in the right places pointed to Colonel Gibbs, Signal Corps Officer, as the proper person to whom I should present my ideas."

This was Colonel George S. Gibbs, later chief signal officer.

* * *

Page 35 [12]: "The War College sits back about a quarter of a mile beyond the parade grounds. I hurried past the guard who let me by at the mention of Van Deman and in a few moments stood before the father of Military Intelligence."

This judgment of then Major Ralph H. Van Deman (1865–1952) is widely held.

* * *

Page 40 [16]: "Upon investigation, I learned that a copy of the War Department code book had been stolen in Mexico during our punitive expedition in 1916 and that a photograph of this was reported to be in the hands of the German Government."

This was the War Department Telegraph Code 1915, a one-part code.

* * *

Page 41 [16]: "I promptly chose a man in the State Department Code Room whom I considered best qualified to follow my directions, and tempted him with a commission. I wished him to take immediate charge of a subsection which would compile codes and ciphers."

This is said to be Captain A. E. Prince, though his name cannot be found in the State Department *Biographical Register.*

* * *

Pages 41–42 [17]: "The compilations of codes and ciphers was, by General Orders, a Signal Corps function, but the war revealed the unpreparedness of this department in the United States. How much so is indicated by a talk I had with a higher officer of the Signal Corps who had just been appointed a military attaché to an Allied country . . . When the new attaché, a veteran of the old Army, appeared, I handed him a brochure and rapidly went over some of our methods of secret communication. He listened impatiently, then growled: 'That's a lot of nonsense. Whoever heard of going to all that trouble? During the Spanish-American War we didn't do all those things. We just added the figure 1898 to all our figure code words, and the Spaniards never did find out about it.'"

This was General George O. Squier, a retired chief signal officer, who had just been appointed military attaché to Italy.

* * *

Page 43 [17–18]: "Amazing as it may seem, his [Squier's] attitude was characteristic, even at the Front. One of the young officers whom we had trained confirmed this when he arrived at General Headquarters in France. He had received his instruction and practical experience in my bureau. Having observed the necessity for revising the War Department's communications in this country, he was eager to learn whether the codes and ciphers of General Pershing in use at the Front were safe."

The officer was Lieutenant J. Rives Childs, later U.S. ambassador to Ethiopia and Saudi Arabia and a world authority on Casanova. He did not solve the American cryptosystem in its entirety, as Yardley suggests but, as a test of a proposed American cryptosystem, merely stripped a superencipherment from a code given to him. He demonstrated that the cryptosystem—an encoding using a small codebook followed by an encipherment of the triliteral codewords using a table—was inadequate. It was not put into service.

* * *

Pages 43–44 [18]: "The first thing which this young officer [Childs] did after arriving in France was to induce his superiors to intercept by wireless our own radio code and cipher messages and by those who employed them they were considered safe . . . Without any knowledge of the American method of encipherment, the young officer solved these messages within a few hours . . . From these wireless intercepts he learned the disposition of troops along the St. Mihiel salient, the number and names of our divisions, and, finally, the actual hour at which the great American offensive would be launched. This, then, the enemy knew!"

Yardley errs here. The information about the American troops was gained, not from Childs' solution, which dealt with made-up messages, but from an American monitoring of American field telephone conversations. These revealed serious lapses in security, and permitted the monitor to reconstruct the American order of battle for the reduction of the salient. He missed the time of attack by 24 hours only because one signalman had misstated it. But Yardley's conclusions—that the Germans also listened to these conversations and withdrew their troops from the St. Mihiel salient in an anticipation of an American attack—seems to be unwarranted; at least, no source is known for this statement.

* * *

Pages 47–48 [21]: In setting up MI-8, the cryptologic section of Army General Staff military intelligence, "it seemed obvious that a Military Intelligence should control its own communications if it were to be held responsible for its vital secrets. Therefore I commissioned another man from the Department of State Code Room, drew up a plan of organization, cut in direct wires to the cable points, employed a corps of code clerks and telegraph operators and within a few weeks we had a subsection which rivaled, in speed, accuracy and economy of transmission of cables, that of the Associated Press."

The man was First Lieutenant James E. McKenna.

* * *

Pages 55–57 [26–28]: ". . . Van Deman called me to his office and handed me a folded sheet of ordinary blank writing-paper. 'Secret ink?' I asked. 'Probably. See what you can do with it,' he ordered, and then dismissed me . . . I immediately telephoned the National Research Council, which kept a list of scientists, and asked them for the name of the most skillful chemist in Washington. Within an hour he was in my office . . . within a half-hour we were buried in the basement. There, in our improvised secret-ink laboratory, the experiments began." Heat brought out the invisible writing, which proved to be a request in modern Greek to a man in San Antonio telling him where to get $119,000.

This letter was not developed by a chemist in Washington but by the U.S. military attaché in Mexico City, Lieutenant Colonel Robert M. Campbell, by applying heat from a small electrical stove.

* * *

Page 60 [29]: "I . . . drafted a cable . . . requesting that the British Government . . . send at once one of their best chemists to the United States to act as an instructor. We received an immediate reply, stating that Dr. S. W. Collins, England's foremost secret-ink chemist, would sail as soon as possible."

This was Stanley W. Collins, chief chemist of British censorship.

* * *

Page 77 [39]: Quoting a Collins speech to chemists in MI-8's secret ink laboratory: "The last words of my superiors just before I sailed, were: 'For God's sake, find this general reagent [that would develop any secret ink]. Beg America to join us in our researches.'"

British and French chemists discovered the general reagent—iodine vapor—in 1915, not after 1917, when Collins visited the United States.

* * *

Pages 88–89 [47]: After pointing out the need to forge seals used on diplomatic documents, Yardley says that "two of the most adept criminals who had been convicted for forgery and counterfeiting were sought out and their particular skill incorporated with that of the Secret-Ink Subsection of MI-8."

No evidence for this statement exists in the official histories. Collins, however, told the Americans that the British had used two paroled forgers in their similar work.

* * *

Page 89 [47–48]: "We were asked to open and photograph the contents of a letter addressed to General Carranza, President of Mexico. Before opening this letter, our counterfeiter made a copy of the seal, but after opening the letter, photographing the contents, and resealing the envelope, we discovered that the duplicate seal which had been made was too defective to be used. We were at a loss to know what to do. Finally the counterfeiter told us that he could approximate the original by engraving a seal. While this move was under discussion, he made a closer examination of a portion of the original seal and discovered, happily enough, that it had been made with an old and rare Spanish coin. This simplified a distressing problem in engraving, for it was only necessary to obtain one of these coins from an obliging collector to make a perfect seal."

The letter was not to Carranza but to a high Mexican official and the coin was an old Mexican centavo. The replacement of the seal was not done by a counterfeiter but by Lieutenant A. J. McGrail, head of the secret-ink laboratory at the office of the Military Intelligence Division at 1330 F Street, Northwest, Washington, D.C. (a site now occupied by the National Press Building). Another military intelligence secret-ink laboratory was in New York.

* * *

Page 90 [49]: "Though she [Madame Maria de Victorica] had been sought by the British Secret Service since 1914, it was the Secret-Ink Bureau of MI-8 that finally proved her nemesis."

She was arrested in April, 1918, and this led to the discovery of her secret-ink messages, not the other way round.

* * *

Page 102 [57]: "Through the records at Kirkwall, England, where all passengers are closely scrutinized, and those of our own immigration authorities, we learned a great deal more about Madame Victorica."

This was Kirkwall, Scotland.

* * *

Page 117 [67]: "This famous spy was of royal birth."

More precisely, the spy was of Junker birth.

64

* * *

Page 117 [67]: "As early as 1910 she was received by the German Minister for Foreign Affairs and Prince von Bülow, and invited to enter the Secret Service."

The minister was Gottlieb von Jagow, state secretary of the Foreign Ministry from 1913 to 1916. Prince Bernhard von Bülow was Reich chancellor from 1900 to 1909.

* * *

Pages 120–139 [69–83]: Yardley gives a clear exposition of the solution of two code messages in five-figure groups transmitted from Germany to Mexico that offered Mexico a loan provided she stayed neutral and offered Mexico plans to manufacture rifles. The messages proved, after solution, to be encoded in the English-French half of a bilingual dictionary.

The messages were not solved by MI-8, since military intelligence had obtained a copy of the French-English dictionary used in encoding them and MI-8 used it to read the messages in the same way as the legitimate recipients.

* * *

Page 147 [89]: "How does one go about deciphering a transposition cipher? If in the spring of 1918 you had searched the libraries of the world you would not have discovered so much as one word that would give you the least idea how to attack such a problem. Even the pamphlet used by the United States Army for instruction in codes and ciphers would have given you no clues."

Not so.

* * *

Page 149 [90]: "Our own spies . . . reported . . . that high German officials, such as Jahnke (Chief of German Secret Service), Von Eckhardt (the German Minister), and the German Consul-General to Mexico were extremely friendly and operated openly with President Carranza."

Kurt Jahnke, a German-American, headed German navy espionage in Mexico; in the Third Reich, he was a member of the SD (Sicherheitsdienst, the espionage service of Heinrich Himmler's SS). Heinrich von Eckardt, who has no "h" in his name, was the minister. The consul general was one Grunow.

***

Page 153 [93]: Referring to a message MI-8 had solved directing German consuls in Mexico to "immediately burn without remainder, and destroy the ashes of, all papers connected with the war, the preservation of which is not absolutely necessary," Yardley comments that "This German cipher message, officially designed PQR, is without question the frankest and most open document treating on the subject of espionage, excepting the Soviet spy document in Chapter XIII, that I have ever seen."

PQR was solved by David Stevens, a member of MI-8 who became a high official of the Rockefeller Foundation in New York.

***

Page 154 [94]: Referring to the long message in 10-letter groups found on a suspected German spy whose passport read Pablo Waberski, Yardley writes that ". . . several cryptographers, under the direction of Captain Manly, were busily engaged in piecing the message together."

John Manly, with his assistant Edith Rickert, solved the Waberski cipher on May 18, 1918, after a week of preliminaries and two weeks of analysis.

***

Page 168 [105]: "It was daylight before the message was completely deciphered and translated."

Presumably May 19, 1918.

***

Page 171 [107]: "Finally in August, 1918, Pablo Waberski, whose real name was Lather Witcke, was tried before military court. He was charged with being a German spy. The trial lasted two days. He was found guilty, and the court sentenced him to be hanged by the neck until dead."

Not Lather Witcke but Lothar Witzke. Manly testified at the trial and his solution helped incriminate Waberski. On 4 June 1920, President Wilson commuted the sentence to life imprisonment, and Waberski/ Witzke was deported to Germany on 23 November 1923. He may have served in the Abwehr (the German military espionage service) in World War II.

***

Page 172 [108]: "One morning my correspondent at the Department of State called me on the telephone and asked me to come over as soon as possible . . . He was positively the most mysterious and secretive man

I had ever known in my sixteen years of experience with the United States Government. Although I dealt personally with him for several years, I know less about the man now than I did the first day I saw him. He was almost a human sphinx and when he did talk his voice was so low that I had to strain my ears to catch the words."

This was Leland Harrison (1883–1951), who during World War I had handled intelligence matters for the Department of State and who later served as technical head of the American delegation to the 1928 international telegraph conference, as an assistant secretary of state and as minister to Sweden, Uruguay, Rumania and, during World War II, Switzerland, where he worked closely with Allen Dulles, head of the Office of Strategic Services bureau in Bern.

* * *

Page 176 [111]: "Van Deman had been ordered abroad. We had a new Director of Military Intelligence now, General Churchill. As he was very close to the Chief of Staff, General March, he was to have a freer hand than Van Deman."

These were Marlborough Churchill and Peyton March.

* * *

Page 177 [111]: "The State Department called me over this morning. They are restless about these Spanish messages."

Typescript has "Harrison called me over . . ."

* * *

Page 179 [112]: "When I entered his room I had a most obvious reason for believing that the Captain was an excellent judge of beauty. Most of his types were blondes, but this girl was brunette. She was dressed in a dark elegant suit and small close-fitting hat. Her eyes were brown and large." She was to help get information that would enable Yardley to solve the Spanish codes.

Two sources identify her as a Miss Wilson, but not the Miss Ruth Willson who was a cryptanalyst specializing in Spanish codes and remained with Yardley in codebreaking until 1929.

* * *

Page 184 [116–117]: Yardley describes a German open code system used by Madame de Victorica that encoded the plaintext message in the *ABC Code* and then represented these numbers by the initial consonant of successive words according to a key, in which, for example, 1 = *d* and *t*.

German naval documents show that this ingenious system was used for German clandestine communications in general, not just for Victorica.

Page 192 [121]: "Boyd [an American agent in South America] had stolen into the Consulate at night, opened the steel safe which protected the diplomatic code, but had been unable to decipher the messages which we had cabled . . . We were not surprised . . . Miss Abbott had already supplied us with detailed reports regarding all phases of the Spanish diplomatic codes . . . According to Miss Abbott's reports, and of course confirmed by cryptographic analysis, the Spanish Government was using in all twenty-five codes."

In addition to photographs of the code later supplied by Boyd and the information from "Miss Abbott," MI-8 was greatly helped by Britain's giving Yardley, late in 1918, copies of two of the Spanish codes, 253 and 301, both used for communication with Berlin. With these as a basis, Ruth Willson reconstructed the others.

* * *

Page 201 [128]: "MI-8 had been on good terms with the Navy Signal Office which compiled naval codes and ciphers. In fact this office had submitted several messages encoded in their battle codes and asked if, in our opinion, their methods were safe . . . The Navy system was a most elaborate one, and at first it looked as if I would need a great deal of luck. But after several clerks had compiled elaborate statistics which required thirteen hundred pages and six hundred and fifty thousand entries, the messages were readily solved."

The solution was actually only of the superencipherment, since Yardley had been asked to test only that and had been given the underlying code.

* * *

Page 203 [128]: "The fact of the matter is (as we shall see later on), there is no such thing as an indecipherable code or cipher constructed along conventional lines."

The meaning of this depends upon how one construes "along conventional lines." For the unbreakable cipher does exist. As Yardley himself says on page 365 [244], "The only indecipherable cipher is one in which there are no repetitions to conceal." This may be an oblique reference to the requirement of randomness and endlessness of key in a one-time pad.

68

***

Page 210 [135]: "I arrived in London the latter part of August, 1918, and presented my credentials to Colonel Slocum, American Military Attaché."

This was Herbert J. Slocum.

COL. RALPH H. VAN DEMAN.

***

Page 210 [135]: "Colonel Tolbert, American Military Attaché at Copenhagen, was in London on a special mission and dropped in an hour or so later."

This was Oscar N. Solbert (not Tolbert).

***

Page 211 [136]: "I saw Colonel French of the British War Office the following morning and Edward Bell, First Secretary of the American Embassy, in the afternoon."

Edward Bell (1882–1924), a career Foreign Service officer who died after a fall in Peking, was a key person in the American liaison with British intelligence. I cannot identify French.

GEN. MARLBOROUGH CHURCHILL.   MAJ. GEN. DENNIS E. NOLAN.

* * *

Page 215 [138]: "Finally Captain Brooke-Hunt of the British War Office submitted to me for examination a combination substitution and trans-position cipher."

This was G. L. Brooke-Hunt of the Royal Engineers.

* * *

Pages 217–218 [138]: "Admiral Hall had given this message to Edward Bell, who cabled it to the Secretary of State, who in turn gave it to the President. Diplomatic procedure would require that such sensational in-formation be transmitted by the Foreign Office to Ambassador Page, but Admiral Hall did as he pleased."

The solved intercept of the Zimmermann message was shown with British Foreign Office approval by Captain Reginald Hall, the Admiralty's direc-tor of naval intelligence, to Bell on 22 February 1917 and was formally presented the next day by Arthur Balfour, the British foreign secretary, to Walter Hines Page, the U.S. ambassador, for transmission to the American government. The intercept played a major role in pushing the United States into World War I and is generally regarded as the most important single cryptogram solution in history.

Photos opposite page: Above: Colonel Ralph H. Van Deman, "the father of American military intelligence," who hired Yardley to set up the cryptologic section of military intelligence that became MI-8. Below, left,

General Marlborough Churchill, Van Deman's successor as director of military intelligence. Below, right, General Dennis E. Nolan, first executive officer and then director of military intelligence after Churchill.

* * *

Page 218 [140]: Hall "insisted that everything be transacted on a personal basis, and though he remained firm in his refusal to give me any information about the German diplomatic codes used for wireless messages between Berlin and Madrid, he finally consented to give me, personally, several copies of a certain neutral government's diplomatic codes and a copy of a German Naval code in two volumes."

The neutral was Spain, as mentioned in the note to Page 192.

* * *

Page 219 [140–141]: "As late as 1921, Clarence H. Mackay, President of the Postal Telegraph Company, testifying before a Senate Committee on cable landing licenses, said, 'Since censorship ceased the British Government have required us to turn over all messages 10 days after they have been sent or received.'"

Typescript has Newcomb Carlton, president of the Western Union Telegraph Co. The use of Mackay may represent a correction.

* * *

Page 219 [141]: "Though I wanted to see Captain Hitchings, who, according to his superiors, was worth four divisions to the British Army, Colonel Van Deman advised against this . . ."

This was Oswald Thomas Hitchings, in civilian life a teacher of music and modern languages.

* * *

Page 222 [142]: "When I explained my mission to Colonel Cartier, he immediately called in Captain Georges Painvin, the great cipher genius of France."

This was Francois Cartier, head of the War Ministry cipher section.

* * *

Page 223 [142–143]: "The finest tribute I ever heard paid a cipher expert was a lecture given by Colonel Frank Moorman, a Staff Officer at American General Headquarters, who said in part: 'Captain Georges Painvin, the chief code expert of the French, an analytical genius of the highest order, was a regular wizard in solving codes . . . On the basis of this single message he worked out a complete system of this new code.'"

Moorman was head of G.2 A.6, the radio intelligence section of the American Expeditionary Force. The new code that Painvin solved was a German trench code called the Schlüsselheft ("key booklet") with a superencipherment called the Geheimklappe ("secret flap"). The single message was intercepted by an American listening post in two versions, one encrypted in the new Schlüsselheft-Geheimklappe system, the other encrypted in the old code, apparently because some German station had not yet received the new system. The old code had been solved, giving Painvin the plaintext of the message which he used as a wedge to break down the new system. Painvin (1886–1980) became the greatest cryptanalyst of World War I. An outstanding cellist, he graduated from the Ecole Polytechnique in Paris (a French super-M.I.T.) and taught at schools of mines until 1914. After the war he had an extremely successful business career in metals mining.

* * *

Page 223–224 [144]: "In order that I may keep history straight, I must add that his [Painvin's] greatest achievement, although he had just recovered from a long and serious illness (the fate of most cryptographers), was the solution of the difficult ADFGVX cipher, which the Germans suddenly sprang on the Allied cipher experts on the eve of the long-heralded German push of March 1918. This cipher was called ADFGVX because only those letters occurred in the cipher messages. The Germans first enciphered a message, one letter at a time, by writing two cipher letters for each German letter. When the message was completely enciphered the cipher message contained twice as many letters as the original German text. The Germans now separated these pairs of letters and mixed them up by a prearranged key. This key changed every day. The system, then, constituted: first, a substitution; second, a division; third, a transposition. This cipher was so extremely difficult to solve that many have marveled at the brain that originally discovered the underlying principles of solution."

Originally the system used only five letters, ADFGX. They were chosen by its inventor, Lieutenant Fritz Nebel, a German signal corps officer, because he had observed that student radiotelegraph operators learned their Morse forms more quickly, presumably because of the distinctiveness of the Morse equivalents, than other letters. The five letters stood at the top and at the side of a 5×5 square of plaintext letters. Thus any plaintext letter inside the square could be represented by two of the outside letters, serving as coordinates. The division that Yardley mentions did not exist as a separate process; the transposition—technically a single irregular columnar transposition—effectively divided the letters of each pair. On June 1, the plaintext square was expanded to 6×6 with the addition of the 10 digits, the V being added to the external letters. In other respects, the system remained the same. Painvin's solution was instrumental in halting the third—and last—of Germany's supreme offensives of 1918, that of July.

* * *

Page 226 [145]: "I explained my difficulty and asked if he could arrange for me to see M. Pichon, French Minister for Foreign Affairs."

This was Stephan J. M. Pichon.

* * *

Page 226 [145]: "I gave Ambassador Sharp letters addressed to him . . ."

This was William Graves Sharp, U.S. ambassador to France.

* * *

Page 226 [145]: "I explained my mission to M. Pichon; that I had seen Colonel Cartier, who informed me that the War Office decoded only military messages and sent the diplomatic messages to the Foreign Office, where they were decoded. He replied without hesitation that that was not the case; that the German Berlin-Madrid messages under discussion were decoded by Cartier before they reached the Foreign Office; and finally that the Foreign Office did not even have a Cipher Bureau."

Pichon was lying. Like other French foreign ministers, he got a great deal of information from the Foreign Office cipher bureau, probably dealt intimately with its representatives, and almost certainly knew where it was.

* * *

Page 227 [146]: "After a conference with our Military Attaché, Major Warburton, and Colonel Van Deman, we decided to address a letter to Colonel Herscher, Clemenceau's secretary."

This was Barclay H. Warburton. Herscher is also identified as head of the military secretariat.

* * *

Page 227 [146]: "This letter he referred to General Mordacq, Chief of Cabinet, Ministry of War."

This was General Jean J. H. Mordacq.

* * *

Page 227 [146]: "He [Mordacq] consented, however, to transmit to our State Department, through the French Ambassador in Washington, all messages that seemed of any interest to the United States. This in itself was an admission that the War Office controlled La Chambre Noire [the Black Chamber]."

This is not true. The Foreign Office jealously maintained the independence of its codebreaking bureau from other agencies' bureaus to the extent of hindering cooperation—even during wartime. But the War Ministry cipher section solved some diplomatic messages, in particular those of Spain.

* * *

Page 230 [148]: " . . . it was by now obvious to everyone that France had no intention of permitting me to have even a peek into La Chambre Noire."

In his unpublished memoirs, General Marcel Givierge, head of the codebreaking agency of French general headquarters, says that the French lied to Yardley about the information available because they thought him indiscreet.

* * *

Page 232 [149]: " . . . I hope that when the authentic history of the World War is written, this small bureau will receive its rightful share of glory in the part that the American Expeditionary Forces played in the winning of the war."

Yardley refers to the unit designated G.2 A.6, the radio intelligence unit of the A.E.F., which Moorman (page 223) headed and to which Childs (page 46) belonged.

* * *

Page 240 [156]: "Following the reasoning in Poe's 'Purloined Letter' I selected as a home for the Black Chamber a four-story brownstone in the East Thirties, just a few steps from Fifth Avenue—the very heart of New York City."

It was at 3 East 38th Street, a brownstone, the former home of a socialite, T. Suffern Tailer. The house has since been demolished. After only a few months there, the organization moved to a townhouse at 141 East 37th Street, where it remained for several years. This building still stands.

Yardley's apartment was on the top floor in both houses. Later in the 1920s the organization moved to an office building at 20 Vanderbilt Avenue and the Yardleys moved to Jackson Heights, a section of Queens, one of the boroughs of New York City.

* * *

Pages 240–241 [156]: "I . . . had been offered several attractive positions in the business world. My heart, however, was with codes and ciphers; so when the government offered to pay me seven thousand five hundred dollars per annum and assured me a future in cryptography, I agreed to direct the activities of this group."

The original salary was $6,000; it was later raised to $7,500.

* * *

Page 241 [156]: "Accordingly, after being demobilized (I had been promoted to the rank of Major), I led this small group of men and women to the brownstone front in New York City—the new home of the American Black Chamber."

The organization was officially called the Cipher Bureau. During its first year, it consisted of the following people: Yardley; Frederick Livesey of G.2 A.6, an outstanding linguist; John C. Meeth of G.2 A.6, who became 234chief administrative clerk; Charles J. Mendelsohn, as a captain the head of German codesolving in MI-8 and professor of history at the College of the City of New York, who taught there in the mornings and cracked codes in the afternoons; Victor Weiskopf, an employee of the Department of Justice who had a stamp business on the side; Edna Ramsaier, a clerk, later to become the second Mrs. Yardley; Claus Bogel, Dorothea B. Jachens, Nellie A. Simpson, and Ruth Willson, all former MI-8 cryptanalysts; and Robert Arrowsmith, Henry D. Learned and seven clerks.

* * *

Page 241 [156]: "But there were now no code and cipher telegrams to work on! The cable censorship had been lifted and the supervision of messages restored to the private cable companies. Our problem was to obtain copies of messages. How? I shall not answer this question directly."

Telegrams were obtained from the Western Union Telegraph Company and the Postal Telegraph Company, whose presidents had agreed to cooperate with Yardley. *Cf.* page 219.

* * *

Pages 242–245 [159–161]: Referring to seven sheets of five-letter groups in cipher taken from the occupants of a German airplane forced to land in Latvia and passed to U.S. authorities after the Latvian government failed to solve the cryptograms, Yardley notes, "The messages are of course from a Soviet secret agent, probably in Berlin, to his superiors in Russia–the aeroplane was en route to Soviet Russia. It seems obvious that all the names are aliases, for the second message ends with 'My name is now Thomas. Regards, James.'"

Among the persons who can be identified in the messages, for which the ciphertexts and translations of the German plaintext into English are given, are Klara Zetkin, a chief founder of the German Communist Party, Karl Radek, a leader of the Communist International, and Nikolai Bukharin, a member of the Central Committee of the Communist Party in Soviet Russia. For solutions of the cryptograms, see William M. Bowers (pseudonym ZEMBIE), "The 'Soviet Spies' Ciphers," *The Cryptogram*, 30 (September–October 1962), 3–5, (November–December 1962), 32–34, (January–February 1963), 58–61.

* * *

Pages 267–268 [175]: In trying to get help in solving the Japanese codes, Yardley sought to trick the Japanese into sending a message whose plaintext contents he would know. "'Well,' I tried again, searching desperately for an example, 'suppose' we dig up the name of someone who has recently come to the United States from Tokyo, a Russian for instance. Now draft a cable something like this, 'Any information that you or the Japanese War Office may have regarding the political activities while in Tokyo of one Herbert Charley or Hubert Yardley, a Russian subject, reported as sailing from Yokohama to San Francisco on November first, is urgently requested.' The ideal repetition is one where the difference is between similar beginnings and endings. Can't you see how simple it would be for me to find these names in the code message? I'm sure a telegram along these lines would enable me to break into the code. Do you think a bona fide can be found?' The idea intrigued Churchill for he was born for espionage. Later, however, he told me that they had been unable to find a real case that would fit."

In fact, the idea was put into practice, and the Japanese military attaché, Inouye, received a cable from Tokyo whose contents he communicated to the assistant to the director of U.S. military intelligence on 26 February 1920. But it arrived after Yardley had independently solved the code.

Lieutenant John Manly—The Professor Who Became Yardley's Chief Assistant.

* * *

Page 269 [176]: "Finally one night I wakened at midnight, for I had retired early, and out of the darkness came the conviction that a certain series of two-letter code words absolutely must equal Airurando (Ireland)."

This seems to have taken place during the night of Saturday–Sunday 13–14 December 1919.

* * *

Page 271 [177]: "For an hour I filled in these and other identifications until they had all been proved to my satisfaction. Of course, I have identified only part of the kana–that is, the alphabet. Most of the code is devoted to complete words, but these too will be easy enough once all the kana are properly filled in. The impossible had been accomplished! I felt a terrible mental let-down. I was very tired. I finally placed my papers in the safe, locked it and leaned back in my chair, checking up my blunders, and at the same time wondering what this would mean to the United States Government. What secrets did these messages hold? Churchill would want to know of my accomplishment. Should I telephone him at this hour? No, I would wait and dictate a letter."

DAVID A. SALMON—YARDLEY'S SUPERIOR.

LELAND HARRISON—"A HUMAN SPHINX."

J. RIVES CHILDS—SOLVED ENCIPHERMENT.

FRANK MOORMAN—HEAD OF G.2 A.6.

Though Livesey in the morning added some identifications that further confirmed Yardley's work, the solution was Yardley's own. Charles Mendelsohn, his colleague, called it "a pretty piece of work," and Yardley, in the letter to Churchill he mentions, said of it: "With the exception of clerical assistance I have worked practically alone and it is the first thing that I have ever done which I really feel proud of."

* * *

Page 272 [179]: "After dictating the letter I instructed my secretary to tell my cleverest cryptographer, Charles Mundy (I shall call him this for want of a better name, for he now holds a position that might be jeopardized were his past history known) that I wanted to see him."

This was Frederick Livesey, by then an economic advisor in the State Department.

* * *

Page 273 [180]: "'How are the Russian codes progressing?' I asked Livesey. 'We're still working on the typescript,' he said. 'The code doesn't look very difficult.'"

Perhaps not, but it was not read.

* * *

Page 276 [181]: In looking for someone to translate his Japanese solutions, Yardley, after much searching, "finally discovered a retired missionary of some sixty years of age who I was told was one of America's best Japanese scholars . . . I selected the largest room available, placed our long-whiskered missionary and thick-spectacled cryptographer [Livesey] at adjacent desks, and changed the locks and keys."

The missionary was the Reverend Irvin H. Correll, an Episcopalian, who was believed to have had the longest continuous service of any Christian missionary in the Japanese empire; he and his wife had become missionaries right after their marriage in 1873. His command of the Japanese language was such that he wrote books in it. He died in 1926.

* * *

Page 279 [184]: "We learned that they had employed a Polish cipher expert to revise their code and cipher systems."

This was Captain Jan Kowalefsky. During the Russian-Polish War of 1920, he solved Russian cryptograms that helped the Poles drive the Russians out of Poland. He was sent to Japan, like Poland a traditional antagonist of Russia, to help the island empire improve its cryptography, presumably to deter the formidable Russian cryptanalysts.

* * *

Pages 279–280 [184]: "The Polish cryptographer seemed to specialize on army codes, for the Japanese Military Attaché's codes suddenly became more difficult than those of any other branch of the Japanese Government. This system was elaborate and required ten different codes."

Actually 11. What made the system especially difficult to solve was that the codegroup that in one code meant to switch to another code had a plaintext meaning in the second, rendering its behavior in the cryptograms extremely confusing.

* * *

Page 282 [186]: "General Nolan, our new executive, came to New York to look us over."

This was Dennis E. Nolan.

* * *

Page 283 [187]: "The Japanese Ambassador and Lord Curzon were discussing the Anglo-Japanese Alliance that was of such tremendous concern to the United States."

This was George Nathaniel Curzon, first Marquess Curzon of Keldeston, British foreign secretary since 1919. A brilliant and vigorous administrator, he had served as viceroy in India and leader of the House of Lords. The post-World War I Anglo-Japanese alliance was aimed at the United States. Great Britain feared that the World War I growth of the U.S. Navy threatened the Royal Navy's position as the world's mightiest fleet and ruler of the waves. Japan wanted to consolidate the expansion she had made through her gain of former German islands in the Pacific.

* * *

Page 284 [188]: "The following Japanese telegram No. 386 from Washington to Tokyo, July 10, 1921, is the first definite word we have of the American Secretary of State's plans for a conference for the reduction of armaments."

The secretary of state, since 1921, was Charles Evans Hughes, former governor of New York, losing presidential candidate in 1916, from 1930 to 1941 chief justice of the United States.

Pages 289–290 [191–192]: "At this stage of the discussion, the Japanese suddenly switched to a new code for a few of their telegrams . . . But to our consternation, the code was of an entirely new type . . . Our difficulty in breaking this code was due to its scientific construction. Although the code messages were on their face the same as others (they were all in groups of ten letters) we could not discover the real length of the code words. Heretofore the code words had been of two-letter and four-letter length . . . Finally we discovered that three-letter code words were interspersed throughout the messages . . . However, once we had discovered the three-letter elements, we quickly solved the messages, and within forty days after their receipt were reading current telegrams almost as rapidly as the Japanese themselves."

Following Yardley's original solution of December, 1919, the Cipher Bureau had solved four codes (Ja, Jb, Jc, and Jd) by the start of May 1920, two military attaché codes (Jf and Jk) by September, another military code (Jm) by January 1921, and an English-language code (Jh) and a Japanese-language syllabary (Jg) by the spring of 1921. About 200 groups of the diplomatic code Jl had been solved and preliminary work on the five-letter naval code Ji had begun by then. The first message in Jp was received in the Cipher Bureau on 18 July 1921 and, after intense efforts, the first solution was achieved by 23 August on the basis of only 15 messages. Though Yardley says that three-letter groups delayed this solution, other documents suggest that this technique was actually used in Jg and that the delay in solving Jp was due, according to what Yardley wrote at the time, to the fact that Jp actually consisted of "twenty-four different small codes instead of the usual one."

* * *

Page 300 [199]: "'On August 3rd I called on Premier BRIAND at his request . . .'"

This was Aristide Briand, 11 times premier of France, co-winner of the 1926 Nobel Peace Prize.

* * *

Page 305 [202]: "A representative arrives to arrange for daily courier service [of the Japanese intercepts] to the capital. 'Every one happy in Washington?' I ask. 'Sure,' he smiles. 'They all read the messages before they have their morning coffee.'"

The representative might have been Arthur Bliss Lane, a Foreign Service officer who had succeeded William Lee Hurley as the State Department liaison with the Cipher Bureau.

* * *

Page 307 [203]: "Admiral Kato, the Japanese plenipotentiary, cabled his government . . ."

This was Admiral Baron Tomosaburo Kato, then navy minister, later prime minister.

THE REVEREND IRVING H. CORRELL, YARDLEY'S JAPANESE TRANSLATOR, WHO, HOW-
EVER, HAS NO WHISKERS.

* * *

Page 309 [205]: "Briand's remarks to Saburi, outlined in the following telegram, are especially enlightening."

This was Sadao Saburi, in the Japanese delegation.

* * *

Page 310 [206]: "'You will be informed of the circumstances of the discussion from the report of Major-General TANAKA.'"

This was Major General Kunishige Tanaka, a delegate.

* * *

Page 318 [212]: "During the Armament Conference the Black Chamber had turned out over five thousand decipherments and translations."

The record shows 1,600 solutions.

141 EAST 37TH STREET, NEW YORK, WHERE YARDLEY SOLVED THE JAPANESE DIPLOMATIC CODE.

* * *

Page 320 [213]: "In June, 1922, I returned from Arizona in excellent health, but found my most valuable assistant in a frightful condition."

This was Livesey, but he is reported to have laughed when he first read this account.

* * *

Page 324 [216]: "Washington was especially concerned that I keep away from congressional investigations. During the investigation of Secretary of Interior Fall, my correspondent in Washington telephoned me for God's sake to lie low for if I was called upon to decipher the Fall messages we would be ruined."

Yardley refers to the Teapot Dome scandal. The secretary, Albert B. Fall, was eventually convicted of accepting a $100,000 bribe in connection with leasing that oil naval reserve land. Solutions of his coded messages were made public during a Senate investigation; the cryptanalyst who testified was William F. Friedman, then head of the U.S. Army Signal Corps code section.

* * *

Pages 325–326 [217]: "In spite of all the precautions to maintain secrecy regarding our activities, we were once nearly given away through our kindness in giving a helping hand to Bruce Bielaski while he was conducting under-cover investigations of rum-runners off the Atlantic coast."

Bielaski preceded J. Edgar Hoover as head of what was then the Justice Department's Bureau of Investigation.

* * *

Page 331 [221]: ". . . the office door was forced, cabinets rifled, and papers scattered all over the place."

Two independent sources state that this episode never occurred. On the other hand, an attempt may have been made, which may have led to the move of the Cipher Bureau from the townhouse on 37th Street to the office building on Vanderbilt Avenue.

* * *

Page 332 [222]: "The Black Chamber did not deal solely with the diplomatic codes of Japan. We solved over forty-five thousand cryptograms from 1917 to 1929, and at one time or another, we broke the codes of Argentina, Brazil, Chile, China, Costa Rica, Cuba, England, France, Germany, Japan, Liberia, Mexico, Nicaragua, Panama, Peru, Russia, San Salvador, Santo Domingo, Soviet Union and Spain."

San Salvador is the capital of El Salvador; Santo Domingo, of the Dominican Republic. Of this list, no British, French, or German systems were solved after 1921, and no Russian or Soviet foreign office code was ever solved by MI-8 or the Cipher Bureau, though Yardley includes a

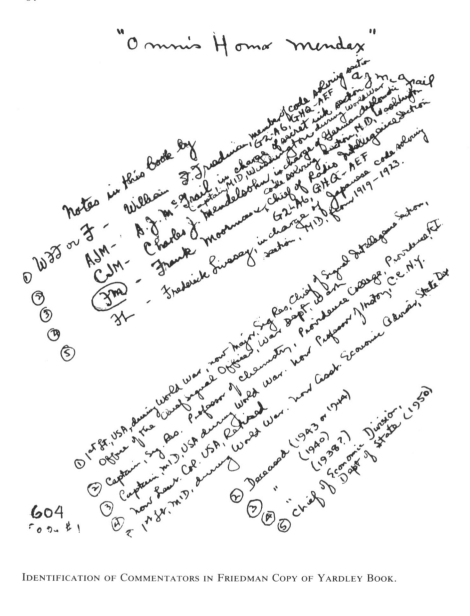

IDENTIFICATION OF COMMENTATORS IN FRIEDMAN COPY OF YARDLEY BOOK.

this secret formula for developing all kinds of inks, the life of every one of our spies who uses secret writing hangs by a thread. In this respect we are helpless. It is useless for us to develop new inks. But once we discover this general reagent, we doubtless will discover a defense against its successful use.

"The last words of my superiors just before I sailed, were: 'For God's sake, find this general reagent. Beg America to join us in our researches.' "

La Fayette we are here.

There was and is no general Developer for Military Secret Inks if the proper precautions are taken.

This lecture of Collins is concocted by Yardley out of Collins Report, brought by him in May 1918 The report contained elaboratory procedures for developing Secret-Writing — as well as accounts of many cases which Collins and his staff worked up. They included the Bacon case and others cited by Y. The original Collins Report was missing as early as 1929. It is my firm belief that Yardley has thus original. This chapter convinces me in this belief. Collins did give a lecture at MID to all officers of that Dunn in July 1918. While here he lost his whisky flask. Has Y that also? AJ.McG.

Of this whole chapter it is only necessary to say that the name of the dictionary was furnished MID by underground channels. There was no "solution" whatever! A mere matter of getting the dictionary and reading the messages! ... . O.J.W.
W.J.J.

CHAPTER VI

TWO GERMAN WIRELESS INTERCEPTS

BY JANUARY, 1918, the Code and Cipher Solution Subsection of MI-8 had grown to ambitious proportions. We not only had to train students for our own use, but were also required to teach recruits for General Pershing's Cryptographic Bureau in France. This double function severely handicapped us, for we felt that in justice to the American Expeditionary Forces we should send abroad the students who showed the greatest promise for successful code and cipher attack. I regret to say that not more than two of all those we sent to France distinguished themselves, but this was not the fault of MI-8.

By far the larger number of officers (not recruits) were trained at Riverbank under my direction. We had several classes, one containing about 60 officers in grade from 2d Lieut to major. W.J.J.

The successful cryptographer requires a type of mind difficult to describe. The work is absolutely foreign to anything he has ever done. To excel, he not only needs years of experience but great originality and imagination of a particular type. We call it "cipher brains." I know of no better description. We were never able to formulate an intelligence test that would indicate the future of a student. The most successful students, when put on their own responsibility were, more often than not, utterly worthless, except for clerical work. I was later to have the unusual opportunity of studying under the British, French and Italians. I learned that they too

120

PAGE 120 OF YARDLEY BOOK WITH COMMENTARY BY CHARLES J. MENDELSOHN AND WILLIAM F. FRIEDMAN.

photograph of a presumably stolen Russian code, and his unit did solve at least one Soviet spy cipher (page 242–245). In some cases, the codes were not cryptanalyzed but were furnished by spies or friendly countries.

* * *

Page 333 [222–223]: "The new Director, his executive officer and I were lunching at the Army and Navy Club, when the Director asked: 'Yardley, what code do you plan to solve next?' 'I don't know, but the Vatican code telegrams rather intrigue me. Our preliminary analysis shows that they can be read . . .' I noticed with amazement that the Director's face went very white."

This was Nolan.

* * *

Page 344 [213]: "I . . . received a long-distance call . . . 'Come down on the midnight train and be at the State Department at nine A.M.' He spoke rapidly."

The typescript of *The American Black Chamber* has, instead of "State Department," "G's office" and an explanation by Yardley that "By G he meant Under Secretary of State Joseph Grew," who held that post from 7 March 1924 to 18 May 1927. Grew was ambassador to Japan from 1932 to 1941, when war broke out.

* * *

Page 345 [231]: "I arrived at the State, War and Navy Building the next morning a few moments before nine . . ."

The typescript has: "I arrived at Grew's office . . ."

* * *

Page 352 [236]: An official at the State Department, talking to Yardley about a message to be solved quickly, says: "'S.D. gave the message to me under the most secretive conditions . . .'"

Typescript has, "'H gave the message to me . . .' By H he meant Under Secretary of State Harrison." Harrison (*cf.* page 172) was never under secretary but was assistant secretary of state from 31 March 1922 to 25 February 1927.

* * *

Page 355 [237]: The coded message that Harrison gave the official, given on page 351, begins: 8453207440 5400000001 19977 NCOTRAL

SECRETARY OF STATE HENRY L. STIMSON.
He closed Yardley's black chamber, on the ground that "Gentlemen do not read each other's mail."

2116388212 . . ., has as its plaintext: "'No. 37.1. Last night I had dinner alone with STABLER. After dinner he told me . . .'"

This was John Herbert Stabler, a former chief of the State Department's Latin American Division.

* * *

Page 356 [238]: "When I sent the complete decipherment of this message to Washington, word came back that a certain official in the Department of State wished to see me."

Typescript has "Harrison."

* * *

Page 357 [239]: Harrison tells Yardley: "'Now we have a report that the Mexican Government is deciphering our messages. There is a terrible scare about it. Imagine—using a code that even Mexico can solve . . .'"

This report turned out to be false. The alleged solutions were forged.

* * *

Page 357 [239]: After hearing Harrison's (legitimate) complaints about poor State Department codes, Yardley writes, "I made no comment to all this, but I was confident I knew what would be the subject of the State Department official's conversation."

Typescript has "Harrison's conversation." Presumably Yardley means that Harrison would, when they next met, urge adoption of more secure cryptosystems. He was a specialist in communications.

* * *

Pages 363–364 [243]: In talking to Harrison about this, Yardley says, "'During the war the American Telephone and Telegraph Company invented a machine that automatically enciphered and transmitted a message over the wire by merely striking the letters of the message on a typewriter keyboard, while the machine at the other end of the wire automatically deciphered the message and at the same instant typed it. Had the enemy at any point between these two machines tapped the wire, he would have intercepted nothing but a jumble of letters. In cases where instantaneous transmission and decipherment was not practicable the operator first enciphered the message by striking the letters on the keyboard and turned the resultant cipher message over to the cable company. When the cipher telegram reached the addressed, he adjusted his machine, struck the cipher letters on the keyboard and the original telegram appeared before him. This machine filled every requirement of simplicity of operation, speed and accuracy. But it was not indecipherable.'"

Yardley is describing the machine invented in 1917 by Gilbert S. Vernam of the American Telephone and Telegraph Company. The strength of the cipher it produces depends entirely upon the keys used. If the key consists of a random sequence of characters that never repeats, that is, is as long as all the characters in all the plaintext messages ever to be sent, the system is unbreakable. If, however, the key is not entirely random, as will be the case if it is generated from two subkeys, the system can be broken. During World War I the Army used this method—which relieves the problem of generating enormous quantities of keys—with the Vernam machine on some East Coast circuits and test cryptograms enciphered that way were solved by William Friedman and others. It is evidently to this method that Yardley is referring when he says the machine was not indecipherable.

* * *

Page 365 [244]: "'The only indecipherable cipher is one in which there are no repetitions to conceal.'"

This is another way of saying that the key must be patternless and endless.

* * *

Page 367 [245]: "Well, in any case, I must hurry back to New York. The Department of State wanted to know what secrets the Peruvian Ambassador had been whispering in Washington."

Typescript has "Harrison wanted to know . . ."

* * *

Page 368 [246]: "In the latter part of 1928 the newspapers were full of the Anglo-American naval race. The British in 1927 had walked out on Hugh Gibson at the conference at Geneva . . ."

Gibson was then American minister to Switzerland and chairman of the U.S. delegation to the Geneva conference for the limitation of naval armaments.

* * *

Page 369 [247]: "The new Secretary of State had already taken office . . ."

This was Henry L. Stimson [Secretary of War during World War II].

* * *

Page 370 [247]: "When informed of the Black Chamber he had totally disapproved of our activities and ordered that all State Department funds be withdrawn from our support, and that the State Department have absolutely nothing to do with our organization."

Stimson later put his view in the lapidary expression, "Gentlemen do not read each other's mail."

* * *

Page 371 [248]: "The next day I received official notice of the closing of the Black Chamber, and was ordered to come to Washington at once."

Though work on codebreaking stopped almost immediately upon Stimson's order, issued when he was first given the solved intercepts in May, 1929, the books were not closed until October 31, 1929, in part to allow the rather specialized personnel time to find other jobs. In fact, by May, 1929, the personnel had been reduced to half a dozen or so, some working only part time, and the bureau's output [reduced] to a bulletin of intercepts every few days. One of the main reasons for this decline was the difficulty of obtaining foreign code messages, owing to the growing reluctance of the cable companies to violate the privacy of their customers' communications. Moreover, most of the material in the bulletin was of interest to the State Department, and as a consequence the Army had decided to transfer its cryptanalytic work to the Signal Corps, where Friedman was heading the cryptographic work, so that all would be centralized. The Army had decided to do this in April of 1929, but before the decision could be carried out Stimson had precipitated the closing of the Cipher Bureau. Upon the closing, its files were transferred to the Army, with Friedman going to New York to supervise the shipment. None of the personnel went to Army cryptology. The Cipher Bureau had, in its ten years of existence, cost the War Department $98,808.49 and the State Department $230,404—just under a third of a million dollars for a decade of codebreaking.

* * *

Page 372 [248]: "I had at last reached the office of my immediate supervisor."

This was Assistant Secretary of State Wilbur J. Carr.

PHOTO CREDITS

Cipher Center: Walther Seifertvia, David Kahn. State, War, Navy Departments: Library of Congress. Van Deman, Churchill, Nolan: U.S. Army Military History Institute Collection. John Manly: University of Chicago. Salmon, Harrison: Library of Congress. Childs: Randolph-Macon College. Moorman: Mrs. Frank Moorman via David Kahn. 141 East 37th Street: Louis Kruh. Correll: Archives of the Episcopal Church. Stimson: Library of Congress.

Memories of Friedman
by Louis Kruh

AUTHOR—Needs info on Col William Friedman, USAR. Lived in Washington, D. C. 1918. Worked on breaking Japanese code. Received cash gift from Congress. Cornell grad. Write Capt. Robert -------, USN-Ret.

Sixteen people, including this writer, responded to the above notice in *Retired Officer* magazine, September 1978.

The retired captain of the United States Navy who placed the notice had lived in the same apartment house as the Friedmans in the early 1920's; their families played bridge together. The notice, however, merely sought to determine if Friedman had been a member of the order of Free and Accepted Masons and was therefore eligible for inclusion in a Masonic directory the captain was compiling. This information was provided in a circular letter that he sent to all who had responded to his appeal and that included their names and addresses. I was disappointed, for I had hoped that the notice meant that a definitive biography of Friedman was planned to fill in the large gaps left by Ronald Clark in his less than adequate work, *The Man Who Broke Purple.*

Staring at the list of the 15 other people who had written the captain, I decided to ask for their cooperation in developing an article on Friedman which would tell more about the man than Clark did. I prepared a lengthy letter which outlined the idea and gave my credentials as a writer and as a person beyond reproach and sent it out. Unfortunately, despite the logical approach and the resource people who should have been available, the responses, with rare exceptions, ranged from the useless to the paranoid. Details follow.

After two mailings, 10 people had replied. One reported that the Friedman papers were donated to the Marshall Foundation Library in

From *Cryptologia*, Vol. 4, No. 1, Jan. 1980.

Lexington, Virginia; another called my attention to *The Codebreakers*! A retired major said, "All my information about WFF is 2d- and 3d-hand. I was at Fort Meade, but left just about when WFF was arriving there. Anything I might want to write would be from reading, not from first-hand knowledge." A retired navy captain indicated that he was for many years with the National Security Agency and its predecessor, the Armed Forces Security Agency. "It was during this period that I worked along-side, as it were, but not with Billy Friedman. We were friends and co-workers but I really knew little of the details of his work, probably because I have not the slightest interest in cryptography."

A response from a retired air force colonel was somewhat more pertinent. In 1937, as a Signal Corps reserve 2nd lieutenant, he was selected to attend the signal staff officer's course at Fort Monmouth, New Jersey. After graduation, having been given credit for completion of all extension courses up to major, he wrote, "This started me into cryptography and cryptanalysis which followed by taking special work under the Chief Signal Officer until my being ordered to active duty in the summer of 1940 to the Army Air Corps. After about three months . . . I received War Department orders immediately transferring me to the Cryptographic Section, Chief Signal Officer, in Washington, D. C. The week before I was supposed to report, I visited Washington to see about housing, etc. When I met Bill Friedman for the first time, he said that he detected that I was not altogether happy with my new assignment. This surprised me somewhat, so I told him that although I enjoyed cryptographic work as a hobby, I did not want to do this 12 to 14 hours a day. He then said that he didn't want anyone assigned to his section unless their heart and soul was in cryptography and he would see that my orders would be cancelled if that was my wish. I thanked him and said I would prefer to stay in my current assignment in Air Defense." Subsequently, the colonel found a friendly personnel sergeant who omitted all references from his records regarding his extensive training in cryptography and cryptanalysis.

Frederick Goff of the Library of Congress wrote that, "He [WFF] was a frequent reader in the Rare Book Division of the Library of Congress, of which I was Chief from 1945–1972. Naturally he made frequent use of the Fabyan Collection which was given to the Library through bequest in 1939(?). The Library made an extensive loan of material from the Fabyan Collection to the U. S. Army during the War for his use . . . I recall one luncheon with him in Verner W. Clapp's office. (Mr. Clapp was Chief Assistant Librarian of Congress at the time.) Colonel Friedman at that time expressed his intention of giving his library on cryptography to the Library of Congress through bequest. I do not know why he changed his mind. At the luncheon in response to my question about his bookplate, which I have never seen, he explained that it contained a cypher. While he and his wife were writing their book on the Bacon-Shakespeare question, they used the reading room of the Rare Book Division, at that time in my charge, almost daily . . . When he and his wife moved to Capital Hill I was quite often invited for cocktails . . . I talked more frequently with Mrs. Friedman who told me of their relationship with Colonel Fabyan."

Another retired navy captain provided some information about his own career. As a young ensign in 1931 he took a Navy crypto course and found out that cryptanalysis was not for him. His subsequent work was basically in "Special Operations (ELINT)" with assignments at the Naval Security Group in Washington and finally at NSA. "The last time I saw the Friedmans was in Frankfurt/M, Germany, when they gave me a personally autographed copy of their new book (1957) *The Shakespearean Ciphers Examined* . . . Please do not mention my name anywhere."

The eighth note came from a retired colonel, who wrote that he knew Friedman while he was assigned to NSA, 1955–1958, "but not on any kind of an intimate basis. I remember him as a gentleman—and one who was still young in heart and zeal for his work . . . I prefer anonymity—even when I acknowledge that I have given you no solid information."

A retired air force colonel, who was apparently a close associate of Friedman in the mid-1950's, sent a note that was sufficiently offensive to cause me to pick up the telephone and call him in Florida to express my resentment at the tone of his letter. He said he was suspicious of what I was after and piqued that I had his address. I expressed my surprise at his attitude, pointing out that he had voluntarily answered the original notice and it was the person he wrote to that had made his and everyone else's addresses known. (My letter did not disclose anyone's location.) In the course of the conversation he revealed that he had been a career intelligence officer stationed in Moscow, among other sensitive places, always subject to various approaches which made him naturally suspicious of letters like mine. He wound up agreeing that I sounded like a sincere person but he still preferred not to cooperate.

One of the rare exceptions, which also became a pleasant experience, resulted from a letter from Shirley Silverman, daughter-in-law of Verna Lehman, who was mentioned near the beginning of Clark's biography as a girl friend of Friedman's during the summer of 1913. Clark used two of her photographs in his book. Coincidentally, Mrs. Silverman's son and his wife are both members of the American Cryptogram

Association. In 1974, when I was co-chairman of the ACA annual convention at Pace University, her daughter-in-law won a prize in the solving contest. Mrs. Silverman said that Mrs. Lehman "is now eighty-five years young and remembers Will Friedman with great affection" and suggested that I might like to talk to her and see the letters Friedman wrote to her and the photographs she still treasures. I visited Verna Lehman on December 12, 1978. She is a very alert person and has fond memories of William Friedman.

In 1913, her family was spending the summer in a boarding house in Cold Spring Harbor, about 40 miles east of New York City. A man who lived in the house and worked with Friedman at the Carnegie Institution's Department of Experimental Evolution in Cold Spring Harbor told her of a nice young man and introduced them. He came to see her every evening. She remembers him bringing her one long-stemmed American Beauty rose. He was working during the summer as part of his studies at Cornell. He apparently enjoyed his work and had ambitions to be another Luther Burbank after graduation.

FIGURE 1.
At Cold Spring Harbor, at least one snapshot was taken of them which she still has.

FIGURE 2.
After the job was over, near the end of August her parents invited him to stay in their house in Brooklyn for a few days before he had to be back in Cornell. During that time, the family took pictures and included him in at least one, dated August 24, 1913.

In late 1967, Mrs. Lehman's son and grandson attended a meeting where they heard David Kahn talk about some of the people and events in his then new book, *The Codebreakers*. Since Friedman's name was familiar to them, they told Mrs. Lehman about the book and the stories about him and the PURPLE code that they had heard. Mrs. Lehman wrote to Friedman about it and he responded in a letter dated 11 December 1967 in which he said:

> Do I know the Kahn book? Of course, but it has brought me nothing but some slight amount of amusement and many headaches—people want to interview me or try to get information out of me—but I'm not granting interviews or answering letters from people wanting more information. Kahn got <u>none</u> out of me though he tried hard, very hard.

> I was retired from active service (civil [or] military) after my 2nd heart attack in 1955 but I've got plenty of work to do—but not nearly as much energy as I need.

Listening to Verna Lehman reminisce about her fond memories of William F. Friedman 56 years ago somehow made this rather unsuccessful project very worthwhile.

FIGURE 3.
Another photograph that Mrs. Lehman has kept through the years is marked "Oct. 1913 Ithaca" and was apparently sent by Friedman to her from Cornell. None of these photographs has ever been published before.

Reminiscences of a Master Cryptologist
by Louis Kruh

Who's Who in America capsulizes Frank B. Rowlett's career as follows. Cryptanalyst, U. S. Govt., 1930–58; spl. asst. to dir. Nat. Security Agy., 1958–65, comdt. Nat. Cryptologic Sch., 1965; lectr., cons. communications spltys., 1966–. Served to col., Signal Corps, AUS, 1942–46. Decorated Legion of Merit; Order Brit. Empire; Distinguished Intelligence Medal U. S. Govt., 1957; Exceptional Civilian Service award Nat. Security Agy., 1960; Congl. award for cryptologic inventions and patents, 1964; President's award for distinguished fed. civilian service, 1965; Nat. Security medal, 1966. Patentee cryptographic devices and equipments.

In addition, Rowlett was a member of the group that broke the Japanese Purple machine before Pearl Harbor. In fact, knowledgeable people insist he was the key cryptanalyst but he maintains it was a team operation.

It was an exciting event for me to visit Frank Rowlett, the senior member of the outstanding cryptologic group recruited by William F. Friedman in 1930, during a visit to Florida this past April.

What I had hoped would be at least a 15–30 minute visit lasted for 3½ hours. But it seemed like just 15 minutes.

His library contains many contemporary works on cryptology. I only became envious when he showed me a complete set of Riverbank Publications, each inscribed to him by Friedman. The book shelves also had a first edition of Hitt's *Manual*, Friedman's *Elements of Cryptanalysis*, an autographed copy of Yardley's *American Black Chamber* and others of that genre.

The reminiscences that follow stemmed in most instances from questions I asked.

From *Cryptologia*, Vol. 4, No. 1, Jan. 1980.

FRANK B. ROWLETT—APRIL 1979.
Rowlett is soft spoken, professorial in appearance, looking a little like Burl Ives since he added a neatly trimmed beard.

A few times he cautioned me about names or exact dates, noting that it had been many years since he had given thought to the matters under discussion.

Late in 1929, and after Yardley's Black Chamber was abolished, steps were taken to form the Signal Intelligence Service and the Chief Signal Officer was given the authority to hire four junior cryptanalysts. Each was to have a knowledge of at least one of four modern languages—German, French, Spanish and, most important, Japanese. Since there was no Civil Service register for junior cryptanalysts in existence at that time (indeed, such a register was never established at any time), Friedman was allowed to select candidates from the standing junior mathematicians register which had been brought up to date by an examination offered on August 10, 1929. Friedman found candidates for three of the four languages but none for Japanese. Solomon Kullback, Abraham Sinkov and myself had college credits in Spanish, French and German, respectively, and the three of us were offered employment. I reported for duty on April 1, 1930, Sinkov about ten days later and Kullback joined us on or about the twenty-first of April. By this time, Friedman was almost convinced that further search for someone with mathematical training who had a knowledge of Japanese was a hopeless task.

The selection of the fourth member of the group is an interesting example of how good fortune can sometimes provide a solution where the logical approach has failed. In late April 1930, Congressman Joe Shaffer of the Ninth Congressional District of Virginia called the Chief Signal Officer, indicating that he had learned from the Civil Service Commission that the Army was looking for a Japanese linguist. The Congressman told the Chief Signal Officer that his nephew, who was considered to be highly proficient in Japanese, was looking for a job, and that he would like to have his nephew interviewed for the vacancy. The Chief Signal Officer responded that he would make arrangements for the Congressman's nephew to be interviewed and to be given an examination in Japanese in strict accordance with Civil Service regulations.

The Chief Signal Officer then turned the matter over to Major David M. Crawford who was Chief, War Plans and Training Division and Friedman's boss, since the Signal Intelligence Service was at that time a part of the War Plans and Training Division. At first, Major Crawford and Friedman were not very hopeful about the likelihood of the Congressman's nephew satisfying the requirements of the position, since the approach had some of the earmarks of a member of congress using his influence to get a government job for a member of his family. Nonetheless, they set up a time for an interview and made arrangements for Major Creswell, G-2's Japanese expert, to conduct the language examination.

When the Congressman's nephew reported for the interview, both Crawford and Friedman were disappointed with his lack of qualifications in mathematics. However, they decided to go ahead with the language examination and had the young man escorted to the G-2 area in the Munitions Building where he was left with Major Creswell. About three hours later, Creswell called Crawford and told him the examination was over and that it was most important that he meet immediately with Crawford and Friedman to discuss the results. Crawford invited Creswell to his office, and when Creswell arrived he quickly annnounced in all his experience he had never met a non-Japanese who was as proficient in the Japanese language as the young man he had just examined. In fact, his first words on entering Crawford's office were: "If you don't hire this man, you'll be making a great mistake." When Friedman pointed out that the young man was not qualified in mathematics, Creswell responded that dozens of mathematicians could be found but that Japanese linguists of this caliber were a great rarity, especially when only native born Americans had to be considered.

And that is how John B. Hurt of Wytheville, Virginia, was selected to become the fourth member of our group. Although his mathematical background was not as complete as ours, his proficiency in Japanese more than made up for it, and he became the key individual in all aspects of our work involving Japanese linguistics. I regret that he never received the full recognition for his work that he so richly deserved, and I am sure that Congressman Shaffer never realized what an important contribution he made to his nation when he called the Chief Signal Officer about a job for his nephew.

* * *

One of the handicaps that Friedman had to overcome in developing our training program in 1930 was the lack of adequate texts on cryptology. The Riverbank Publications, Hitt's *Manual*, and *The Elements of Cryptanalysis* (Signal Corps Training Pamphlet Number Two) are all that I can recall that were in print at that time. The text for *Elementary Military Cryptography*, the first of the Signal Corps extension courses on cryptology, was at that time being set in type at the Government Printing Office, and only one copy of the typewritten draft was available for Sinkov, Kullback, Hurt and myself to study. This copy was almost illegible; it must have been at best the fifth carbon copy. I was the first of the group to receive the copy, and it was so bad that frequently I had to interrupt Friedman to ask him to clarify the portions which were illegible. Fortunately for the others, the notes I made on the illegible portions of the draft were helpful when their turns came to study the text.

* * *

Foreign language texts on cryptology were also scarce. One of my first tasks was to read two books in German; one was by Kasiski (*Die Geheimschriften und die Dechiffrirkunst*) and the other by Figl (*Systeme des Chiffrierens*). While the grammar was easy and the vocabularies tolerable, the descriptions of the code and cipher systems in both texts were long winded and ponderous. Fortunately, the descriptions were accompanied by precisely worked out examples, and I soon found out that it was a lot easier for me to figure out how the systems operated by following the examples than to plough through the turgid descriptions of the principles on which they were based.

When I reported to Friedman that I had worked my way through the texts by studying the examples and more or less ignoring the long-winded descriptive passages, he was amused, and remarked that he had followed the same procedure with the two books. He then mentioned that he had been thinking of having the few foreign texts that were available translated, and asked me if I would like to undertake the translation of Kasiski and Figl. I told him that I thought it would be more useful to extract the examples and draft a simple explanation in English for each, than to undertake literal translations of the texts of the two books. He responded that he rather liked this idea, but that there were certain advantages to a full translation. He concluded by saying that he would give the matter further thought and that we would discuss it later. I was pleased that he did not instruct me to go ahead with the translation of the two books, partly because I was not too sure of my ability in German and partly because I did not want to spend a lot of time at translating while there seemed to be so many more interesting tasks for me to work on.

* * *

In his cryptanalytical work, William F. Friedman was always a very methodical individual. He usually tried to design his attack on a difficult system as a program of step-by-step operations which ultimately would lead to success. A good example is the approach he laid out for attacking a set of test messages enciphered by the ITT cipher machine designed by Colonel Parker Hitt. He arranged to keep notes indicating the exact moment the work began, the instant each test started and ended, the exact time each message was solved, time out for interruptions, and so on. He also laid out and rehearsed the procedures we were to follow. Two teams were set up, with Sinkov and himself forming one and Kullback and myself the other.

The test messages were enciphered at the State Department and delivered to Friedman by messenger. After recording the exact time of delivery, he assigned one of the messages to Kullback and myself and he and Sinkov started working on the other; the remaining messages were set aside for later analysis. It took Kullback and myself only a few minutes to identify the last two letters of the ten-letter key for our message as "O N." I do not remember which of us got the inspiration, but Kullback and I proposed that we immediately try WASHINGTON as the key for our messsage without any further testing. Friedman at first turned down our suggestion, indicating that we were to continue with his planned program until more of the letters of the key were identified. When we argued that if our assumption was correct, the time required for solving the first message would be tremendously shortened, he gave in reluctantly. Luckily, our guess was right and the message was decipherable without the need for further work on it.

I got the distinct feeling that Friedman was disappointed that our short-cut approach was successful, for he insisted that all the remaining test messages be dealt with as he had planned until there was no doubt about the identity of the key for each. In many other cases he showed that he wanted to avoid the possibility of being accused of having achieved the solution through a "lucky guess" and chose to follow the exhaustive analytic approach rather than to take the intuitive or short-cut route.

* * *

Sinkov, Kullback, Hurt and I spent some time trying to solve the Beale Cipher, and as I recall, this was in relation to our training program. I have encountered at least two other legends of this sort and I believe all three are hoaxes. One of the other legends also involves enciphered instructions for locating a rich silver mine in Southwest Virginia, just a few miles from the famous Cumberland Gap. This mine is known as the Swift Silver Mine. The third legend is much more nebulous and to my knowledge does not involve any cipher texts; however, there is a consistency in the circumstances of this last legend with the Beale and Swift legends that leads me to the conclusion that all three are fabrications.

* * *

Friedman always treated Sinkov, Kullback and myself equally and never favored one over the other. However, the Signal Intelligence Service [SIS] was an administrative unit within a military organization, and some-one had to take over Friedman's administrative duties when he was absent. Because I had been the first of the group to report for duty, I was considered to be the next in seniority. Formal administrative matters were almost invariably handled by one of the officers of the War Plans and Training Division and we, as civilians, dealt mainly with the technical work of the SIS.

I worked more closely with Friedman and probably got to know him better than any other person in the SIS. For several years we shared the same office or our desks were located in adjacent rooms and he kept me fully informed on all the SIS activities. In addition to the normal SIS work in which we were all involved, Friedman and I also collaborated in certain cryptographic inventions.

* * *

The successful cryptanalysis of the Japanese Purple system was accomplished by a team of Army cryptanalysts. At first, it was a joint Army-Navy project, but after a few months the Navy withdrew its cryptanalytic resources to apply them to the Japanese naval systems. The Navy did, however, continue to provide some intercept coverage of diplomatic traffic.

The Chief Signal Officer, General Joseph O. Mauborgne, was personally interested in the Purple effort and supported our work to the fullest degree possible. He liked to refer to us as his magicians and called the translations of the messages we produced by the name "Magic."

Friedman played a signal role in the selection and assignment of personnel and participated in the analytical work on a part-time basis.

* * *

The Japanese diplomatic systems included two machine ciphers which they called "Cipher Machine, Type A" and "Cipher Machine, Type B." For some time after we broke into the "A Machine" which preceded the "B Machine" by several years, we referred to it in our conversations and official reports as the "A Machine." Friedman soon recognized that this practice was very poor security, and proposed that we assign a cover name to the machine which would be used at all times instead of the true Japanese designation. After considerable discussion of what might be the most suitable cover names for not only the "A Machine" but also the other machines known to us at that time (Enigma, Kryha, Hagelin, etc.), we concluded that the colors of the spectrum would be the most satisfactory choice. We selected the first color of the spectrum as the cover name for the "A Machine" and from that time on it was known as the Red machine. By the time we encountered and identified the "B Machine," we had assigned the remaining colors of the spectrum to other devices. But we thought it wise to continue identifying cipher machines by colors, and of all the non-spectrum colors, Purple seemed more appropriate than any other we could imagine as the cover name for such an important cipher machine.

* * *

It is difficult to compare the American recovery of the Purple cipher machine system with the British exploitation of the Enigma, because both were very significant cryptanalytic and intelligence achievements. Also, my opinion on this might not be considered as totally objective. However, aside from the importance of the intelligence information enciphered in the two systems and without intending to denigrate the superb technical work of the British on the Enigma, I consider that the recovery of the Purple was the greater cryptanalytic achievement. The main reason for this conclusion is that the British knew the cryptanalytic principles incorporated in the Enigma (they had a machine), while we had no knowledge of the principles employed in the Purple machine until we had reconstructed them from a study of the intercepts.

* * *

Clark's biography of Friedman does not do him justice. He deserves better. The book should have been written by someone who knew more of what went on after the Signal Intelligence Service was formed. The early years of Friedman's career were excellently characterized but the biography was very weak during the period after 1930.

A good deal of misinformation has been written about U. S. cryptologic work and, unfortunately, succeeding writers such as Clark pick up that kind of incorrect material with the result errors are perpetuated and are eventually accepted as facts.

* * *

It seems that most writers are concerned with the breaking of other nation's ciphers. Isn't it more important and even more of a feat to make your own systems secure against foreign cryptanalysts.

* * *

The day is past when one person, working alone, can break a sophisticated cipher system. The state of the cryptographic art is now so advanced that a well-designed system can be expected to resist all the efforts of a well-organized team supported by computers to solve it.

A Failure of Radio Intelligence: An Episode in the Battle of the Coral Sea
by John B. Lundstrom

From *Cryptologia*, Vol. 7, No. 2, April 1983.

On the morning of 6 May 1942, while he sailed the warm, blue waters of the Coral Sea, Rear Admiral Frank Jack Fletcher, on board his flagship, the U.S.S. *Yorktown,* bent over his charts to assess the situation. At the moment, his Task Force 17, whose heart was the aircraft carriers *Lexington* and *Yorktown,* was refueling, steaming southeast into the wind to do so. Fletcher had the mission of destroying Japanese naval forces threatening to invade Port Moresby in eastern New Guinea, 700 miles to the northwest. Three days before, the Japanese, in the opening move of their offensive, had swooped down on little Tulagi Island in the southern Solomon Islands and set up a vital seaplane base there. Fletcher the next morning had roared up from the south and attacked with *Yorktown* aircraft. Thereafter, there was a short lull in what was becoming known as the Battle of the Coral Sea. Both sides redeployed their forces for the next phase, the Japanese assault on Port Moresby, which was certain to bring the American and Japanese carriers into battle with each other.[1]

In charting his next move, Fletcher felt he had a good idea of the enemy's strength, approximate location, and, most importantly, what the Japanese planned to do. His estimate of Japanese intentions derived partly from conventional sources, such as aircraft sighting reports, but mainly depended on radio intelligence furnished primarily by his superior at Pearl Harbor, Admiral Chester W. Nimitz, Commander-in-Chief, United States Pacific Fleet (CINCPAC). Naval cryptanalysts at Pearl Harbor, Washington, and Brisbane had solved portions of Japanese Naval Codebook D. Thus they read with varying degrees of completeness a fair number of Japanese naval communications, including some high-level operational despatches. Combining these solutions with traffic analyses, brilliant deductions, and just plain guesses, they provided vital information on enemy fleet movements and general intentions obtained largely from the mouths of the Japanese themselves. By spring 1942, this intelligence enabled the U.S. Pacific Fleet to anticipate every major enemy strategic move.[2]

In this instance, however, Frank Jack Fletcher's strong reliance on the special intelligence based on solutions actually placed his Task Force 17 in jeopardy that morning of 6 May. The Japanese carriers were not where Fletcher thought they were, and the enemy commanders entertained ideas as to what they were going to do that differed from what the intercepts themselves suggested. Though radio intelligence proved immensely useful in strategic matters, in the fast-moving, tactical situations in which Task Force 17 found itself, much of it turned out to be incomplete or incorrect and very misleading. For Task Force 17, ostensibly good intelligence sources had failed. This article will demonstrate how

Rear Admiral Frank Jack Fletcher—Almost Trapped by Incomplete Radio Intelligence.

this failure came about by examining Japanese planning and operations in the Coral Sea and how the Americans perceived them through radio intelligence.

BACKGROUND OF THE CORAL SEA BATTLE

Looking southward in early 1942 from his newly conquered bastion of Rabaul, Vice Admiral Inoue Shigeyoshi set a number of necessary goals in the Coral Sea region for his South Seas Force (the operational title of the Fourth Fleet). The first, Lae and Salamaua on New Guinea, he gained early in March. Inoue next planned to capture Tulagi and then Port Moresby, the valuable Allied air base on the south coast of New Guinea. Port Moresby in Japanese hands would round out the defensive perimeter by guarding the approaches to Rabaul. Japanese air power operating from Port Moresby would be able to range far into the Coral Sea and even strike northeastern Australia.

The threat of carrier attack, made real when on 10 March two U.S. carriers damaged some of his ships badly, as well as increased Allied land-based air opposition in the area, forced Inoue to ask the high command for increased carrier support. In early April, Admiral Yamamoto Isoroku, commanding the Combined Fleet, agreed to provide South Seas Force with carriers for the so-called MO, or Moresby, Operation. However, Yamamoto stipulated that the Port Moresby and Tulagi invasions take place early in May—well before his intended June assault on Midway. Combined Fleet at first offered Inoue use of the carrier *Kaga,* then on 12 April replaced that vessel with *Zuikaku* and *Shokaku* of the 5th Carrier Division under Rear Admiral Hara Chuichi. South Seas Force had already secured the services of the newly commissioned light carrier *Shoho.*

Hara's flattops were returning to Japan via the East Indies after helping to trounce the British in the Indian Ocean. Orders went forth from Yamamoto detaching Hara from the Carrier Striking Force and assigning him to Inoue's command. In response, Hara on 13 April informed Inoue that he would proceed to Bako on Formosa for fuel and a short refit. He indicated he expected to depart there about 28 April for Truk.[3] The message was intercepted and tackled independently by American and British cryptanalysts. On 15 April, the British Admiralty forwarded a tentative solution to OP-20-G, Captain Laurence F. Safford's radio intelligence unit serving under the Chief of Naval Operations in Washington. Safford confirmed the reading and sent it to Nimitz in the Pacific. Safford's communication provided the Japanese message almost in full, but inferred erroneously that the carriers *Zuikaku* and *Shokaku* would arrive around 28 April at Truk.[4] Despite this error, the general time frame revealed that Japanese offensive operations south of Truk were imminent. Carriers would not assemble there and operate under South Seas Force control for nothing. Nimitz began taking steps to counter the Japanese threat.

The 5th Carrier Division separated from the Carrier Striking Force on 14 April and shaped course for Formosa. Three days later, Inoue unwittingly made the false Allied rendition of the 13 April message true when he ordered Hara to depart immediately for Truk rather than dallying in Formosa until near the end of the month. On 18 April, because of the Doolittle air raid on Japan, Yamamoto roused much of the Combined Fleet and hurled it eastward in a vain attempt to overtake the American carriers responsible for the outrage. Hara touched briefly at Bako for fuel, then on 19 April joined the chase. Shortly thereafter, he received orders to head directly to Truk. The Doolittle raid did not delay preparations for the MO Operation.

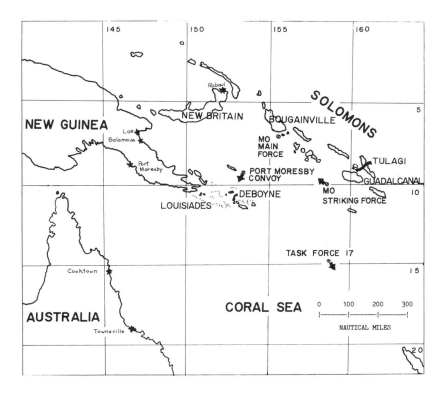

POSITIONS OF FORCES AT 0800 6 MAY 1942. TASK FORCE 17 IS HEADING SOUTHEAST INTO THE WIND TO FUEL. (MAP BY SANDRA LUNDSTROM.)

On 23 April, Inoue's South Seas Force issued Operations Order No. 13, the basic directive for the MO Operation.[5] Headquarters at Truk broadcast a summary of the lengthy document, but the transmission likely escaped interception and certainly cryptanalysis by the Allies. Inoue set the invasion of Port Moresby, X-Day, for 10 May, with Tulagi to fall on X–7 Day (3 May). Conducting the invasions was MO Attack Force, comprising the troop convoy, escorts, and auxiliary forces under Rear Admiral Goto Aritomo. A task group within MO Attack Force was MO Main Force under Goto's direct command. This consisted of four heavy cruisers, a destroyer, and the light carrier *Shoho*. American analysts knew of the attachment to South Seas Force of the converted flattop *Shoho*, but they wrongly read the Kanji characters making up her name as *Ryukaku*.

His two fleet carriers Inoue incorporated into MO Striking Force led by newly promoted Vice Admiral Takagi Takeo, commander of the 5th Cruiser Division. Hara became Takagi's air commander. Takagi's primary mission was to protect the invasion forces from carrier attack. Inoue also felt it was vital to use MO Striking Force to knock out Allied air bases. The basic premise behind the MO Operation was one of surprise, and Inoue predicated his plan on the belief that the American carriers would not be in position to intervene immediately. Operations Order No. 13 specified that if American carriers were thought not to be present in the Coral Sea, then Takagi was to raid Townsville in northeastern Australia to help neutralize Allied land-based air strength. Then, if the American carriers still had not appeared, MO Striking Force was to launch further air strikes either on Cooktown (also in Australia) or Port Moresby itself.

Hara was not at all pleased with the proposed air strikes on northeastern Australia. Upon his arrival on 25 April at Truk, he studied Operations Order No. 13 and raised a number of objections. First of all, he thought it perilous to execute air strikes against well defended bases out of support range of Japanese land-based aviation. Also, the approach to the launch point would take the ships through reef-studded waters, and the thought of high-speed operations made Hara want more than the one fleet oiler assigned to MO Striking Force. He was not shy and voiced his concerns to Takagi, South Seas Force, and even Combined Fleet. Ignoring his subordinate's arguments, Takagi on the basis of Inoue's directive issued MO Striking Force Operations Order No. 1 on 28 April. It called for the Townsville strike to take place on X–3 Day (7 May) and allowed for possible follow-up attacks on Cooktown and Port Moresby.[6] Rear Admiral Yano Shikazo, South Seas Force chief of staff, reacted on 29 April to Hara's complaints by reiterating Operations Order No. 13: "The attacks on Townsville, Cooktown, and Port Moresby should proceed as ordered."[7] He did give Takagi discretion to cancel the strike if he suspected an enemy carrier force operated in the Coral Sea or if Allied search planes discovered him on the way in. Yano made it clear, however, that South Seas Force counted on the air strikes being executed if at all possible.

Hara's note of caution did strike home at Combined Fleet. On 29 April, Rear Admiral Ugaki Matome, Combined Fleet chief of staff, sent on behalf of Yamamoto the following order to Fourth Fleet (South Seas Force) and other concerned commands:[8]

> Combined Fleet Secret Radio No. 907: As for the operations of MO Striking Force with reference to South Seas Force Secret Order No. 13, said force should restrict itself to dealing with the enemy striking forces. It is thought advisable that the force should be sufficiently cautious, in light of its strength and the situation in the waters north of Australia, in executing strikes on important bases in that country. It is advised that you should utilize requisite Base Air Force strength and concentrate its operations on destroying enemy land-based air strength.

In essence, Yamamoto told Inoue to rely on his own land-based air strength to deal with the Allied air bases and forget about using the carriers against northern Australia, at least until after they had dealt with the American carriers. Hara had won the first round.

Inoue on 30 April cancelled the proposed carrier air strikes on Townsville, Cooktown, and Port Moresby, but in turn ordered Takagi to do his part to reinforce Japanese air units at Rabaul.[9] Takagi agreed to transport nine Zero fighters on board his carriers from Truk to within air ferry range of Rabaul. After flying off the fighters to Rabaul, he intended to take station north of Tulagi to support the forces undertaking that invasion on 3 May. After refueling on 4 May, MO Striking Force was to pass around the southern tip of the Solomons chain and patrol the waters about 300 miles southwest of Tulagi, there to watch for the approach of Allied warships, especially American carriers.

THE CORAL SEA: PRELIMINARY MOVES

It was mainly through traffic analysis—studying message originators and addresses—that American naval radio intelligence officers outlined the Japanese build-up at Truk and Rabaul. There was little actual cryptanalyzed information to go on: nowhere did there appear in the solved intercepts a definite statement of Japanese strengths or even objectives. Still, Nimitz decided to concentrate all his available carrier strength in the Coral Sea, at first two carriers under Fletcher to be joined in mid-May by two more. On 1 May, Fletcher rendezvoused with reinforcements sent from Pearl Harbor and made ready to fight in the Coral Sea. For the Japanese, the MO Operation had already begun, as in the last days of April task forces had departed from Rabaul and elsewhere to erect seaplane bases in the Solomons, capture Tulagi, and build a seaplane anchorage at Deboyne in the Louisiade Archipelago to cover the advance of the invasion convoy on its voyage toward Port Moresby. Takagi's MO Striking Force sailed on 1 May from Truk.

On 30 April (Hawaiian time—1 May in the Coral Sea), Commander Joseph J. Rochefort's radio intelligence unit (codename HYPO) at Pearl Harbor partially solved a message sent by Inoue to his Fourth Fleet, Takagi's 5th Cruiser Division, Hara's 5th Carrier Division, and other commands.[10] It corrected the communications plan of Operations Order No. 13 and mentioned, among other places, Cooktown and Townsville as reference points. The message helped to pinpoint Port Moresby as a major objective and indicated Japanese interest in northeastern Australia. Rochefort late the same day summarized the situation as he saw it. He had detected the MO Operation and noted that Port Moresby appeared to be the immediate objective. Major forces readily available included the 5th Carrier Division and the 5th Cruiser Division, which were already in the Rabaul region or en route. He added, "Despite message giving Townsville as reference point do not believe Australia involved in immediate future except for submarine operations."[11]

That same day, however, the Pearl Harbor cryptanalysts started work on an intercepted message which proved to be the 29 April operations order from Combined Fleet to South Seas Force restricting the mission of the Japanese carriers to wiping out the American flattops (see text previously quoted).

On 1 May, Rochefort's unit provided a decrypt of the message with an analysis.[12] [See figure below for reproduction of message report.]

The recorder of the Pacific Fleet's *Greybook* (diary of the War Plans Division) noted for 1 May the gist of the message as the CINCPAC staff took it to be: "To keep our forces from interfering, the Japanese plan to raid such places as Cooktown, Townsville, and Horn Island [off northern Australia], and may raid as far east as ROSES [Efate], Noumea, Fiji, and Samoa."[13]

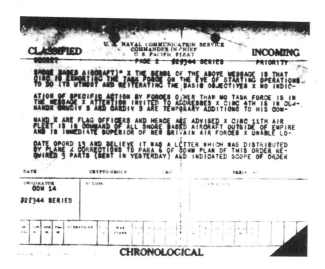

After pondering the message one day, Nimitz, late on 2 May (Hawaiian time), transmitted to Fletcher and others the following message [see below] based on the decrypt of the 29 April order from Combined Fleet to South Seas Force:[14]

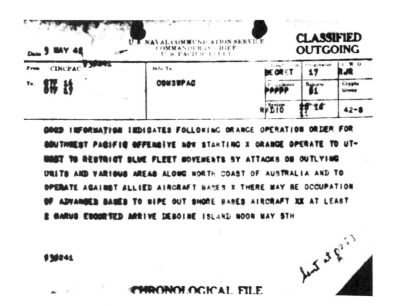

REPRODUCTION OF CINCPAC TO CTF 16,17; INFO COMSOWPAC 030241 OF MAY 1942.

Thus Fletcher, cruising in the Coral Sea out of enemy air search range, learned on 3 May (local time) that the enemy would likely conduct a series of raids on northern Australia and also South Pacific island air bases to pin down Allied naval forces. But, as shown, the Combined Fleet order actually instructed the Japanese carrier commanders to concern themselves with hunting down their American counterparts. Allied misconception stemmed from an erroneous solution of a complex Japanese operational despatch, due mainly, as HYPO's transmittal message noted, to a "lack of code groups" already solved.

MO Striking Force's first order of business after departing Truk was to transport the nine Zero fighters to reinforce the air units at Rabaul. On 2 May, Takagi, from 240 miles northeast of Rabaul, despatched the nine fighters, flown by his own carrier pilots, and seven torpedo planes to bring back the pilots. Bad weather forced them back. Takagi loitered in the area and tried the next day with equally dismal results. He had delayed his move southward toward Tulagi (captured on 3 May) and consequently was out of support range of Japanese naval forces there. He planned to refuel on 4 May, then resume his southward advance according to plan.

Concerned by the delay in obtaining the vitally needed Zero fighters at Rabaul, South Seas Force on 3 May revived the idea of executing a carrier strike to soften up Port Moresby. Yano, the chief of staff, that day radioed MO Striking Force [15]:

Depending on the situation of the enemy planes remaining at Port Moresby, it has been agreed informally that MO Striking Force would by X–3 or the dawn of X–2 [7 May or dawn 8 May] move to a point southeast of Port Moresby, and by special order attack the enemy base at Port Moresby. Be prepared to do this.

Presumably Takagi and Hara retained the right to disregard this order if they felt threatened by enemy forces, this being specified in the 29 April order from Combined Fleet. As of 4 May, the Japanese had no doubt that an American carrier force lurked in the area. That day, *Yorktown* carrier planes several times struck at Japanese vessels near Tulagi. Thus South Seas Force's "informal agreement" became academic, as Hara, for one, had no intention of hitting shore bases when American carriers were loose.

American radio intercept stations at Brisbane and in the Hawaiian Islands recovered the 3 May message from Yano to Takagi and Hara. They furnished a transcription to the cryptanalysts.

Lieutenant Rudolph J. Fabian's BELCONNEN radio intelligence groups at Brisbane came up with the following message:[16]

BELCONNEN to COMB 050150 of May 1942.

SOKA 3 306 Message originated by _____.

"With regard to _____ in the RZP area hereafter the MO Fleet _____(will operate?) in the following manner. On X–2 or X–3 (dashes mean minus?) you are ordered to _____ in the area on the southeast of RZP and attack the enemy bases in the RZP area. With regard to this order wish you to confer prior to arrival."

The message addressed to COMCARDIV 5 and COMCRUDIV 5.

Rochefort's HYPO unit at Pearl Harbor likewise studied the same intercept and offered this rendering:[17]

COM 14 to COMB 050322 of May 1942.

SOKA SOKA 3 Serial 306 to COMCRUDIV 5, COMCARDIV 5 for action.

"From CINC 4th. In order to wipe out enemy air bases in the RZP (Moresby) area the MO Striking Force will launch attacks (from) a south easterly direction (direction not sure but looks like easterly or southerly in other traffic) on bases in Moresby area on X minus 3 days and/or X minus 2 days. This order in effect until its successful completion. Commence preparations."

Best estimate here of X Day is 10 May based on previous messages saying gunboat division leaving Marshalls X minus 7 and units going to Deboyne X minus 5.

The Pearl Harbor cryptanalysts offered a more complete solution, probably because they had solved more code groups, but neither achieved the full sense of the message. Rochefort's analysis noted that the order was binding: "in effect until its successful completion."[18]

Based on the Rochefort unit solution, Pacific Fleet headquarters on 4 May (Hawaiian date) despatched the following message to Fletcher and other concerned commanders:[19]

CINCPAC to CTF 16,17; INFO COMSOWESPAC 050345 of May 1942.

Reliable indications on 3 May:

ORANGE Moresby striking Force composed of CRUDIV 5 and CARDIV 5 will launch attacks on Allied bases Port Moresby area on X minus 3 or X minus 2 days. Attacks to be launched from southeast (fairly good but not certain). X Day not known but one indication points to 10 May as X Day. Above attacks to be carried out until successful completion by ORANGE.

In the Coral Sea the date was 5 May when Fletcher's communicators logged in the CINCPAC transmission. Task Force 17 had retired south after attacking Tulagi. That morning *Yorktown* and her escorts rejoined the rest of the task force, which included Rear Admiral Aubrey W. Fitch with the carrier *Lexington*.

Almost simultaneously with the above quoted message, another had arrived from Nimitz which also contributed enormously to Fletcher's view of the situation. This decrypt originated with new orders issued on 4 May by Inoue to counter the American carrier force that had just appeared off Tulagi. Inoue did not know whether the enemy flattop was north of Tulagi or south of it in the Coral Sea proper. He allowed for either contingency.[20] Rochefort's cryptanalysts solved one of these orders as follows:[21]

COM 14 to COMB 050208 of May 1942.

MOO MOO Serial 847.

"If location of the enemy striking force is determined to be in _____ the MO Striking Force will operate as follows:
Pass (NNK) (NNE?) of RX thence south. At 0600 5 May after arrival at _____ proceed in accordance with further orders. If no further orders received proceed to RXB.
If plane search is required in southern and _____ sectors COM-CARDIV 5 will send carrier bombers to RXB at dawn.
_____ will proceed to RXE after taking on stores."

Believe RX is Bougainville, RXB is Tulagi. This message sent to MO Striking Force for action.

Nimitz passed this information to Fletcher which he likewise received the afternoon of 5 May:[22]

CINCPAC to CTF 16,17; INFO COMSOWESPAC 050329 of May 1942.

Jap Commander Moresby Striking Force (COMCRUDIV 5) indicates 4 May that if BLUE striking force is determined in Coral Sea (questionable location) ORANGE Striking Force will proceed north northeast of Bougainville thence southward. At 0630 Item 5 May after arrival unknown place will proceed accordance further orders. If no further orders will go to Tulagi. If plane search in southern and another sector needed Carrier Div 5 to send his bombers to Tulagi at daybreak.

Thus Fletcher on 5 May obtained what appeared to be two concrete statements concerning Japanese carrier movements. One message indicated that if the Japanese found the American carriers in the Coral Sea, MO Striking Force with the two big flattops *Shokaku* and *Zuikaku* would proceed north-northeast of Bougainville—evidently to offer close support to the invasion convoy either at Rabaul or still near by. Even before he read the two messages, Fletcher had excellent reason to believe this condition had already been fulfilled. The morning of 5 May, Task Force 17's combat air patrol shot down a Japanese flying boat which had apparently shadowed Fitch's ships to the rendezvous with Fletcher. There was no question the enemy snooper had had ample opportunity to spot both American carriers, and Fletcher felt certain the Japanese had reported him. He was wrong. For some unexplained reason, the flying boat crew had never established contact with headquarters, and it was only hours later after the aircraft had failed to return to Tulagi that the Japanese deduced it might have run afoul of the Americans south of the Solomons.

The second item of intelligence information vouchsafed to Fletcher on 5 May informed him that MO Striking Force would on 7 or 8 May strike Port Moresby from the air. To do this, the Japanese carriers had to approach within attack radius (about 200 miles) of the target. Geography indicated the southeast as the likely direction from which to attack Port Moresby. A look at the chart would confirm that the orders, such as outlined in the CINCPAC 050345 message, seemingly restricted severely the options open to the Japanese carrier commander. The timing would compel him to run southward from Bougainville toward the Louisiades. In doing so, MO Striking Force would thus sweep ahead along the seaward flank of the invasion convoy plodding southward from Rabaul.

In the interpretation by Rochefort's analysts "This order is effect until its successful completion,"[23] rendered to Fletcher as "Above attacks to be carried out until successful completion by ORANGE,"[24] appeared to offer the Japanese commanders little discretion. So it was natural for the Americans to assume that MO Striking Force would remain relatively close to the convoy, using air searches to locate the American warships if they were present, and also steam toward the launch point (conveniently in the convoy's path) designated for the ordered air strikes on Port Moresby. The American realized that the sooner the Japanese carried out their orders and hit Port Moresby, the sooner they could begin searching out the American carriers.

How did the admirals on the spot piece together the various items of intelligence provided them? The clearest statement is in Fitch's after-action report for Coral Sea. The designated air task group commander, he noted that on 6 May he and Fletcher agreed that the invasion convoy and the carrier they thought was *Ryukaku* were nearing the Louisiades from the north. As for the other two enemy flattops, Fitch wrote that as of 6 May, "two additional CV's [aircraft carriers], probably Carrier Division FIVE, were reported in the vicinity of BOUGAINVILLE ISLAND."[25] He added that his proposed air search for 7 May would cover the Louisiades to pinpoint the invasion convoy and extend northward "to locate Carrier Division FIVE, which it was expected would run southward from the vicinity of BOUGAINVILLE and might be within striking distance on the morning of 7 May."[26] Thus Fletcher and Fitch, on the morning of 6 May, felt strongly that their principal opponents, the two big flattops of the 5th Carrier Division, were in Bougainville waters far out of immediate attack range. They reached this belief on the basis of intelligence reports received from Pearl Harbor.

Fletcher's plans for 6 May were to top off his ships with fuel, requiring a brief interval of steaming into the wind—southeast, or away from the enemy, then to race to the northwest to gain a favorable predawn position from which to launch an air search and follow up attack on 7 May. He arranged to leave his fleet oiler *Neosho* and a destroyer behind in what he thought were secure waters to the southeast. Even though he felt the enemy carriers were far away, Fletcher sent two air searches 275 miles to the north and northwest, one in the morning and one that afternoon. The search crews, hindered by bad weather, sighted no enemy vessels. Bothering Task Force 17 that morning was another Japanese flying boat, but the fighters could not corner it. Fletcher again concluded that the enemy knew his location, this time correctly, but he carried out his plans and made ready for likely action the next day. He hoped his 7 May dawn search would locate the 5th Carrier Division as well as the convoy; then he could hit the Japanese carriers with his full air attack force. Perhaps he might catch the enemy flattops while their aircraft raided Port Moresby. If not, Task Force 17 would be in for a struggle, but Fletcher hoped at least to smash the Japanese first, so they could not retaliate as hard.

Unfortunately for Fletcher and Fitch, their impressions of Japanese intentions and movements, so carefully formed from the intelligence summaries furnished them, were based on incomplete and sometimes erroneous information. The 5th Carrier Division was not in the Bougainville area. The decrypted message relayed by CINCPAC (message 050329 of May 1942) which seemed to place *Shokaku* and *Zuikaku* there did not, after all, even refer to MO Striking Force. Inoue's 4 May orders, which had been intercepted and partially solved by the Americans, pertained instead to Rear Admiral Goto's MO Main Force with the light carrier *Shoho* (wrongly labelled *Ryukaku* by the Americans). American naval intelligence was actually unaware of the existence of MO Main Force; in this instance they confused it with MO Striking Force. Until the 4 May attack on Tulagi, Goto's operations had proceeded according to plan. Upon receipt of Inoue's 4 May order, the one partially solved by HYPO (message COM 14 to COM 050208 of May 1942), Goto retired in the direction of Bougainville. The next day (5 May) and for all of 6 May, MO Main Force remained near Bougainville and covered the advance of the slow Port Moresby invasion convoy.[27] Allied search planes spotted

Goto's force on 4 May and both succeeding days, reporting its location to Fletcher.

Although *Shoho* (*Ryukaku* to the Americans) was about where Fletcher on 6 May expected she was, MO Striking Force definitely was not. On 4 May when *Yorktown's* aircraft pounded the Tulagi invasion ships, Takagi and Hara lay to the north, far out of support range, delayed by the fiasco of trying to fly the Zero fighters off to Rabaul. Their ships had just started refueling when they learned of Fletcher's air strike. Inoue ordered Takagi to "operate according to plan,"[28] so MO Striking Force suspended fueling and steamed southeastward along the northern edge of the Solomons, on 5 May swung around the tip of that island chain and headed westward into the waters west of Guadalcanal. Takagi planned on 6 May to resume the fueling interrupted two days before and also to fly the vitally needed fighters to Rabaul. After that his carriers would be free to hunt down the troublesome American carrier. The carrier attack on Port Moresby was shelved, at least for the time being.

The 6 May contact report by the Japanese flying boat which had found Task Force 17 reached MO Striking Force at 1050. The message placed the Americans about 350 miles south of Takagi, but it was in error. Actually Fletcher's carriers lay only 300 miles south. A follow-up message from the flying boat indicated the Americans were steaming south at 20 knots. Takagi's force was again caught unprepared because of refueling, and this time there was no question of rushing southward immediately because the destroyers were very low on fuel. Takagi decided to detach Hara's 5th Carrier Division and two destroyers to lead the pursuit, while he would follow with the rest of the ships when he could. Hara departed at 1200.

The 5th Carrier Division and its small escort steamed southward at high speed, but Hara already held certain misgivings as to the efficacy of the pursuit. His ships entered a band of extremely bad weather (which hid them from Fletcher's afternoon search), and Hara had no idea how far south it extended. If the overcast covered the target area, his strike planes might never even find the enemy. Then too, there were no amplifying messages from the flying boat supposedly shadowing the enemy. The last Hara heard, the Americans were heading away from him at 20 knots. The odds in this instance seemed very much against his overtaking the enemy. He felt reluctant to launch his own air search, because he did not want to alert the enemy to the presence of carrier planes (therefore carriers) in the vicinity before he was ready to attack. He thought it better to seek out and smash the Americans early the next morning. At 1930, he radioed Takagi that he had received no additional news of the enemy's location and situation. Therefore he planned to retire north and suggested a rendezvous between him and Takagi for 0600 the next morning 280 miles southwest of Tulagi. Hara reversed course at 2000 and headed north. Takagi himself had decided on his own that the Americans had eluded Hara and likewise turned northward. Both Japanese admirals expected on 7 May to renew the search and offer battle under circumstances which they felt would be more favorable to them.

Actually, had they been more persistent, the Japanese could not have had a better opportunity to smash Task Force 17. MO Striking Force threw away a golden chance to surprise the Americans. Instead of steaming away, as Hara was led to believe, Fletcher was far closer than the Japanese thought. Despite the first reports of the flying boat crew, the Americans had not steamed south, but had remained roughly in the area where they were first sighted. During the afternoon, Hara's carriers swiftly covered the distance between themselves and the unsuspecting Americans. Task Force 17 that day sailed in the open, as the band of clouds and rain squalls abruptly terminated just north of it. Hara's search planes, had he bothered to launch any, would likely have located Fletcher without difficulty.

By late afternoon the two carrier forces had closed to within ridiculously short distances of each other. At 1800 they were only 90 miles apart. After dark, at 2000, when Hara finally reversed course, Fletcher was only 70 miles away! Hara, of course, knew the Americans lay somewhere to the south of him, but never dreamt they were so near. Fletcher, on the other hand, had no inkling the Japanese flattops were anywhere in the neighborhood. His intelligence sources, after all, placed them near Bougainville![29]

On 7 May the search reports came early, fast, and furious. That morning aircraft from MO Striking Force discovered the fleet oiler *Neosho* and destroyer *Sims* marking time in the supposedly secure area where Fletcher had parked them. The Japanese search crews mistook the long, low oiler for a carrier. Hara hit the two hapless vessels with all he had. After all, he had thought all along the American carrier force was still to the south of him, when actually it lay to the west. Task Force 17 aviators near the Louisiades likewise erred in reporting enemy ships, and Fletcher hurled his air groups northward against what he believed were *Shokaku* and *Zuikaku,* which *he thought* all along were to the north of him. The American attack planes had to settle for the light carrier *Shoho* north of the Louisiades, and soon sent the small flattop beneath the waves. Misconceptions as to the enemy's location, fostered the previous day, had

U.S.S. Lexington in the Battle of the Coral Sea.
An explosion aboard the U.S.S. *Lexington* flings an airplane from the flight deck during the Battle of the Coral Sea, which took place despite the failure of radio intelligence to tell American forces where the Japanese were. (U.S. Navy photo.)

misdirected both sides' strikes. Only on 8 May did the two main opponents find each other and square off for a fight. The Americans lost *Lexington,* but they roughed up *Shokaku* and forced the Japanese to withdraw and postpone the Port Moresby invasion.

CONCLUSION

There seems little doubt that Task Force 17 escaped what might have been a devastating attack on it the afternoon of 6 May. Fletcher himself acted on the basis of special intelligence estimates furnished from Pearl Harbor and aircraft sighting reports relayed from Brisbane. The forecasts of Japanese intentions and movements, derived largely from interpretations of partially solved enemy radio messages and traffic analysis, decisively influenced his deployment of Task Force 17. He took careful precautions, but on 6 May poor weather to the north screened the Japanese from his own air searches.

Mainly responsible for Fletcher's erroneous views were three items of intelligence. The first Fletcher received the afternoon of 3 May. It told him the Japanese would attack Allied "outlying units and various areas along the north coast of Australia," and would "operate against Allied aircraft bases."[30] In fact, the original intent of the Japanese message (Combined Fleet Serial 907 of 29 April 1942) was to cancel planned Japanese carrier raids on northern Australia and Port Moresby in order to restrict MO Striking Force to the mission of destroying American carrier forces.

The afternoon of 5 May Fletcher heard from Pearl Harbor the second item: that the Japanese carriers had orders to strike Port Moresby on 7 or 8 May. This, of course, fitted in well with the previously cited message which forecast raids "against Allied aircraft bases." Unfortunately, neither Fletcher nor the CINCPAC analysts could know that his opposite number on the MO Striking Force flagship was not bound by these "orders" in view of the overriding mission of hunting down the American carriers. With Fletcher's 4 May assault on the Tulagi invasion ships, the Japanese carriers had no other objectives than smashing Task Force 17.

The final piece of information was the incorrect attribution by the codebreakers of orders to MO Striking Force when they in fact applied to MO Main Force. That is, Inoue had ordered MO Main Force to retire toward Bougainville should the American carrier force be discovered on 5 May to be operating in the Coral Sea. It seemed logical to Fletcher and Fitch that MO Striking Force would take station between them and the invasion convoy in order to provide close support. Also, there were the just cited orders ("to be carried out until successful completion") for MO Striking Force to attack Port Moresby. The pieces all fitted together, but for Fletcher it turned out to be the wrong puzzle. To him the Japanese fleet carriers on 6 May had to be well to the northwest near Bougainville, when in fact they lay just out of attack range to the north.

Radio intelligence was responsible for the American carriers being in the Coral Sea in the first place, and this provided Nimitz with a tremendous strategic advantage in knowing in a general way his opponent's future moves. The Pacific Fleet, however, had no magic looking glass which mapped out for them just what the enemy would do and where. They still had to go out, fight, and win the battles enshrouded in the "fog of war." Radio intelligence as yet lacked the sophistication to provide reliable information in many cases to those who utilized it. Partially solved messages offered only confused, sometimes downright misleading glimpses of the enemy's complex high-level policy decisions. Under these conditions, incomplete, erroneous, or tardy intelligence could actually be detrimental for fast developing tactical situations. For the commander who operated on the basis of radio intelligence, there was always the peril that the situation was not what the codebreakers and analysts believed or that the enemy commanders simply might not follow their superior's orders. Both circumstances befell Frank Jack Fletcher on 6 May in the Coral Sea. He was fortunate he did not have to pay the consequences.

ACKNOWLEDGEMENTS

Dr. Dean C. Allard of the Operational Archives Branch, Leo Johnson, Museum Photographer, and Sandra Lundstrom.

NOTES

1.   For the Battle of the Coral Sea, see the sources cited in: John B. Lundstrom, *The First South Pacific Campaign: Pacific Fleet Strategy, December 1941–June 1942.* (Annapolis, 1976), 215. The best source on operations is: Japan Self Defense Force, War History Series *(Senshi Sosho), Nantohomen Kaigun Sakusen* (Southeast Area Naval Operations), Volume I (Operations up to the Guadalcanal Counteroffensive). (Tokyo, 1971) 163–330 (in Japanese, hereafter *Senshi Sosho*).
2.   Background on U.S. naval radio intelligence, see: W. J. Holmes, *Double-Edged Secrets.* (Annapolis, 1976); David Kahn, *The Codebreakers: The Story of Secret Writing.* (New York, 1967); Rear Admiral Edwin T. Layton, USN (Ret.), Note in *United States Naval Institute Proceedings* (June 1979), 99–101.
3.   *Senshi Sosho,* 187–188.
4.   OPNAV [Chief of Naval Operations] to CINCPAC 152049 of April 1942, in U.S. Pacific Fleet Secret and Confidential Message Files, microfilm held by Operational Archives Branch, Naval Historical Center, Washington, D.C. Message times are all in Greenwich Civil Time (GCT), with the date first and the hours second. Local time for Pearl Harbor was GCT 9½ hours plus; in the Coral Sea, GCT minus 11 hours.
5.   Text in *Senshi Sosho,* 176–185.
6.   *Ibid.,* 189–191.
7.   *Ibid.,* 186.
8.   *Ibid.*
9.   *Ibid.*
10.   COM 14 to COMB Addresses, 010810 of May 1942, in Pacific Fleet Message Files. COM 14 is the 14th Naval District, COMB refers to Combined Addresses of COPEK messages.
11.   COM 14 to OPNAV, BELCONNEN, COM 16, Information CINCPAC, 011108 series of May 1942, in Pacific Fleet message files.

12. COM 14 to COMB, 020344 series of May 1942, in Pacific Fleet message files: CofS is Chief of Staff, COMCRUDIV 5 is Commander, Cruiser Division 5, COMCARDIV 5 is Commander, Carrier Division 5.
13. CINCPAC Greybook (War Diary of War Plans Division), 1 May 1942, in Classified Operational Archives.
14. CINCPAC to CTF 16, 17, INFO COMSOWESPAC, 030241 of May 1942, Pacific Fleet message files. CTF is Commander, Task Force, COMSOWESPAC is Commander Southwest Pacific Area (General Douglas MacArthur).
15. *Senshi Sosho,* 230.
16. BELCONNEN to COMB, 050150 of May 1942, in Pacific Fleet message files.
17. COM 14 to COMB, 050322 of May 1942, in Pacific Fleet message files.
18. *Ibid.*
19. CINCPAC to CTF 16, 17, INFO COMSOWESPAC, 050345 of May 1942, in Pacific Fleet message files.
20. *Senshi Sosho,* 233–235.
21. COM 14 to COMB, 050208 of May 1942, in Pacific Fleet message files.
22. CINCPAC to CTF 16, 17, INFO COMSOWESPAC, 050329 of May 1942, in Pacific Fleet message files.
23. COM 14 to COMB 050322 of May 1942, in Pacific Fleet message files.
24. CINCPAC to CTF 16, 17, INFO COMSOWESPAC, 050345 of May 1942, in Pacific Fleet message files.
25. Action Report, CTG 17.5 (Rear Admiral A. W. Fitch) to CTF 17 (Rear Admiral F. J. Fletcher), for Coral Sea (May 7–8, 1942), dated 18 May 1942, in Classified Operational Archives.
26. *Ibid.*
27. *Senshi Sosho,* 233–235.
28. *Ibid.,* 235.
29. On 6 May operations, see especially *Senshi Sosho,* 239–245.
30. CINCPAC to CTF 16, 17, INFO COMSOWESPAC, 030241 of May 1942, in Pacific Fleet message files.

[*Ed. note:* Newly declassified material on U.S. Navy codebreaking may include more information on the operations of the radio intelligence units but will not include any more decrypts for the period dealt with in this article. The sources used in it—chiefly the *Greybook* and the secret and confidential message files of the Pacific Fleet—include all intelligence messages to Fletcher from Nimitz; the numeration is complete. After June of 1942, this intelligence material no longer appeared in those sources, perhaps as a consequence of the news story revealing the Japanese order of battle that appeared in the *Chicago Tribune* (for this episode, see Kahn, 603–604, and Larry J. Frank, "The United States Navy *v.* the *Chicago Tribune,*" *The Historian* (1980), 284–303). Ronald Lewin's book, *The American Magic: Codes, Ciphers and the Defeat of Japan* (New York, 1982), contains no new information that would affect this study. The Battle of the Coral Sea is not mentioned in the official history by F. H. Hinsley *et al., British Intelligence in the Second World War,* Vol. 2, (London and New York, 1981).]

Enigma: The Dropping of the Double Encipherment
by Gilbert Bloch and Ralph Erskine

The double encipherment of the message key was a fatal flaw in the keying procedures adopted by the German armed forces for the Enigma cipher machine before May 1940. Marian Rejewski, the Polish cryptanalyst who first penetrated Enigma, described it as "the third secret" of military Enigma.[1] As well as helping him to reconstruct rotors I to III in 1932 and to develop cryptanalytical methods for reading messages, it was also the weak point that was later exploited by the Polish electro-mechanical bombes and the perforated sheets.[2]

In July 1939, the Poles handed over the design of the perforated sheets to the British and French, along with reconstructed copies of Enigma and other important material.[3] By mid-December 1939, a British team led by John Jeffreys had accomplished the enormous task of producing two full sets of the sheets at Bletchley Park (BP), the new home of the Government Code and Cypher School. Fortunately, the sheets were still as effective against the Enigma in wartime as they had been in peace. [4]

In early 1940, the start of an Enigma signal (after the sender's and receiver's call signs) took the following form (using the example in the 13 January 1940 instructions)[5]:

1755—135 wep ulznu hfikl bsgex unfo . . .

where

the first four figures (1755) were the time of origin (Zeitgruppe) of the message;

the next three figures (135) gave the number of letters, including

From *Cryptologia*, Vol. 10, No. 3, July 1986.

the recognition group (Kenngruppe) and the message key (Spruch-schlüssel), but excluding the starting position (Grundstellung) (see below), in the enciphered message;

the first three letters (wep) were the starting position of the rotors (Grundstellung);

the next five letters (ulznu) contained the Kenngruppe[6], which indicated the net to which the message belonged;

the message key (Spruchschlüssel)[7] followed immediately after the Kenngruppe, as letters 6 to 11 (hfiklb).

After the message key came the cipher text proper (sgex unfo . . .).

Some time in May 1940, BP suffered a major setback. The part of a signal from the Zeigruppe on changed, so that a typical example read as follows (again, the example is taken from the German operating instructions):

1755—129—wep hfi ulznu sgexu nfo . . .

The first three items (Zeitgruppe, letter count and Grundstellung) were the same as before (although the letter count now excluded the message key). But the three letters (hfi) immediately before the Kenngruppe were new: they consisted of the enciphered message key—now enciphered once only. [8] In consequence, the perforated sheets had become useless against virtually all traffic. Before May, BP had been breaking Enigma from early 1940, mainly with the aid of British versions of the Zygalski perforated sheets. With the change to single encipherment, BP became blind against the important Red net, which was being used by the Luftwaffe and was, with Yellow, one of the few useful keys which had until then been broken by BP and the Poles.

It is well known that BP eventually circumvented the difficulties caused by the change to the single encipherment of the message key[9], but authors disagree on the date when it occurred. Gordon Welchman, a key member of GCCS, relying on a 1981 essay by Jean Stengers[10], says that it took place on 10 May, when the German campaign on the Western front opened.[11] A later paper by Stengers, citing firsthand Polish accounts, suggests 15 May[12]. Wladyslaw Kozaczuk gives the same Polish dates as Stengers, quoting the documents.[13] Curiously, no one refers to the British official history, which states that "on 1 May [1940], in preparation for the French campaign, the German authorities introduced new indicators for all Enigma keys except the Yellow"—a slightly elliptical way of describing the change.[14]

A recent (May 1985) visit to the Militärgeschichtliches Forschungsamt (Military History Research Office) in Freiburg-im-Breisgau gave

Gilbert Bloch the opportunity to ask the officials there what Enigma documents were held in the archives. Three documents were very kindly supplied by them. Two were well known (Gebrauchsanleitung für die Chiffriermaschine Enigma[15], of 12 January 1937, and Schlüsselanleitung zür Chiffriermaschine Enigma[16] of 13 January 1940), but the third seems until now to have been unnoticed. It consisted of Deckblätter (amendments) 1 to 8 of the Schlüsselanleitung of January 1940. And the Deckblätter modified the procedures set out in the January instructions by requiring the message key to be enciphered only once. The Deckblätter were distributed in April 1940, and "Gültig ab 1. V. 1940," that is, they specifically state that they took effect on 1 May 1940 (see Part I of the Appendix). They were issued to all three branches of the German armed forces, like the 1940 instructions. In particular, part of amendment number 2 reads, in translation, as follows (see Part II of the Appendix for the original):

"Paragraphs 11 and 12 on page 9 are entirely canceled and replaced by the following text—

11. The message key chosen by the operator, for example XFR (24.06.18), must be typed *once* [our emphasis] on the Enigma cipher machine, the settings of the machine being those indicated for the day [by the relevant monthly list of settings] and the starting position being chosen by the operator. The three resulting letters that are illuminated on the lampboard must be included in the heading of the message after the three letters giving the starting position [Grundstellung]."

[Paragraph 12 is not relevant for present purposes.]

Taken together with Hinsley, the amendments leave no room for doubt that the change to the singly enciphered message key occurred on 1 May 1940. Fighting was, however, then taking place in Norway, making it difficult—perhaps impossible—to distribute them to units on the Yellow net in operation there, which continued to use the old procedure until 15 May.[17]

BP did not reenter the Red traffic until 22 May. It then proceeded to read messages on Red at the rate of 1,000 each day "during the remainder of the campaign in France."[18] The number of messages decrypted by BP while that campaign lasted, possibly exceeding 20,000, may be significantly higher than any figure featuring in the French and Polish accounts[19], if Hinsley is referring to complete signals (as distinct to parts of messages[20]). It reinforces Welchman's comments on the value of the pre-1 May traffic and the Polish contribution.[21] Without the Poles, BP would almost certainly have been unable to read Enigma before 1 May.[22] If that had been the position, BP would have taken much longer, perhaps even years, to have broken Enigma after 1 May 1940.

April 1940   Nr. S 336

Geheim

Deckblätter Nr. 1—8

ʒu H. Dv. g 14 — M. Dv. Nr. 168 — L. Dv. g 14

»Schlüſſelanleitung ʒur Schlüſſelmaſchine Enigma vom 13. 1. 40«

Berichtigung iſt gemäß Vorbemerkung 6 bei H. Dv. 1a — M. Dv. 1a — L. Dv. 1 v. 1. 6. 1935 auszuführen.

Gültig ab 1. 5. 1940

1) ʒu S. 6. — 2) u. 3) ʒu S. 9. — 4) ʒu S. 11. — 5) ʒu S. 12.
6) ʒu S. 13. — 7) ʒu S. 10. — 8) ʒu S. 11.

Seite 6 ſtreiche die geſamten Ʒeilen 6, 7 und 8 von oben und überklebe ſie mit nachſtehendem Deckblatt:

PAGE 1 OF DECKBLÄTTER

PAGE 1 OF DECKBLÄTTER.

Seite 9 streiche die gesamten Ziff. 11 und 12 und überklebe sie mit nachstehendem Deckblatt:

11. Der vom Schlüßler gewählte Spruchschlüssel, z. B. X F R (24 06 18), wird auf der nach dem Tagesschlüssel und der gewählten Grundstellung eingestellten Schlüsselmaschine Enigma einmal getastet, die dabei aufleuchtenden 3 Geheimbuchstaben werden den im Spruchkopf eingesetzten 3 Buchstaben der Grundstellung angefügt.

12. Der Schlüßler stellt nunmehr in den Fenstern die als Spruchschlüssel gewählten Buchstaben, z. B. X F R (24 06 18), ein und tastet den Klartext. Die hierbei aufleuchtenden Buchstaben werden auf das Spruchformular hinter die 5 Buchstaben der Kenngruppe als 6., 7., 8. usw. Buchstaben geschrieben und alle Buchstaben zu fünfstelligen Buchstaben gruppen zusammengefaßt.

Deckblatt Nr. 2

DECKBLÄTT No. 2.

ADDENDA

This article was submitted on 30 August 1985, before the publication of an article by the late Gordon Welchman in which, having regard to Polish documents, he suggests that the change to single encipherment took place on 15 May 1940.[23]

The authors hold firmly to 1 May: Welchman simply did not have access to all the evidence, especially the amendments found in Freiburg im Breisgau and analyzed above. Welchman states (note 62) that "To me the Yellow crypto net is still a puzzle": he therefore cannot ascribe a net to the daily keys of 1–14 May 1940 which are shown as broken in his Table 2. Those keys almost certainly belonged to "Yellow," which operated in Norway, and to which the new procedure did not apply.[24]

A recently published French source also supports 1 May. Writing on the breaking of Enigma by the Poles and BP (which had been successful for most of the daily keys in April), Colonel Paul Paillole states that "*brusquement, le 2 Mai* [1940], *c'est le silence.*"[25] Paillole bases his statement on the "*Journal de marche*" (campaign diary) of Colonel Louis Rivet[26] who, as head of the "*5ième Bureau*" (*2ième Bureau* in peacetime), i.e., the Services de Renseignements et de Contre-Espionnage militaire[27], was in almost daily touch with the Polish-British attack on Enigma.

NOTES

1. Marian Rejewski, in Wladyslaw Kozaczuk (Christopher Kasparek ed. and trans.), *Enigma: How the German Machine Cipher Was Broken and How It Was Read by the Allies in World War Two* (Frederick, MD, 1984), 251. The message key took various forms, depending on the period of Enigma's history under consideration. For example, instructions of 13 January 1940 required the machine's operator to pick a random group of three letters as an individual message key for each message (or part of a message—a message of more than 250 letters had to be divided into parts, each not exceeding 250 letters). These were entered twice (say XFR XFR) on the machine: the resulting six letters (for example HFI KLB) were noted and sent, in their enciphered form, as part of the signal.

2. The perforated sheets were invented by Henryk Zygalski, one of Rejewski's colleagues. Both the bombes and the sheets defeated the procedural changes made by the Germans on 15 September 1938 (under which the operator was allowed to choose the rotor starting position for each message; until then there had been a common starting position for all messages transmitted on any one day). It was only with the introduction of two additional rotors (IV and V) on 15 December 1938 that the Poles virtually ceased to read Enigma. The bombes then lost much of their usefulness, as 60 bombes were then required (there were only six). The difficulties facing the Poles were compounded when, on 1 January 1939, the number of plugboard connections was increased from between 5 and 8 pairs to between 7 and 10, depriving the bombes of much of their power: Rejewski, in Kozaczuk, 242, 268. The perforated sheets still worked, but the Poles only had two sets—again, they needed 60.

3. F. H. Hinsley, with E. E. Thomas, C. F. G. Ransom and R. C. Knight, *British Intelligence in the Second World War: Its Influence on Strategy and Operations,* Volume 1 (London, 1979), 492.

4. Hinsley, 1:493.

5. Para. 23.

6. The Kenngruppe consisted of three letters (the first two in the block of five were nulls): para. 8 of the January 1940 instructions. Welchman calls the Kenngruppe *the discriminant*: Gordon Welchman, *The Hut Six Story: Breaking the Enigma Codes* (New York, 1982), 52.

7. Welchman calls the message key *the indicator,* 46.

8. Welchman, 97.

9.   See Welchman, 98–102; Kozaczuk, 117, note 11, although we have reservations about the detailed descriptions of the "sillies" in Welchman and of the meteorological reports in Kozaczuk.

10.   Jean Stengers "La guerre des messages codés (1930–1945)," *L'Histoire* 31 (February 1981), 19.

11.   Welchman, 96.

12.   Jean Stengers "Enigma, the French, the Poles and the British, 1931–1940," in *The Missing Dimension,* Christopher Andrew and David Dilks, eds. (London, 1984), 135.

13.   Kozaczuk, 115, note 2; *cf.* 105.

14.   Hinsley, 1:109; *cf.* Peter Calvocoressi, *Top Secret Ultra* (London, 1980), 70.

15.   Instructions for using the Enigma cipher machine.

16.   Instructions for keying messages on the Enigma cipher machine.

17.   As to the likely explanation of the inconsistency in the dates, which is more apparent than real, see Ralph Erskine "Ultra and the Polish Contribution," *Cryptologia,* 9 (1985), 322.

18.   Hinsley, 1:144.

19.   General Gustave Bertrand, the French intelligence officer who worked closely with the Poles from 1931 to 1942, states that 4789 messages were decrypted by the Poles between 28 October 1939 and 14 June 1940 (these dates obviously refer to the transmission of the messages, not their decryption): Gustave Bertrand, *Enigma: ou la plus Grande Enigme de la Guerre, 1939–1945* (Paris, 1973), 79.

20.   The substantial difference between Bertrand's figure of 4789 and the 20,000 or so implied by Hinsley may perhaps reflect a difference in the meaning of "message." Bertrand indicates (79, note 1) that, on average, each message was made up of three to four parts, so that "about 15,000 radiograms have been intercepted and read." In Hinsley's "thousand messages a day" (1:144) "message" may also mean only a part of a message. On the other hand, Hinsley may be referring to complete "signals" (as elsewhere in his work), with the difference being attributable to a higher intercept rate by BP than by the French, especially after 10 May (see Marian Rejewski "Remarks on Appendix 1 to *British Intelligence in the Second World War* by F. H. Hinsley," *Cryptologia,* 6 (1982), 82; *cf.* Hinsley's description of the Yellow traffic in Norway as being voluminous and Bertrand's figure of 768 messages read on that net by the Poles: Hinsley, 1:137; Bertrand, 79). Colonel Stefan Mayer, the prewar head of Polish military intelligence, states that 83 percent of the decrypted keys were broken by BP at this time: Hinsley, 1:493.

21.   Welchman, 164, 165.

22.   Hinsley's suggestion (1:494) that the Polish gifts of July 1939 to BP gained the British only seven months cannot be sustained: see Ralph Erskine, review of Volume 3(1) of Hinsley, *Annals of the History of Computing,* 7 (1985), 187.

23.   Gordon Welchman, "From Polish Bomba to British Bombe: The Birth of Ultra," *Intelligence and National Security,* 1 (1986), 71.

24.   Hinsley, 1:109. The Germans would have been apprehensive that changing procedures in the middle of a battle would lead to chaos, a factor which also militates against Welchman's choice of 15 May.

25.   Paul Paillole, *Notre Espion chez Hitler* (Paris, 1985), 183.

26.   Personal communication from Colonel Paillole to Gilbert Bloch.

27.   The functions of Section D (head, Commandant Gustave Bertrand) of the *5ième Bureau* included codebreaking.

Part II

Machines and their Solutions

The Cryptology of Multiplex Systems
by Greg Mellen and Lloyd Greenwood

ABSTRACT: Multiplex systems are a family of cryptosystems whose origin can be traced to Thomas Jefferson. They were not used extensively, however, until the period just prior to World War II. The characteristic feature of a multiplex system is that it permits the encipherer to select the ciphertext from among 25 alternatives, reducing the likelihood that the same block of plaintext will result in identical blocks of ciphertext.

This paper traces the history of multiplex systems and examines both their cryptographic and their cryptanalytic aspects. The computer simulation of one system, U.S. Army Signal Corps Cipher Device, Type M-94, is described.

PART 1: CRYPTOGRAPHY

Background

Multiplex systems are a family of cryptosystems which use the same algorithm for converting plaintext (*pt*) to ciphertext (*ct*). The distinctive feature of the algorithm is that, for a given block of *pt,* the encryptor is free to choose the *ct* from among 25 variants.

The earliest extant reference to a multiplex system is in the papers of Thomas Jefferson, probably dated 1790. [1] Jefferson describes a "wheel cypher" comprised of 36 discs, each bearing an alphabet on its rim, mounted on a central shaft. Possibly the idea was inspired by padlocks of similar appearance dating from the seventeenth century or ear-

From *Cryptologia*, Vol. 1, No. 1, Jan. 1977 (Part 1); Vol. 1, No. 2, April 1977 (Part 2).

lier, the principle of which persists in the familiar numerical lock of attaché cases. [2]

In 1891 Major Etienne Bazeries, apparently unaware of Jefferson's work, proposed a nearly identical device of 20 discs for use by the French Army. Though rejected, the "Bazeries cylinder" continues to give its name to one form of multiplex system. [3]

The algorithm was again "invented" in 1914 by Captain Parker Hitt, USA, this time as a "strip cipher." [4] Hitt's idea was adopted (in cylinder form) as the Army's field cipher in 1922 by William F. Friedman, then chief Cryptanalyst of the Signal Corps. Friedman was the first to use the term "multiplex system" to describe the algorithm. [5]

In the late thirties, the U.S. State Department chose a multiplex system as its most secret means of communication. During World War II, both Allied and Axis powers used variations, and as late as the mid-sixties, the U.S. Navy employed a version. [6]

Though obsolescent if not obsolete in a world of computers, multiplex systems would be a proper object of study if only for their colorful history. Yet their study illuminates areas of cryptographic strengths and weaknesses which hold true for computer-based cryptosystems.

Basic Principles

Figure 1 illustrates the strip-cipher multiplex system. A rigid frame holds 25 strips which may slide with respect to one another. Each strip bears a different mixed alphabet. Each alphabet is repeated on the strip, so that regardless of the relative positions of the strips, there are always at least 26 complete columns. An index line at the center of, and attached to, the frame bisects the strips.

(In practice, the number of strips, or alphabets, may vary from 20 to 30; the number is invariant within messages and normally invariant among messages for the prevailing cryptoperiod. [7] For convenience, 25 alphabets are assumed for all examples in this paper.)

To encrypt a message, the strips are permuted in accord with the current key, perhaps derived from a keyword. For example, if the key is *codex byzantium,* the key letters are repeated until they number 25; the letters are then numbered in alphabetical order:

```
c  o  d  e  x b  y  z  a  n  t  i  u  m c  o  d  e  x b  y  z  a  n  t
5 15  7 9 20  3 22 24  1 13 17 11 19 12  6 16 8 10 21  4 23 25  2 14 18
```

Thus the two a's become 1 and 2, the two b's become 3 and 4, and so on. The strips are then arranged in the frame in order of the final sequence.

INDEX LINE

1	A	B	C	E	I	G	D	J	F	V	U	Y	M	H	T	Q	K	Z	O	L	R	X	S	P	W	N	A	B
2	A	C	D	E	H	F	I	J	K	T	L	M	O	U	V	Y	G	Z	N	P	Q	X	R	W	S	B	A	C
3	A	D	K	O	M	J	U	B	G	E	P	H	S	C	Z	I	N	X	F	Y	Q	R	T	V	W	L	A	D
4	A	E	D	C	B	I	F	G	J	H	L	K	M	R	U	O	Q	V	P	T	N	W	Y	X	Z	S	A	E
5	A	F	N	Q	U	K	D	O	P	I	T	J	B	R	H	C	Y	S	L	W	E	M	Z	V	X	G	A	F
6	A	G	P	O	C	I	X	L	U	R	N	D	Y	Z	H	W	B	J	S	Q	F	K	V	M	E	T	A	G
7	A	H	X	J	E	Z	B	N	I	K	P	V	R	O	G	S	Y	D	U	L	C	F	M	Q	T	W	A	H
8	A	I	H	P	J	O	B	W	K	C	V	F	Z	L	Q	E	R	Y	N	S	U	M	G	T	D	X	A	I
9	A	J	D	S	K	Q	O	I	V	T	Z	E	F	H	G	Y	U	N	L	P	M	B	X	W	C	R	A	J
10	A	K	E	L	B	D	F	J	G	H	O	N	M	T	P	R	Q	S	V	Z	U	X	Y	W	I	C	A	K
11	A	L	T	M	S	X	V	Q	P	N	O	H	U	W	D	I	Z	Y	C	G	K	R	F	B	E	J	A	L
12	A	M	N	F	L	H	Q	G	C	U	J	T	B	Y	P	Z	K	X	I	S	R	D	V	E	W	O	A	M
13	A	N	C	J	I	L	D	H	B	M	K	G	X	U	Z	T	S	W	Q	Y	V	O	R	P	F	E	A	N
14	A	O	D	W	P	K	J	V	I	U	Q	H	Z	C	T	X	B	L	E	G	N	Y	R	S	M	F	A	O
15	A	P	B	V	H	I	Y	K	S	G	U	E	N	T	C	X	O	W	F	Q	D	R	L	J	Z	M	A	P
16	A	Q	J	N	U	B	T	G	I	M	W	Z	R	V	L	X	C	S	H	D	E	O	K	F	P	Y	A	Q
17	A	R	M	Y	O	F	T	H	E	U	S	Z	J	X	D	P	C	W	G	Q	I	B	K	L	N	V	A	R
18	A	S	D	M	C	N	E	Q	B	O	Z	P	L	G	V	J	R	K	Y	T	F	U	I	W	X	H	A	S
19	A	T	O	J	Y	L	F	X	N	G	W	H	V	C	M	I	R	B	S	E	K	U	P	D	Z	Q	A	T
20	A	U	T	R	Z	X	Q	L	Y	I	O	V	B	P	E	S	N	H	J	W	M	D	G	F	C	K	A	U
21	A	V	N	K	H	R	G	O	X	E	Y	B	F	S	J	M	U	D	Q	C	L	Z	W	T	I	P	A	V
22	A	W	V	S	F	D	L	I	E	B	H	K	N	R	J	Q	Z	G	M	X	P	U	C	O	T	Y	A	W
23	A	X	K	W	R	E	V	D	T	U	F	O	Y	H	M	L	S	I	Q	N	J	C	P	G	B	Z	A	Y
24	A	Y	J	P	X	M	V	K	B	Q	W	U	G	L	O	S	T	E	C	H	N	Z	F	R	I	D	A	Y
25	A	Z	D	N	B	U	H	Y	F	W	J	L	V	G	R	C	Q	M	P	S	O	E	X	T	K	I	A	Z

S	P	W	N	1
R	W	S	B	2
T	V	W	L	3
Y	X	Z	S	4
Z	V	X	G	5
V	M	E	T	6
M	Q	T	W	7
G	T	D	X	8
X	W	C	R	9
Y	W	I	C	10
F	B	E	J	11
V	E	W	O	12
R	P	F	E	13
R	S	M	F	14
L	J	Z	M	15
K	F	P	Y	16
K	L	N	V	17
I	W	X	H	18
P	D	Z	Q	19
G	F	C	K	20
W	T	I	P	21
C	O	T	Y	22
P	G	B	Z	23
F	R	I	D	24
X	T	K	I	25

FIGURE 1. STRIP CIPHER.

Next, the strips are slid so as to align the *pt* to the right of the index line (Figure 2-A): p e t e r p i p e r . . . The *ct* is then taken off by reading down any other, arbitrarily selected, column: S D N M B Y Z G M L . . .

To decrypt, the process is reversed (Figure 2-B). The strips are set up with the *ct* to the right of the index line, and the other columns are scanned to find the one column which yields *pt*.

With but minor variations, this is the principle of all multiplex systems. It will be noted that the *pt* is encrypted and the *ct* decrypted in blocks of 25 letters. The *ct* is a form of polyalphabetic substitution. Polyalphabetic substitution, in contrast to the monoalphabetic substitution of newspaper cryptograms, provides two or more cipher substitutes for each *pt* character.

Most polyalphabetic cryptosystems, by rule or by mechanism, rigorously specify the cipher substitute to be used at each stage of encryption. A multiplex sysem, as has been shown, permits the user to choose arbitrarily one of 25 different substitutes for the first *pt* letter of each block. (Selecting the substitute for the first letter of course determines the substitutes for the remaining letters in the block.)

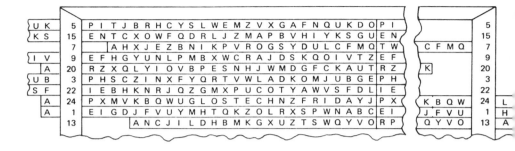

FIGURE 2. STRIP CIPHER. (A) ENCRYPTMENT. (B) DECRYPTMENT.

Cryptographic Considerations

Friedman, in the body of his patent for a strip-cipher device [8], states "The letters on the alphabet strips may be in normal order or in disarranged order; if the latter, the various alphabets may or may not be different." However, it can be demonstrated rather easily that for any degree of security worthy of the name, the alphabets must be different.

First, if all alphabets are the same and in normal order, any *ct* column is but a Caesar cipher of the *pt*; the *pt* may be recovered merely by running down the alphabet. Thus:

```
ct: L   A   P   A   N     L   E   L   A   N   . . .
    m   b   q   b   o     m   f   m   b   o   . . .
    n   c   r   c   p     n   g   n   c   p   . . .
    o   d   s   d   q     o   h   o   d   q   . . .
pt: p   e   t   e   r     p   i   p   e   r   . . .
```

Second, if all alphabets are the same but in disarranged order, though the *pt* cannot be recovered by running down the normal alphabet, the recovery of the *pt* is still rather easy. Consider the following short message:

```
T J N C J   I V W S D   G T O R V   W G S F G   S F J T S   J G Q A J
D N Y H J   X N Z G N   P J X N M   N D Z E N   K L S B T   R W U J I
X Q J B L   U B Y J L   U P V W L   A X O P F   Q P A L X   F G G D L
U D A L G   L G G Q K   N J T T L   X I A K L   Y I M I H   X L J S J
P Q M I X   C A D M T   S D Y D Q   C R D W D   T S D O N   G T R V D
T W X J A   O A L E Z   A L E K T   E Y K C C   G E E K B   R N R O Q
F B O G E   R G H O E   R X A N E   E N G R R   D V J R I   R Z J K B
R A R J J   R P K V A   Y Q R F R   P Z F Y S   F A Q R P   W U Z V L
Q R U P I   U P I F Z   F H F P M   J G Q A F   G H B H G   I T A P H
E A F Q H   D C V F I   C W C V X   U W H N X
```

Careful examination reveals three isomorphs, i.e., *ct* patterns which recur with different constituent letters. They have been underscored above:

(1) T J N C J I V W S D G T O R V W G S F G S F J T
    Z F Y S F A Q R P W U Z V L Q R U P I U P I F Z

(2) W U J I X Q J B L U B Y J L U P V W
    N R O Q F B O G E R G H O E R X A N

(3) Z G N P J X N M N D Z E N
    C A D M T S D Y D Q C R D

By chaining, we derive the following partial sequences for each group:

(1) T-Z; J-F-I-A; N-Y; C-S-P; O-V-Q; D-W-R-L; G-U.

(2) W-N; U-R; J-O; I-Q-B-G; P-X-F; L-E; Y-H; V-A.

(3) Z-C; G-A; N-D-Q; P-M; J-T; X-S; M-Y; E-R.

We will attempt to recovger the mixed alphabet by a geometrical technique. [9] We assign the chains of group 1 to the X-axis and the chains of group 2 to the Y-axis. Much in the manner of a crossword puzzle, we begin to interlock the chains and at an early stage have:

```
C S P
  X
J F I A
O
```

The relative position of "X" and "S" (X-S is one of the chains of group 3) establishes that the chains of group 3 run diagonally upward from right to left. This fact permits us, piece by piece, to add the remaining chains to the diagram. After removing redundant letters (else we would end up with a 26 × 26 array), we have:

```
V Q - G U N Y E C S P J F I A B D W R L H M T Z X O
A B D W R L H M T Z X O V Q - G U N Y E C S P J F I
- G U N Y E C S P J F I A B D W R L H M T Z X O V Q
D W R L H M T Z X O V Q - G U N Y E C S P J F I A B
```

Adding the missing letter (obviously "K"), we obtain the single 26-letter sequence:

A B D W R L H M T Z X O V Q K G U N Y E C S P J F I

Decimation of this sequence at interval 17 reveals the original mixed alphabet, based on the key *codex byzantium*:

C O D E X B Y Z A N T I U M F G H J K L P Q R S V W

One can now read the original message by running down this alphabet. Moreover (an important point when we later attempt to recover unknown alphabets), the undecimated sequence may also be used: The order in which the generatrices are recovered is immaterial so long as they maintain proper relative separation.

This example, manipulated as it is for reasons of space, clearly shows that to avoid isomorphism, the mixed alphabets of a multiplex system must differ from one another. There being approximately 4×10^{26} mixed alphabets, one need not fear a shortage.

Another phenomenon of cryptographic interest arises from the freedom of the encryptor to choose from among 25 *ct* variants. With proper coordination the identical *pt* message, enciphered in the same key, can result in two or more apparently unrelated *ct* messages. One could indeed create 25 different *ct* messages from the same *pt* in the same key. There are circumstances where this characteristic could be used advantageously.

Yet if an unauthorized recipient had the 25 different *ct* versions of a given *pt* message, he could read the *pt* without effort and without knowing anything of the underlying cryptosystem. Since multiplex systems are noncrashing (no *pt* letter may be substitute for itself in the *ct*), the *pt* character in any position would be the letter absent from the set of *ct* characters for that position.

A final point of cryptographic interest is the total unsuitability of multiplex systems for the second stage in superencipherment, that is, the encipherment in another system (or key) of text which has already been enciphered. Successful decryptment depends on the ability of the decipherer, whether man or machine, to recognize the *pt* generatrix.

Selection of Cryptoperiod

Shannon [10] has shown that for all cryptosystems save one (the one-time random key), there is a critical mass of identically keyed *ct* which in theory would permit an enemy to analyze and solve the system. In simple substitution, for example, this minimum amount is on the order of 27 to 30 characters.

The user of a cryptosystem, then, should change the key frequently enough so that an enemy is unlikely to get enough text in one key so as to be able to read that set of messages. The use of the term "unlikely" correctly implies we are dealing with probabilities and not certainties. The important factor is the amount of text encrypted by a single key. But practical considerations of the operating environment dictate that keys be changed on the basis of time rather than volume of text.

The ideal would be a new key for every message, with the maximum length of a single message strictly specified. As will be demonstrated later, the ideal is rather easy to implement in the computer. For practical use among manual users, however, the ideal may be considered unattainable. A World War II text outlines the problem:

Messages cryptographed by the same sequence of alphabet[s] can remain secure against solution by a well-organized and efficient enemy cryptanalytic section for only a relatively short time. It is impossible to state exactly how long, because solution depends upon a number of variable factors; a conservative estimate would place the minimum at six hours, the maximum at two or three days. [11]

Once set up in a given key, a multiplex system may be thought of as simple substitution with 25 variants and a different alphabet for each position in the block. Hence, once an enemy has about 30 *ct* blocks from the same generatrix, he has, in theory, sufficient material to solve that generatrix. With that large an entry, a number of the other generatrices may be solved as well. Nor need the generatrices be recovered in their original order. As the solution by isomorphs has shown, any decimation of the correct order will suffice to break the key.

In theory, if the encryptor selects the *ct* generatrices at random, an enemy who intercepts 520 *ct* blocks in the same key has an even chance that at least 30 blocks are derived from the same generatrix. [12] In other words, a user who encrypts 13,000 or more characters in the same key is giving the enemy an even chance of reading that set of messages. Most users will, of course, demand far better security than that.

Cipher Device, Type M-94

The multiplex system adopted by Friedman for Army field use in 1922, and which saw service until the middle of World War II, is embodied in the U.S. Army Signal Corps Cipher Device, Type M-94 (Fig. 3). The device consists of an endplate bearing a central shaft upon which 25 aluminum discs are mounted and secured by a knurled nut on the end of the shaft. Each disc has a different alphabet engraved on its outer rim. The endplate has a guiderule which projects over the rims of the discs, and which serves the same purpose as the index line in the strip cipher. When assembled, the M-94 forms an aluminum cylinder 12 cm long and 3.6 cm in diameter, weighing about 100 [grams].

The alphabets on the discs are identical to those in Figure 1. They have been attributed to Signal Corps' Lt. Joseph O. Mauborgne, and in general show no method to their construction. The "R" and "Y" alphabets (see below) are minor exceptions in that they incorporate the words ARMY OF THE US and FRIDAY respectively.

The alphabets, ordered A-B, A-C, . . . , A-Z, are known as the B, C, . . . , Z alphabets. Each disc has its alphabet letter plus a number

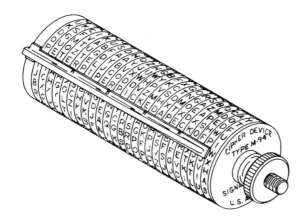

FIGURE 3. U.S. ARMY SIGNAL CORPS CIPHER DEVICE, TYPE M-94.

from 1 to 25 (corresponding to B through Z) stamped on its inner surface for identification. The inner surface of each disc is also dentated, so that when the nut is tightened, each disc locks with its neighbor, the end disc locking with the end-plate, and the cylinder is immobilized.

To use the M-94, the discs are ordered on the shaft in the manner described above for the strip cipher, i.e., in accord with some key. To encrypt a *pt* block, the nut is loosened and the *pt* is aligned with the guiderule by rotating the discs. Thereupon the cylinder is locked, and any legal generatrix is selected for the *ct*.

Standing Signal Corps orders prohibited using the generatrix immediately above the *pt* for the *ct*, presumably to encourage greater randomness in its selection. In addition, the guiderule obscures the two generatrices beneath it. Thus, the M-94 effectively provides only 22 useable *ct* generatrices.

Tests by the Signal Corps showed that the average speed of encryption by the M-94 was 1.75 five-letter groups/minute, and the average speed of decryption, 1.78 five-letter groups/minute. Of the six types of encoding and encipherment tested in the series, the M-94 was the slowest. The fastest was a keyboard-equipped electrical printing cryptograph, which had an average speed of 30.00 five-letter groups/minute for encryption and 25.00 five-letter groups/minute for decryption. [13] Despite the speed disparity, the small size and zero power requirement of the M-94 recommended its use under difficult combat conditions.

NOTES AND REFERENCES

1. Kahn, David, *The Codebreakers*, New York: Macmillan, 1967, p. 192.

2. The authors are indebted to Louis Kruh of the New York Telephone Company for this suggestion.

3. Kahn, *op. cit.*, pp. 245*ff.*

4. *Ibid.*, p. 493.

5. Friedman, William F., *Several Machine Ciphers and Methods for Their Solution*, Riverbank Publication No. 20, Geneva, IL: Riverbank Laboratories, 1918.

6. Additional details of the history of multiplex systems may be found in: Kruh, Louis, "The Cryptograph That Was Invented Three Times," *The Retired Officer*, April 1971.

7. A cryptoperiod is the time, e.g., one day, during which a given key is in effect.

8. U.S. Patent 2,395,863. This is a curious patent in light of the prior three "inventions" of the system. There appear to be only three elements not found in earlier literature: a secondary frame which permits subsets of strips to be permuted in groups; a transverse hinge which permits the main frame to be folded; and feet for the frame to prevent slippage. Yet the patent claims cover the entire system.

9. An alternate method of alphabet recovery may be found in: Gaines, Helen Fouche, *Elementary Cryptanalysis*, American Photographic Publishing Company, 1943, pp. 178*ff.* This volume was reissued in paperback under the title *Cryptanalysis* by Dover Publications in 1956.

10. Shannon, C. E., "Communication Theory of Secrecy Systems," *Bell System Technical Journal*, Vol. 28, October 1949.

11. TM 11-485, *Advanced Military Cryptography*, Washington, D.C.: War Department, 8 June 1944, par. 65. No author is given but internal evidence suggests the writer is William F. Friedman.

12. This is a "worst-case" assumption in that the 30 blocks from the same generatrix would not be identifiable as such. For a comprehensive mathematical treatment of the criteria and probabilities of identification, see: Kullback, Solomon, *Statistical Methods in Cryptanalysis*, National Security Agency, reprinted 1967, pp. 88–92.

13. TM 11-485, par. 75b(1).

PART 2: SIMULATION AND CRYPTANALYSIS

M-94 Simulation Program

To facilitate study of cryptologic and cryptanalytic aspects of multiplex systems, a program simulating the M-94 was developed. The program, written in FORTRAN V, is most effectively executed from a keyboard/display terminal in conversational mode.

The 25 mixed alphabets are stored in the program as a fixed two-dimensional array. Each line of the array, representing one disc, is five words in length; the corresponding alphabet is stored in these words, beginning with the letter A, in field data format.

This basic array, called DEV 1, represents the device in its initial state, with the discs in numerical order on the shaft and rotated so as to align A with the guiderule.

There are two other arrays which represent the device in later states of encryption and decryption (see Figure 4). The second array, DEV 2, is derived from DEV 1 and the key phrase. It represents the device with the discs reordered on the shaft as determined by the key phrase (e.g., disc order 5, 15, 7, 9, 20, . . . for the key codex byzantium).

The third array, DEV 3, is derived from DEV 2 and the *pt* for encryption, and from DEV 2 and the *ct* for decryption. It represents the device with the discs in key order and rotated so as to align the *pt* (or *ct*) with the guiderule.

Encryption requires three operator entries: the key phrase, the *pt*, and the number of the *ct* generatrix (02–26) for transmission. Decryption requires the key phrase and the *ct*. How the program derives the *pt* from *ct* will be described following additional details on the operation of the program.

Encryption:

1) The program solicits the key phrase, then stores it and checks it for legality. The program presumes that the first space encountered marks the end of the key. All characters must be alphabetic. One character

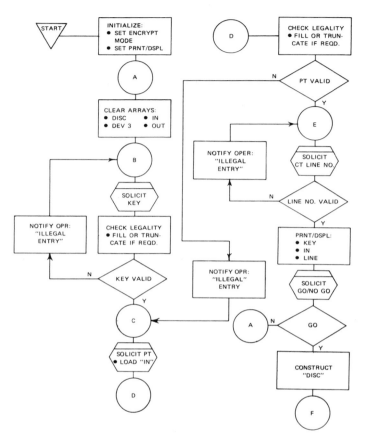

FIGURE 4. FLOW CHART, M-94 SIMULATOR (SHEET 1 OF 2).

will be accepted as a legal key. A lengthy phrase is truncated to 25 characters. If less than 25 characters are entered, the block is filled out by repeating the key phrase.

2) The order of the discs is derived by scanning the key and testing for the presence of K_i, where K_i is successively A, B, C, . . . Detection of one or more A's is noted by entering 1, 2, 3, . . . in the corresponding position(s) in a 25-word linear array, DISC. K_i is then incremented and the process is repeated until DISC is full. DEV 2 may now be loaded by copying the lines of DEV 1 in the order of the entries in DISC.

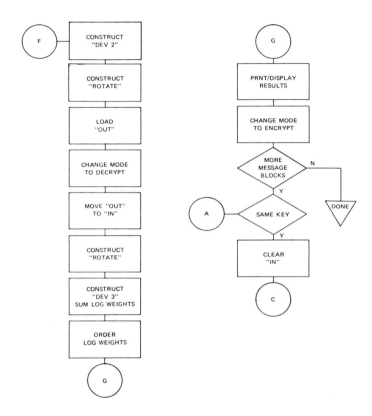

FIGURE 4. FLOW CHART, M-94 SIMULATOR (SHEET 2 OF 2).

3) The program solicits the *pt* (or *ct*, since the operation for both is identical), and stores it in array IN. Legality checking is performed as in step 1, except that if less than 25 characters are entered, the block is completed with random characters (this, in disregard of M-94 field orders, which stipulated that the last block of a message be left short if the text did not fill it).

4) Each line of DEV 2 is scanned in search of the characters in the corresponding position of IN. For each line, a count is maintained of the spaces scanned, and when a match is found the count (termed the "offset") is recorded in the corresponding position of array ROTATE. When completed, ROTATE contains the number of spaces each disc

must be rotated from home position to align the *pt* (or *ct*) with the guiderule.

5) DEV 3, the third and final representation, is constructed by loading those characters from DEV 2 which lie at the offsets specified in ROTATE.

6) The *ct* generatrix for transmission is operator-selected from DEV 3 and copied into array OUT, thus completing the encryption process.

Decryption:

7) The *ct* block in OUT is copied into IN and processed in a manner identical to that for encryption. The final DEV 3 is similar to the encrypting DEV 3, except the *ct* is aligned with the guiderule instead of the *pt*.

8) As described below, the decryption algorithm sorts the generatrices of DEV 3 in decreasing order of probability of their being *pt*. By operator selection, any number of lines of the resulting decryption matrix, from 1 to 26, may be printed out. There is greater than 99 percent probability that line 1 will be the correct *pt*.

The decryption algorithm takes advantage of a method described by Sinkov [14], that of log weights. In a more simple cryptanalytic process, a measure of the probability of a block of 25 letters being *pt* can be obtained by assigning each letter a weight corresponding to the percentage of its occurrence in normal text: Thus E might be assigned weight 13.0, T, weight 9.3, and so on. By adding the percentages, a figure of merit is arrived at, with the generatrix having the highest sum presumably being the *pt*.

The log weight method is similar but more sensitive in that it substitutes the multiplication of probabilities of occurrence for their addition, in conformity with the underlying theory. The log of the percentage is substituted for the percentage itself, and the logs are summed. Thus, E is assigned weight 2.114; T, weight 1.969, and so on.

As mentioned above, the log weight method successfully recovers the *pt* in more than 99 percent of the cases. It is of interest that "Jabberwocky" ("'Twas brillig and the slithy toves. . .") was recovered.

It may also be of interest that *pt* not recovered included the "hundred-letter thunderwords" from *Finnegan's Wake* and the familiar "The quick brown fox jumped over the lazy . . ." In all cases, failure resulted of course from the unusual occurrence of so many infrequent letters.

Though "The quick brown fox . . ." did fail, in no instance did the *pt* occur later than the seventh generatrix (key: *uniservo*) and in one instance occurred on the second generatrix (key: *multiplex systems*).

The log weights for English were also used successfully to recover *pt* in Italian, French, Latin, German, and Spanish. Had it been necessary, though, it would have been a trivial task to replace the English log weights with their equivalents in other languages.

Cryptanalysis

An old recipe for rabbit stew advises the would-be chef, "First, catch a rabbit." Slightly altered, the advice is apt for the would-be cryptanalyst: First, find the system. Identification of the general cryptosystem by analysis of the *ct* alone is usually difficult. Given sufficient *ct,* however, it is sometimes possible to diagnose a multiplex system from the idiopathic pattern it produces in the *ct*. Generally, the longer repetitions (say, those of four or more letters) will be separated by some multiple of the block length; in the case of our examples, by 25, 50, . . ., letters. Repetitions not in the same message will tend to begin in the same position in each block. (We will refer to the positions in the block as byte 1, byte 2, . . ., byte 25.) Thus a polygram starting with character 80 in one message may be repeated in a second message starting with character 30, indicating that in both instances the same underlying *pt* occurred in byte 5 of the message block.

Having tentatively identified a corpus of *ct* as being in a multiplex system, the next step is to solve it. We examine three cases in order of increasing difficulty.

Case 1: Known Alphabets; Known Crib

A multiplex system is most easily broken when the alphabets are known and the analyst has a known or suspected crib. A certain source may be known to use the M-94, and the analyst may have information that messages from that source have the stereotyped beginning: m e s s a g e c e n t e r s e r i a l n u m b e r.

(A fair question is how the analyst acquired the crib. One possibility is that messages from the same source, enciphered in other systems or in other M-94 keys, may have been solved previously. Another possibility is "practical" cryptanalysis, which is to say theft, bribery, or wastebasket inspection of sender or receiver.)

The general method for this case was originated by the Marquis de Viaris in 1893 [15] and elaborated upon by Friedman [16]; accessing the original documents is difficult; it appears worthwhile to describe the procedure here.

The following start of message in the M-94 system is available for examination. No previously recovered key gives results:

DYPPC KPFJG HJLCS GRLCH CCXFW

TJOCV NPEBO SYURX JBXDS XKOZP ...

We place the crib over the first block of *ct*:

message center serial number

m e s s a g e c e n t e r s e r i a l n u m b e r

DYPPC KPFJG HJLCS GRLCH CCXFW

Taking each *pt/ct* pair in turn beginning with m/D, we record in a table the offset of each pair on each M-94 disc:

	Disc Number																								
	1	2	3	4	5	6	7	8	9	10	11	12	13	14	15	16	17	18	19	20	21	22	23	24	25
m/D	20	17	㉓	16	11	⑭	21	3	8	19	11	20	㉓	4	21	10	12	㉕	⑨	1	2	⑬	19	20	11
e/Y	8	12	10	21	㉒	⑭	12	2	4	20	19	16	20	3	21	⑤	21	12	11	20	1	17	⑦	10	12

If the crib is correct, all pairs have the same offset. But offset 23 appears only for m/D and not for e/Y. We circle it as impossible. Offset 14 is also impossible; it appears for both pairs but on the same disc. Similarly, we eliminate offsets 5, 7, 9, 13, 22, 23, and 25. Line by line we continue, each time eliminating more offsets. After seven iterations, we have:

	Disc Number																								
	1	2	3	4	5	6	7	8	9	10	11	12	13	14	15	16	17	18	19	20	21	22	23	24	25
m/D													4												
e/Y						4																			
s/P										4									4						
s/P										4									4						
a/C					4												4								
g/K				4												4	4								
e/P					4										4										

Perhaps offset 4 is correct. (If we continued through the block, offset 4 might well be eliminated also, proving the crib incorrect.) To test it, we list under each *pt/ct* pair the disc numbers which yield an offset of 4:

											Byte Number													
1	2	3	4	5	6	7	8	9	10	11	12	13	14	15	16	17	18	19	20	21	22	23	24	25
m	e	s	s	a	g	e	c	e	n	t	e	r	s	e	r	i	a	l	n	u	m	b	e	r
D	Y	P	P	C	K	P	F	J	G	H	J	L	C	S	G	R	L	C	H	C	C	X	F	W
14	9	11	11	5	4	6	2	1	8	5	1	3	4	8	22	5	12	12	6	14	9	13	10	1
	19	19	18	17	16	11	2	16	9	2	20		21		6		25		15	20				12
			18		24	13	21		13						7				21					
					17	23			17						16				22					
					20		20																	

The table may be greatly simplified. Disc 9 is required for byte 2; it thus cannot be among the choices for byte 11, so disc 5 goes with byte 11. Disc 3 appears only under byte 13, so disc 20 is really not a candidate for that position. The process is straightforward and by carrying it through to completion the table is reduced to:

											Byte Number													
1	2	3	4	5	6	7	8	9	10	11	12	13	14	15	16	17	18	19	20	21	22	23	24	25
m	e	s	s	a	g	e	c	e	n	t	e	r	s	e	r	i	a	l	n	u	m	b	e	r
D	Y	P	P	C	K	P	F	J	G	H	J	L	C	S	G	R	L	C	H	C	C	X	F	W
14	9	11	11	18	17	16	24	2	23	5	2	3	4	8	22	7	12	25	6	15	21	13	10	1
	19	19						20			20													

The correct key, if our crib is valid, must be one of the four permutations of the discs which can be obtained from this table. Any of the four will yield the original crib, but only one can result in good *pt* from the remainder of the message. A little experimentation with line 2 and we obtain (at offset 21, though this is immaterial):

											Byte Number													
1	2	3	4	5	6	7	8	9	10	11	12	13	14	15	16	17	18	19	20	21	22	23	24	25

	Disc Number																								
14	9	19	11	18	17	16	24	2	23	5	20	3	4	8	22	7	12	25	6	15	21	13	10	1	
T	J	O	C	V	N	P	E	B	O	S	Y	U	R	X	J	B	X	D	S	X	K	O	Z	P
n	i	n	e	f	o	u	r	f	i	v	e	s	t	o	p	r	e	f	e	r	e	n	c	e

In the absence of a crib, probable words and phrases may be tested in an attempt to recover a partial key. When a trial results in a disc sequence which yields acceptable *pt* on succeeding lines of *ct,* we take it as correct and try to extend the *pt* on any one line of *ct* while ensuring that the best possible *pt* continuation results on other lines. At first, when only a few digits of the key are known, the process is time consuming. False starts are common but from the vantage point of an interactive terminal, the task is tolerable.

Case 2: Alphabets Unknown; Crib Known

For comfortable solution when the alphabets are unknown, a crib of 1000–1500 characters is desirable. Shorter cribs of several hundred letters can be used but prolong the effort. Even with the longer crib, it is unlikely that the alphabets will be recovered completely. That will come only with the application of recovered alphabet fragments to additional *ct.* (A crib of 1000–1500 letters may come either from "practical" cryptanalysis or from the situation where the same message is enciphered in two different systems and one of the systems is broken.) For reasons of space, all details for this case cannot be shown, but the short example below permits the general outline to be made clear.

[See table given directly below], we have again paired *pt* and *ct.* A careful study gives rise to these observations:

1) Lines 6 and 8: Byte 2 is identical; hence these lines are from the same generatrix.

2) Lines 2 and 8: Byte 3 is identical. These lines are from the same generatrix, to which line 6, by the law of transitivity, also belongs.

3) Lines 3 and 4: Byte 6 has the complementarity t/N and n/T. Hence the offset of line 4 is complementary to that of line 3, mod 26.

4) Lines 2 and 5: Byte 9 is reciprocal; the offset of line 5, then, is complementary mod 26 to that of line 2, and from (2) above, to that of lines 6 and 8.

5) Lines 1 and 7: Byte 14 is reciprocal; the offset of these lines is also complementary mod 26.

Byte Number

Line	1 2 3 4 5 6 7 8 9 10 11 12 13 14 15 16 17 18 19 20 21 22 23 24 25
(1)	v e s s e l s i n d i s t r e s s s h a l l u s e E Q Z I A T Z Y X N B K I S H W E O E G D W V R M
(2)	t h e r a d i o t e l e g r a p h a l a r m s i g E E G K K J W P S V Z V Z C Y V S N G S W V G R D
(3)	n a l o r t h e r a d i o t e l e p h o n e a l a I H B X B N W J H P Y T E N J Q G A N B C Y Q C X
(4)	r m s i g n a l t o s e c u r e a t t e n t i o n M F K W Y T S B C G F L V O B I J X N W J C X V F
(5)	t o d i s t r e s s c a l l s a n d m e s s a g e F R I O J Y D R T P S H D Y J T O Q C K J P U M O
(6)	s t h e r a d i o t e l e g r a p h a l a r m s i O U B A N W R F E B V J V V T U Z B D J X G D V G
(7)	g n a l w h i c h i s d e s i g n e d t o a c t u P O E C G J H E X A X I H R G K X Y Z K V U X X Z
(8)	a t e t h e r a d i o t e l e g r a p h a u t o a N U G U X O J K R P U M V E F P W N A V X M B S U
(9)	U E G Q N T N R T P P Z K Z Y S F V G K Z A Y B R
(10)	D W N L R Y V A Y D D R Z U S I N B K C R E Q A C
(11)	M K Z M B S L I N E G A F C R O A

These clues in hand, we set out for solution. We draw the basic framework of a multiplex cipher, with alphabet (disc) numbers across the top and generatrices down the side. The space below the line at generatrix 25 will be used for scratch-pad storage in the course of work. It will be understood that the disc and generatrix numbers are arbitrary assignments, useful for keeping the solution orderly but probably not related to the disc numbers and generatrices of the original device, of which nothing is known.

We begin with line 2. Since each byte of a *pt/ct* line has the same offset as every other byte in that line, we ascribe offset 1 to line 2 and write the *pt* and *ct* as generatrices 0 and 1:

	Disc Number																								
Gen.	1	2	3	4	5	6	7	8	9	10	11	12	13	14	15	16	17	18	19	20	21	22	23	24	25
0	T	H	E	R	A	D	I	O	T	E	L	E	G	R	A	P	H	A	L	A	R	M	S	I	G
1	E	E	G	K	K	J	W	P	S	V	Z	V	Z	C	Y	V	S	N	G	S	W	V	G	R	D
. . .																									

Letters from lines 6 and 8, which have the same offset as line 2, may now be added. They are entered on the main diagram where possible. Where not, they are entered in the temporary working area. In the main diagram, we are attempting to reconstruct the original matrix of mixed alphabets (or a decimation thereof), and the vertical and horizontal relationship are both significant. In the scratch-pad area, only the vertical relationships have meaning. The analyst should not be misled by the happenstance that adjacent letters make good *pt*. That results from making most economical use of the working space, and the *pt* will disappear as letters are moved up into the main diagram by column only, as shown [below].

	Disc Number																								
Gen.	1	2	3	4	5	6	7	8	9	10	11	12	13	14	15	16	17	18	19	20	21	22	23	24	25
25																							U		
0	T	H	E	R	A	D	I	O	T	E	L	E	G	R	A	P	H	A	L	A	R	M	S	I	G
1	E	E	G	K	K	J	W	P	S	V	Z	V	Z	C	Y	V	S	N	G	S	W	V	G	R	D
. . .																									

```
                                           P           O
      S T H E R A D I O T E L E G R A P H A L A R M S A
      O U B A N W R F E B V J V V T U Z B D J X G D V U
              J
      A     T H E   A D I O T   L E   R       H     T
      N     U X O   K R P U M   E F   W       V     B
```

So far we have been working with the letter pairs of lines 2, 6, and 8 to which we arbitrarily assigned offset 1. The offset of line 5 is complementary mod 26 to the offset of these pairs, i.e., line 5 has offset 25. Hence we can add the letters of line 5 to the skeleton, linking them wherever possible with chains already present and forming new chains when necessary. We omit the slow evolution of the final diagram. The reader interested in reconstructing the work will find that when the letters of line 5 are added, disc 15 will provide a clue permitting the letters of line 4 to be added at offset 2, following which the letters of line 3 can be placed at the complementary offset of 24. Discs 7 and 10 will then indicate that the offset of line 7 is 3; line 1 may then be added at the complementary offset of 23. This exhausts the information to be gotten from the crib, and we have gained the partial tableau shown below.

Here the case must rest. But if one considers that the mixed alphabets were totally unknown at the start, and that the crib was only one-fifth as long as one would have liked, our progress may be judged satisfactory. We put the work aside and will be watchful for additional *ct* apparently enciphered in the same key.

Gen.	1	2	3	4	5	6	7	8	9	10	11	12	13	14	15	16	17	18	19	20	21	22	23	24	25
													Disc Number												
. . .																									
22																G				A					
23		A												S		–		G		–					
24	Q	–		H											–		E		–		–				
25	F	–	–			–									–	G	–			–		U			I
0	T	H	E	R	A	D	I	O	T	E	L	E	G	R	A	P	H	A	L	A	R	M	S	I	G
1	E	E	G	K	K	J	W	P	S	V	Z	V	Z	C	Y	V	S	N	G	S	W	V	G	R	D
2	–	A				–			–		C					K		P						–	
3	–			E		H																		O	
4	V																							S	
5																									V
. . .																									

Disc Number

Gen.	1	2	3	4	5	6	7	8	9	10	11	12	13	14	15	16	17	18	19	20	21	22	23	24	25
	S	T	H	E	B	A	D	Y	O	T	E	L	C	G	R	T	P	H	A	L	A	R	M	M	X
	O	U	B	A	-	W	R	-	E	B	V	J	E	V	T	A	Z	B	D	J	X	G	D	G	-
		-	R		J	-					V	Y	B	U						-					A
	I	R	L	T	N	E		I	H	I	O	D	O				R	Q	-	H	C	P	T	C	U
	A	O		U		O	Z	F	D	P	U	T	H	L	H	E	W	D	Z	V	-	S	B	-	-
	N	I		H		A	R	S		M	E	J	-						N					L	-
		M	D	L	X	N	-	A	X	A	S	I	D		S	I	A	T	C	T	-	T	V		Z
	R	-			Y	S	K	-		C		L	U	E				-	-	M	-	J	-	-	T
	-	F	Z	-	J	T			-	O	F	H		-	F	Q	J	X		-	S	C	Q	-	M
	M	-	C	S	-		C	N	-	X	A	I	O		-					T	K		U	-	-
		N	-				-		J		G			-	I	L	O	E	E	E	O	Y	A	X	O
	G	-	S	X	W	L		R			Y	K	-	N	-		N	-	N	-	-	-			E
	-	-	-	-	-			E		N	-	-	T	-	-	W	-	-	-	W	-	E	C		
	-	O	K	O	-				-	D	-		T	G	-	-	Y	H		V		I			N
	P		I	G			L		-	S				-	X				B		W	-			-
		-	-				D	B						S		O		-	D	-	X				F
		W	Y		B				-						-				-	L					
		S							-						-				O	-	-				
							I								S						L				

Case 3: Alphabets Unknown; Crib Unknown

When the alphabets are unknown and there is no crib, the successful cryptanalysis of a multiplex system depends wholly on having sufficient *ct* with which to work. A multiplex system may be considered a cipher with period 625 (25 alphabets times 25 generatrices). The overall period is comprised of 25 subperiods (the generatrices) which follow each other in random order. To make sense of it, the randomness must be eliminated.

In examining the question of a suitable cryptoperiod, we stated that if an analyst has about 520 *ct* blocks in the same key, he had an even chance that at least 30 were from the same generatrix, permitting solution of at least that generatrix. (In practice, because of the high probability of errors in classifying the generatrices, more material is desirable and perhaps necessary.)

In distributing the generatrices into 25 families, the analyst will use long repetitions and such statistical tools as the index of coincidence and cross-correlation. After 30 or more *ct* blocks have been accumulated in one family, he will attack that family on the basis of frequency distributions. Sooner or later, the instinct of the analyst or sheer plod of computer will solve the family as shown in the short extract below, thus giving a solid foothold for solving other families:

Family

```
1 I P K G J   Y P F O Y   R X V D G   O O V X K   G E S T W
    a l m o s   t e v e r   y w o r d   i n t h e   e n g l i

1 I D X N B   V P H X I   D V L K S   P F E T A   E Q L R T
    a s a r u   l e c i p   h e r d e   v i c e s   o r m a c

1 V G U B G   O P H X I   H V I A Z   F N S T A   F L H C Y
    i f t h e   r e c i p   i e n t a   g r e e s   n o t t o

1 M E F I D   S W Z L X   T X V D D   O O D C P   L D C B O
    f a l l i   n g i n t   o w o r k   i n g m a   c h i n e
```

Family

```
? M Q O L R   Y J K Z D   Z A X D O   Y C S M V   T Y Y A Z

? L Z A E L   X O F Q E   K V C N V   Z D H L U   J K E O E

? O F D J I   V N U H J   A P B H P   H R S V Q   L I R W K
```

NOTES AND REFERENCES

14. Sinkov, Abraham, *Elementary Cryptanalysis: A Mathematical Approach*, New York: Random House, 1968. This volume is now part of the New Mathematical Library, published by the Mathematical Association of America, Washington, D.C., 20036.

15. Reported by Kahn, *op. cit.*, pp. 247–249.

The Typex Cryptograph
by Louis Kruh and Cipher A. Deavours

I. INTRODUCTION

In 1919 the Government Code and Cypher School was established by the British as an inter-service organization. Its main tasks were to study cipher communication methods used by other countries and to advise all government departments on cryptographic security.

In 1926 an inter-departmental committee was formed to consider the use of cipher machines to replace the bulk systems in use by the army, navy, and air services. All available cryptographic devices including the Hebern, Kryha, and German Enigma, two of which were purchased in 1928, were studied for almost ten years. In January 1935 the committee recommended the construction of Enigma type cipher machines improved through the use of "Type X" attachments. This was the genesis of the Typex machine which was used successfully by the three services and other governmental departments for many years.

The War Office and Air Ministry immediately adopted it so that by 1939 the Typex was widely used by the Army and the RAF. The Admiralty did not adopt the Typex until 1941 when the insecurity of its codes became evident.

The design of the Typex indicates that the British not only copied the commercial Enigma but also embodied some elements of Willi Korn's Enigma patents which include features not found in the production models of the machine.

It becomes clearer as time passes that the commercial Enigma of post-World War I days had a profound effect on cipher machine design in many countries throughout the succeeding decade. It was realized quite early, however, that the commercial Enigma had one glaring cryp-

From *Cryptologia*, Vol. 7, No. 2, April 1983.

tographic defect—infrequent and largely regular movement of all rotors other than the rightmost (entrance) rotor. This feature of the machine led readily to cryptanalysis using probable plaintext to locate "isomorphs" generated during message encipherment.[1] The Italian naval Enigma, which appears to have been essentially identical to the commercial version of the Enigma, was read using this method until the Italians switched to the Hagelin C-36 during June 1941. The purpose of the "Enigma variations" which came after the original model was largely the desire to rid the machine of its isomorphic weaknesses.

In a sense, a line of descent exists between the commercial Enigma and its progeny as the following table illustrates:

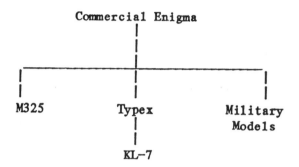

The American M-325 was William Friedman's unsuccessful attempt to develop a tactical level rotor machine based on Enigma principles.[2] Friedman's design was constructionally different from the Enigma but cryptographically similar. The M-325 had 3 rotors and a fourth reflecting rotor (reflector on the right here in contrast to the Enigma and Typex). The isomorph problem was handled by causing each rotor to step its neighbor five steps during one of its own revolutions. In this manner, isomorphs were broken up somewhat and the "baton method" was more difficult to apply. The rotor movement table shows an example of the M-325's movement. Unfortunately, the rotor movement is really not good enough to prevent analysis, and in addition, the period is so shortened by the faster rotor stepping that heavy traffic would result in numerous keying overlaps.

When it was learned that the Germans had introduced a plugboard in their military model of the Enigma, M-325 models were also built with a plugboard. This version of the machine, used correctly, would probably have served as well as the M-209 did as a tactical level cipher machine.

However, slowness of operation and operational difficulties rendered the machine unsuitable for service.

The German military introduced the well known plugboard to remedy the isomorph attack. This works well if 5 or more plugs are in use and was indeed a giant stride forward in design. The keying methods used were disastrous to say the least, and, as we all now know, the machine was solved on a regular basis by Allied cryptanalysts (but not without difficulty).

In its Typex design, the British provided a much more irregular rotor movement and introduced some other features. Strangely, the Typex incorporated many features from the Enigma patents of Willi Korn which were not used by the Germans themselves in their improvements of the machine! Not only were Korn's ideas used, but it appears that the mechanical construction of the Typex is taken directly from the commercial machine. (Examples of Korn's Patents: US Patent Office #1,705,641, #1,733,886.) The Typex and Enigma designs were so similar that Bletchley Park used the Typex in its Enigma work and a British machine, captured by the Germans during Dunkirk, was converted into an Enigma by an enterprising German Signal Officer who was short of equipment.

THE TYPEX CRYPTOGRAPH.

TYPEX WITH TOP OPEN.
Inscription on plate reads, "IMPORTANT." The handle must always be given a few turns without depressing a key at the completion of operation and on every occasion before inserting a set of drums.

II. PHOTOGRAPHIC ANALYSIS

Our analysis of the Typex is based largely on the accompanying photographs of the Mark III model of the machine. There were, of course, other models of the machine—some apparently bearing little resemblance to the model pictured.

The Typex was electrically powered and, in the model shown, output was via a paper tape printer located in the rear. The machine contained five interchangeable rotors and a sixth reflecting rotor (on the left). The rotor design and the rotor cage are nearly identical to that of both the commercial and later military Enigmas. The inscription plate visible in one photo shows that the large crank on the right of the device

Ratchet Wheels Removed from Typex.

was used to power an impulse generator for the printer and shift key functions.

The Typex (and Enigma) rotor movement is obtained by two ratchet wheels on each rotor. One ratchet wheel has 26 notches and lies on the left of the rotor when inserted in the machine (the driving ratchet wheel). The second ratchet wheel contains a number of irregularly spaced notches and lies on the rotor's left side when inserted (the control ratchet wheel). A turning rotor drives its left neighbor in the following manner: as the rotor turns, its control ratchet wheel is carried around until at a certain point of the revolution the opposing pawl (which rocks forward with each letter enciphered) enters the notch of that rotor's control ratchet wheel simultaneously engaging the driving ratchet wheel of the lefthand rotor thus driving both rotors forward one step. This mechanical construction, which is quite simple, introduces an anomaly into the rotor movement so that when it is time for the rotor left of a given rotor to move, that rotor itself must move. This results in a rotor taking two steps in succession at this time. Rotor movements of this sort do not produce maximal periods; further, the exact period length depends on the rotor starting positions. It is interesting to note that Hebern's machine, a contemporary of the Enigma, had control ratchets separate from the rotors themselves and did not possess this "multi-step" property. The pawls for driving rotors I, II, III (reading left to right) are clearly visible in the rotor cage photo just above the rotors themselves. Rotors IV and V have no corresponding visible constructions.

On the Enigma, the control ratchet had only one notch per rotor in the Army model (two on some Naval rotors) while in the Typex rotor shown there are nine such notches. The question arises as to whether all of the Typex control ratchet wheels are identical. The following table shows the notch pattern for the control ratchet in the photo (the letters N and O are just visible under the ratchet). The visible control ratchet notches from the rotor cage photo are also entered in the table. (+ = notch at this rotor position, − = no notch present, blank = cannot be determined from photo.)

	A	B	C	D	E	F	G	H	I	J	K	L	M	N	O	P	Q	R	S	T	U	V	W	X	Y	Z
	+	−	+	−	+	−	−	−	+	−	−	−	−	+	−	−	+	−	−	+	−	+	−	−	+	−
I	+	−	+	−	+																			+	−	
II													+	−	−	+	−	−	−	+						
III	+	−	+	−	+	−	−	−																		
IV	+	−	+	−	+																			+	−	
V										−	−	+	−	−	−											

The conclusion we draw from this table is that all of the control ratchet wheels are identical and that the alphabet rings are rigidly connected to the control ratchets. Further, rotor IV shows to the right of positions B and C a releasable catch (copied again from the Enigma) which allows the control ratchet wheel to be rotated with respect to the body of the cylinder. The coding cylinder itself is seen to be readily detached from the body of the rotor. Since the control ratchets are identical, the purpose intended here seems to be use of a large number of easily changed rotor wiring rather than allowing permutation of control ratchets and coding cylinders. This construction also allows sets of differently notched control ratchets to be used with the same rotor wirings. In one of his patents, Korn suggests multi-notched control ratchets and the interchangeability of these with the coding cylinders although German designers never exploited this idea fully. Largely due to these detachable coding "slugs" we have indicated the Typex to be the ancestor of the U.S. developed NATO machine of postwar years, the KL-7.

A unique Typex feature is the double rows of rotor contacts. Referring to the keyboard, we see a shift key is provided so that numerals and certain other characters may be enciphered as well as alphabetic text. The primary purpose here was encipherment of numeric code rather than mixing alphabet and numeric encipherments in one message.

It would appear that the original purpose of the double contact set was to provide separate and switchable wirings for the shift encipherment. However, corresponding contacts are electrically connected and the shift function is carried out via the following rather artificial device. The space bar and the "X" key are connected so that word divisions are enciphered as X's. The figures shift is connected to the letter "Z" while the letters shift is also "V"; thus, the letters "Z" and "V" are entered via their shifted equivalents as visible on the keyboard while these two letters indicate the required shift functions in the text.

Entrance rotors IV and V are stators as evidenced by the absence of opposing pawls. Thus, where German cryptographers introduced the plugboard, the British provided two stators to perform the same function. The combined stator substitution is not, as in the Enigma, reciprocal. (Actually, the Germans introduced a "uhr" box late in the war to make the plugboard nonreciprocal.) The middle rotor, III, is the "fast" rotor on this machine. Rotor III in turn drives rotor II which drives the "slow" rotor, I.

With the cover of the machine closed, three rods are seen to project near the pawls of rotors I, II, and III. Their function is unknown but they may have been used to lock the rotors in position for making key settings or adjusting the counter. The accompanying rotor comparison chart shows a typical Typex rotor stepping sequence in comparison with other machines of its day.

III. MATHEMATICS OF THE ENIGMA/TYPEX ROTOR MOVEMENTS

The type of rotor movement used in the three machines discussed in this article presents some interesting mathematical aspects. If each of n rotors moves a number of steps relatively prime to 26 for each revolution of its neighbor, then the period of the ciphertext will have its maximal value 26^n. A Hebern type device with control ratchet wheels divorced from the coding cylinders is capable of this type of rotor movement. When the control ratchet wheel of a rotor is rigidly attached to the driving ratchet as in the case we have here, the result is a nonmaximal period. In the Army Enigma, for example, each control ratchet wheel had only one notch. This meant that each revolution of that rotor's right neighbor drove the rotor one step forward except at one position when the control ratchet's notch was engaged at which time the rotor stepped two successive positions. Since this puts the rotor one place ahead of where it would be for a maximum period cycle the basic machine cycle is $26 \times 25 \times 26$ instead of 26^3. What happens to the missing rotor positions not in this cycle? While there are 26^3 starting positions for the cryptogram, some of these positions have no predecessors in the keying cycle. Let us suppose that the control ratchet has a single notch such that as the rotor moves between position "A" and "B" on the alphabet ring it drives its neighbor which has a similar control ratchet. No starting position of the form "A?" can ever be repeated in the subsequent keying cycle if "?" is any starting position except "B". The reason for this is plain to see: the previous position of the right rotor was not A; therefore, as it stepped it could not have driven the left rotor. On the other hand, the left rotor could not have been at position A previously or it would have moved itself. Thus, no position of the form "A?" has a predecessor if "?" is not position "B". In addition, there is one position, "ZZ", which has only position "AA" as a predecessor and thus, if we start the rotors at position "AA", two steps are taken before we enter the main keying cycle. For these two rotors the keying sequence is composed of 0, 1, or 2 steps followed by a repeating cycle of length 25×26. For a three rotor combination we see that every 25 revolutions of rotor III will cause one revolution of rotor II which in turn requires 26 revolutions to rotate rotor I once resulting in the previously stated length $26 \times 25 \times 26$ after the main cycle is entered. (Note that the leftmost rotor has no pawl engaging its control ratchet wheel and is then stepped only by its right neighbor.)

With more than one notch on the control ratchet wheel, the situation is more complicated but still similar. With the 9-notch control ratchet wheel shown in the photos, each revolution of a rotor drives its left neighbor between 11 and 16 steps forward. (The designers were apparently aiming at about ½ revolution of the rotor per revolution of the driving rotor.) As shown in the illustrative rotor movement table, a rotor can step more than twice in succession at certain positions. Exactly what happens depends not only on the number of notches present but upon their location:

1. For control ratchet wheels having an odd number of notches (excluding 13) the maximum cycle attainable for two rotors is $(26-N) \times 26$. In this case, $26-n$ revolutions of the right rotor are required to return the left neighbor to its initial position.

2. For control ratchet wheels having an even number of notches, n, the maximum cycle attainable for two rotors is $((26-n)/2) \times 26$ or half the corresponding maximal cycle length of odd-number ratchet wheels.

On the Typex, for example, a two rotor combination has cycle length equal to $(26-9) \times 26 = 442$ compared with a maximal cycle of 676. Additionally, there are 234 starting positions not in the basic two rotor cycle and of these, 153 have ISL's (initial segment lengths) of 1 position, 81 have ISL's of 2, with none longer. The M-325 control ratchets are 5-notched to produce a maximal two rotor cycle of $(26-5) \times 26 = 546$ with 105 ISL's of 1 and 25 with ISL's of 2. Putting the notches in

TYPEX 2-ROTOR CYCLE STRUCTURE

CYCLE LENGTH= 442
 153 INITIAL SEGMENTS OF LENGTH 1
 81   INITIAL SEGMENTS OF LENGTH 2

```
 2 -1   2 -1   2 -1 -1 -1   2 -1 -1 -1 -1   2 -1 -1   2 -1 -1   2 -1   2 -1 -1   2 -1
-1  1 -1   1 -1   1 -1 -1 -1   1 -1 -1 -1 -1   1 -1 -1   1 -1 -1   1 -1   1 -1 -1   1
 2 -1   2 -1   2 -1 -1 -1   2 -1 -1 -1 -1   2 -1 -1   2 -1 -1   2 -1   2 -1 -1   2 -1
-1  1 -1   1 -1   1 -1 -1 -1   1 -1 -1 -1 -1   1 -1 -1   1 -1 -1   1 -1   1 -1 -1   1
 2 -1   2 -1   2 -1 -1 -1   2 -1 -1 -1 -1   2 -1 -1   2 -1 -1   2 -1   2 -1 -1   2 -1
-1  1 -1   1 -1   1 -1 -1 -1   1 -1 -1 -1 -1   1 -1 -1   1 -1 -1   1 -1   1 -1 -1   1
 1 -1   1 -1   1 -1 -1 -1   1 -1 -1 -1 -1   1 -1 -1   1 -1 -1   1 -1   1 -1 -1   1 -1
 1 -1   1 -1   1 -1 -1 -1   1 -1 -1 -1 -1   1 -1 -1   1 -1 -1   1 -1   1 -1 -1   1 -1
 2 -1   2 -1   2 -1 -1 -1   2 -1 -1 -1 -1   2 -1 -1   2 -1 -1   2 -1   2 -1 -1   2 -1
-1  1 -1   1 -1   1 -1 -1 -1   1 -1 -1 -1 -1   1 -1 -1   1 -1 -1   1 -1   1 -1 -1   1
 1 -1   1 -1   1 -1 -1 -1   1 -1 -1 -1 -1   1 -1 -1   1 -1 -1   1 -1   1 -1 -1   1 -1
 1 -1   1 -1   1 -1 -1 -1   1 -1 -1 -1 -1   1 -1 -1   1 -1 -1   1 -1   1 -1 -1   1 -1
 1 -1   1 -1   1 -1 -1 -1   1 -1 -1 -1 -1   1 -1 -1   1 -1 -1   1 -1   1 -1 -1   1 -1
 2 -1   2 -1   2 -1 -1 -1   2 -1 -1 -1 -1   2 -1 -1   2 -1 -1   2 -1   2 -1 -1   2 -1
-1  1 -1   1 -1   1 -1 -1 -1   1 -1 -1 -1 -1   1 -1 -1   1 -1 -1   1 -1   1 -1 -1   1
 1 -1   1 -1   1 -1 -1 -1   1 -1 -1 -1 -1   1 -1 -1   1 -1 -1   1 -1   1 -1 -1   1 -1
 2 -1   2 -1   2 -1 -1 -1   2 -1 -1 -1 -1   2 -1 -1   2 -1 -1   2 -1   2 -1 -1   2 -1
-1  1 -1   1 -1   1 -1 -1 -1   1 -1 -1 -1 -1   1 -1 -1   1 -1 -1   1 -1   1 -1 -1   1
 1 -1   1 -1   1 -1 -1 -1   1 -1 -1 -1 -1   1 -1 -1   1 -1 -1   1 -1   1 -1 -1   1 -1
 2 -1   2 -1   2 -1 -1 -1   2 -1 -1 -1 -1   2 -1 -1   2 -1 -1   2 -1   2 -1 -1   2 -1
-1  1 -1   1 -1   1 -1 -1 -1   1 -1 -1 -1 -1   1 -1 -1   1 -1 -1   1 -1   1 -1 -1   1
 2 -1   2 -1   2 -1 -1 -1   2 -1 -1 -1 -1   2 -1 -1   2 -1 -1   2 -1   2 -1 -1   2 -1
-1  1 -1   1 -1   1 -1 -1 -1   1 -1 -1 -1 -1   1 -1 -1   1 -1 -1   1 -1   1 -1 -1   1
 1 -1   1 -1   1 -1 -1 -1   1 -1 -1 -1 -1   1 -1 -1   1 -1 -1   1 -1   1 -1 -1   1 -1
 2 -1   2 -1   2 -1 -1 -1   2 -1 -1 -1 -1   2 -1 -1   2 -1 -1   2 -1   2 -1 -1   2 -1
-1  1 -1   1 -1   1 -1 -1 -1   1 -1 -1 -1 -1   1 -1 -1   1 -1 -1   1 -1   1 -1 -1   1
```

the wrong places can have disastrous cryptographic results. For example, if 5 notches are placed in successive positions on the control ratchet the cycle length is found to be only 130 with the remaining 546 starting rotor positions belonging to initial segments whose lengths vary from 1 to 115 positions before the main cycle is entered. In general, adjacent placement of notches causes such abnormalities in rotor movement.

With an even number of notches present on the control ratchet, the maximum cycle splits into two disjoint cycles each of ½ the corresponding length in the odd numbered case. For example, if the control ratchet has 8 notches cut so that the rotor stepping is at positions: A, D, H, K, M, P, T and W, then there are two cycles each of length 234 with 208 noncyclic starting positions (144 with ISL's of 1 and 64 with ISL's of 2). It might be supposed that even-numbered ratchet wheels would be avoided in usage, but the Typex is known to have used even notched ratchet wheels on occasion.

The overall cycle length can be calculated from consideration of the two rotor cycle lengths. With rotors I–IV moving in the manner indicated the overall cycle length would be $26 \times (26-9) \times 26 = 11,492$. Most rotor starting positions in this case have 0, 1, or 2 ISL's.

The two accompanying tables [preceding directly above] show graphically the two rotor cycle structures generated by the M-325 and Typex control ratchet wheels. The fastest moving rotor position is given as a row coordinate and the slower one as a column coordinate. A value of -1 indicates that that rotor pair lies in the main cycle; a positive number indicates a rotor pair lies outside the main cycle and represents the number of steps taken before the main cycle is entered.

IV. CRYPTANALYSIS

We now outline a statistical method of cryptanalysis which might be used with cryptographs of the Enigma/Typex variety. The method is based on the fact that rotor encipherment of text with non-random statistical properties results in ciphertext having non-random properties. Consider the rotor table for Enigma rotor I [above]. This table shows the 26 simple substitutions generated as the rotor turns. Also shown are the theoretical frequencies we should expect for 1000 characters of standard English text enciphered with such a rotor. Note that the predicted frequencies, while not varying as much among themselves as the input frequencies, are still non-random.

M325 2-ROTOR CYCLE STRUCTURE

CYCLE LENGTH= 546
105 INITIAL SEGMENTS OF LENGTH 1
25 INITIAL SEGMENTS OF LENGTH 2

ENIGMA ROTOR I

PREDICTED OUTPUT FREQUENCIES IN A 1000 CHARACTER TEXT

A 40 B 43 C 36 D 36 E 33 F 37 G 33 H 38 I 36 J 40 K 42 L 41 M 31 N 46 O 45 P 35
Q 40 R 46 S 36 T 28 U 44 V 44 W 44 X 42 Y 41 Z 26

MINIMUM VARIANCE ROTOR

PREDICTED OUPUT FREQUENCIES IN A 1000 CHARACTER TEXT

A 38 B 41 C 38 D 37 E 36 F 40 G 41 H 37 I 36 J 39 K 38 L 38 M 37 N 39 O 36 P 39
Q 40 R 41 S 37 T 36 U 40 V 41 W 38 X 39 Y 39 Z 39

```
   A B C D E F G H I J K L M N O P Q R S T U V W X Y Z
A  * * * * * * * * * * * O P Q R S T U V W X Y Z A B
B  N Z Y X W V U T S R Q P O N M L K J I H G F E D C B A
C  Y X W V U T S R Q P O N M L K J I H G F E D C B A Z
D  W V U T S R Q P O N M L K J I H G F E D C B A Z Y X
E  U T S R Q P O N M L K J I H G F E D C B A Z Y X W V
F  S R Q P O N M L K J I H G F E D C B A Z Y X W V U T
G  Q P O N M L K J I H G F E D C B A Z Y X W V U T S R
H  O N M L K J I H G F E D C B A Z Y X W V U T S R Q P
I  M L K J I H G F E D C B A Z Y X W V U T S R Q P O N
J  K J I H G F E D C B A Z Y X W V U T S R Q P O N M L
K  I H G F E D C B A Z Y X W V U T S R Q P O N M L K J
L  G F E D C B A Z Y X W V U T S R Q P O N M L K J I H
M  E D C B A Z Y X W V U T S R Q P O N M L K J I H G F
N  C B A Z Y X W V U T S R Q P O N M L K J I H G F E D
O  A Z Y X W V U T S R Q P O N M L K J I H G F E D C B
P  Z Y X W V U T S R Q P O N M L K J I H G F E D C B A
```

If we pick any two rotor positions in this table, there is a certain probability, which can be readily calculated, that letters enciphered at these two positions will coincide. For example, using the first two rows of the table as an example, whenever plaintext "A" is enciphered at rotor position 1 and plaintext "C" is enciphered at rotor position 2 the ciphertext letter "E" results. If no other rotors of our cryptograph move between these encipherments, the "E"s emerge as some other coincident letter, say "K", in the cryptogram. The probability of coincidence ciphertext letters which were enciphered at different rotor positions depends on the rotor wiring. While in general the average probability of coincidence is about $1/26 = .038$, some pairs of positions are more or less than this. The index of coincidence distribution table shows what happens when we run through all the possible pairs of positions for rotor I, calculating for each pair the corresponding index of coincidence. As expected, most of the values obtained hover around the random index value of .038. However, certain pairs of positions are abnormally high or low by virtue of the particular rotor wiring used. Whenever the predicted IC exceeded .046 or was less than .030 a separate tally was prepared. Rotor positions "A" and "O" show, for example, an abnormally high tendency to produce coincident ciphertext while rotor positions "C" and "R" are the reverse. Given a cryptogram, we can then compare positions expected to be high or low with the predicted characteristics for each rotor in use and hope to learn both the rotor identity and starting position for the entrance rotor. Using this method on the Hebern machine or commercial Enigma requires only about 250 characters of ciphertext to be conclusive.

Before continuing, let us consider how we might choose our rotor wirings to avoid this attack. The output frequencies of the rotor would be more equidistributed if each column of the rotor table contained each letter of the alphabet only once. Physically this could be achieved if the rotor wiring could be chosen so no displacement from input to output contact on the rotor were to appear more than once. Thus, the displacements of the rotor contacts would be, in some order, 0, 1, 2, 3, . . . , 25. (A wiring from input "A" to output "A" is a displacement of 0, "A" to "B", a displacement of 1, etc.) If the rotor has an even number of contacts, this type of wiring is physically impossible and the best we can do is to repeat one displacement twice. We shall term rotors wired in this manner "minimum variance rotors" since the variability of their coincidence distributions should be the smallest possible under the circumstances. An index distribution for a minimum variance rotor is included for comparison. As expected there are fewer extremely high or low tails on the distribution curve but the inherent nonuniformity still

INDEX OF COINCIDENCE DISTRIBUTION

```
IC > .046      IC < .030

AO .0472996
AR .0467292
AT .0460732
CG              .0297288
CR              .0292661
CZ .0468315
DO .0465519
DS              .0296439
DT .0486026
DX .0495018
EN .0507753
EU              .0266391
EV .0492735
FI              .0290378
FK              .0293595
FT .0466284
FX .0529884
GN .0508526
HJ              .0299742
HO              .0276279
HS .0501309
IR              .0298509
IT              .027569
JQ              .0296013
KV .0526745
LR .0465224
LT .0487338
LX .0478696
MQ              .0297675
MX              .0296226
NP              .0296511
OS              .0281325
OW              .0295094
RT .0465959
RW .0490812
SX .0471751
WZ              .0296407
```

COINCIDENCE DISTRIBUTION

```
 0 .0260
 4 XXXX.0287
26 XXXXXXXXXXXXXXXXXXXXXXXXXX.0313
36 XXXXXXXXXXXXXXXXXXXXXXXXXXXXXXXXXXXX.0340
55 XXXXXXXXXXXXXXXXXXXXXXXXXXXXXXXXXXXXXXXXXXXXXXXXXXXXXXXXX.0367
61 XXXXXXXXXXXXXXXXXXXXXXXXXXXXXXXXXXXXXXXXXXXXXXXXXXXXXXXXXXXXXXX.0393
47 XXXXXXXXXXXXXXXXXXXXXXXXXXXXXXXXXXXXXXXXXXXXXXXXX.0420
37 XXXXXXXXXXXXXXXXXXXXXXXXXXXXXXXXXXXXX.0447
23 XXXXXXXXXXXXXXXXXXXXXXX.0473
 6 XXXXXX.0500
 5 XXXXX.0527
```

ENIGMA ROTOR #I

INDEX OF COINCIDENCE DISTRIBUTION FOR MINIMUM VARIANCE ROTOR·

IC > .046   IC < .030

AF .0475552   .0275312
AQ .0471931
BG .0471931   .0285516
BR
BW .0460577
CH .0467299   .0275047
CM
CX .0482569   .027696
DN
DY .0482137   .0286099
EO   .0295448
GU   .0275047
PZ   .0296471
RW   .0295409
SX

COINCIDENCE DISTRIBUTION

0 .0260
6 XXXXXX.0287
9 XXXXXXXXX.0313
65 XXXXXXXXXXXXXXXXXXXXXXXXXXXXXXXXXXXXXXXXXXXXXXXXXXXXXXXXXXXXXXXXXX.0340
64 XXXXXXXXXXXXXXXXXXXXXXXXXXXXXXXXXXXXXXXXXXXXXXXXXXXXXXXXXXXXXXXX.0367
76 XXXXXXXXXXXXXXXXXXXXXXXXXXXXXXXXXXXXXXXXXXXXXXXXXXXXXXXXXXXXXXXXXXXXXXXXXXXXXXXXXX
.0393
42 XXXXXXXXXXXXXXXXXXXXXXXXXXXXXXXXXXXXXXXXXX.0420
23 XXXXXXXXXXXXXXXXXXXXXXX.0447
12 XXXXXXXXXXXX.0473
3 XXX.0500
0 .0527

persists. Thus, for 26 contact rotors (or 36 contact rotors such as in the KL-7) our proposed attack can be frustrated to some degree but not rendered useless. We should add a note here that while minimum variance rotors may seem desirable from some standpoints, they make the problem of reconstructing unknown rotor wirings from ciphertext much simpler and are undesirable in that light.

Cryptanalysis using the data from the coincidence table is illustrated by the two accompanying tables. A cryptogram of somewhat less than 500 characters enciphered on a plugboardless Enigma is analyzed to determine the position of its entrance rotor. Analysis begins by testing for each possible rotor. Only the correct rotor table is shown here for brevity. Given a rotor, we encipher the cryptogram at each of the 26 possible starting positions. This removes the entrance rotor encipherment. For each of the resulting 26 enciphered cryptograms we calculate the average index of coincidence of the message at (1) the high coincidence positions and (2) the low coincidence positions.

This must be done 26 times assuming for each calculation a different position for the alphabet ring of that rotor. For example, assuming the starting rotor position was "A" we find the average of the 26 IC's is .0262 for the high IC group and .0529 for the low IC group.

The idea behind this calculation is that the correct position should be one of the highest in the high IC group and, simultaneously, one of the lowest in the low IC group. Since the alphabet ring setting on the rotor determines just where the adjacent rotor moves which, in turn, determines if the coincidence pair should be counted or not, we try all ring settings. Clearly, any high or low coincidence pair which straddles a stepping position of the second rotor should be omitted from the IC calculations. The final average IC, in the correct rotor starting position, is computed from 1 correct ring setting and 25 incorrect ones but even the incorrect ones contain a number of correct coincidence positions which make the average value stand out from the incorrect starting position calculations.

In the table shown, each average high IC and low IC is shown. These values are then ranked in descending order for the high IC's and descending order for the low IC's. The average of the two ranks then gives a good indication of the correct starting position; a low average rank is indicative of a value which is near the top of the high group and near the bottom of the low IC group. In the case of the message enciphered, the rotor starting position was "C" which has an average rank of 2.5—clearly the favored choice since the next average rank is 7.5. In this case, 500 characters is much more data than would be needed for good results. When the message is very short or a large number of

STARTING POSITION	IC HIGH	IC LOW	RANK HIGH	RANK LOW	AVERAGE RANK
A	.0262	.0529	24	25	24.5
B	.0561	.0425	1	16	8.5
C	.0549	.0286	2	3	2.5
D	.0489	.0335	6	9	7.5
E	.04	.0388	16	13	14.5
F	.0355	.0307	19	5	12
G	.0482	.0395	8	14	11
H	.0484	.0359	7	11	9
I	.0274	.0479	23	22	22.5
J	.0284	.0456	22	18	20
K	.0491	.0419	5	15	10
L	.0405	.0459	15	20	17.5
M	.04	.0444	16	17	16.5
N	.0418	.0476	14	21	17.5
O	.0286	.0489	21	23	22
P	.0362	.0255	18	1	9.5
Q	.0477	.068	9	26	17.5
R	.0456	.0357	10	10	10
S	.0426	.0457	12	19	15.5
T	.0497	.0321	4	8	6
U	.0332	.0275	20	2	11
V	.0419	.0316	13	7	10
W	.0364	.0311	17	6	11.5
X	.0545	.0381	3	12	7.5
Y	.0418	.0506	14	24	19
Z	.0451	.03	11	4	7.5

DETERMINING THE ENTRANCE ROTOR STARTING POSITION BASED ON HIGH AND LOW COINCIDENCE POSITIONS

RING POSITION	IC HIGH	IC LOW	RANK HIGH	RANK LOW	AVERAGE RANK
A	.0555	.0222	6	5	5.5
B	.0555	.025	6	8	7
C	.05	.025	10	8	9
D	.0472	.025	12	8	10
E	.0531	.0222	8	5	6.5
F	.0531	.0194	8	1	4.5
G	.0531	.0224	8	6	7
H	.0589	.0224	5	6	5.5
I	.0537	.0224	7	6	6.5
J	.0537	.0196	7	2	4.5
K	.0649	.0196	3	2	2.5
L	.0649	.0199	3	4	3.5
M	.0649	.0199	3	4	3.5
N	.0649	.0225	3	7	5
O	.0734	.0197	1	3	2
P	.0678	.0308	2	10	6
Q	.0647	.0337	4	11	7.5
R	.0647	.0308	4	10	7
S	.0505	.0308	9	10	9.5
T	.0475	.025	11	8	9.5
U	.0446	.025	13	8	10.5
V	.0446	.025	13	8	10.5
W	.0418	.025	14	8	11
X	.0389	.025	16	8	12
Y	.0389	.025	16	8	12
Z	.0412	.0278	15	9	12

DETERMINING THE STEPPING POSITION OF THE ENTRANCE ROTOR

possible rotors must be tested, this approach yields a small group of probable candidates from which to proceed.

Once the correct starting position is known, the alphabet ring setting of the entrance rotor can often be found by examining the 26 IC's which went into its average. For the case under discussion, these 26 values are shown and ranked as before. The table indicates that the second rotor stepped between "O" and "P" which is indeed correct. As we approach the correct ring setting the high IC values tend to rise and the low IC values fall as expected.

The example just presented is a simple one. In the case of the Typex the frequent rotor stepping as well as the two entrance stators make application of the frequency spectrum method more difficult. The essential point here is that while the tests involved in adapting the method to the Typex might require a great deal of calculation, the necessary computations can be done beforehand and the tests themselves are co-incidence type calculations which are rapidly performed. The frequent rotor stepping means that we must limit our analysis to adjacent or nearby positions in the coincidence spectrum, or, perhaps, consider a two rotor group as a combination rotor of period 17×26 in positions II and III of the machine.

The similarity of the Typex to its father, the Enigma, also implies that methods used in the analysis of the Enigma should be of use with the Typex. For example, Turing's approach of deriving plain/cipher loops is suitable for a sequential machine calculation. In this attack, probable plaintext is used as shown below to find cycles.

```
PLAINTEXT:   P A R T T W O O F T W O P A R T S...
CIPHERTEXT:  T Q W Z O O R P E X X G Y E E F W...
             1 2 3 4 5 6 7 8 9 0 1 2 3 4 5 6 7...
    Loop 1:  P  →  T  →  O  →  P
             1     5     8
    Loop 2:  W  →  O →  R  →  W
             6     7     3
```

The presence of a loop is independent of the stator transformation in the Typex (or plugboard in the Enigma). Thus, if we could exhaustively test all possible positions using the three moving rotors, (I, II, III), then, we could check for the presence of loops at the correct positions. Again, the frequent rotor movement hampers this process much more than in the Enigma. We should note here that the British Bombe used in Enigma analysis contained a "diagonal board" invented by Gordon Welchman and in this form could not be adapted to the Typex since the stator transformation is not reciprocal as was the Enigma plugboard.

V. THE SIGABA CONNECTION

During World War II, communication between British and American high command dictated a common cipher system. The corresponding American cryptograph was the M134 series of machines commonly (and incorrectly) referred to as the Sigaba. A U.S. Navy adaptation of the Sigaba rotor basket along with a special adaptor which fit over the Typex allowed communication between the two machines. This was even more remarkable since the M134 machines were not reciprocal. In fact, it would be difficult to find two more dissimilar rotor machines than these two.

VI. CONCLUDING REMARKS

It is tempting to compare the relative advantages of the Enigma versus the Typex. Before doing so, however, one must bear in mind that such comparisons are likely to be misleading since, in practice, the care (or carelessness) with which a device is used is the determining factor in the security attained. The German Enigma was adequate in its day to resist cryptanalysis had it been used properly.

The strong point of the Typex over the Enigma is, of course, the frequent rotor stepping. The interchangeability of the wiring slugs (which could also be inserted reversed) and the ratchet wheels is another ingenious development in the Typex. There is some evidence that this construction came some time after the initial models were introduced.

The Enigma plugboard offers more security, in spite of its reciprocal nature, than the two stator setup in the Typex. While the Army Enigma and the Typex are roughly comparable in design and cryptographic strength, the German Naval Enigma probably possessed an edge over the Typex due to the introduction of the three "thin" reflector rotors which, in effect, made the machine a four rotor device (the reflector was a stator however). Also, the naval model had, as we have noted, multinotched rotors in addition to the standard army issue (rotor #'s I–V). At the conclusion of the war, some newer Enigma's had plug-in reflectors. This would have given the Enigma an additional edge over the Typex.

VII. THE PROGRAM

The computer program shown [immediately following] is an emulation of a Typex machine written in PASCAL '80 (for the TRS-80). As the text is enciphered, the current rotor positions are shown at the top of the screen so that the movement may be observed. None of the number shift features of the Typex have been implemented in this demonstration program.

REFERENCES

1.   Deavours, C. A., La Methode des Batons. *Cryptologia*. 4:240–247.
2.   Kruh, L., Cipher Equipment: The M-325. *Cryptologia*. 1:143–149.

```
0000 PROGRAM TYPEX;
0003 TYPE ALPHABET= 'A' .. 'Z' ;
000C      WIRING = ARRAY(.ALPHABET.) OF ALPHABET;
0012 VAR
0012    C,D : CHAR;
001A    I,J,K,L,MOVE1,MOVE2 : INTEGER;
0032    N,P : ARRAY(.1..5.) OF INTEGER;
0040    R,RR : ARRAY(.1..5.) OF WIRING;
004E    REFLECT : WIRING;
0052    TURNOVER : ARRAY(.0..25.) OF CHAR;
005C    TEXT : ARRAY(.1..500.) OF CHAR;
0066
0066 PROC DATA;
```

```
006F BEGIN
0075 TURNOVER:='010000100100101001010100';
0096 RR(.1.):='EKMFLGDQVZNTOWYHXUSPAIBRCJ';
00BF RR(.2.):='AJDKSIRUXBLHWTMCQGZNPYFVOE';
00E8 RR(.3.):='BDFHJLCPRTXVZNYEIWGAKMUSQO';
0111 RR(.4.):='ESOVPZJAYQUIRHXLNFTGKDCMWB';
013A RR(.5.):='VZBRGITYUPSDNHLXAWMJQOFECK';
0163 REFLECT :='YRUHQSLDPXNGOKMIEBFZCWVJAT';
0184 END;
0185
0185 PROC SHIFT( VAR I : INTEGER );
018D VAR J : INTEGER;
0192 BEGIN
0197    IF I<0 THEN I:=I+26;
01B1    J:=ORD(C)+I;
01C2    IF J>90 THEN J:=J-26;
01DE    C:=CHR(J)
01E6 END;
01EC
01EC PROC SUBSTITUTE( VAR ALPHA : WIRING );
01F4 BEGIN
01FA    C:=ALPHA(.C.);
0211 END;
0212
0212 PROC ROTOR( VAR I : INTEGER; ALPHA : WIRING);
021E VAR J : INTEGER;
0223 BEGIN
0228    SHIFT(I);
022E    SUBSTITUTE(ALPHA);
0234    J:=-I;
0240    SHIFT(J);
0246 END;
0247
0247 PROC MOVE;
024B VAR L,K : INTEGER;
0254 BEGIN
0259    IF( TURNOVER(.P(.3.).)= '1') THEN MOVE2 :=1
027E                   ELSE MOVE2 := 0;
0289    IF ( TURNOVER(.P(.2.).) = '1') THEN
02A8         BEGIN MOVE1 := 1; MOVE2 := 1 END
02B8    ELSE MOVE1 := 0;
02C1 P(.3.) :=( P(.3.)+1) MOD 26 ;
02E5 IF( MOVE2 <> 0 ) THEN P(.2.) := (P(.2.) +1) MOD 26 ;
0314 IF( MOVE1 <> 0 ) THEN P(.1.) :=( P(.1.) + 1) MOD 26;
0343 L:=15377; FOR K:=1 TO 3 DO BEGIN POKE(L,CHR(P(.K.)+65));
0379                                 L:=L+3 END;
038B END;
038C
038C PROC INVERSE;
0390 BEGIN
0396 FOR I:=1 TO 5 DO
03AA    BEGIN
03AA    FOR C:= 'A' TO 'Z' DO
03BE       BEGIN
03BE       D:=R(.I.)(.C.); RR(.I.)(.D.):=C END;
0403    END;
0406 END;
0407
```

```
0407 PROC INPUT;
040B BEGIN
0411 L:=1;
0419 REPEAT
0419    READ(TEXT(.L.)); L:=L+1
0438 UNTIL EOF;
0442 L:=L-1
044D END;
0452
0452 PROC CIPHER;
0456 BEGIN
045C        C:=TEXT(.I.);
0473        FOR J:=5 DOWNTO 1  DO ROTOR(P(.J.),R(.J.));
04AA        ROTOR(K,REFLECT);
04B6        FOR J:=1 TO 5 DO ROTOR(P(.J.),RR(.J.));
04ED END;
04EE
04EE BEGIN
04EE    DATA;CLS;
04F2    WRITELN('ENTER ROTOR ORDER (E.G. 3,4,2,1,5):');
0522    READ(N(.1.),N(.2.),N(.3.),N(.4.),N(.5.));
0569    FOR K:= 1 TO 5 DO R(.K.):= RR(.N(.K.).);
05A9    WRITELN('ENTER ROTOR STARTING POSITIONS (LEFT TO RIGHT)');
05E4    FOR I:= 1 TO 5 DO BEGIN READ(C); P(.I.) := ORD(C) - 65 END;
061E    CLS;WRITE('ROTOR POSITIONS: ');
0636    FOR I:=1 TO 5 DO BEGIN C:= CHR(P(.I.)+65);
0666                               WRITE(C,'   ') END;
0678    INVERSE;
067B    WRITELN;WRITELN('ENTER TEXT (END WITH CLEAR KEY):');
06AF    INPUT;
06B2    K:=0;
06B8    FOR I:= 1 TO L DO
06CE    BEGIN
06CE    IF TEXT(.I.) <> ' ' THEN
06E5      BEGIN
06E5         MOVE;
06E8         CIPHER;
06EB         WRITE(C);
06F2      END;
06F2    END;
06F5 END.
00:02:21 COMPILATION COMPLETE
```

Uncaging the Hagelin Cryptograph
by Elliot Fischer

ABSTRACT: A modification of the cage of the Hagelin (M-209) cipher machine is shown to make the modified cipher secure against the Morris Known Plaintext Attack.

0. INTRODUCTION

In [1], Morris presents a method for reconstructing the internal settings of the Hagelin (M-209) cipher machine from known plaintext. In this note it is shown that an expansion of the cage of the M-209, easily realized as a ROM or PROM, makes the cipher secure against the Morris attack.

In Section 1 a brief description of the M-209 is given, while Section 2 describes the weakness and the exploitation of this weakness by the Morris method. Section 3 describes the modification of cage expansion and discusses security with respect to the Morris attack.

1. M-209 DESCRIPTION

The description of the M-209 will be restricted to its salient mathematical features. Basically, the Hagelin generates a pseudo-random keystream of numbers between 0 and 25. Successive elements of the keystream are added, mod 26, to the numerical equivalent (A = 0, B = 1, etc.) of the plaintext to produce the ciphertext. It is the construction of this keystream that is of immediate concern.

There are six key wheels bearing, respectively, 26, 25, 23, 21, 19, 17 pin positions. These positions are either active (=1) or inactive (=0). Each key wheel is rotated by one position after the encipherment of each

From *Cryptologia*, Vol. 7, No. 1, Jan. 1983.

letter. A key wheel returns to its starting position after one complete rotation. Since the periods of the six wheels are all relatively prime, the six wheels do not all return simultaneously to their starting positions until $26 \times 25 \times 23 \times 21 \times 19 \times 17$ ($= 101,405,850$) encipherments.

Each configuration of the six wheels corresponds to a six-component binary vector. For example, if the pins in the starting (first) position of all 6 rotors were active, this would correspond to the vector $(1,1,1,1,1,1)$. On rotation, the sequence might be active, active, inactive, inactive, active, active and this would correspond to $(1,1,0,0,1,1)$.

To generate the keystream, the current vector is passed through the "cage." This part of the machine received its name from its mechanical appearance, although it may be described as follows mathematically. To produce a displacement between 0 and 25, the scalar product of the above described binary 6-vector and a 6-vector with carefully chosen components, called the cage vector, is taken. For example, if the cage vector is

$$(1,5,12,10,3,2)$$

the scalar product of $(1,1,0,0,1,1)$ and the cage vector yields

$$1 + 5 + 3 + 2 = 11$$

and this would be added to the plaintext mod 26. To further complicate matters, overlaps are employed so that if certain combinations of the components of the cage vector are rendered active by the binary 6-vector, the effect on the scalar product is less than the sum of the two separate components. This tends to make the distribution of keystream displacements more uniform and detracts somewhat from the linearity of the process. For example, in the above cage, positions 2 and 3 might have an overlap of 3, positions 3 and 4 an overlap of 2, and positions 5 and 6 an overlap of 1. Then if the pins on wheels 2 and 3 were both active, their combined effect would be $14(5 + 12 - 3)$. Similarly, if pins 3 and 4 were both active their combined effect would be $20(12 + 10 - 2)$ while if pins 5 and 6 were both active their combined effect would be $4(3 + 2 - 1)$. Although the inclusion of overlaps is intended to make the keystream generation process nonlinear, enough linearity remains that the cipher may be exploited by a known plaintext attack, as discussed in the next section. To set up the machine to encipher a message requires specification of the 131 pins and the cage vector.

2. THE MORRIS KNOWN-PLAINTEXT ATTACK

The Morris Known Plaintext Attack [1] assumes that a sufficient number (approximately 75) of the successive keystream numbers are known. The settings (active or inactive) of the 131 pins on the six wheels are first recovered, and then the cage is reconstructed. The pin settings are recovered as follows.

Consider, say, wheel 4 with the cage with overlap as described in the previous section. Wheel 4 has a period of 21, and an active pin on wheel 4 contributes 10 to the displacement, unless wheel 3 is also active, and then there is an overlap of 2. Given 75 keystream displacements, arrange the key sequence in columns with period 21, and form the average of each row. For example, the first row would contain key displacements 1, 22, 43, 64. The second row would contain displacements 2, 23, 44, 65 etc. Each row contains displacements where the pin corresponding to a particular row number is always active or inactive. For example, in row 1 the first pin is always in the same position, in row 2 the second pin, etc.

A plot of the averages of these rows (rounded to the nearest integer) has a bimodal distribution with two peaks: one peak occurs where the pins were active (and thus contributed 10 to the keystream) and one peak where the pins were inactive (and contributed 0 to the keystream). Active and inactive pins may be recognized from examination of the plot. In practice, a plot must first be made of all 6 wheels to determine which distribution shows the greatest tendency toward bimodality. The pin settings over the wheel of this distribution may be determined, and the effects of these pins on the displacements caused by pins on the other wheels removed, until all 131 pin settings are recovered. As the pin settings are recovered, the cage elements can be reconstructed until all the machine settings (pins, cage vector, and overlaps) are determined. The reader is referred to [1] for details.

3. CAGE MODIFICATION

The Morris method exploits the fact that the key displacement is an almost linear function of the pin settings. This was apparently a mechanical constraint on the construction of the machine. However, if one views the cage as a mapping from a binary 6-vector to (0, 25) there is no reason, especially in the current era of high-speed electronic chips, to restrict this mapping.

Consider, then, the binary 6-vector as a number between 0 and 63 in binary notation. Expand the cage to a 64-component array, where each component is a number between 0 and 25. These numbers are put in the cage array randomly, 14 numbers appearing twice and 12 appearing 3 times. The key displacement is found by generating the binary 6-vector using the 6 wheels as before and then taking as the key displacement the number in the component of the cage array corresponding to the binary vector. For example, if the binary vector were (1,1,0,0,0,1), this converts to 49 decimal and the key displacement would be the number in the 49th component of the cage array.

By randomizing the cage in this way, the Morris method is thwarted because the effect of an individual pin is not necessarily the same when the wheel has gone through a full rotation. There is no bimodal distribution to facilitate pin reconstruction. In fact, using the central limit theorem (see, for example, [2, pp. 266–267]), it can easily be shown that if the plots made previously for the Morris attack are made for the randomized cage, the distribution is not bimodal but in fact approaches a normal distribution (with mean equal to the average of the 64 cage entries) as the number of known key displacements used becomes larger and larger. Computer experiments using 100 key displacements have verified this trend toward a normal distribution with the appropriate mean.

This randomized cage can easily be realized by an electronic ROM or PROM, and an electronic version of the resulting cipher could be an effective cryptographic machine. An analysis of such a machine's cryptographic weaknesses would be an interesting and very challenging undertaking.

REFERENCES

1.   Morris, R. (1978), The Hagelin Cipher Machine (M209)—Reconstruction of the Internal Settings. *Cryptologia.* 2: 267–289.

2.   Papoulis, A. (1965), *Probability, Random Variables, and Stochastic Processes.* New York: McGraw-Hill.

Statistical Analysis of the Hagelin Cryptograph
by Ronald L. Rivest

We derive here a formula which estimates how much ciphertext is needed to solve a cryptogram produced by a Hagelin cryptograph, using the cryptanalytic technique presented by Barker.[1] We shall see that no more than 8000 characters of ciphertext are needed to solve a Hagelin Model C-48 (or U.S. Army M-209) cryptogram. The Hagelin cryptograph was invented in the 1930's by Boris Hagelin; many thousands of these machines were produced in the subsequent decades.

I. THE ENCRYPTION PROCESS

We let the letters of the alphabet used (both for plaintext and ciphertext) be denoted $a_1, a_2, \ldots, a_\lambda$, where λ is the number of letters (typically $\lambda = 26$).

A typical Hagelin machine has w keywheels, or wheels, where wheel i has t_i pins. For the C-48 we have $w = 6$ wheels of 17, 19, 21, 23, 25, and 26 pins, respectively. Each pin can either be pushed left or right. Each wheel rotates past a sensor; at a given moment the w sensors can determine which of the w wheels have "left"-pins under the sensor, and which have "right"-pins. Therefore one of 2^w possible sensor readings will occur; this sensor reading is used to select a monoalphabetic substitution to encrypt the plaintext letter. Each wheel then advances one position before the encryption of the next letter.

The detailed operation of the machine is described in Barker.[1] A substitution selected by a given sensor reading may be the same as substitutions selected by other sensor readings; this will not affect our analysis. (For example, on the C-48 we have $2^w = 64$ different readings possible, but only 26 monoalphabetic substitutions available, so some substitutions will be selected by more than one reading.)

From *Cryptologia*, Vol. 5, No. 1, Jan. 1981.

II. THE CRYPTANALYTIC PROCEDURE

We assume that we must make a "ciphertext only" attack; no partial plaintext or probable words are available to us. We assume, however, that the plaintext is English (or another nonrandom source of characters). For English military text we can expect frequency counts per 1000 characters as shown in Table 1 (from [1, p. 109]). The frequency of "Z" is high because the Hagelin machines are not equipped with a "space" character, so Z is conventionally used in its place.

A-62	H-28	O-63	V-13
B-8	I-62	P-22	W-13
C-26	J-1	Q-3	X-4
D-35	K-2	R-64	Y-16
E-109	L-31	S-51	Z-162
F-24	M-21	T-77	
G-14	N-67	U-22	

TABLE 1. ENGLISH MILITARY TEXT FREQUENCIES (per 1000).

The fact that the plaintext has a non-uniform distribution causes the ciphertext also to have a non-uniform distribution; this enables us to determine the pin settings using statistical tests on the ciphertext.

Suppose we wish to determine the pin-settings on wheel 1 (the other wheels can be handled similarly). Although a very large number of characters must be enciphered before the sequence of sensor readings repeats itself (this number is the least common multiple of $t_1,...,t_w$), the pins passing under wheel 1's sensor will repeat every t_1 letters. If C_1, C_2,..., is the sequence of ciphertext letters available, then pin 1 was used to encipher letters C_1, C_{t_1+1}, C_{2t_1+1},..., while pin 2 was used to encipher letters C_2, C_{t_1+2}, C_{2t_1+2},..., etc.

We wish to determine if pin i on wheel 1 has been pushed in the same direction as pin j on wheel 1, for all i and j, $i \neq j$. To do this we can compare the frequencies of the ciphertext letters produced using pin i with those produced using pin j. For example to compare pins 1 and 2 we can make a table such as is given in Table 2.

	a_1	a_2	$\cdots$	a_λ	←Ciphertext Letter
pin 1	f_1	f_2	$\cdots$	f_λ	n
pin 2	g_1	g_2	$\cdots$	g_λ	n
total	f_1+g_1	f_2+g_2	$\cdots$	$f_\lambda+g_\lambda$	$2n$

TABLE 2. SAMPLE FREQUENCY TABLE.

Here, f_i is the number of a_i's in $C_1, C_{t_1+1}, C_{2t_1+1}, \ldots$, while g_i is the number of a_i's in $C_2, C_{t_1+2}, \ldots$, etc. We have assumed for simplicity that the available ciphertext has length $t_1 \cdot n$, so that each pin of wheel 1 is used exactly n times.

If pins 1 and 2 are in the same position (i.e., either both left or right), we would expect the f_i's and g_i's to have the same distribution. On the other hand, if the pins are in different positions, the underlying non-uniformity of the plaintext distribution will result in a statistically significant difference in the distribution of the f_i's and the g_i's.

The χ^2 test [2, p. 447] will detect significant differences between the f_i's and the g_i's. We compute

$$\chi^2 = \sum_{i-1}^{\lambda} (f_i - g_i)^2/(f_i + g_i); \tag{1}$$

This statistic will follow the χ^2 distribution with $\lambda - 1$ degrees of freedom if the f_i's and the g_i's have the same distribution. Thus [2, p. 234],

$$E(\chi^2) = \lambda - 1, \text{ and} \tag{2}$$

$$\mathrm{Var}(\chi^2) = 2(\lambda - 1). \tag{3}$$

If the f_i's and the g_i's are *not* from the same distribution, we can expect that $\chi^2 \to \infty$ as $n \to \infty$.

When

$$\chi^2 > E(\chi^2) + 2\sqrt{\mathrm{Var}(\chi^2)} = \lambda - 1 + \sqrt{8(\lambda - 1)} \tag{4}$$

we may assume that the deviation is statistically significant.

Once we have enough ciphertext we will be able to determine which pins on wheel 1 are set in the same manner; that is we will have divided the pin positions into two groups, where every pin in a group is set in the same direction. Other simple techniques (see [1]) can then be used to decide which group is "left" and which "right". From there on determining the pin settings on the other wheels, etc., is relatively straightforward (see [1] for more details).

III. HOW MUCH CIPHERTEXT IS NEEDED?

Although the cryptanalytic procedure given above was published by Barker [1], no estimate was given there for the amount of ciphertext required to solve a cryptogram. The analysis given here uses only elementary techniques, and arrives at an answer which seems "reasonable" in comparison with the examples given in [1].

We first solve the following problem. Let p_i (respectively q_i) denote the probability of letter a_i occurring in the ciphertext when pin 1 (respectively pin 2) of wheel 1 is under the sensor. Then we want to know how much ciphertext is required to determine that the p_i's are different from the q_i's (assuming that they are different). The answer will of course depend on how different the two distributions are.

The distribution of f_i thus follows a binomial distribution with probability of success p_i:

$$\text{Prob } (f_i = k) = \binom{n}{k} p_i^k (1 - p_i)^{n-k} \tag{5}$$

$$E(f_i) = np_i \tag{6}$$

$$\text{Var}(f_i) = np_i(1 - p_i). \tag{7}$$

Similarly g_i follows a binomial distribution with probability q_i of success.

We assume that $p_i \approx q_i \approx 1/\lambda$ for all i in what follows. That is, we assume that each ciphertext letter will be (to a first-order approximation) equally likely; the χ^2-test will however measure the second-order effects of any differences. Using this assumption in (1) to conclude that $f_i + g_i \approx 2n/\lambda$, we obtain

$$E(\chi^2) \approx (\lambda/2n) \sum_{i=1}^{\lambda} E((f_i - g_i)^2). \tag{8}$$

Furthermore,

$$E((f_i - g_i)^2) = E(f_i^2) + 2E(g_i^2) - 2E(f_i)E(g_i) \tag{9}$$

since f_i and g_i are independent random variables. Also,

$$E(f_i^2) = \text{Var}(f_i) + (E(f_i))^2. \tag{10}$$

Combining equations (6)–(10):

$$E(\chi^2) \approx (\lambda/2n) \sum_{i=1}^{\lambda} E(n \cdot (p_i(1 - p_i) + q_i(1 - q_i)) + n^2(p_i - q_i)^2). \tag{11}$$

Using our assumption that $p_i \approx q_i \approx 1/\lambda$ to simplify the coefficient of n in (11), we obtain

$$E(\chi^2) \approx (\lambda - 1) + (\lambda n/2) \sum_{i=1}^{\lambda} E((p_i - q_i)^2). \qquad (12)$$

Note that this agrees with (2) when $p_i = q_i$ for all i; we obtain $E(\chi^2) = \lambda - 1$ as we should. When the two distributions are different the excess of χ^2 over λ increases linearly with n and with the sum of the squares of the differences in the corresponding probabilities. This completes our answer to our first problem for given probabilities p_i, q_i, since we can now calculate how large n must be for (4) to hold.

In order to use the above result we need to calculate $E((p_i - q_i)^2)$. Note that p_i and q_i are random variables; they depend on how the pins are set on wheels $2,...,w$. Once we know the distribution of p_i and q_i we can calculate $E((p_i - q_i)^2)$, since

$$E((p_i - q_i)^2) = \text{Var}(p_i - q_i) = 2\text{Var}(p_i). \qquad (13)$$

This follows since $E(p_i) = E(q_i) = 1/\lambda$, so that $E(p_i - q_i) = 0$, and since $\text{Var}(p_i - q_i) = \text{Var}(p_i) + \text{Var}(q_i)$, where $\text{Var}(p_i) = \text{Var}(q_i)$ since p_i and q_i will have the same distribution.

How is p_i determined? With pin 1 of wheel 1 in a fixed position, the other $w-1$ wheels can produce 2^{w-1} distinct sensor readings, each of which selects some monoalphabetic substitution. Since the recommended usage of the Hagelin machine is to set about half of the pins on each wheel in each direction, each of the 2^{w-1} substitution functions is equally likely to be used.

Let $\pi_1, \pi_2,...,\pi_\lambda$ denote the respective probabilities of occurrence of $a_1, a_2,...,a_\lambda$ in the plaintext. (For English military text these can be obtained from Table 1.) To determine the probability p_i of letter a_i occurring in the ciphertext when pin 1 is used, let $a_{j_1}, a_{j_2},...,a_{j_{2^{w-1}}}$ be the list of 2^{w-1} plaintext letters, the kth of which causes a_i to be produced as the ciphertext when substitution k is used. (There may be repetitions in this list.) Then,

$$p_i = (1/2^{w-1}) \sum_{k=1}^{2^{w-1}} \pi_{j_k}; \qquad (14)$$

p_i is the mean probability of the 2^{w-1} plaintext letters which can produce a_i.

Let π be a random variable which is equally likely to take any one of the values $\pi_1, \pi_2, ..., \pi_\lambda$. Then,

$$E(\pi) = 1/\lambda, \text{ and} \tag{15}$$

$$\text{Var}(\pi) = \sigma_0^2, \tag{16}$$

for some value σ_0^2. From Table 1 we have $1/\lambda = .03846$ and $\sigma_0^2 \approx .001344$.

Equation (14) says that p_i is the mean value of a sample of 2^{w-1} values of π, so that

$$E(p_i) = E(\pi) = 1/\lambda \tag{17}$$

$$\text{Var}(p_i) = \text{Var}(\pi)/2^{w-1} = \sigma_0^2/2^{w-1} \tag{18}$$

Thus, although p_i and q_i both have expected value $1/\lambda$, the underlying nonuniformity of the distribution of the plaintext ($\text{Var}(\pi) \neq 0$) will cause p_i and q_i to be samples from a distribution with non-zero variance. If pins 1 and 2 are set in the same manner, then $p_i = q_i$ is forced, but if they are set differently, we may assume that p_i and q_i are independent, so that from (13) and (18) we obtain a non-zero $E((p_i-q_i)^2)$:

$$E((p_i-q_i)^2) = 2\text{Var}(p_i) = \sigma_0^2/2^{w-1}. \tag{19}$$

Plugging this into (12) we obtain for the case that pins 1 and 2 are in different positions:

$$E(\chi^2) \approx (\lambda - 1) + ((\lambda^2\sigma_0^2)/2^{w-1}) \cdot n. \tag{20}$$

In order for this to be a significant deviation we want (4) to hold, so that

$$((\lambda^2\sigma_0^2)/2^{w-1}) \cdot n \geq 2\text{Var}(\chi^2) = \sqrt{8(\lambda - 2)}. \tag{21}$$

Since $t_1 n$ is the total amount of ciphertext required to produce n ciphertext letters enciphered under each pin of wheel 1, we can rewrite (21) as

$$\text{Amount of ciphertext} \approx (t_i 2^w \sqrt{2(\lambda - 1)})/(\lambda^2\sigma_0^2); \tag{22}$$

this amount of ciphertext should produce sufficient statistical evidence to determine all the pin settings.

Formula (22) is our main result. If we assume that we are trying to break a w-wheel Hagelin cryptogram where one of the wheels has length $t_1 = 17$, then we can calculate the amount of ciphertext required as estimated using (22) with $\lambda = 26$ and $\sigma_0^2 = .001344$:

Number of Wheels	Amount of Ciphertext
1	264 Characters
2	529 Characters
3	1058 Characters
4	2117 Characters
5	4233 Characters
6	8468 Characters

TABLE 3.

The amount of ciphertext required doubles with each additional wheel, reaching approximately 8000 characters for a six-wheel machine.

How realistic is this result? By way of comparison, Barker [1] provides a set of four six-wheel problems to be solved. Since they all have the same pin settings, they can be combined for statistical purposes into a single problem of 3245 characters. Barker also solves as an example a 4-wheel problem of 770 letters in length.

We conclude that our analysis is probably a bit conservative; our estimates may be a factor of two to four too large. While we believe our analysis to be correct, several considerations may reduce the actual amount of ciphertext required:

(1) Our assumption that the χ^2 statistic must be 2 standard deviations above its expected value in order to be considered significant is probably conservative; a cryptogram might still be easily breakable if the expected deviation in the case that the pins were set differently were only one standard deviation. This would reduce our estimates by a factor of two.

(2) There is a "snowballing" effect once several of the pin settings on a wheel have been correctly identified, since the statistics from the known settings can be combined to yield improved accuracy in the determination of the remaining settings.

(3) There may be characteristics of the Hagelin machines which we have ignored which permit more powerful statistical tests to be used. For example, it may be useful to know that if pins 1 and 2 are set in different positions, then the substitutions selected under pin 2 are all shifted by the same amount from the substitutions

selected under pin 1 (this is the "lug setting" for wheel 1). In our analysis we assume that the substitutions were all randomly selected.

We leave as open problems the precise analysis of considerations (1)–(3). Since these considerations all tend to reduce the amount of ciphertext required, our estimate of 8000 characters to break a C-48 cryptogram should be taken as an upper bound. The reader is urged to devise improved statistical techniques and analyses which would provide an improved estimate of the amount of ciphertext required.

ACKNOWLEDGEMENTS

This research was supported by NSF grant MCS76-14294 and by the Xerox Corporation.

REFERENCES

1.   Barker, W. G. (1977), *Cryptanalysis of the Hagelin Cryptograph.* Laguna Hill, CA: Aegean Park Press.
2.   Cramer, H. (1974), *Mathematical Methods of Statistics.* Princeton, NJ: Princeton University Press.

The Hagelin Cipher Machine (M-209): Reconstruction of the Internal Settings

by Robert Morris

Bell Laboratories
Murray Hill, New Jersey 07974

ABSTRACT: It is an interesting and useful cryptanalytic problem to try to reconstruct the internal settings of the M-209 cipher machine, given the text of a message which has been obtained both in clear and enciphered form. Then it is considerably easier to decipher any further messages encrypted with the same internal settings. It turns out to be possible to do this reconstruction for rather short messages, of the order of 75 characters or so. Partial or incomplete solutions are generally possible with as few as 50 characters [1,2].

The Hagelin C-48 cipher machine, also known as the M-209 Converter by the U.S. Army Signal Corps, was designed and built to encipher and decipher messages for mililtary, diplomatic, and similar purposes. This machine was in wide use in the U.S. Army for tactical purposes until the early 1950's.

The cryptograms produced by the machine consist of polyalphabetic substitutions based on a key with period of length $26 \times 25 \times 23 \times 21 \times 19 \times 17$ ($=101,405,850$). The encipherment is effected letter by letter in such a way that the key number (an element in the key sequence) for each letter of the plain text indicates a displacement in a given alphabetic sequence.

The internal operations of the machine produce a sequence of pseudo-random numbers with this long period. Much of the apparent security of the machine lies in the extraordinary length and apparent randomness of this sequence. The burden of this paper is to show that

From *Cryptologia*, Vol. 2, No. 3, July 1978.

the entire sequence of 101,405,850 outputs can generally be reconstructed from any given subsequence of 75 or more elements of it.

PHYSICAL DESCRIPTION

The machine is adequately described in Kahn [3] pp. 425–434, and the description which follows is presented primarily to establish a vocabulary for discussing its operation.

The periodic key sequence is a sequence of numbers from 0 to 27 produced by a prearranged set-up comprising:

(1) Six *key wheels* each bearing a different number of letters with no common divisor (*viz.* 26, 25, 23, 21, 19, 17). Each key wheel is rotated by one step after the encipherment of each letter. A key wheel returns to its starting position after its period. The six key wheels do not all return simultaneously to their starting positions before the period of $26 \times 25 \times 23 \times 21 \times 19 \times 17$ encipherments.

(2) A *keyword* of 6 letters which is easily changed as an external setting and is normally changed for each message and transmitted as part of the message. The letters of the keyword are engraved on the key wheels and they determine the starting position of the wheels.

(3) *Pins* on the periphery of the key wheels which may be made "active" or "inactive," each pin corresponding to a letter on one of the six key wheels. There are, in all, $26 + 25 + 23 + 21 + 19 + 17 = 131$ pins.

(4) A cylinder (called the *cage*) composed of 27 sliding bars bearing projections (called *lugs*) in one of six positions corresponding to the six key wheels. The cage rotates through an entire revolution to encipher each letter, and in doing so, each bar is engaged if a lug is present in the same position as an active pin. These bars, when engaged, serve as so many teeth on the left end of the cage and the cage itself therefore acts as a gear with a variable number of teeth.

The number of teeth thus formed determines for each enciphering operation, the *displacement number* (amount of shift in the sequence) for that operation.

The six key wheels have pins which can be active (1) or inactive (0). One pin on each key wheel is in a position to affect the encryption of the current letter. That pin will be called the *current pin* on that wheel and the set of current pins will be called *current sextuplet*. After each letter is enciphered, each of the key wheels is advanced one click and the next letter is enciphered with a new set of active and inactive pins, the new *current sextuplet*. The first wheel comes to its original position after 26 encipherings and similarly for the other five wheels with their respective periods (25, 23, 21, 19, 17). The pins on the key wheels form a changing sextuplet of 0's and 1's and the displacement is determined by this sextuplet.

The cage has twenty-seven bars and each bar is a sextuplet of 0's and 1's. The 1's are called *lugs*. Each bar has at most two lugs on it. There are then only 22 different possible lug patterns for each bar, 15 with two lugs, 6 with 1 lug and 1 with no lugs at all.

To produce a displacement (an element of the key sequence) each of the 27 bars is compared with the current sextuplet present at the wheels. If for a given bar, at least one active pin hits a lug on the bar (i.e., if the logical AND of the bar and the current wheel sextuplet is nonzero) then that bar is *engaged*. The number of bars that are engaged is the displacement for that pin pattern; it can range from 0 to 27.

This displacement is produced between the *indicator disk* of the apparatus on which the plaintext letter is entered and the *printing disk* from which the corresponding cipher letter is printed.

The cipher alphabet is the reverse of the plaintext alphabet, as

Plaintext: ABCDEFGHIJKLMNOPQRSTUVWXYZ
Cipher: ZYXWVUTSRQPONMLKJIHGFEDCBA

When the key displacement is 0, then A→Z, B→Y, and so forth. If the displacement is not zero then the two alphabets are shifted with respect to each other by the amount of the displacement. Here is the correspondence for a displacement of 5:

Plaintext: ABCDEFGHIJKLMNOPQRSTUVWXYZ
Cipher: EDCBAZYXWVUTSRQPONMLKJIHGF

Since the two alphabets are the reverse of each other, the encryption process is reciprocal (symmetric) and if a given letter (say K) is enciphered by V, then V is also enciphered by K. Therefore the operations of enciphering and deciphering are identical.

In fact, the machine has settings for deciphering and enciphering and they have the following action. When enciphering, all letters are printed and spaces are inserted so that the cipher text is broken up into 5-letter groups. When deciphering, no such space is inserted but the letter Z is not printed. Thus if Z is used as a space when enciphering (as is usually done), the output appears as normal words with word spacing but the letter Z will not be printed even within words and must be supplied from context.

The wheels have letters engraved on them, but the correspondence between these letters and the pins is irrelevant unless we wish to recover the actual literal keys that were used. They have no other cryptologic significance.

CRYPTOGRAPHIC DESCRIPTION

The machine produces a sequence of digits between 0 and 27 which is called the *key sequence* or *displacement sequence*. The plaintext alphabet is a standard alphabet and the ciphertext alphabet is a reverse standard alphabet. They coincide at $Z=A$. The elements of the key sequence cause a displacement of the ciphertext alphabet. The elements 26 and 27 cause the same output as 0,1 respectively. If the displacement is 0 then $A\rightarrow Z$, $B\rightarrow Y$, $C\rightarrow X$, etc; if the displacement is 1, then $A\rightarrow A$, $B\rightarrow Z$, $C\rightarrow Y$.

Suppose that the letters of the alphabet are given numerical values in the normal order, $A=1$, $B=2$, . . . When the key displacement has the value n, then the value y of the cipher letter resulting from the cleartext letter, whose value is z, is

$$y = 27-z+n,$$

subtracting multiples of 26 as necessary. On rearranging, we get

$$z = 27-y+n,$$

which shows that decryption is identical to encryption.

Here is an example of the encipherment produced by a key sequence:

Plain:	A	L	L	Z	I	S	Z	D	I	S	C	O	V	E	R	E	D
Key:	22	0	5	18	14	17	24	15	13	3	15	1	8	1	1	24	14
Cipher:	V	O	T	S	F	Y	Y	L	E	K	M	M	M	W	J	T	K

Since there are sixty-four possible sextuplets and only 28 displacements, some distinct sextuplets produce identical displacements. However during the encryption of a single message (i.e., if the internal settings are constant) the same sextuplet always produces the same displacement. The lug settings can be viewed as a mapping of the 64 sextuplets onto the displacements, and it is this mapping that we wish to know.

Here is a representation of a cage in the form of a set of 27 sextuplets of 0's and 1's:

1	(100000)	10	(001000)	19	(000010)
2	(100000)	11	(000100)	20	(000010)
3	(100000)	12	(000100)	21	(000010)
4	(100000)	13	(000110)	22	(000010)
5	(100000)	14	(000110)	23	(000011)
6	(100000)	15	(000010)	24	(000001)
7	(100000)	16	(000010)	25	(000001)
8	(110000)	17	(000010)	26	(000001)
9	(010010)	18	(000010)	27	(000001)

Permutations among the cage bars make no difference. Therefore the numbering of the cage bars is irrelevant. With the cage bar table shown the wheel pin sextuplet (010110) will produce the displacement 15.

One sextuplet of pins will be said to *dominate* another when it has 1's in all the positions where the other does. Then if one sextuplet dominates another, the displacement it causes is at least as great. A special case is the sextuplet (000000) which always causes the displacement 0.

The effect of having more than one lug on each bar is that the contributions of the different wheels on the displacement cannot just be added. The most we can say is that the displacement produced by active pins on two wheels is no greater than the sum of the displacements produced by each active pin individually. This *overlap* contributes considerably to the cryptographic security of the machine.

Table 1 is a graphic description of the set of wheels showing the pins as active (1) or inactive (0).

Suppose that the top pin in each position is one presented for the first encipherment operation, in other words, that the keyword used was AAAAAA. The wheels are lettered slightly differently on the actual Hagelin machine, in that the letter W is skipped on wheels 2 and 3.

We can obtain a paper-and-pencil simulation of the action of the M-209 in the following way. To produce a letter of the keying sequence, each of the 27 bars is compared with the pattern presented by the key wheels. If, for a given bar, at least one active pin hits an active lug, i.e., if both the bar and wheels share a 1 in any position, then the bar is counted as engaged. The number of engaged bars is the displacement for that pin pattern; it can range from 0 to 27. This displacement is then reduced modulo 26 and used as described above to encrypt the current letter. For the encryption of the next letter, the next pin in each column

	1	2	3	4	5	6
A	0	1	0	1	1	0
B	1	0	1	0	0	0
C	1	1	1	1	0	1
D	0	1	0	1	0	1
E	0	1	0	0	0	1
F	1	0	0	0	1	1
G	1	1	1	0	0	0
H	0	0	0	0	0	0
I	0	0	0	1	0	1
J	0	0	1	1	0	0
K	0	0	1	0	0	1
L	1	0	0	1	0	1
M	1	1	0	0	0	1
N	0	1	1	1	1	1
O	1	1	0	1	0	1
P	0	1	1	1	0	1
Q	0	0	1	0	0	0
R	1	0	0	0	0	
S	0	1	1	1	1	
T	1	0	0	1		
U	0	1	0	0		
V	1	1	0			
W	1	0	1			
X	0	1				
Y	1	0				
Z	0					

TABLE 1. TABLE OF ACTIVE AND INACTIVE PINS BY WHEELS.

is used. The last pin in any column is followed by the top pin in that column.

Table 2 is a sample encryption using the pins and lugs above, showing the active pins, the displacement, the cleartext letter, and the ciphertext letter.

pins				pins			
010110	15	A	O	011101	12	E	H
101000	9	L	X	001000	1	D	X
111101	19	L	H	100000	8		I
010101	11	Z	L	011110	16		K
010001	7	I	Y	100111	26		O
100011	24	S	F	010001	7		C
111000	10	Z	K	110101	18		M
000000	0	D	W	101001	14		O
000101	9	I	A	010100	6		F
001100	5	S	M	101110	23		W
001001	6	C	D	011001	8		I
100101	17	O	C	000000	0		L
110001	14	V	T	110001	14		A
011111	20	E	P	110001	14		L
110101	18	R	A	011101	12		H

TABLE 2. SAMPLE ENCRYPTION.

The resulting cipher message reads:

oxhly fkwam dctpa hxiko cmofw ilalh

The missing cleartext is left as an exercise for the reader.

THE CRYPTANALYTIC PROBLEM

Given a segment of cipher text and the corresponding cleartext, or some other means of determining the displacement sequence, we want to determine the settings of the cage bar lugs and the wheel pins.

It will generally be sufficient to determine the internal settings well enough that further messages using the same internal settings can be read. It is often possible to obtain such *partial solutions* even when the settings of all of the pins and lugs cannot be determined.

A Naive Approach

Arrange the key sequence in columns with period 26 and form the average of each of the 26 resulting rows. Each row represents a collection of displacements for which the corresponding pin on the 26-wheel was the same pin and thus active for all or inactive for all. If there are any lugs at all in position 1, then the average displacement will be greater for those rows in which the pin is active. With sufficiently long displacement sequences, we can immediately conclude that those pins with large displacements are active and those with small displacements are inactive. The same can be done for the other periods (wheels).

The amount of text required for this approach to supply the complete internal settings is very large indeed, in general, of the order of a thousand characters would be needed. If only a few hundred characters of the displacement sequence are available, the results of such an analysis are nearly valueless. Yet the successful method about to be described is merely the application of a set of improvements of and extensions to the fundamental and trivial observation just made.

Some Preliminaries

There are sixty-four possible pin configurations for the enciphering of a letter, and, given the cage setting, the displacement depends only on the pin configuration. There are only 28 different displacements (0–27 inclusive) and so the same displacement will be produced by several different pin configurations.

In our analysis, we will not be able to make any strong arguments that depend on any particular configuration having occurred, since with only 50 displacements, the probability that some particular configuration occurred is only about even (54%) and this probability increases to 69% with a sequence of 75 characters and to 79% with a sequence of 100 characters. None of these probabilities is very close to certainty. (I assume, as is generally true, that active and inactive pins occur with approximately equal frequencies.)

It is possible to proceed towards a solution by making inferences such as that the largest observed displacement must have been caused by a configuration with all six pins active. Although such inferences can be valuable, methods which depend entirely on chains of such inferences seem to require much longer sequences and they leave one at a loss as to how to proceed when early guesses are wrong.

There are some combinatorial facts that are used either explicitly or implicitly through the analysis:

Any ambiguous displacement which contacts an active pin in a position with at least two lugs set must be 26 or 27.

Any ambiguous displacement which contacts an inactive pin in a position with at least two unshared lugs must be 0 or 1.

When there exists a displacement smaller than the number of lugs in a position, the corresponding pin is inactive.

When there exists a displacement larger than $27 - L$, where L is the number of unshared lugs, then the corresponding pin must be active.

A Practical Solution

Suppose we have obtained, by some means, the following sequence of displacements:

```
22 *0  5 18 14 17 24 15 13  3 15 *1  8 *1 *1 24 14 15 18  2
 3 18 20 13 18  4 16 21 25 *1  4 *1 20 14 23  4 24 19 15 15
18  3 12 20  3  2 16 16 14 *1 23 18 12 18  9 11 16 23 14 16
15 15  9 *1 13  6  3  4  9 21 24 15 14 16 23
```

In this section, we will proceed from this displacement sequence, which was selected at random, and go through all the steps necessary to determine the internal settings of the machine that produced the sequence. The reader is warned that it does not make particularly good bedtime reading. It is essential to an understanding of the method to follow the example in considerable detail, preferably recreating from scratch each of the tables which are presented here only in final form. Such a reconstruction, even for an expert, requires several hours of hard work and a considerable amount of scratch paper.

Arrange the key sequence in columns with period 26 and form the average of each of the 26 positions. Do the same for periods 25, 23, 21, 19, 17. The six tableaux correspond to wheels 1, 2, ... , 6. There are 131 lines in these six tableaux and each line corresponds to one of the 131 pins. The positions with a displacement of 0 or 1 must be ignored for the moment; these have been marked above with an ∗. For each of the 131 rows, the average displacement has been computed.

pin #	wheel 1 disp's	avg.	wheel 2 disp's	avg.	wheel 3 disp's	avg.
1	22 16 12	16.7	22 4 23	16.3	22 13 16 21	18.0
2	*0 21 18	19.5	*0 16 18	17.0	*0 18 16 24	19.3
3	5 25 9	13.0	5 21 12	12.7	5 4 14 15	9.5
4	18 *1 11	14.5	18 25 18	20.3	18 16 *1 14	16.0
5	14 4 16	11.3	14 *1 9	11.5	14 21 23 16	18.5
6	17 *1 23	20.0	17 4 11	10.7	17 25 18 23	20.8
7	24 20 14	19.3	24 *1 16	20.0	24 *1 12	18.0
8	15 14 16	15.0	15 20 23	19.3	15 4 18	12.3
9	13 23 15	17.0	13 14 14	13.7	13 *1 9	11.0
10	3 4 15	7.3	3 23 16	14.0	3 20 11	11.3
11	15 24 9	16.0	15 4 15	11.3	15 14 16	15.0
12	*1 19 *1	19.0	*1 24 15	19.5	*1 23 23	23.0
13	8 15 13	12.0	8 19 9	12.0	8 4 14	8.7
14	*1 15 6	10.5	*1 15 *1	15.0	*1 24 16	20.0
15	*1 18 3	10.5	*1 15 13	14.0	*1 19 15	17.0
16	24 3 4	10.3	24 18 6	16.0	24 15 15	18.0
17	14 12 9	11.7	14 3 3	6.7	14 15 9	12.7
18	15 20 21	18.7	15 12 4	10.3	15 18 *1	16.5
19	18 3 24	15.0	18 20 9	15.7	18 3 13	11.3
20	2 2 15	6.3	2 3 21	8.7	2 12 6	6.7
21	3 16 14	11.0	3 2 24	9.7	3 20 3	8.7
22	18 16 16	16.7	18 16 15	16.3	18 3 4	8.3
23	20 14 23	19.0	20 16 14	16.7	20 2 9	10.3
24	13 *1	13.0	13 14 16	14.3		
25	18 23	20.5	18 *1 23	20.5		
26	4 18	11.0				

pin #	wheel 4 disp's	avg.	wheel 5 disp's	avg.	wheel 6 disp's	avg.
1	22 18 12 *1	17.3	22 2 15 23	15.5	22 15 23 18 9	17.4
2	*0 20 20 13	17.7	*0 3 15 14	10.7	*0 18 4 12 21	13.8
3	5 13 3 6	6.8	5 18 18 16	14.3	5 2 24 18 24	14.6
4	18 18 2 3	10.2	18 20 3 15	14.0	18 3 19 9 15	12.8
5	14 4 16 4	9.5	14 13 12 15	13.5	14 18 15 11 14	14.4
6	17 16 16 9	14.5	17 18 20 9	16.0	17 20 15 16 16	16.8
7	24 21 14 21	20.0	24 4 3 *1	10.3	24 13 18 23 23	20.2
8	15 25 *1 24	21.3	15 16 2 13	11.5	15 18 3 14	12.5
9	13 *1 23 15	17.0	13 21 16 6	14.0	13 4 12 16	11.2
10	3 4 18 14	9.8	3 25 16 3	11.8	3 16 20 15	13.5
11	15 *1 12 16	14.3	15 *1 14 4	11.0	15 21 3 15	13.5
12	*1 20 18 23	20.3	*1 4 *1 9	6.5	*1 25 2 9	12.0
13	8 14 9	10.3	8 *1 23 21	17.3	8 *1 16 *1	12.0
14	*1 23 11	17.0	*1 20 18 24	20.7	*1 4 16 13	11.0
15	*1 4 16	10.0	*1 14 12 15	13.7	*1 *1 14 6	10.0
16	24 24 23	23.7	24 23 18 14	19.8	24 20 *1 3	15.7
17	14 19 14	15.7	14 4 9 16	10.8	14 14 23 4	13.8
18	15 15 16	15.3	15 24 11 23	18.3		
19	18 15 15	16.0	18 19 16	17.7		
20	2 18 15	11.7				
21	3 3 9	5.0				

The first task is to identify that wheel (or wheels) with the greatest number of lugs set against it on the cage. At the same time, it will be helpful to resolve as soon as possible the ambiguities between 0,26 and 1,27, respectively. Remember that until the ambiguities have been resolved, these displacements (marked above with a *) will not be used in forming the averages. To this end, the tableau of averages is arranged as a bar chart for each wheel. Each x represents one appearance of approximately the average represented by its horizontal position. The averages have been rounded to the nearest integer.

```
wheel 1        X                   X
               X             X   X X
               XX XX   X   X   X X
         XX    XX XX XX XX   X X

0 2 4 6 8 10 12 14 16 18 20 22 24 26

wheel 2                    X   X
                           X   X
               XX X   X   XX   X X
               X X XX XX XX XX   X XX

0 2 4 6 8 10 12 14 16 18 20 22 24 26

wheel 3                       X
                  X           X
               X XX       X X
               XXX XX XX   X XX XX XX   X

0 2 4 6 8 10 12 14 16 18 20 22 24 26

wheel 4        X
               X             X
               X       X   XX   X
         X X X X   X   XX XX X   XX       X

0 2 4 6 8 10 12 14 16 18 20 22 24 26

wheel 5                    X
                  X        X
                  X X   X        X
         X    XX XX XX XX XX X XX

0 2 4 6 8 10 12 14 16 1820   22 24 26

wheel 6           XX X
               X XX X     X
               XX XX XX XX       X

0 2 4 6 8 10 12 14 16 18 20 22 24 26
```

If the displacement sequence were much longer, then the distribution of the x's in these bar charts would be distinctly bimodal (it would have two peaks). Moreover, the tendency to bimodality is strongest for those positions with the most lugs. The reason for the bimodal distribution runs as follows: each x that corresponds to an inactive pin just reflects the average displacement contributed by the other positions; each x that corresponds to an active pin reflects that average plus the contribution from the wheel it is on. We are here dealing with a sequence so short that the problem is only barely solvable and the tendency to bimodal distributions has entirely disappeared for the positions with few lugs set. We must work with the positions with the most lugs set since the disturbance produced by other positions is then rather small. Typically a displacement sequence longer than about 100 elements is enough to permit easy identification of the position that has the most lugs set and of the setting of essentially all of the pins on that wheel.

The distance between the two peaks in the bimodal distribution is equal to or very slightly less than the number of lugs set in the position. It turns out empirically that if the position being considered has at least one third of the total number of lugs, then about two complete periods of the displacement sequence are enough to be able to guess about one half of the pins in that position with considerable confidence. That amounts to 52 displacements in position 1 and 34 displacements in position 6. With four complete periods of the displacement sequence, essentially all of the pins can be guessed with great confidence.

Glancing at the six distributions, it seems that wheels 3 and 4 have the greatest tendency to bimodality and it is reasonably safe to assume that one of these two positions has the greatest number of lugs set. In fact this guess need not be accurate and we will not need to backtrack provided only that the selected position has more than an average number of lugs set against it. Seldom will this initial guess lead us astray.

Thus we will begin work with position 4 and we will assume for the moment that position 4 has more than 6 lugs because the two peaks are 7 apart. And so if any individual displacement in position 4 is less than 7, we suppose with great confidence that the corresponding pin must be inactive. The conclusion that a very large individual displacement implies that the corresponding pin is set is a weaker conclusion because many lugs may be shared with other positions.

Yet we will still guess that pins with large *average* displacement are active and pins with small *average* displacement are inactive. Since the two distributions are not clearly separated, we had better make the guesses for only some of the pins to reduce the number of wrong choices. Experience has shown that trying to guess about two-thirds of the pins based on average displacement will on the one hand provide enough information to continue the analysis and on the other hand will result in few, if any, errors.

On the basis of average displacement, we can guess that

pins 1, 2, 7, 8, 9, 12, 14, 16 are active

pins 3, 4, 5, 10, 13, 15, 21 are inactive

Inspecting those rows that have displacements less than 7, we can make the additional conclusion that pin 20 is inactive.

Given that pin 15 is inactive, it is likely that displacement #15 is 1 and we so assume. It could equal 27 only if position 4 had no unshared lugs and would even then be unlikely. Of the remaining ambiguous displacements, all but one correspond to active pins and we can say with certainty that these are displacements of 26 or 27 rather than 0 or 1, assuming, of course, that the assignment of active and inactive pins is correct. The only remaining ambiguous displacement is #32. At this point, the averages can be revised to reflect these assignments.

It is not clear whether we should try to make more guesses or to go to the next step since there will be the devil to pay if we make any wrong guesses so early in the game. But on the other hand we have scant information to go on. It turns out that continuing to the next step is profitable and no more guesses are needed in this stage.

The assumptions so far lead to this assignment of active pins

4   11000x1110x10101xxx00

where "x" stands for a pin that has not received a value.

The next step is to try to remove, to the extent possible, the effect of the pins on wheel 4 on the displacements caused by pins on the other wheels. For instance, if we choose only those displacements for which wheel 4 has an inactive pin, and inspect the other wheels, we will be looking at results without the extraneous effects of wheel 4. We can then try to select the remaining wheel with the most lugs set against it. If we proceed in this way, we have only half the data to work with. We could consider separately the displacements for which the pin on wheel 4 is active and get separate but confirming evidence. As we are working with nearly the minimum data for which any solution is possible, we will get little comfort from this approach.

Let us rather try to merge the two sets of data. We do this by trying to infer what the displacements would have been if all of the pins on wheel 4 had been inactive. We take the set of displacements for which a pin on wheel 4 is inactive (call it S_0) and the set of displacements for which a pin on wheel 4 is active (call it S_1). Arrange the numbers in the two sets of displacements in order like this

1 2 2 3 3 3 3 3 4 4 4 4 5 6 8 9 9 13 14 14 14 15 16 16 18 18 18 18
11 12 13 13 14 15 15 18 18 20 20 20 21 21 22 23 23 23 23 24 24 24 24
25 26 27 27 27 27 27

We set up a correspondence of each displacement in S_1 with one in S_0. If there are n elements in one of the sets and we are looking at the ath element in it, we say that its *relative rank* in the set is the quotient a/n. The correspondent of each displacement in S_1 is the element of S_0 whose relative rank is closest to it. Although this is the proper way to do the job, generally a linear correspondence is much easier and will suffice unless we get into deep trouble.

In this case, the elements in S_1 range from 1 to 18 and those in S_0 from 11 to 27. We know, however, that the respective ranges are in fact 0 to 18 and 11 to 27. A quick way to set up the correspondence and to merge the two sets of data is to subtract 10 from every displacement for which we know that a pin on wheel 4 was active. It is pure luck that in this case a mere subtraction happened to be appropriate. In general we need a relation of the form $y = ax + b$ for some constants a and b. In this case, a happened to be equal to 1. The displacements for which we know a pin was inactive keep the same value. Those displacements for which we did not make a guess are ignored for the moment. No great accuracy is required in this process because in what follows we are still looking for the twin peaks of a bimodal distribution and if we are on the right track, an error of 1 or 2 will make no difference at all.

We can estimate now that position 4 has approximately 11 lugs because the minimum displacement we found for an active pin is 11 and it is likely that this displacement was produced by inactive pins in all the other positions. We can further estimate that 9 of these pins are unshared because the maximum displacement that we found for an inactive pin was $18 = 27 - 9$ and this maximum displacement was likely produced by active pins in all of the other positions. These estimates are not needed now, but they supply some comforting evidence that we are on the right track.

The proper way to have made the correspondence gives slightly different results, but the difference doesn't matter. We then inspect the pins on the other five wheels in order to discover which remaining position has the most lugs set, to resolve more ambiguous displacements, and to guess some of the active and inactive pins on another wheel.

Here is the display of reduced displacements. The (.) entries are places where the setting of the corresponding pin on wheel 4 is as yet unknown.

wheel 1			*wheel 2*			*wheel 3*			*wheel 5*			*wheel 6*		
12	.	.	12	4	13	12	13 16	11	12	2	. 13	12	. 13 18	.
16	11	8	16	.	18	16	18	. 14	16	3	. .	16	. 4	. 11
5	15	9	5	11	.	5	4	4 5	5	8 18	.	5	2 14	8 14
18	17	1	18	15	8	18	. 17	14	18	10	3 .	18	3	. 9 5
14	4	16	14	17	9	14	11 13	.	14	13	2 15	14	8	. 1 14
.	.	13	.	4	1	.	15 18	13	.	18 10	9	.	10	. 16 .
14	10	.	14	.	16	14	17	.	14	4	3 17	14	13 18	13 13
5	14	.	5	10	13	5	4	8	5	.	2 3	5	18	3 .
3	13	.	3	14	.	3	.	9	3	11 16	6	3	4	2 .
3	4	15	3	13	.	3	10	1	3	15	. 3	3	. 10	.
.	14	9	.	4	.	.	14	16	.	17	4 4	.	11	3 15
17	.	17	17	14	15	17	13	13	17	4 17	.	17	15	2 9
8	.	3	8	.	9	8	4	.	8	.	13 11	8	17	16 17
17	.	6	17	.	17	17	14	.	17	10 18	14	17	4	. 3
1	18	3	1	.	3	1	.	.	1	14	. 5	1	. 4	6
14	3	4	14	18	6	14	.	15	14	13	8 14	14	10 17	3
.	2	.	.	3	3	.	.	9	.	4	9 .	.	14 13	4
.	10	11	.	2	4	.	18	17	.	14	1 13			
.	3	14	.	10	.	.	3	3	.	. 16				
2	2	5	2	3	11	2	2	6						
3	16	14	3	2	14	3	10	3						
8	.	.	8	16	5	8	3	4						
10	4	13	10	.	14	10	2	.						
13	17		13	4	.									
18	13		18	17	13									
4	18													

We can form the row averages in this tableau as was done before and prepare five bar charts for these remaining wheels. We see immediately from these bar charts (which are not shown) that the most promising position is position 3. The distribution of the averages on this wheel is clearly bimodal, they have the greatest dispersion, and as confirming evidence, the variance within rows is very small indeed, as if most of the lugs were accounted for by wheels 3 and 4. Here is the bar chart for position 3 with those pins omitted for which only one reduced displacement is known.

```
wheel 3
       x
      x x              x x
     x  x x           x  x x  x
     x x x x          x  x x  x x
─────────────────────────────────────
  0  2  4  6  8 10 12 14 16 18 20 22 24 26
```

The dispersion and bimodality of the reduced displacement on wheel 3 are so great that we can confidently specify the state of almost all of the pins on it. Let us try to do so for every row that has at least 2 entries. Here is the assignment of active pins on wheel 3.

3   11011110001101x1x100000

At the same time, we can resolve the last ambiguous displacement, namely that displacement #32 is 1.

This in turn determines that pin 11 on wheel 4 is active. Now as we derive this new information, we have to amend the previous tables not only to make further inferences, but also to make sure that no conflicts arise. We now have the following pin assignments on wheels 3 and 4.

3   11011110001101x1x100000
4   11000x1110010101xxx00

Now that we have made most of the pin assignments on wheel 3, we are done with the reduced displacements and we are ready to go to the next step.

We now write down the original displacement sequence along with the assignments we have made in positions 3 and 4.

22 11	24 11	4 00	2 00	15 ..
26 11	14 ..	1 00	16 10	15 10
5 00	15 1.	20 01	16 1.	9 .0
18 10	18 0.	14 10	14 01	27 11
14 10	2 00	23 11	27 11	13 01
17 1.	3 00	4 00	23 11	6 00
24 11	18 01	24 11	18 10	3 00
15 01	20 01	19 ..	12 10	4 00
13 01	13 10	15 1.	18 01	9 0.
3 00	18 10	15 ..	9 00	21 11
15 10	4 00	18 10	11 01	24 11
27 11	16 1.	3 00	16 10	15 01
8 00	21 11	12 01	23 11	14 10
27 11	25 11	20 01	14 0.	16 10
1 .0	27 11	3 00	16 1.	23 11

For all those displacements for which we have the pin assignment in positions 3 and 4, we make scatter diagrams of a new sort showing the range of individual displacements for each of the four possible configurations of active and inactive pins on the two wheels. The table for "01," for example, refers to the displacements for which the pin on wheel 3 is inactive and the pin on wheel 4 is active. Each x represents a displacement equal to the number represented by its horizontal position.

```
00  x
    x x
    x x
    x x x
 x x x x x x  x x
 _____
 0  2  4  6  8  10 12 14 16 18 20 22 24 26
```

```
01                          x
             x    x    x  x
          x  x x  x x     x  x
 _____
 0  2  4  6  8 10  12   14   16 18 20  22 24 26
```

```
10                      x
             x  x   x
             x x  x   x
          x x  x x  x    x
 _____
 0  2  4  6  8 10 12  14  16 18 20 22 24 26
```

11

```
                          X
            X X    X
            X X    X
        X   X X    X
        X  XX XX  XX
_____
0 2 4 6 8 10 12 14 16 18 20 22 24 26
```

Now we have a self-consistent assignment of pins on the two wheels. The lack of any outlying points on these scatter diagrams is a strong indication that we have made no errors so far. We can already estimate that there are approximately 9 bars that are not accounted for in these two positions by observing that the maximum displacement in the "00" table is equal to 9. Position 3 has approximately 12 lugs set, of which about 7 are unshared. Position 4 has approximately 11 lugs, of which about 9 are unshared. These estimates are made by simple inspection of the scatter diagrams; the number of lugs is probably the minimum displacement that occurs when the wheel has an active pin; the number of unshared lugs is probably the maximum displacement that occurs when the wheel has an inactive pin. Not only are these interesting facts in themselves, but (if true) they seem to justify the earlier assignments. Indeed this is circular reasoning, but we have at least made a large number of tentative assignments with no conflicts.

By comparison of the two preceding tables, we can make reasonable inferences of the pin assignments for displacements #6, 15, 18, 19, 27, 39, 48, 59, 60, 63, 69. Displacement #6 is either a type 10 or a type 11 and if we try to fit a displacement of 17 into the scatter table, it fits in the 10-table but not in the 11-table. And so on for the rest of them.

The crucial step is to fill in these pin assignments in the remaining places in the table. Not only do they make a consistent pattern but they permit us to make a complete assignment of the pins in positions 3 and 4. The scatter diagrams should be filled in; when they are, the new entries all fall within the range of the old. The complete assignment on wheels 3 and 4 is

3   110111100011010101001000000
4   1100001110010101101010100

It is a bit unusual to get a complete assignment of pins at any stage in the process. This results from the fact that each of these positions has more lugs than the total number of lugs of the other four positions put together. If the lugs were more evenly spread, we would undoubtedly have a very partial solution for the pins at this point, but on the other hand, the overall problem would be no harder to solve. The next step is again to form reduced displacements in order to discount the combined effect of positions 3 and 4. Strictly, we should use the relative rank to reduce the displacements, but it will suffice that we can merge the data by subtracting 11 from each displacement that has a pin set on one of the two wheels, and subtracting 20 from the displacements which have pins set on both of the wheels.

Having done this, we inspect the pins on the other four wheels using the new reduced displacements.

wheel 1	wheel 2	wheel 5	wheel 6
2 5 1	2 4 3	2 2 4 3	2 4 3 7 9
6 1 7	6 5 7	6 3 4 3	6 7 4 1 1
5 5 9	5 1 1	5 7 7 5	5 2 4 7 4
7 7 0	7 5 7	7 9 3 4	7 3 8 9 4
3 4 5	3 7 9	3 2 1 4	3 7 4 0 3
6 1 3	6 4 0	6 7 9 9	6 9 4 5 5
4 9 3	4 1 5	4 4 3 7	4 2 7 3 3
4 3 5	4 9 3	4 5 2 2	4 7 3 3
2 3 4	2 3 3	2 1 5 6	2 4 1 5
3 4 4	3 3 5	3 5 5 3	3 5 9 4
4 4 9	4 4 4	4 7 3 4	4 1 3 4
7 8 7	7 4 4	7 4 7 9	7 5 2 9
8 4 2	8 8 9	8 1 3 1	8 7 5 7
7 4 6	7 4 7	7 9 7 4	7 4 5 2
1 7 3	1 4 2	1 3 1 4	1 1 3 6
4 3 4	4 7 6	4 3 7 3	4 9 7 3
3 1 9	3 3 3	3 4 9 5	3 3 3 4
4 9 1	4 1 4	4 4 0 3	
7 3 4	7 9 9	7 8 5	
2 2 4	2 3 1		
3 5 3	3 2 4		
7 5 5	7 5 4		
9 3 3	9 5 3		
2 7	2 3 5		
7 3	7 7 3		
4 7			

Either by inspection or by making a scatter table of the averages of these lines, we can see that the nicest looking positions are 2 and 5, with wheel 2 having somewhat greater dispersion and more pronounced bimodality.

When we look at the table for the four wheels we also see that the rows of the wheel-1 table and the wheel-6 tables are chaotic, with both very high and very low reduced displacements on individual pins. This shows that the wheel involved has not accounted for the majority of the remaining lugs. Wheels 2 and 5 are considerably better in this respect, with wheel 2 slightly better than wheel 5. We can proceed now to try to work on wheel 2; if this fails to work, we know that it is reasonable to backtrack and work on position 5 instead.

Given the deep gap in the scatter diagram of the new row averages for wheel 2, we could make virtually all the pin assignments right now, but it would be better to make [for example,] two thirds of them. Then we will be able to proceed with much less chance of backtracking. The assignments are

pins 2, 4, 5, 13, 14, 16, 19, 23, 25 are active
pins 1, 3, 6, 7, 9, 15, 17, 18, 20, 21, 24 are inactive

and we have the following pin assignment for position 2:

2   0101100x0xxx110100100x101

Now we go back to the original displacements and the pin settings determined so far on positions 2, 3, and 4:

22 011	24 111	4 000	2 000	15 .01
26 111	14 001	1 000	16 .10	15 .10
5 000	15 010	20 .01	16 110	9 100
18 110	18 101	14 010	14 001	27 111
14 110	2 000	23 .11	27 111	13 001
17 010	3 000	4 .00	23 011	6 100
24 011	18 .01	24 .11	18 110	3 000
15 .01	20 101	19 101	12 010	4 000
13 001	13 010	15 110	18 101	9 100
3 .00	18 110	15 001	9 100	21 011
15 .10	4 000	18 110	11 001	24 011
27 .11	16 110	3 000	16 010	15 .01
8 100	21 011	12 001	23 .11	14 110
27 111	25 111	20 101	14 001	16 010
1 000	27 111	3 000	16 .10	23 111

We now look at how the displacements are distributed among the eight different arrangements of the pins on these three wheels simply by copying the data out of the table above in the following form, which shows first the pin arrangement, and then the list of displacements which occur for that arrangement.

```
000   5 1 2 3 4 4 1 3 3 2 3 4
001   13 14 15 12 14 11 14 13
010   17 15 13 14 12 16 16
011   22 24 21 23 21 24
100   8 9 9 6 9
101   18 20 19 20 18
110   18 14 18 16 15 18 16 18 14
111   26 27 24 25 27 27 27 23
```

From these two tables, we could safely determine the pin settings for displacements #10, #12, #22, #33. The remaining pins cannot be assigned with any degree of confidence. In fact, we have enough information that we can afford to ignore the whole thing and simply proceed with the information we have without making use of these assignments. Notice that we can make reasonably accurate guesses as to the number of lugs in each of the three positions.

We form reduced displacements again and display them in the usual way:

wheel 1	wheel 5	wheel 6
2 3 0	2 2 2 .	2 3 . 5 4
4 1 3	4 3 5 4	4 3 . 0 1
5 3 4	5 . 5 .	5 2 . 3 4
5 5 1	5 5 3 .	5 3 4 4 .
1 4 4	1 1 2 .	1 . 2 1 1
5 1 .	5 5 5 4	5 5 5 4 4
4 . 4	4 4 3 5	4 1 5 . 1
3 . .	3 1 . 1	3 4 2 .
3 2 3	3 1 3 1	3 5 . 5
5 5 1	5 . 5 4	5 4 3 3
1 5 3	1 2 0 .	1 1 4 1
2 3 4	2 . 3 1	2 . 5 3
4 2 4	4 . 4 4	4 2 3 4
3 5 1	3 . 1 1	
3 3 4	3 4 4	
2 2 .		
3 . 1		
5 4 1		
1 5		
5 3		
4 5		

It doesn't take any scatter diagram to see that wheel 5 is next. (A fact we knew even at the previous step!) Here is the pin assignment for position 5, as usual not trying to assign more than about two thirds of the pins:

5   0111011xxx11x10x1xx

Again we display the displacements and the current settings of pins on wheels 2, 3, 4, and 5:

22 0110	24 111 .	4 0001	2 000	15 .011
26 1111	14 0011	1 000 .	16 .10 .	15 .100
5 0001	15 010 .	20 .011	16 110 .	9 1001
18 1101	18 101 .	14 0100	14 0011	27 1111
14 1100	2 0000	23 .11 .	27 1111	13 001 .
17 0101	3 0001	4 .001	23 011 .	6 100 .
24 0111	18 .011	24 .11 .	18 1101	3 000 .
15 .01 .	20 1011	19 101 .	12 0100	4 0001
13 001 .	13 0100	15 1100	18 101 .	9 1001
3 .00 .	18 1101	15 0011	9 1001	21 011 .
15 .101	4 0001	18 1101	11 001 .	24 0111
27 .111	16 111 .	3 0001	16 010 .	15 .010
8 100 .	21 011 .	12 0010	23 .110	14 110 .
27 1111	25 111 .	20 1011	14 0011	16 0101
1 0000	27 1111	3 0001	16 .101	23 111 .

and here is the distribution of these displacements among the 16 possible settings of the pins on wheels 2, 3, 4, and 5:

0000	1 2	1000		
0001	5 3 4 4 3 3 4	1001	9 9 9	
0010	12	1010		
0011	14 15 14 14	1011	20 20	
0100	13 14 12	1100	14 15	
0101	17 16	1101	18 18 18 18	
0110	22	1110		
0111	24 24	1111	26 27 27 27 27	

Apparently wheel 5 has 3 lugs set. Of the remaining two positions, one has only one lug set and the other no more than two lugs. The total effect of these remaining positions cannot exceed 3 and is in fact probably 2. This makes it rather easy to make further pin assignments on wheels 2, 3, 4, and 5.

We can fill in the pin assignments for the following numbers:

22 32 33 36 46 56 57 61 73 75

When we fill in the resulting pin assignments where they go in the table, we can settle the pin settings on these four wheels for almost all of the remaining displacements.

We get the following assignment of pin settings for positions 2, 3, 4, and 5:

2   0101100100011101001001101
3   110111100011010101000000
4   11000011100101010110100
5   01110110xx110100101

By going through the (by now) usual process of finding reduced displacements to remove the effect of wheels 2, 3, 4, and 5, we soon find (details omitted) that it is wheel 6 that has most of the remaining lugs set. We can also in the process make the following assignment of active pins on wheel 6.

6   101001x0x101x1x1x

Here is the table of displacements and pin assignments on wheels 2–6:

22 01101	24 11101	4 00011	2 00001	15 00111
26 11110	14 0011.	1 0000.	16 110..	15 11000
5 00011	15 01001	20 10111	16 110.1	9 10011
18 11010	18 10110	14 0100.	14 0011.	27 1111.
14 11000	2 00001	23 01101	27 11111	13 00101
17 01011	3 00010	4 00010	23 0110.	6 100..
24 0111.	18 10110	24 11101	18 11011	3 000.1
15 10100	20 10111	19 10110	12 01000	4 0001.
13 001..	13 0100.	15 11000	18 10101	9 10011
3 000.1	18 11010	15 00111	9 10010	21 01100
15 01010	4 0001.	18 1101.	11 00100	24 01111
27 11111	16 11001	3 00010	16 01011	15 10100
8 1000.	21 011.0	12 0010.	23 1110.	14 11000
27 11111	25 111.1	20 10111	14 00110	16 01011
1 0000.	27 1111.	3 00010	16 0101.	23 1110.

and the distribution of the displacements for the thirty-two possible arrangements of active pins on wheels 2–6:

00000	01000 12	10000	11000 14 15 15 14
00001 2 2	01001 15	10001	11001 16
00010 3 4 3 3	01010 15	10010 9	11010 18 18
00011 5 4	01011 17 16 16	10011 9 9	11011 18
00100 11	01100 21	10100 15 15	11100
00101 13	01101 22 23	10101 18	11101 24 24
00110 14	01110	10110 18 18 19	11110 26
00111 15 15	01111 24	10111 20 20 20	11111 27 27 27

Since there is only one remaining position, there can be at most two different displacements for each pin assignment in the table above. If there are two different displacements for a pin assignment, the larger represents a displacement for which the pin on wheel 1 is active and the smaller a displacement for which the pin on wheel 1 is inactive.

Since the remaining position has only one lug set, the two different displacements for a pin assignment cannot differ by more than one.

With this information, we can readily discover the pin assignments for displacements #10, #24, #28, and #34. This is enough to determine the settings of all the pins on wheels 2, 3, 4, 5, and 6.

Here again is the table of displacements and pin assignments on wheels 2-6 after all assignments have been made:

22 01101	24 11101	4 00011	2 00001	15 00111
26 11110	14 00111	1 00000	16 11001	15 11000
5 00011	15 01001	20 10111	16 11001	9 10011
18 11010	18 10110	14 01001	14 00110	27 11111
14 11000	2 00001	23 01101	27 11111	13 00101
17 01011	3 00010	4 00010	23 01101	6 10000
24 01110	18 10110	24 11101	18 11011	3 00001
15 10100	20 10111	19 10110	12 01000	4 00011
13 00101	13 01000	15 11000	18 10101	9 10011
3 00001	18 11010	15 00111	9 10010	21 01100
15 01010	4 00011	18 11010	11 00100	24 01111
27 11111	16 11001	3 00010	16 01011	15 10100
8 10001	21 01100	12 00101	23 11100	14 11000
27 11111	25 11101	20 10111	14 00110	16 01011
1 00000	27 11111	3 00010	16 01011	23 11100

and again the distribution of the displacements for the thirty-two possible arrangements of active pins on wheels 2–6. Duplicates have been omitted.

00000	1	01000	12 13	10000	6	11000	14 15
00001	2 3	01001	14 15	10001	8	11001	16
00010	3 4	01010	15	10010	9	11010	18
00011	4 5	01011	16 17	10011	9	11011	18
00100	11	01100	21	10100	15	11100	23
00101	12 13	01101	22 23	10101	18	11101	24 25
00110	14	01110	24	10110	18 19	11110	26
00111	14 15	01111	24	10111	20	11111	27

From this table, we can assign settings to pins on wheel 1 in the following way. Displacement #1 = 22 has pin settings 01101 and that pin setting in turn produces displacements equal to both 22 and 23. Therefore displacement #1 has an inactive pin on wheel 1. If we continue in this vein, we obtain the settings of all but four pins on wheel 1 and these settings are

1   0x1x01x011011110010000x110

Here is the table of assignment of lugs on the bars to positions, presented in the form of sextuplets:

(100000)	(001000)	(000100)
(010000)	(001000)	(000100)
(010000)	(001000)	(000100)
(011000)	(001000)	(000100)
(011000)	(001100)	(000100)
(011000)	(001100)	(000010)
(001000)	(000100)	(000010)
(001000)	(000100)	(000011)
(001000)	(000100)	(000001)

and here is the table of active and inactive pins for all positions:

1   01110110110111100100001110
2   01011001000111010010011101
3   11011110001101010100000
4   110000111001010110100
5   0111011000110100101
6   10100100110111011

The reconstruction of the internal settings is complete.

PARTIAL SOLUTIONS

It is seldom possible, even theoretically, to reconstruct the internal settings completely from a displacement sequence of fewer than about 60 characters. In general, such a short sequence will not completely determine the internal settings. In other words, many different internal settings can give rise to the same displacement sequence if the sequence is very short.

Even if a complete solution cannot be obtained, it is often possible to obtain a partial solution which is close to the actual solution. A few mis-set pins will cause occasional garbled characters. A few misplaced lugs will cause small errors in the displacements at more frequent intervals. Such partial solutions can be made complete when further information becomes available.

PRACTICAL APPLICATIONS

The source material for cryptanalysis consists almost entirely of radio intercepts. It is to be expected that under tactical conditions, the error rates will be rather high. Moderate error rates (say 5%) do little harm to the intelligibility of a message to the intended recipient, but they make life considerably more difficult for the cryptanalyst. On the other hand, experience has shown that even the best run signal establishment will make occasional blunders which result in the enemy obtaining both cleartext and ciphertext of the same message or the ciphertext of the same message encrypted with different keys or with different systems. This may seem like unexpected gravy, but in fact it is the lifeblood of cryptanalysis.

Although it would be possible to conceal the starting key and thus make it more difficult to read all of the messages sent with the same internal settings, apparently no great attempt was ever made to do this. And therefore, a reconstruction generally made all traffic sent with the same internal settings immediately available to the enemy with no further analytic work.

Many (and perhaps most) establishments that used the M-209 found it necessary to supply guidelines for selecting internal settings. It can hardly be imagined that these guidelines would remain secret from the enemy and they could be very useful. One actual practice was to choose active and inactive pins essentially by a coin-tossing process, but runs of more than five active or five inactive pins on the same wheel were forbidden. The lugs were set with the following notable constraint. The lug settings were to be made so that every displacement 0–27 was possible for some configuration of the pins. The remarkable and very useful result of this constraint was that some position *had to have* exactly one lug in it. Another position had to have either one or two, and so forth. This constraint also implies that some position had to have at least seven lugs. This kind of information, when available, would make life much more comfortable for the cryptanalyst.

The only further observation that we need to make is that the lug in position 1 is not shared. Since the pin configuration (11101) produces two different displacements, the lug in position 1 is not shared with any of positions 2, 3, 4 or 6. Since the pin configuration (00010) produces two different displacements, the lug in position 1 is not shared with position 5. Therefore the contribution from position 1 is simply additive; if it is set, the displacement is increased by 1, regardless of the rest of the configuration.

We can now settle the setting of all remaining pins and obtain the complete pin assignment for the given displacement sequence.

22 001101	24 011101	4 000011	2 000001	15 100111
26 111110	14 000111	1 100000	16 011001	15 111000
5 100011	15 101001	20 110111	16 011001	9 010011
18 111010	18 010110	14 001001	14 100110	27 111111
14 011000	2 000001	23 101101	27 111111	13 100101
17 101011	3 000010	4 100010	23 101101	6 110000
24 101110	18 010110	24 011101	18 011011	3 100001
15 010100	20 110111	19 110110	12 001000	4 000011
13 100101	13 101000	15 111000	18 110101	9 010011
3 100001	18 111010	15 100111	9 110010	21 101100
15 001010	4 000011	18 111010	11 100100	24 001111
27 111111	16 011001	3 000010	16 001011	15 010100
8 110001	21 101100	12 000101	23 111100	14 011000
27 111111	25 111101	20 110111	14 100110	16 001011
1 100000	27 111111	3 000010	16 001011	23 111100

We can now go through the last table, taking out the effect of position 1 precisely and develop a table of displacements produced by each of the pin configurations that we have evidence for. We need not display that part of the table for which wheel 1 has an active pin.

000000	0	001000	12	010000	5	011000	14
000001	2	001001	14	010001	7	011001	16
000010	3	001010	15	010010		011010	17
000011	4	001011	16	010011	9	011011	18
000100		001100	20	010100	15	011100	22
000101	12	001101	22	010101		011101	24
000110		001110		010110	18	011110	
000111	14	001111	24	010111	19	011111	26

We can read off the following information from this table:

Since (010000) → 5, position 2 has 5 lugs
Since (001000) → 12, position 3 has 12 lugs
Since (000010) → 3, position 5 has 3 lugs
Since (000001) → 2, position 6 has 2 lugs
Since (000011) → 4, positions 5 and 6 share one lug. Because (011100) → 22 and (011111) → 26, positions 5 and 6 share no lugs with any other positions.

Therefore the effect of positions 5 and 6 is separable from the effect of the other positions as follows:

if neither is set +0
if only position 6 is set +2
if only position 5 is set +3
if both positions 5 and 6 are set +4

We can now use this information to fill in the rest of the table.

Now that we know the settings of all of the pins and the displacements caused by the 64 possible pin arrangements, the cryptographic problem is completed. It is nearly an afterthought to determine the arrangement of lugs on the cage bars. Here is the information that is needed:

position 4 has 10 lugs set
positions 2 and 3 share 3 lugs
positions 3 and 4 share 2 lugs

DISCUSSION OF THE METHOD

The methods used in the reconstruction are mainly statistical and not algebraic in nature. It is indeed possible to use algebraic techniques, but some guesswork is always necessary and the algebraic methods do not work well in the presence of bad guesses. These statistical methods seem to survive bad guesses and what is more important, errors such as would be encountered in real-life situations. It would be too much to expect that even if the plaintext and the ciphertext of the same message were obtained, that they would be free of errors of transmission and transcription.

The method seems to work easily and without fail for displacement sequences of length 100 or more. Seldom is any backtracking needed and the solution goes forward rapidly. The method seems to be rather difficult for sequences of length less than 75. Considerable backtracking and revision of previous guesses is needed and the solution is very time-consuming.

Here are the crucial steps in the analysis. At each stage, we identify which of the remaining positions has the most lugs. In that position, we guess the setting of as many pins as can be done with small chance of error. Then the collection of displacements corresponding to active pins are modified so that the effect of the active pins is removed as precisely as possible. The new collection of reduced displacements is used both to fill in any unassigned pin settings from previous stages and to identify the next position to be treated.

It seems to be advisable when using this reconstruction method to make as few guesses as possible while still being able to progress from step to step. Ordinarily the results of a later step confirm the guesses of an earlier step and make it possible to fill in settings that were doubtful earlier. Wrong guesses early in the reconstruction (i.e., in important positions) almost always lead to chaos so soon that little time is lost. Wrong guesses late in the reconstruction (i.e., in less important positions) seldom do any harm and are usually found at the end.

As the solution proceeds, the emphasis gradually shifts from statistical reasoning to combinatorial reasoning. The methods suggested for computing reduced displacements are essentially useless by the fifth wheel, but by then the solution is easy to complete by combinatorial reasoning.

SOME PROBLEMS IN RECONSTRUCTION

(1) Suppose that you have obtained by surreptitious means, the following sequence of characters and that you have been assured by your informant that they resulted from encipherment of a series of *a*'s using this week's M-209 settings.

whzmv mmpqi dkapa btqdx   cjxac   vmohu ambac iktyo
qvjha jcooo aiwau ugmto   mqowa indmw hqqmm tlumx
adqud ihvwl kugpo mhwam

You should find it possible to reconstruct the internal settings for this week from the resulting displacement sequence (which begins 23 8 . . .). Notice that only a partial solution is possible and two of the pins cannot be determined from the information given.

(2) The following sequence, obtained in the same way, comes from a machine with internal settings quite different from the previous:

squsu lpvjn vxjit wxvsu tuoum qsrvj ueovt yupmu
xxsmt sngjw vvstt oqtto qxqws gqusr ptxuo vwqqt
wjoor oovlw

(3) Here is a problem considerably closer to a real-life situation. On the front cover of the New York Times Magazine of May 16, 1976, David Kahn published the cryptogram:

kzwxo yax?f opxjh e?pmj nekai
xeu?j wxllb nbolq hylna op?ut
zwsp? gsjft vagla qabxa w?t?z
?p?jo h

where the question marks are characters that were totally illegible. There were other characters which were doubtful. Kahn claimed that this was an M-209 encipherment of the message:

"N.S.A. is America's phantom ear.
And sometimes it has eavesdropped on the wrong things."

If you suppose that Kahn used "z" for blank and that punctuation is omitted, the numbers of characters in the plaintext and ciphertext match. You have to use your judgement as to whether you believe that Kahn made no errors in enciphering the text! It is possible to obtain almost all of the internal settings that Kahn used, but it is a very difficult task to come anywhere near a complete solution.

(4)   You have received the following intercept of a radio message:

fhdgej xazty bkhcd qsbcq uneiq xmwjl ndrxm huyit
framb bidfk yvwxy wcuqn rhhms

There is good reason to believe that the message contains the cleartext fragment:

"rmation contradicts idea that german concentration"

which was found on a charred fragment of paper in a garbage dump just outside of Homs, Libya on the day after the intercept. As a result of statistical tests, the staff statistician has informed you that the message was very likely enciphered with an M-209 and that the alignment between them is

fhdgej xazty bkhcd qsbcq uneiq
           rm ation zcont

and so forth.

You should be able to get a partial soltuion that determines all but a few pins on the four most important wheels. You can use the given cleartext to check and complete the solution if necessary. Suppose further that the first group is the keyword. Decipher the following message which was intercepted on the same day.

ppcpna eluag asvnn dphgc syymw uavxi sqnqb

ACKNOWLEDGEMENTS

I am indebted to Louis Kruh and James Reeds for supplying me with copies of reference material on the M-209. I was helped in the description of the operation of the M-209 by reading various unpublished notes by James Reeds.

REFERENCES

1.   Yves Gylden, "Analysis, from the point of view of cryptanalysis of 'Cryptographer Type C-36,' provided with 6 Key Wheels, 27 slide bars, the latter having movable projections, single or multiple," Stockholm, May 9, 1938. (Tr. from the French and annotated by W.F.F.).
Gylden demonstrates that the kind of analysis done in this paper is impossible. His motives for writing the paper are not clear.

2.   Howard T. Oakley, "The Hagelin Cryptographer (Model C-38)—Converter M-209: Reconstruction of the Key Elements," Mimeographed notes dated May 12, 1950.

Oakley attacks the same problem treated in this paper. His methods require a good deal more trial and error and also require at least 200–300 characters to have any great probability of finding a complete solution.

3.   David Kahn, *The Codebreakers,* Macmillan, New York (1967).

The M-209 and similar machines constructed by Boris Hagelin are described on pp. 425–434. There is a drawing of the M-209 on p. 429. There are minor errors in Kahn's description of the M-209.

Solving a Hagelin, Type CD-57, Cipher
by Wayne G. Barker

In the July issue of *Cryptologia* [1], Louis Kruh presented an interesting description of a more recent Hagelin Cryptograph, the Hagelin Pocket Cryptographer, Type CD-57. At the same time, he offered readers a "chance to test their cryptanalytic skills" by solving two given messages, both enciphered with the Hagelin, Type CD-57 cryptographic machine.

We have solved both messages; and thinking that readers perhaps might be interested in how solution was accomplished, this paper has been written.

THE PROBLEM

The following two messages were given:

Message Number One

```
P Z U Y V  N B I Y E  R K G N L  N L E B O  Q Z D W Q  Z V V R D
G Y K N P  R Q X S M  Q T A I G  Y F Z Z V  K X U T N  X K R G I
L Z O Z Q  Q S C O X  E Z N J A  W A T R M  B F C W A  W K E N Q
H H X Z I  W Y X G P  O Y X I D  N T E W N  D N F T P  A R L K H
T F T N C  C Z C Z W
```

Message Number Two

```
O C C A G  J Y Q Y M  U Z K K N  B K E Y K  F E E P Q  Z Y W N N
G D Z L G  Q Y U Z P  L T U A M  T R F W B  C Z R K D  G F T N L
Z C O G F  K X R W R  Y W A Y S  W Z B G M  S G A N D  E Q Y D A
R R X N L  Q X F W S  S E R E A  G Q T A M  Q D T H B  Q A M H O
F N L F U  W W A S K
```

From *Cryptologia*, Vol. 2, No. 1, Jan. 1978.

The following information concerning the two messages was also provided:

"The key wheels used have 26, 38, 42, 34, 46, and 25 pins respectively, and less than 50% of each are in active positions. In addition, the key setting of the second half of Message One overlaps with the key setting of the first half of Message Two and the word *artillery* is in both of these sections. Other clues may be discerned in the photographs accompanying the text."

STEPS IN SOLUTION

In this problem—as the two messages overlap—we are given, in essence, two messages "in depth" and accordingly our plan of attack in two steps will be the following:

(1) In the first step we shall attempt to recover or "strip off" as much keying sequence as possible.

(2) In the second step, having [we hope] recovered a portion of the keying sequence, we shall attempt to determine the amount of lug displacement, or "kick," of each wheel, identify the effectiveness of the pin settings of each wheel, and read the messages.

THE CRYPTOGRAPHIC PROCESS OF THE CD-57

Before showing the actual recovery of a portion of the keying sequence, for those readers not acquainted with the "cryptographic process" of the Hagelin Cryptograph, the relationship between the three elements, *plaintext, ciphertext,* and *key,* when dealing with the Hagelin Cryptograph, Type CD-57, will briefly be discussed. Essentially, by means of the following *Beaufort Tableau, given any two elements, the third element may be found.*

Using the above *Beaufort Tableau,* it is seen, for example, that the plaintext letter A and the ciphertext letter R yield a key of 17. As the letters of the *Beaufort Tableau* are reciprocal, it is likewise seen that A + R = 17 is true, whether A is plaintext and R ciphertext, or *vice versa.* One important point with respect to CD-57 key, as can be seen in the tableau, individual keys run from 0 to 40, with certain pairs of the key being equivalent. Thus, for example, the keys of 0 and 26 are effectively the same. Both have the same effect insofar as encipherment or decipherment is concerned. Similarly, the keys of 1 and 27 are the same, 2 and 28, etc.

Beaufort Tableau

		A	B	C	D	E	F	G	H	I	J	K	L	M	N	O	P	Q	R	S	T	U	V	W	X	Y	Z
	0/26	A	Z	Y	X	W	V	U	T	S	R	Q	P	O	N	M	L	K	J	I	H	G	F	E	D	C	B
	1/27	B	A	Z	Y	X	W	V	U	T	S	R	Q	P	O	N	M	L	K	J	I	H	G	F	E	D	C
	2/28	C	B	A	Z	Y	X	W	V	U	T	S	R	Q	P	O	N	M	L	K	J	I	H	G	F	E	D
	3/29	D	C	B	A	Z	Y	X	W	V	U	T	S	R	Q	P	O	N	M	L	K	J	I	H	G	F	E
	4/30	E	D	C	B	A	Z	Y	X	W	V	U	T	S	R	Q	P	O	N	M	L	K	J	I	H	G	F
	5/31	F	E	D	C	B	A	Z	Y	X	W	V	U	T	S	R	Q	P	O	N	M	L	K	J	I	H	G
	6/32	G	F	E	D	C	B	A	Z	Y	X	W	V	U	T	S	R	Q	P	O	N	M	L	K	J	I	H
	7/33	H	G	F	E	D	C	B	A	Z	Y	X	W	V	U	T	S	R	Q	P	O	N	M	L	K	J	I
	8/34	I	H	G	F	E	D	C	B	A	Z	Y	X	W	V	U	T	S	R	Q	P	O	N	M	L	K	J
	9/35	J	I	H	G	F	E	D	C	B	A	Z	Y	X	W	V	U	T	S	R	Q	P	O	N	M	L	K
	10/36	K	J	I	H	G	F	E	D	C	B	A	Z	Y	X	W	V	U	T	S	R	Q	P	O	N	M	L
	11/37	L	K	J	I	H	G	F	E	D	C	B	A	Z	Y	X	W	V	U	T	S	R	Q	P	O	N	M
	12/38	M	L	K	J	I	H	G	F	E	D	C	B	A	Z	Y	X	W	V	U	T	S	R	Q	P	O	N
Key	13/39	N	M	L	K	J	I	H	G	F	E	D	C	B	A	Z	Y	X	W	V	U	T	S	R	Q	P	O
	14/40	O	N	M	L	K	J	I	H	G	F	E	D	C	B	A	Z	Y	X	W	V	U	T	S	R	Q	P
	15	P	O	N	M	L	K	J	I	H	G	F	E	D	C	B	A	Z	Y	X	W	V	U	T	S	R	Q
	16	Q	P	O	N	M	L	K	J	I	H	G	F	E	D	C	B	A	Z	Y	X	W	V	U	T	S	R
	17	R	Q	P	O	N	M	L	K	J	I	H	G	F	E	D	C	B	A	Z	Y	X	W	V	U	T	S
	18	S	R	Q	P	O	N	M	L	K	J	I	H	G	F	E	D	C	B	A	Z	Y	X	W	V	U	T
	19	T	S	R	Q	P	O	N	M	L	K	J	I	H	G	F	E	D	C	B	A	Z	Y	X	W	V	U
	20	U	T	S	R	Q	P	O	N	M	L	K	J	I	H	G	F	E	D	C	B	A	Z	Y	X	W	V
	21	V	U	T	S	R	Q	P	O	N	M	L	K	J	I	H	G	F	E	D	C	B	A	Z	Y	X	W
	22	W	V	U	T	S	R	Q	P	O	N	M	L	K	J	I	H	G	F	E	D	C	B	A	Z	Y	X
	23	X	W	V	U	T	S	R	Q	P	O	N	M	L	K	J	I	H	G	F	E	D	C	B	A	Z	Y
	24	Y	X	W	V	U	T	S	R	Q	P	O	N	M	L	K	J	I	H	G	F	E	D	C	B	A	Z
	25	Z	Y	X	W	V	U	T	S	R	Q	P	O	N	M	L	K	J	I	H	G	F	E	D	C	B	A

RECOVERING A PORTION OF THE KEYING SEQUENCE

We are given the important fact by Louis Kruh that "the key setting of the second half of Message One overlaps with the key setting of the first half of Message Two." If we take this fact to be literally correct, since each message contains exactly 130 letters, we can say that the last 65 letters of Message One have been enciphered with the same keying sequence as the first 65 letters of Message Two. Further, and again with kind thanks to Louis Kruh, we know that the word *artillery* occurs within the overlap portion of both Message One and Message Two.

Therefore, appropriately overlapping the two messages, we can run the plaintext word *artillery* through Message Two, simultaneously obtaining resultant text in Message One. When "good" plaintext occurs in Message One, we will know that we have found the correct position of the word *artillery* in Message Two. The following is the result of this tabulation:

Position in Message Two	Message Two	Message One	Resultant plaintext in Message One when word "artillery" occurs in Message Two
1	O	Q	Y B T U U Q D U N
2	C	S	K R F R Q K H G K
3	C	C	A D C N K O T D W
4	A	O	M A Y H O A Q P X
5	G	X	J W S L A X C Q P
6	J	E	F Q W X X J D I R
7	Y	Z	Z U I U J K V K Z
8	Q	N	D G F G K C X S Y
9	Y	J	P D R H C E F R D
10	M	A	M P S Z E M E W A
11	U	W	Y Q K B M L J T A
12	Z	A	Z I M J L Q G T I
13	K	T	R K U I Q N G B H
14	K	R	T S T N N O A S
15	N	M	B R Y K N V N L Y
16	B	B	A W V K V W Y R A
17	K	F	F T V S U F E T Y
18	E	C	C T D R F L G R Q
19	Y	W	C B C C L N E J P
20	K	A	K A N I N L W I X
21	F	W	J L T K L D V Q M
22	E	K	U R V I D C D F D
23	E	E	A T T A C K S W I
24	P	N	C R L Z K Z J B D
25	Q	Q	A J K H Z Q O W A
26	Z	H	S I S W Q V J T D
27	Y	H	R Q H N V Q G W P
28	W	X	Z F Y S Q N J I A
29	N	Z	O W D N N Q V T Y
30	N	I	F B Y K Q C G R V
31	G	W	K W V N C N E O P
32	D	Y	F T Y Z N L B I K
33	Z	X	C W K K L I V D W
34	L	G	F I V I I C Q P Y
35	G	P	R T T F C X C R O
36	Q	O	C R Q Z X J E H C
37	Y	Y	A O K U J L U V X
38	U	X	X I F G L B I Q O
39	Z	I	R D R I B P D H C

Position in Message Two	Message Two	Message One	Resultant plaintext in Message One when word "artillery" occurs in Message Two
40	P	D	M P T Y P K U V Y
41	L	N	Y R J M K B I R B
42	T	T	A H X H B P E U K
43	U	E	Q V S Y P L H D A
44	A	W	E Q J M L O Q T G
45	M	N	Z H X I O X G Z E
46	T	D	Q V T L X N M X Y
47	R	N	E R W U N T K R U
48	F	F	A U F K T R E N L
49	W	T	D D V Q R L A E Y
50	B	P	M T B O L H R R Y
51	C	A	C Z Z I H Y E R Y
52	Z	R	I X T E Y L E R H
53	R	L	G R P V L L E A V
54	K	K	A N G I L L N O B
55	D	H	W E T I L U B U K
56	G	T	N R T I U I H D F
57	F	F	A R T R I O Q Y H

Success! It is seen that when the word *artillery* begins in position 23 in Message Two, the resultant plaintext in Message One is *attacks wi*. The overlap of Message One and Message Two appears as follows:

```
key—
#1— Q S C O X E Z N J A W A T R M B F C W A W K
#2— O C C A G J Y Q Y M U Z K K N B K E Y K F E
      1 2 3 4 5 6 7 8 9 10 11 12 13 14 15 16 17 18 19 20 21 22
```

```
key—   4 6 9 7 9 7 17 4 4
#1— E N Q H H X Z  I W Y X G P O Y X  I D N T E W
     a t t a c k s  w i
#2— E P Q Z Y W N N G D Z L G Q Y U Z P L T U A
     a r t i l l e r y
    23 24 25 26 27 28 29 30 31 32 33 34 35 36 37 38 39 40 41 42 43 44
```

```
key—
#1— N D N F T P A R L K H T F T N C C Z C Z W
#2— M T R F W B C Z R K D G F T N L Z C O G F
    45 46 47 48 49 50 51 52 53 54 55 56 57 58 59 60 61 62 63 64 65
```

We have now recovered a small portion of the keying sequence, the keys between positions 23 and 31. Using a "trial-and-error" process, we shall attempt to recover additional keying sequence. Thus, we may attempt to guess plaintext in one message and confirm the guess by obtaining "good" plaintext in the other message. For example, we may guess that the word *enemy* is in front of the word *attacks* in Message One; and the confirming letters *clude* are obtained in Message Two! And, of course, we have not forgotten that the word *artillery* also occurs somewhere in Message One! In this manner, some 39 consecutive keys are recovered:

```
key—                                         6 9 4 8 8
#1— Q S C O X E Z N J A W A T R M B F C W A W K
                                             e n e m y
#2— O C C A G J Y Q Y M U Z K K N B K E Y K F E
                                             c l u d e
    1 2 3 4 5 6 7 8 9 10 11 12 13 14 15 16 17 18 19 20 21 22
```

```
key—    4 6 9 7 9 7 17 4 4 17 4 6 6 7 6 8 19 7 4 17 9 4
#1— E N Q H H X Z I W Y X G P O Y X I D N T E W
    a t t a c k s w i t h a r t i l l e r y f i
#2— E P Q Z Y W N N G D Z L G Q Y U Z P L T U A
    a r t i l l e r y o f v a r i o u s t y p e
    23 24 25 26 27 28 29 30 31 32 33 34 35 36 37 38 39 40 41 42 43 44
```

```
key—    4 7 4 9 9 9 4 9 4 10 15 10
#1— N D N F T P A R L K H T F T N C C Z C ZW
    r e r e q u e s t a i r
#2— M T R F W B C Z R K D G F T N L Z C O G F
    s o n e n i c k n a m e
    45 46 47 48 49 50 51 52 53 54 55 56 57 58 59 60 61 62 63 64 65
```

ANALYSIS OF THE RECOVERED KEYS

A frequency distribution of the 39 so-far recovered keys is made:

```
1 2 3  4 5 6 7 8 9 10 11 12 13 14 15 16 17 18 19 20 21 22 23 24
       11  5 6 2 8 2              1     3        1
```

This frequency count of the recovered keys brings to light the interesting fact that the number of different keys appears to be limited! Thus, the two keys 4 and 9 account for almost 50% of all keys used; and the seven keys 4, 6, 7, 8, 9, 10, and 17 account for almost 95%.

From the fact that a limited number of different keys appear, it is likely that

(1) As no key of "0" occurs, it is probable that the "outer alphabet ring" of the CD-57 has been turned, so that the letter A does not appear at the very top, the position giving rise to a key of "0" when all wheels are inactive.

(2) Further, as the smallest key to appear is 4 (which occurs 11 times), it would appear that 4 might well represent "all wheels inactive." If this is correct, then the letter E on the "outer alphabet ring" of the CD-57 will be at the very top (instead of the letter A). Quickly turning to the picture of the CD-57 in Kruh's article, it is seen that the letter E of the "outer alphabet ring" is indeed at the top!

(3) Reducing all keys by 4 shows that the following "now-adjusted" keys have appeared in the keying sequence: 0, 2, 3, 4, 5, 6, 11, 14, and 15. This then is the base that we shall work with in the second step leading to our goal of reading the two messages.

(4) One other conclusion that we can reach by examination of the adjusted keys that have so-far occurred in the keying sequence is that it appears that most of the pins of the wheels must be in inactive positions, such that when an adjusted key of 2, 3, 4, 5, or 6 has occurred, it is because only one wheel is active, the others being inactive! Thus, the number of "lugs" on the wheels are very likely 2, 3, 4, 5, and 6—with no wheel containing one lug ([otherwise] an adjusted key of 1 would have occurred).

RECOVERY OF PIN SETTINGS ON INDIVIDUAL WHEELS

In the Hagelin CD-57 system, a key is the result of the summation of the "lugs" displaced on individual wheels. Thus, the amount of "kick" of individual active wheels (wheels are active when their respective pins are in an active position) are added together to arrive at the key. With this in mind, we shall consider the portion of the keying sequence already recovered, with its keys now adjusted (4 has been subtracted from each recovered key):

Position:	18	19	20	21	22	23	24	25	26	27	28	29	30	31	32	33	34	35	36	37
Adjusted key:	2	5	0	4	4	0	2	5	3	5	3	13	0	0	13	0	2	2	3	2

	38	39	40	41	42	43	44	45	46	47	48	49	50	51	52	53	54	55	56
	4	15	3	0	13	5	0	0	3	0	5	5	5	0	5	0	6	11	6

To show the method of recovering individual pin settings, let us examine Wheel 25, the wheel containing the fewest number of pins. The effect of Wheel 25 on the adjusted keying sequence may be shown by the following:

1	2	3	4	5	6	7	8	9	10	11	12	13	14	15	16	17	18	19	20	21	22	23	24	25
2	5	0	4	4	0	2	5	3	5	3	13	0	0	13	0	2	2	3	2	4	15	3	0	13
5	0	0	3	0	5	5	5	0	5	0	6	11	6											

We have already reached the conclusion, see (4) above, that the number of "lugs" on the six wheels are likely 2, 3, 4, 5, and 6—with no wheel containing one lug. If we here assume that Wheel 25 contains 6 lugs, or has a kick of 6, then every adjusted key less than 6 must be the result of Wheel 25 being inactive in that position. Identifying an inactive pin with a minus sign (–), we have the following:

1	2	3	4	5	6	7	8	9	10	11	12	13	14	15	16	17	18	19	20	21	22	23	24	25
2	5	0	4	4	0	2	5	3	5	3	13	0	0	13	0	2	2	3	2	4	15	3	0	13
5	0	0	3	0	5	5	5	0	5	0	6	11	6											
–	–	–	–	–	–	–	–	–		–	–		–	–	–	–	–	–		–	–			

All pins are inactive, except four, [which are] unidentified. Here we take a shortcut! But who can blame the cryptanalyst for not taking the path of least resistance! We turn to take a look at the picture of Wheel 25 in Kruh's article [1]. Knowing that pins turned outward toward the rim of the wheel are active, we copy the active and inactive pins as follows:

```
A B C D E F G H I J K L M N O P Q R S T U V W X Y Z
– – – – – – – + – – + – – – – – – – + – – + – – – –
```

All pins of Wheel 25 are inactive, except four! Will the four active pins now match the four unidentified pins of our identification above? Again, success! Wheel 25 matches perfectly the identification made, and we have the following:

1	2	3	4	5	6	7	8	9	10	11	12	13	14	15	16	17	18	19	20	21	22	23	24	25
2	5	0	4	4	0	2	5	3	5	3	13	0	0	13	0	2	2	3	2	4	15	3	0	13
5	0	0	3	0	5	5	5	0	5	0	6	11	6											
–	–	–	–	–	–	–	–	–	–	–	+	–	–	+	–	–	–	–	–	–	+	–	–	+

```
V X Y Z A B C D E F G H I J K L M N O P Q R S T U
```

In a similar manner, the pins of the remaining five wheels are identified, active or inactive; at the same time, the number of lugs, or the amount of kick, of each wheel is found.

Solution is further assisted by Kruh [having provided] in his article the order of the wheels, 26, 38, 42, 34, 46, and 25, together with several pictures of the open CD-57 machine, showing the "lug settings," beginning with Wheel 25, getting smaller and smaller.

A portion of the complete cryptographic operations is shown as follows:

```
Message One—  Q S  C O  X E  Z N  J A  WA  T R  MB  F C  WA
              r  r e  i n  f o r c e  me n  t s  i f  e  n  e
Message Two—  O C  C A  G J  YQ  YM  U Z  KK  NB  KE  YK
              t  h e  w e  a p o  n s  o f  w a r  i a  c l  u
       Key—   7 9  6 22 10 9  13 4  11 4 8  4 6 10  4 9  10 6 9  4
Reduced Key—  3 5  2 18 6  5 9  0 7  0 4  0 2  6 0  5 6  2 5  0
```

Wheel 25 (6) —	− − − + − − + − − − − − − + − − + − − −
Wheel 46 (5) —	− + − + − + − − + − − − − − − − − + −
Wheel 34 (4) —	− − − + − − − − − − − − − − − − − − −
Wheel 42 (3) —	+ − − + − − + − − − − − − − − + − − − −
Wheel 38 (2) —	− − − − + − − − − − + − − − − − − + − −
Wheel 26 (2) —	− − + − − − − − + − + − + − − + − − − −

Plaintext of Message Two: THE WEAPONS OF WAR IACLUDE
ARTILLERY OF VARIOUS TYPES
ONE NICKNAME FOR THESE GUNS
IS LONG RIFLES THE REASON IS
THAT THEIR RANGE CAN EXTEND
FOR SEVERAL MILES X.

(One "garbled" letter, incidentally, is noted in the fifth word.)

FINAL REMARKS

In many respects this problem of Louis Kruh was easier than it might have been, due to such things as:

(1) The vast majority of pins on the wheels were in an inactive position.
(2) Each wheel contained a limited number of lugs.
(3) Louis Kruh's article provided an overlap between two messages plus the probable word *artillery* in both messages.

(4) Photographs in Kruh's article provided the pin settings on all wheels, the setting of the "outer alphabet ring," and a good indication of the wheels' lug settings.

(5) The order of the wheels was provided in the article.

For readers interested in learning more about the cryptanalysis of the Hagelin, Type CD-57, and the Hagelin Cryptograph in general (the M-209, for example), reference is made to a recent book written by the author of this paper [2].

REFERENCES

1. Kruh, Louis, Cipher Equipment—Hagelin Pocket Cryptographer, Type CD-57, *Cryptologia,* 1(1977), 255–260.

2. Barker, Wayne G., *Cryptanalysis of the Hagelin Cryptograph* (Laguna Hills, CA: Aegean Park Press, 1977.)

Analysis of the Hebern Cryptograph Using Isomorphs
by Cipher A. Deavours

The first known encryption device to embody the wired codewheel principle was built in California by Edward Hebern before the end of World War I. Hugo Koch of Holland and Arthur Scherbius of Germany discovered the same cryptographic principle and embodied it in parallel inventions. Rotary cipher machines were very popular during the World War II period, major examples being Germany's *Enigma,* Britain's *Typex,* and the U.S. *SIGABA.* Most other mechanical encryption devices of that time, excluding on-line machines, used stepping switches (the Japanese "J" machine) or the Hagelin cage principle (the M209 and several other types of German machines).

After the war and well into the 60's the rotor principle was still a widely used principle in the design of cryptographic devices, but emphasis was placed on irregular gear interruption, patch boards, and other variable circuit features. As the reader will see, a straight rotor machine such as Hebern's is not cryptographically secure from a known plaintext attack.

The lines of mathematical analysis which the British used to cryptanalyze the Enigma machine led to the development of the world's first protoelectronic computers during the war years, and, in fact, it was the subsequent advent of the computer age which rendered the rotor principle *passé* among the major cryptographic powers. Rotary machines, perhaps due to the inherent cleverness of the idea involved in their conception, enjoy a reputation for high security. Known facts do not substantiate this viewpoint. The original Hebern device was successfully cryptanalyzed shortly after its introduction. Although the [U.S.] Defense Department still refuses to release Friedman's original report on the Hebern machine

From *Cryptologia*, Vol. 1, No. 2, April 1977.

[1] (after nearly half a century!), it is the author's speculation that the isomorphic peculiarities of the device were among the cryptanalytic roads which Friedman traversed [2].

The most famous example of cryptographic failure and its ensuing consequences is, of course, the British decryptment of the Enigma machine. There is no doubt that the Enigma was the best source of secret information which the British ever had during the war. Rotor machines of other countries, notably France and Italy, were similarly penetrated during the hostilities. The Typex and SIGABA machines appear never to have been successfully cryptanalyzed on an ongoing basis; however, in both of these cases the details of the device itself were able to be kept secret. In addition, the SIGABA utilized a large number of interchangeable rotors—a feature which contributes greatly to the security of the machine. (For the SIGABA, the rotors were chosen from a set of 10 available ones.) If one can draw any conclusion from the meager data available, it is that rotor machines are less secure than commonly supposed and that the need to maintain absolute secrecy concerning construction details of the machine itself is paramount.

In this paper, we shall exhibit several properties of a Hebern type cryptograph which render it susceptible to cryptanalysis. In our sense, the term *Hebern cryptograph* is taken to mean a rotary cipher machine having a variable number, N, of rotors each of which turns in regular parallel order with no irregular motions or interruptions. Starting in a randomly determined position, the first rotor (taken to be the one nearest to the input keyboard) enciphers the first 26 letters of the message, turning forward one step per letter enciphered. As the 27th letter of the message is enciphered, the first rotor returns to its original position and the adjacent rotor steps forward one position. Each complete revolution of this second rotor steps forward the third rotor by one position and so on. In this manner, the second rotor completes a revolution during 26 revolutions of the first rotor. The third rotor completes a revolution in 26 revolutions of the second rotor, etc. The total period of the device is thus 26^N.

Our prototype machine differs in several relatively unimportant details from an actual Hebern cryptograph. The accompanying photos should clarify the situation. In both Hebern's original patent and the particular cryptograph examined, provision is made for a varying number of movable rotors. For example, the pictured cryptograph has rotors 2 and 4 [as] immobile stators. Each revolution of the first rotor (the one nearest the reader in Figure 1) steps forward the fifth rotor by one step. Each subsequent revolution of the fifth rotor steps forward the third rotor. In spite of this construction, the method which we shall describe applies equally well.

FIGURE 1.
Sideview of the cryptograph removed from carrying case. Battery case is directly behind the rotors. The right rachet wheel is clearly visible showing a deep toothcut between the letters "A" and "Y". This rachet wheel moves forward (towards the keyboard) one step with each letter enciphered. When the previously mentioned saw-toothed cut reaches a certain point below the visible portion of its revolution, this notch causes the rotor to step forward one place. The opposite rachet wheel has a similar deepcut notch to move the middle rotor forward one place with each revolution of the 1st rotor.

A second difference between Hebern's actual construction and our prototype machine is that the rachet wheels which can both be set arbitarily before encipherment control the exact point within the 26-letter group at which the rotors besides the first move forward. Thus, the fifth rotor in the pictured machine could step forward during the middle of the first 26-letter encipherment and not at its conclusion. In actual practice, this irregularity causes little delay in cryptanalysis of the cipher generated and so we shall neglect it in our model.

To digress somewhat, pictures cannot convey the beautiful care and precision with which these machines were manufactured. Even the screws appear to be individually sunk. The parts fit together with an ease and preciseness characteristic of a bygone era in human craftmanship. The machine makes a striking appearance, particularly striking among the gray and green landscapes of military hardware. Most of the metal parts of the cryptograph are brass finished in a bright burnished gold color impressed with a typical zigzag *art deco* motif of the late 1920's. The rotors are constructed of a bakelite-type substance and are black. For portability, the machine came housed in an old-fashioned typewriter case lined in blue velvet. Conceptually and artistically, the machine was a triumph. This renders even more poignantly the sad tale told in Kahn's *The Codebreakers* of how a truly inventive and great man was virtually robbed of his invention and its fruits by an uncaring bureaucracy. [3]

During normal periods of use, the machine required no servicing other than occasional replacement of its batteries and indicator lamps. The brass contacts of the rotors also required fairly regular cleaning, and military personnel were frequently furnished with chamois or similar cloths for this purpose. Over long periods of operation, the wires on the back movable plate often came loose and needed to be periodically inspected and tightened. The rear panel of the device slides out, apparently for this very purpose.

FIGURE 2.
Backview of cryptograph with rotors and two back plates removed. Note the flexible brass rotor contacts in the rotor housing. Wiring to the back plate which is movable to the right or left to convert the machine from its "direct" (encipher) mode to its "reverse" (decipher) mode is clearly visible.

Our proposed cipher machine will be composed of a typewriter keyboard having 26 output contacts and N rotors each having 26 input contacts connected randomly to 26 output contacts. The output contacts of the last rotor connect electrically with another fixed plate which leads to a printing device. We shall deal only with cryptograms having a length less than $26^2 = 676$ characters, and thus only the first two rotors will be moving during encipherment. For this reason, the portion of the wiring from the input contacts of the third rotor to the printing device constitutes a fixed monoalphabetic substitution of the input characters involved during an encipherment of a single cryptogram.

FIGURE 3.
Bottom view of cryptograph showing keyboard contacts and back plate wiring. The knob at the lower right shifts the two wired plates relative to one another. The two symmetric projections on each side of the machine serve no function other than to carry wiring from the front to the rear of the machine.

The following pencil and paper representation of a Hebern machine which seems most convenient to our purposes will be used throughout. The wiring of a given rotor is specified by listing the input contacts and the corresponding output positions current for that rotor. For example,

Input Contacts: A B C D E F G H I J K L M N O P Q R S T U V W X Y Z
Output Contacts: F N B R L O U A V T X K D P E S M C W Q H Y Z G J I

This is interpreted to mean that current entering by contact A exits at *location* A of the output contacts. Current entering at B exits at *location* B below, and so on. What we have by this particular mode of representation is the rotor as if it were cut and spread out on a two-dimensional surface. Rotations of the rotor can be represented by sliding it right or left relative to the other rotor strips.

In order to simulate the operation of the machine we prepare paper strips and trace the paths of current during each encipherment of a character. The input keyboard will be taken to consist of the output contacts:

Keyboard: Q W E R T Y U I O P A S D F G H J K L Z X C V B N M

For our sample encipherments, the following rotor wirings are assumed:

Rotor #1
Input Contacts: A B C D E F G H I J K L M N O P Q R S T U V W X Y Z
Output Contacts: F N B R L O U A V T X K D P E S M C W Q H Y Z G J I

Rotor #2
Input Contacts: A B C D E F G H I J K L M N O P Q R S T U V W X Y Z
Output Contacts: H S J P I D T V Q Y O B Z G M K F A C U X N R W E L

Rotor #3 to Output
Input Contacts: A B C D E F G H I J K L M N O P Q R S T U V W X Y Z
Final Output: G M A O Q D I R V K B T L J W S X C U H Y F N Z P E

In the rotor #3 connections, the final monoalphabetic substitution is represented by taking the character directly *below* the corresponding input character as its substitute. Thus, an input to rotor 3 of A results in a final cipher character of G; if the input is B, the output is M, etc.

To facilitate hand use, each rotor arrangement is repeated twice on a strip of paper. The three rotor strips are then placed in order below the keyboard strip and aligned to a given starting position, obtained by placing in a column below the letter Q of the input board the three input letters representing the initial rotor positions.

For example, if the chosen starting rotor positions are AIE the strips are aligned as follows:

```
                    Q W E R T . . .
                    A B C D E . . .
                    F N B R L . . .
        A B C D E F G H I J K L M . . .
        H S J P I D T V Q Y O B Z . . .
            A B C D E F G H I . . .
            G M A O Q D I R V . . .
```

The first letter is enciphered from input to final output and then the second strip is moved to the left one space for the next encipherment. After 26 successive encirpherments the first strip is returned to its starting position and the second strip is moved forward one space to the left and the encipherment continues.

If the starting position had been AAA then Q is enciphered to be G; W is enciphered to be U; E to be N, etc., as the reader can verify from the previously given wirings. In the first case, the input-output sequence is seen to be Q-A-H-AG, the second W-B-C-SU, the third E-C-R-WN.

Suppose now we take the word "CHIFFREMENT" and encipher it beginning at several selected locations. The reader should verify the following results:

		STARTING POSITION
Plaintext:	CHIFFREMENT	
	MANKBVBJDRY	CFL
	UVJNARACGTD	CML
Ciphertext:	QJOLMWMVUGS	CQL
	KIKNKHNRLEO	HFL
	FXFIFTIVGZW	HRB

The above encipherments lead to some interesting observations. The first three cryptograms are *isomorphic,* i.e., they may be transformed into one another by means of a monoalphabetic substitution. In all three of these cases, the reader will note that the starting position of the first rotor was the same. The isomorphic property is independent of the positions of the other rotors provided that they do not move during the encipherment of the plaintext. In fact, rotors 3 to N do not move at all if the message length is less than 677 characters and, hence, perform only a monoalphabetic substitution on the ciphertext input to rotor 3.

The isomorphic property may be seen again in the last two encipherments which are found to be isomorphic to one another but not to the first three cryptograms. Our general conclusion is that *the same plaintext m-gram enciphered beginning at the same position of the first rotor of a Hebern cryptograph always yields isomorphic ciphertext m-grams.* An Achilles heel has thus emerged.

If two relatively long isomorphs can be found in compared cryptograms, we can assume that these isomorphs represent identical plaintext and that the same first rotor was used in both cases. If the wiring of the first rotor is known, probable plaintext can be spotted by successively enciphering the suspected text at all 26 starting locations of the initial rotor and then searching the cipher for isomorphs. The relative positions of the other rotors do not matter in this process. We shall presently show how the placement of relatively small amounts of plaintext can result in complete solution of the cryptogram and reconstruction of the wiring of the second rotor along the way. We wish to emphasize that only the wiring of the first rotor will be needed to place probable text and then to solve the message; *the wiring of the other rotors need never be explicitly known.*

If no rotor wirings are known, an abundance of isomorphs in the ciphertext can be used to reconstruct the wirings of the first two rotors. The process is more difficult than the previous one, but, is often possible with pencil and paper using geometrical techniques and alphabet chaining. The indicated process can succeed often without knowledge of any

FIGURE 4.
Rotors removed showing front, back, and side views. The wire is enameled copper. The indentations where the letters are imprinted contact a metal rod during use which propels the rotors in their revolutions. Rotors may be freely interchanged and even inserted backwards if desired.

plaintext. Surprisingly enough, neither of these processes requires the use of any explicit mathematics, but is more akin to crossword puzzle solution.

Before continuing with examples, we need to briefly investigate the probablistic aspects of locating and ascertaining isomorphs in ciphertext. For instance, we need to know just how long is "long enough" for two ciphertext strings which are isomorphic to be considered encipherments of identical plaintext. We shall first calculate the probability of two isomorphs of length n occurring randomly with no repeated characters.

The number of ways to place n different letters in a sequence without repeating any letter is clearly

$$26 \cdot 25 \cdot 24 \ldots (26-(n-1)).$$

Thus, the number of ways two isomorphic character strings of length n with no repeated characters in either string can be constructed is the square of the previous number. The total number of ways to write down two arbitrary character strings of length n is, obviously, 26^{2n}. The desired probability is therefore

$$(26 \cdot 25 \cdot 24 \ldots (26-(n-1))^2/26^{2n}.$$

A tacit assumption we shall make is that encipherment of differing plaintext segments, or the same plaintext enciphered [by] not beginning at the same position of the first rotor, results in a mathematically random collection of characters.

Isomorphs having no repeated characters are the most difficult to pinpoint (particularly discerning the beginning and end of the isomorph!). For two isomorphic n-grams having exactly one repeated character, there are 26 ways to choose the repeated character and $n(n-1)/2$ positions in which to place the repeat. The remaining $n-1$ different characters can be chosen $25 \cdot 24 \cdot 23 \ldots (25-(n-3))$ ways. We conclude that the probability of two isomorphic n-grams having exactly one repeated character is

$$(n(n-1)/2) \cdot 26^2 \cdot (25 \cdot 24 \ldots (25-(n-3)))^2/26^{2n}.$$

Typical results obtained using the two previous formulas and a similar calculation for two isomorphic n-grams having two repeated characters are shown in Table 1.

TABLE 1.

Length of Isomorph	Probability		
	No Repeats	1 Repeat	2 Repeats
1	1.0000	—	—
2	.9246	.0015	—
3	.7878	.0041	—
4	.6165	.0070	.0000
5	.4414	.0091	.0000
6	.2879	.0098	.0000
7	.1704	.0089	.0002
8	.0910	.0071	.0003
9	.0436	.0048	.0003
10	.0186	.0029	.0003
11	.0071	.0015	.0004
12	.0023	.0007	.0001
13	.0007	.0003	.0001
14	.0002	.0001	.0000
15	.0000	.0000	.0000

Thus, for a cryptogram [of] several hundred characters [in length], an isomorph of 12 or so characters seems necessary (if there are no repeats) to establish identical plaintext encipherment. To illustrate our results briefly, suppose a cryptanalyst has selected two isomorphs of length 8 in a 500-character message and that the isomorphs have one repeated letter. The two isomorphs must be separated by a distance divisable by 26 if the machine motion is regular. The probability of the aforementioned isomorphism is seen to be .0071, or about 7 times in a thousand. If the message is written out in groups of 26 letters, there will be 19 such groups with 6 characters on the last line (500 = 19 × 26 + 6).

How many isomorphic comparisons of length 8 can be tried in this message? There are 19 starting locations on each line for eight-character strings (in general $26 - n + 1$). At each starting location the 19 rows yield 19(18/2) possible comparisons. We therefore arrive at a possible total of $19 \cdot 19 \cdot 18/2 = 3249$ eight-character comparisons. We would then expect about .0071 × 3249 = 23.07 isomorphs of length 8 with one repeated letter to occur purely by chance. The conclusion that the two isomorphs represent identically enciphered plaintext is unjustified in this case. Had the message been 250 letters long the reader can verify by a similar calculation that the number of expected isomorphs falls to 5—a drastic reduction, but one which still leaves the conclusion unfounded.

Isomorphic probabilities also play a crucial role in the placement of probable plaintext. Suppose that we have received the following cryptogram for decipherment:

```
WMWL I A D U L K O U N O B J B I I T X L A Y B K
J L A Q Q B F X W F R P U A E Z C N Q C K Q H Z G U
T U K F E V Z X M I Y Z Q R T S O O S B B C U T Q S
V U M O P H B E D V S R G U W F Y H M R W K I Y Y G
F H K A Y D J Y C Y D M N L M C I C B C J I P M M I
H G S O X Y A E Y W D N S R R Y
```

We have reason to suspect the probable phrases "Minister of Exterior Affaires" and "ten percent." We also suspect that rotor #1 was the first rotor in the machine during encipherment. To locate the shorter of the two phrases, we encipher the characters "TEN PERCENT" at every possible one of the 26 starting locations of rotor 1. The cipher present at the input to rotor 2 is then written down. As the reader will soon see, the relative position of rotor 2's input alphabet does not matter, so we will arbitrarily take it to be "A" (in the actual encipherment, rotor 2 began at "R").

This process yields:

	Plaintext:	T	E	N	P	E	R	C	E	N	T
	A	O	L	F	N	T	U	W	R	P	S
	B	Z	M	Z	X	P	S	K	D	L	V
	C	V	X	N	A	T	E	E	V	P	C
	D	R	T	H	H	R	W	F	G	N	H
	E	V	P	I	M	D	H	Q	Q	Z	Q
	F	T	T	T	V	V	R	M	Q	R	B
	G	F	R	P	G	G	U	I	A	C	U
	H	X	D	L	Z	Q	B	M	F	M	Q
	I	I	V	P	V	T	G	K	O	P	R
	J	S	G	N	W	A	P	W	Z	W	A
	K	V	Q	Z	F	F	A	O	S	B	R
	L	C	T	R	W	O	T	Z	O	K	B
Starting	M	S	A	C	G	Z	P	J	P	V	B
Location	N	R	F	M	G	S	Q	M	Y	O	L
of Rotor 1	O	B	O	P	Q	O	Z	T	P	K	F
	P	U	Z	W	K	P	Q	Y	Z	L	T
	Q	Q	S	B	Y	Y	A	H	Z	U	N
	R	R	O	K	S	P	A	S	J	L	O
	S	A	P	V	T	Z	K	L	D	V	Z
	T	R	Y	O	E	Z	E	H	R	V	V
	U	B	P	K	A	J	S	I	L	Z	R
	V	B	Z	L	W	D	M	R	M	Z	V
	W	L	Z	U	A	R	N	I	X	N	T
	X	F	J	L	Y	L	Y	S	T	H	F
	Y	T	D	V	K	M	U	S	P	I	X
	Z	N	R	V	C	X	Q	C	T	T	T

Repeated letters in each isomorph have been underlined. There are only three character strings with no repeated characters (self-isomorphs); no other character strings are isomorphic to one another. Approximately 88% of the character strings contain at least one repetition of letters and 61% of the strings have more than one repeated letter. This is highly desirable, since the more repetitions in an isomorph, the greater the probability of correctly placing it in the ciphertext. Large numbers of strings with repetitions are not unexpected. If we think of each encipherment as producing essentially a random character, then, only about 14% of the strings should be without repetitions. This is easily seen since the number of ways to write 10 different characters is 26·25·24 . . . 17, making the probability of such a happening:

$$26·25·24 \ldots 17/26^{10} = .14.$$

Similarly, about 36% of the strings should have exactly one repetition (27% actually do in this example), 56% should have two repetitions (38% found here), and 6% should have two repetitions with one letter repeated three times (8% found).

To place probable plaintext, we should start with the strings having the most repeated patterns and try these first. A correct match at the beginning of the testing indicates with high probability a successful placement of plaintext. If more than one phrase is known, the fact that both isomorphs must simultaneously occur consistent with their assumed starting locations of the first rotor usually allows one to place even short isomorphs lacking in repetitions.

In the example at hand, an isomorph for the character string beginning at "J," i.e., SGNWAPWZWA, is to be found in the next to the last line of the cryptogram, . . . JXENRGNQNR . . . The isomorph for the first and longer of the two phrases can be found in similar manner. For reasons of space, we shall omit the calculations involved in this second location of plaintext.

The results of our successful location of plaintext yields the following information:

Plaintext: m i n i s t e r o f e x t e r i o r a f f a i r e s
Ciphertext: L K O U N O B J B I I T X L A Y B K J L A Q Q B F X
Plaintext: t e n p e r c e n t
Ciphertext: J X E N R G N Q N R

Starting position of first rotor is "I."

We are now in a position to begin solution of the cryptogram. Using the probable text which has been placed, we shall construct a polyalphabetic tableau, which will permit decipherment of the remaining ciphertext backwards to the input of rotor 2. With this accomplished, the problem is resolved, since we already know how to decipher from the input of rotor 2 through the first rotor and back to the plaintext, which was present at the input keyboard.

To understand just how this matter may be carried out, consider the equivalent cipher generated in passing from the input of rotor 2 to the input of rotor 3. For the rotor used in the example, the desired tableau:

Input to Rotor	2	A B C D E F G H I J K L M N O P Q R S T U V W X Y Z
	AA	R L S F Y Q N A E C P Z O V K D I W B G T H X U J M
	AB	S M T G Z R · · · · · · ·
	AC	T N U H A · · · · · · · · ·
	.	U O V I · · · · · ·
Relative Po-	.	V P · · · · · · · · ·
sition of Rotors	.	W · · · · · · · · ·
2 and 3	.	·
		· ·
		· · · · · · · ·
		P
	AZ	Q · · · · · · · · · ·

Input to Rotor 3

Any of the 26 rows of input to rotor 3 is, in effect, the wiring diagram for that rotor. As the rotor turns relative to rotor 3, each column generates the normal alphabet in progressive fashion.

If none of the rotors outside the first two move during encipherment, then the final cipher could be obtained by applying a monoalphabetic substitution to each of the 26 rows of the tableau. The monoalphabetic substitution is determined by the relative positions of the rotors from 3 to N and the arrangement of the output unit. The important thing is, however, that the *same* monoalphabetic substitution is applied to every row of the tableau. Furthermore, every column of the enciphered tableau contains the same monoalphabetically enciphered alphabet beginning at a different location. Thus, a great deal of symmetry is present in the tableau.

Full exploitation of the symmetries of the tableau can be expected to be quite useful in many different problems connected with this cryptograph. Alphabet chaining is, of course, the foremost technique of bringing out such properties. In particular,

A. *Chaining any two rows* found at an interval of n lines apart will produce a decimation at interval n of the original columnar sequence of characters; and

B. *Chaining any two columns* will produce a decimation of the original columnar sequence at an interval corresponding to the relative shift between the two alphabets.

From our previous work we have the following data:

Plaintext:	m i n i s t e r o f e x t e r i o r a f f a i r e s
Isomorph at Input to Rotor 2:	X E B O G B Z K Z R R H V X Q L Z E I K B Y Y H G T
Final Ciphertext:	L K O U N O B J B I I T X L A Y B K J L A Q Q B F X

and

Plaintext: t e n p e r c e n t
Isomorph at Input
to Rotor 2:   W K R A E T A D A E
Final Ciphertext: H K A Y D J Y C Y D

    To obtain the isomorph, rotor 2 was taken to begin encipherment of the message at position "A." As mentioned previously, the real starting location of rotor 2 was "R." The same decipherment will be produced in any case, since the relative position only introduces a Caesar shift in the isomorphs present at rotor 2. Physically, what we are saying is that, while we may solve the cipher, we can never know absolutely how the enemy has chosen to label his input contacts. In fact, they serve only as labels to orient the rotors relative to one another.

    Entering the above data into our attempted reconstruction of the enciphered tableau, we have

```
Input to Rotor  2 A B C D E F G H I J K L M N O P Q R S T U V W X Y Z
                1   O     K   N T   J Y   U   A I     X   L   B
                2   A       F B J   L           X         Q
                3
                4
                5 Y   C D       K           A   J       H
                .
                .
```

    The vertical chains X???JL??K????D, NF, and I????OA are immediately evident and could be added to the tableau. Entering these symmetries into the table and using the results to partially decipher the remaining ciphertext yields allows us, in turn, to insert some more probable text with which to expand our tableau. For instance, the beginning of the cryptogram now reads:

    ???AYT?EMINISTEROF...

From the above, we readily conclude that the cryptogram begins with the phrase:

    TODAYTHEMINISTEROF...

The fifth line of the cryptogram now reads:

    ?TENPERCENT??O?E?A?TQ????X.

    Since "U" follows "Q" in English, we may also enter this fact into our tableau. It appears that "X" might serve as a sentence divider in the cryptogram in which case "QU???" is probably a noun ending of the sentence. We could now try to guess the word involved, or, perhaps more rapidly, make use of the fact that the cipher letter "M" appears no less than 4 times in the undeciphered segment of line 5. It is not too difficult to find the correct isomorph which will result in simultaneous high frequency plaintext letters at all four positions. Taking the last "M" in the line to result in plaintext "E" yields the following decipherment of line 5:

  ?TENPERCENTA?OVE?A?TQU?TEX.

We easily fill in the line to read:

  ?TENPERCENTABOVETHELASTQUOTEX.

Entering the above information into our tableau and applying symmetry, we now have the top of the tableau reading as follows:

Input to Rotor 2	A	B	C	D	E	F	G	H	I	J	K	L	M	N	O	P	Q	R	S	T	U	V	W	X	Y	Z
1	O					K		N	T	W		J	Y		U			A	I		M	X		L	D	B
2	A				M		F	B	J		L					D		X				T	Q	K		
3							K	L								Q			I	W		B	O	M		
4				I			M	T								O		W	D	J		K	A			
5	Y		C	D			B		K					N				P	A	J	Q	L	H	M		I
.																										
.																										

The reconstructed vertical alphabet chain is expanded to

  X?WJLTBKM IDQOA???P

We shall not continue this process which is, by this point, obvious to the reader.

To recapitulate, probable plaintext is first placed using the known wiring of rotor 1. This information is then entered into the tableau and further decipherment of the message may be made. More plaintext is then guessed, the corresponding isomorphs for the new plaintext are obtained using rotor 1 and this new data is entered into the tableau. Horizontal and vertical symmetries are at all times exploited as fully as possible using chaining. Gradually the entire tableau and hence the entire message is reconstructed. When the tableau has been fully filled in, the cryptanalyst has the added bonus of having reconstructed the wiring of rotor 2. If the wiring of rotor 2 was previously known then, often, the displacement patterns of its vertical alphabets can be used to speed up the reconstruction.

Some cryptograms may present the would-be cryptanalyst with isomorphs which represent identical but unknown plaintext. In this case, some information towards the reconstruction of the tableau is obtained;

however, the process is much more difficult. As an example, suppose that the isomorphs

IUNXZPFODAUBCSJGJZ

and

ISQLNAUJEBSHKFPXPN

are found in the same position along a line two lines apart in a cryptogram. Then the cryptanalyst knows that in the original tableau the corresponding pairs appear two characters apart and are separated by two rows, e.g.,

I??	U??	N??
? ,	? ,	? , etc.
I	S	Q

This type of information, particularly if many such isomorphs can be found, is useful in reconstructing the tableau. The problem is made more difficult because the relative positions of the letter pairs along each line of the tableau are not known if no rotor wirings are known.

Isomorphic identifications also play a vital role in attacking rotor machines with irregular gear motions. In such cases, the locations of isomorphs found can often give clues to the nature of the irregular gear motions.

We have seen that the Hebern cryptograph is at best a medium-security cryptographic instrument. A typical attack on this machine would consist of obtaining some plaintext for several cryptograms and then using this to reconstruct the wiring of one or more of the rotors. Once this is done, one merely waits until the reconstructed rotors are again used in the first position of the machine. When this happens, probable plaintext can be used to solve the resulting cipher and to reconstruct the second rotor wiring used in the cryptogram. If the Gods of Fortune provide us with a plethora of isomorphs before we have reconstructed any of the rotor wirings, we may be able to break into the machine even without probable plaintext. Of course, there is *always* probable plaintext.

ACKNOWLEDGEMENT

The author wishes to thank Bradford Hardie, David Kahn, Louis Kruh, Greg Mellen, and James Reeds for reading and making many valuable comments on this paper.

REFERENCES

1.   William F. Friedman, *Analysis of a Mechanico-Electrical Crypto-graph,* U.S. Government Printing Office, Part 1 (1934), Part 2 (1935) (Original report, 1925), Washington, D.C.
2.   William F. Friedman, U.S. Patent 1,683,072, Sept. 4, 1928.
3.   David Kahn, *The Codebreakers: The Story of Secret Writing,* New York: Macmillan, 1967.

The Black Chamber:
La Methode des Batons
by Cipher A. Deavours

The story of the commercial version of the Enigma cryptograph is told in [1]. Basically, the public version of the machine was a four rotor device with three regular interchangeable rotors and a reflecting rotor. The reflecting rotor was also movable to any of its possible 26 settings. The rotor movement employed was subject to variations among users but was generally regular with the first rotor stepping once for each letter enciphered, the second rotor stepping once for each revolution of the first, etc. The ratchet wheels on each of the three rotors were rigidly fixed to the body of the coding cylinders (in contrast to the standard Army plugboard model) and the rotors possessed alphabet rings bearing a normal alphabetic sequence. The alphabet rings were rotatable with respect to the body of the coding cylinder and were designed in this manner so that the rotor starting positions could be randomly selected by the transmitter and sent *in the clear* with each message. The ring settings constituted part of the daily key and were altered along with the rotor order.

The commercial Enigma was bought and used by many countries during the 1920's and 1930's. In spite of claims for its security, the machine was repeatedly cryptanalyzed successfully during this time. During the Spanish Civil War of 1936–39, German, Italian, and Franco's forces all used the machine. As described in [2], the German Foreign Office was able to assemble intercepted Enigma messages, probably Italian in origin, in depths of 100 or so and solve for the succession of rotor alphabets generated by the usual polyalphabetic type of analysis. It was then simple for them to reconstruct the rotor wirings involved and to continue to read further messages. Italian keying practices are known from several references to have been bad during this period of time.

From *Cryptologia*, Vol. 4, No. 4, Oct. 1980.

What French cryptanalysts termed "*La Methode des Batons*" was a probable text approach to discovering the rotor order and starting position for known rotors. This method seems to have been discovered by nearly everyone who ever tried to break Enigma ciphers. The somewhat murky account of William Friedman's life in [3] gives the impression that Friedman toiled unsuccessfully trying to resolve this problem of rotor order and starting position for the commercial machine(s) he had purchased in the 1920's. Given W.F.F.'s propensity for "alphabet strip" solution processes, this impression can hardly be true. It is interesting to note that the same source quotes an interesting Dutch Army report of the time as stating the machine to be completely secure against cryptanalysis even if the adversary possesses a copy of the machine. The fact that the Germans found the Enigma vulnerable to probable plaintext attacks was the major reason for their insertion of a plugboard in the military models of the machine.

If R_j^i denotes the ith rotor position of the jth rotor, then, at rotor positions i, j, k, l, the encipherment equation for the Enigma is

$$c = pR_1^i \; R_2^j R_3^k \; Z \; R_{-3}^i \; R_{-2}^j \; R_{-1}^k \tag{1}$$

where Z is the reversing rotor, p is a character of plaintext, c is a character of ciphertext. The permutation generated by rotor j at position i, R_j^i, can be expressed in terms of its permutation at any randomly chosen ground state S_j through the equation:

$$R_j^i = C^i S_j C^{-i}.$$

The corresponding inverse permutation is given by

$$R_{-j}^i = C^i S_j^{-1} C^{-i}.$$

The C^i operators are circular shifts in a known alphabet, usually, the normal sequence ABCDEFGHIJKLMNOPQRSTUVWXYZ or the typewriter alphabet QWERTYUIOPASDFGHJKLZXCVBNM. Additionally, there was a known permutation introduced by the wiring from the keyboard to the first rotor input. On the commercial models of the Enigma, this permutation was that of the standard typewriter keyboard shown above while on German military versions of the Enigma the normal alphabetic sequence was used. We shall assume the normal alphabetic sequence for simplicity. This keyboard permutation enters the equation (1) before R_1^i with its inverse occuring after R_{-1}^i. With the normal alphabet sequence we may omit the keyboard permutation since the normal sequence is the identity transformation.

The polyalphabetic cipher generated as a rotor turns is shown in the tableau of Figure 1. Note that the normal alphabet reproduces itself along the principle diagonals. Two complete revolutions of the rotor are shown. The solution method which we will describe utilized strips for each rotor bearing the columns of the appropriate tableau. The strips were usually glued to wooden rods for ease of use.

	A	B	C	D	E	F	G	H	I	J	K	L	M	N	O	P	Q	R	S	T	U	V	W	X	Y	Z
A	I	L	S	B	M	D	T	J	A	H	K	C	V	G	N	P	O	X	F	E	Q	W	Z	R	Y	U
B	V	J	M	T	C	N	E	U	K	B	I	L	D	W	H	O	Q	P	Y	G	F	R	X	A	S	Z
C	A	W	K	N	U	D	O	F	V	L	C	J	M	E	X	I	P	R	Q	Z	H	G	S	Y	B	T
D	U	B	X	L	O	V	E	P	G	W	M	D	K	N	F	Y	J	Q	S	R	A	I	H	T	Z	C
E	D	V	C	Y	M	P	W	F	Q	H	X	N	E	L	O	G	Z	K	R	T	S	B	J	I	U	A
F	B	E	W	D	Z	N	Q	X	G	R	I	Y	O	F	M	P	H	A	L	S	U	T	C	K	J	V
G	W	C	F	X	E	A	O	R	Y	H	S	J	Z	P	G	N	Q	I	B	M	T	V	U	D	L	K
H	L	X	D	G	Y	F	B	P	S	Z	I	T	K	A	Q	H	O	R	J	C	N	U	W	V	E	M
I	N	M	Y	E	H	Z	G	C	Q	T	A	J	U	L	B	R	I	P	S	K	D	O	V	X	W	F
J	G	O	N	Z	F	I	A	H	D	R	U	B	K	V	M	C	S	J	Q	T	L	E	P	W	Y	X
K	Y	H	P	O	A	G	J	B	I	E	S	V	C	L	W	N	D	T	K	R	U	M	F	Q	X	Z
L	A	Z	I	Q	P	B	H	K	C	J	F	T	W	D	M	X	O	E	U	L	S	V	N	G	R	Y
M	Z	B	A	J	R	Q	C	I	L	D	K	G	U	X	E	N	Y	P	F	V	M	T	W	O	H	S
N	T	A	C	B	K	S	R	D	J	M	E	L	H	V	Y	F	O	Z	Q	G	W	N	U	X	P	I
O	J	U	B	D	C	L	T	S	E	K	N	F	M	I	W	Z	G	P	A	R	H	X	O	V	Y	Q
P	R	K	V	C	E	D	M	U	T	F	L	O	G	N	J	X	A	H	Q	B	S	I	Y	P	W	Z
Q	A	S	L	W	D	F	E	N	V	U	G	M	P	H	O	K	Y	B	I	R	C	T	J	Z	Q	X
R	Y	B	T	M	X	E	G	F	O	W	V	H	N	Q	I	P	L	Z	C	J	S	D	U	K	A	R
S	S	Z	C	U	N	Y	F	H	G	P	X	W	I	O	R	J	Q	M	A	D	K	T	E	V	L	B
T	C	T	A	D	V	O	Z	G	I	H	Q	Y	X	J	P	S	K	R	N	B	E	L	U	F	W	M
U	N	D	U	B	E	W	P	A	H	J	I	R	Z	Y	K	Q	T	L	S	O	C	F	M	V	G	X
V	Y	O	E	V	C	F	X	Q	B	I	K	J	S	A	Z	L	R	U	M	T	P	D	G	N	W	H
W	I	Z	P	F	W	D	G	Y	R	C	J	L	K	T	B	A	M	S	V	N	U	Q	E	H	O	X
X	Y	J	A	Q	G	X	E	H	Z	S	D	K	M	L	U	C	B	N	T	W	O	V	R	F	I	P
Y	Q	Z	K	B	R	H	Y	F	I	A	T	E	L	N	M	V	D	C	O	U	X	P	W	S	G	J
Z	K	R	A	L	C	S	I	Z	G	J	B	U	F	M	O	N	W	E	D	P	V	Y	Q	X	T	H
A	I	L	S	B	M	D	T	J	A	H	K	C	V	G	N	P	O	X	F	E	Q	W	Z	R	Y	U
B	V	J	M	T	C	N	E	U	K	B	I	L	D	W	H	O	Q	P	Y	G	F	R	X	A	S	Z
C	A	W	K	N	U	D	O	F	V	L	C	J	M	E	X	I	P	R	Q	Z	H	G	S	T	B	T
D	U	B	X	L	O	V	E	P	G	W	M	D	K	N	F	Y	J	Q	S	R	A	I	H	T	Z	C
E	D	V	C	Y	M	P	W	F	Q	H	X	N	E	L	O	G	Z	K	R	T	S	B	J	I	U	A

FIGURE 1.

```
F  B E W D Z N Q X G R I Y O F M P H A L S U T C K J V
G  W C F X E A O R Y H S J Z P G N Q I B M T V U D L K
H  L X D G Y F B P S Z I T K A Q H O R J C N U W V E M
I  N M Y E H Q G C Q T A J U L B R I P S K D O V X W F
J  G O N Z F I A H D R U B K V M C S J Q T L E P W Y X
K  Y H P O A G J B I E S V C L W N D T K R U M F Q X Z
L  A Z I Q P B H K C J F T W D M X O E U L S V N G R Y
M  Z B A J R Q C I L D K G U X E N Y P F V M T W O H S
N  T A C B K S R D J M E L H V Y F O Z Q G W N U X P I
O  J U B D C L T S E K N F M I W Z G P A R H X O V Y Q
P  R K V C E D M U T F L O G N J X A H Q B S I Y P W Z
Q  A S L W D F E N V U G M P H O K Y B I R C T J Z Q X
R  Y B T M X E G F O W V H N Q I P L Z C J S D U K A R
S  S Z C U N Y F H G P X W I O R J Q M A D K T E V L B
T  C T A D V O Z G I H Q Y X J P S K R N B E L U F W M
U  N D U B E W P A H J I R Q Y K Q T L S O C F M V G X
V  Y O E V C F X Q B I K J S A Z L R U M T P D G N W H
W  I Z P F W D G Y R C J L K T B A M S V N U Q E H O X
X  Y J A Q G X E H Z S D K M L U C B N T W O V R F I P
Y  Q Z K B R H Y F I A T E L N M V D C O U X P W S C J
Z  K R A L C S I Z G J B U F M O N W E D P V Y Q X T H
```

FIGURE 1 (CONT'D)

1. SOLUTION OF THE FIRST ROTOR

In order to determine the identity and position of the first rotor (i.e., the fastest turning one) we need to locate a segment of probable plaintext enciphered while only that rotor is turning. In this case, the other rotors generate a fixed reciprocal simple substitution and equation (1) becomes

$$c_k = p_k R_1^{i+k} \, U R_{-1}^{i+k}, \ k = 1, 2, \ldots, L \tag{2}$$

where the p_k and c_k are L consecutive characters of plaintext and cipher-text, respectively. U represents the combined substitution of all other rotors.

Applying the permutation R_1^{i+k} to both sides of (2) yields the equivalent equation:

$$c_k R_1^{i+k} = p_k R_1^{i+k} U. \tag{3}$$

Equation (3) shows that when the correct rotor and correct starting position are used to encipher both plaintext and corresponding ciphertext, then the resulting encipherments are related by a fixed reciprocal mono-alphabetic substitution. This property can be used to determine the first rotor from even a short amount of plaintext. For example, if we suspect the parallel plain and cipher text to be

Plain: G E N E R A L
Cipher: L Z H X B T F

In order to test the rotor of Figure 1 to see if it could be the first rotor, we assemble the vertical column strips for that rotor as shown in Figure 2.

```
                                          L
                                       A  C
                                    R  I  L
                                 E  X  V  J
                              N  M  P  A  D
                           E  G  C  R  U  N
                        G  M  W  U  Q  D  Y
Assumed      A          T  C  E  O  K  B  J
Starting     B          E  U  N  M  A  W  T
Position     C          O  O  L  Z  I  L  J
             D          .  .  .  .  .  .  .
             E          .  .  .  .  .  .  .
             F          .  .  .  .  .  .  .
```

FIGURE 2.

This use of strips allows us to generate all 26 possible encipherments of GENERAL using the rotor of Figure 1. If a second parallel set of strips is likewise set up using the ciphertext LZHXBTF, then comparison of the two strips should show isomorphic encipherments at the correct position. Further, the isomorphs must be related by a monoalphabetic substitution that is reciprocal. The 26 sets of encipherments are shown in Figure 3.

Rotor starting position A can be discounted since this requires isomorphism of the sequences:

T C E O K B J
C Z F T V S A

If the mapping U of equation (3) contains the cycle (TC) then it obviously cannot contain the contradictory cycle (CZ) as required here. For position B, we need isomorphism of the sequences:

		G	E	N	E	R	A	L	L	Z	H	X	B	T	F
Assumed	A	T	C	E	O	K	B	J	C	S	F	T	V	S	A
Starting	B	E	U	N	M	A	W	T	L	T	P	I	E	M	F
Position	C	O	O	L	Z	I	L	J	J	C	F	K	C	C	Z
	D	E	M	F	E	R	N	B	D	A	X	D	X	K	I
	E	W	Z	P	Y	P	G	V	N	V	R	V	M	T	G
	F	Q	E	A	H	J	Y	T	Y	K	P	P	O	R	B
	G	O	Y	L	F	T	A	G	J	M	C	W	H	L	Q
	H	B	H	V	A	E	Z	L	T	F	H	Q	Z	V	S
	I	G	F	L	P	P	T	F	J	X	B	G	B	G	L
	J	A	A	D	R	Z	J	O	B	Z	K	O	A	R	D
	K	J	P	X	K	P	R	M	V	Y	I	X	U	B	F
	L	H	R	V	C	H	A	H	T	S	D	V	K	R	E
	M	C	K	I	E	B	Y	W	G	I	S	P	S	J	Y
	N	R	C	N	D	Z	S	Y	L	Q	U	Z	B	D	O
	O	T	E	H	X	M	C	R	F	Z	N	K	Z	B	W
	P	M	D	Q	N	R	N	J	O	X	F	V	T	O	F
	Q	E	X	O	V	L	Y	L	M	R	H	F	D	T	D
	R	Z	N	J	E	U	I	K	H	B	G	V	O	N	X
	S	F	V	Y	C	S	Y	E	W	M	A	N	Z	W	H
	T	Z	E	A	W	N	Q	U	Y	X	Q	H	J	U	S
	U	P	C	T	G	C	K	C	R	P	Y	F	Z	P	D
	V	X	W	L	R	E	I	L	J	J	H	S	R	E	N
	W	G	G	N	C	X	V	J	L	H	F	X	L	G	D
	X	E	R	M	M	P	A	D	K	U	Z	R	J	Z	V
	Y	I	C	G	C	R	U	N	E	Z	J	A	W	R	P
	Z	Y	M	W	I	Q	D	Y	U	T	U	T	B	T	N

FIGURE 3.

```
E U N M A W T
L T P I E M F
```

One contradiction here, for example, is the existence of the cycles (*EL*) and (*EA*). In a similar manner every one of the 26 locations can be ruled out, except starting location *Q*, where the required isomorphism is

```
E X O V L Y L
M R H F D T D
```

Thus, if the plaintext has been correctly placed, then this rotor could have been the first one only if the encipherment begins at rotor position *Q*. The mapping *U* at this encipherment position contains the cycles (*EM*), (*RX*), (*HO*), (*FV*), (*DL*), (*TY*).

If the second rotor moves during the encipherment of our probable plaintext, the mapping U is altered and two different isomorphic pieces will be obtained. With the commercial Enigma this situation is advantageous as will be seen shortly. Since the ratchet wheel in this Enigma model is rigidly fixed to the body of the coding cylinder, then the stepping position is known when the identity of the rotor is known. Suppose our probable text has been expanded to include the matching plain and cipher segments:

G E N E R A L F E L D M A R S C H A L L K E S S E R L I N G
L S H X B T F W U I O V B C A R X S N C V Z Y X N J B F W B

Encipherments of both texts beginning at rotor position Q yield the isomorphs

Q R S T U V W X Y Z	A B C D E F G H I J K L M N O P Q R S T	*Rotor 1 Position*
E X O V L Y L X R U	B D A P R W R L J B S P F Q C H M O O Z	*Output of Rotor 1 (Enciphered Plaintext)*
M R H F D T D R X G	N R W X D A D J L N M Y H X I F S E E T	*Output of Rotor 1 (Enciphered Ciphertext)*

$\underbrace{\hspace{4cm}}_{U_1} \qquad \underbrace{\hspace{6cm}}_{U_2}$

If this rotor is known to step the adjacent rotor as it moves between Z and A then we derive pieces of the mapping U_1 and U_2 from equation (3).

2. SOLUTION OF THE SECOND AND FURTHER ROTORS

After the fastest rotor has been determined, recovery of further rotors can begin. The analysis used here requires known plaintext and corresponding ciphertext at two different locations of the rotor to be identified. In the previous example the movement of rotor 2 generated the mappings U_1 and U_2. We know, partially at least, these two mappings:

U_1: $(EM),(RX),(HO),(FV),(DL),(TY)$;
U_2: $(BN),(DR),(AW),(QX),(JL),(SM),(PY),(FH),(QX),(CI),(EO),(TZ)$.

Denoting

$$p'_k = p_k R^{i+k} \text{ and } c'_k = c_k R^{i+k}$$

in (3) yields

$$c'_k = p'_k U, \qquad k = 1, 2, \ldots, L.$$

This last equation states that the enciphered plaintext and enciphered ciphertext are related by a mapping U which is constant unless the second rotor moves. When the rotor does move, as in the previous example, the mappings U_1 and U_2 correspond to operators:

$$U_1 = R_2^n V R_{-2}^n \quad \text{and} \quad U_2 = R_2^{n+1} V R_{-2}^{n+1}$$

respectively, where n is the (unknown) position of rotor 2 and mapping V is that due to the third and reflecting rotors,

$$V = R_3^m U R_{-3}^m.$$

Since we know some p', p'', c', and c'' for which the equations:

$$c' = p' R_2^n V R_{-2}^n \quad \text{and} \quad c'' = p'' R_2^{n+1} V R_{-2}^{n+1}$$

hold, we can form the equations:

$$c' R_2^h = p' R_2^n V R_{-2}^n R_{+2}^h \quad \text{and} \quad c'' R_2^{h+1} = p'' R_2^{n+1} V R_{-2}^{n+1} R_{+2}^{h+1}$$

for a suspected rotor 2 and a trial rotor position h. The operators:

$$R_{-2}^n R_2^h \quad \text{and} \quad R_{-2}^{n+1} R_2^{h+1}$$

are complicated, but, when $n = h$, both reduce to the identity operator. We then have the equations:

$$d' = c' R_2^h = p' R_2^n V \quad \text{and} \quad d'' = c'' R_2^{h+1} = p'' R_2^{n+1} V$$

satisfied simultaneously. These last two equations can be used to determine the identity and rotor position of the second rotor. In effect, the d' and d'' values result from taking the p' and p'', enciphering them in two successive rotor positions of rotor 2 and then applying an unknown substitution V in both cases. If we reconnect the two alphabets by chaining, the same cycle structure will result as we would have gotten without applying V. For example, using the tableau for rotor 2 and chaining the first two alphabets for positions A and B yields the permutation: (LOZSEP) (ACTGVJYRQ) (BUINWMHFX) (DK). This mapping has four cycles of lengths 6, 9, 9, and 2. Chaining any two successive rotor position alphabets yields a permutation with the same cycle lengths—6, 9, 9, 2—although the letters in each cycle will change. Thus, the cycle lengths serve to identify the rotor. The position of the cycles relative to the plaintext alphabet yield the rotor position. For instance, if the 2 cycle occurs under plaintext letter K and N in the tableau, the rotor positions must be C and D. The mapping V only serves to monoalphabetically encipher the 26 rotor position alphabets and clearly leaves the cycle properties of interest unchanged.

All of this process is easier to do than to say. Consider the following two tables:

U_1 (Rotor Position at left):

	A	B	C	D	E	F	G	H	I	J	K	L	M	N	O	P	Q	R	S	T	U	V	W	X	Y	Z
U_1:			L	M	V		O				D	E		H				X	Y					R	T	
A			K	P	G		Z				T	B		J				I	V					O	H	
B			D	L	V		S				G	U		Y				N	J					Z	F	
C			U	E	J		R				Y	H		C				I	O					S	Q	
D			G	V	H		N				O	Z		E				X	J					C	B	
E			N	H	S		G				R	P		X				L	Y					V	U	
.		.		.		.					.		.				.		.						.	.

U_2 (Rotor Position at left):

	A	B	C	D	E	F	G	H	I	J	K	L	M	N	O	P	Q	R	S	T	U	V	W	X	Y	Z
U_2:			R	O	H		F				J	S		E				D	Z					Q	P	
B			Z	S	Y		C				E	P		U				G	J					R	A	
C			S	R	C		V				L	A		H				Y	R					B	T	
D			C	N	E		I				A	T		Z				O	N					U	S	
E			V	G	X		A				E	D		P				R	G					T	O	
F			U	X	K		Q				G	W		S				A	X					P	H	
.		.		.		.					.		.				.		.						.	.

On the first two lines of each table are recorded the reciprocal mappings U_1 and U_2 for all letters in common. Following this is the encipherment of the second lines of each table for each position of rotor 2. The second table contains the rotor position advanced one with respect to the first table. This process is convenient to do with alphabet strips bearing the columns of the rotor 2 tableau. The fact that strips can be used is what makes the method fast enough for hand use.

We now seek to examine corresponding lines of each table and find patterns isomorphic with the rotor 2 table [see Figure 4].

	A	B	C	D	E	F	G	H	I	J	K	L	M	N	O	P	Q	R	S	T	U	V	W	X	Y	Z
A	L	W	F	T	B	A	X	J	D	S	C	K	P	R	Z	Q	Y	O	E	H	U	G	M	I	V	N
B	O	M	X	G	U	C	B	Y	K	E	T	D	L	Q	S	A	R	Z	P	F	I	V	H	N	J	W
C	X	P	N	Y	H	V	D	C	Z	L	F	U	E	M	R	T	B	S	A	Q	G	J	W	I	O	K
D	L	Y	Q	O	Z	I	W	E	D	A	M	G	V	F	N	S	U	C	T	B	R	H	K	X	J	P
E	Q	M	Z	R	P	A	J	X	F	E	B	N	H	W	G	O	T	V	D	U	C	S	I	L	Y	K
F	L	R	N	A	S	Q	B	K	Y	G	F	C	O	I	X	H	P	U	W	E	V	D	T	J	M	Z
G	A	M	S	O	B	T	R	C	L	Z	H	G	D	P	J	Y	I	Q	V	X	F	W	E	U	K	N
H	O	B	N	T	P	C	U	S	D	M	A	I	H	E	Q	K	Z	J	R	W	Y	G	X	F	V	L
I	M	P	C	O	U	Q	D	V	T	E	N	B	J	I	F	R	L	A	K	S	X	Z	H	Y	G	W
J	X	N	Q	D	P	V	R	E	W	U	F	O	C	K	U	G	S	M	B	L	T	Y	A	I	Z	H
K	I	Y	O	R	E	Q	W	S	F	X	V	G	P	D	L	K	H	T	N	C	M	U	Z	B	J	A
L	B	J	Z	P	S	F	R	X	T	G	Y	W	H	Q	E	M	L	I	U	O	D	N	V	A	C	K
M	L	C	K	A	Q	T	G	S	Y	U	H	Z	X	I	R	F	N	M	J	V	P	E	O	W	B	D
N	E	M	D	L	B	R	U	H	T	Z	V	I	A	Y	J	S	G	O	N	K	W	Q	F	P	X	C
O	D	F	N	E	M	C	S	V	I	U	A	W	J	B	Z	K	T	H	P	O	L	X	R	G	Q	Y
P	Z	E	G	O	F	N	D	T	W	J	V	B	X	K	C	A	L	U	I	Q	P	M	Y	S	H	R
Q	S	A	F	H	P	G	O	E	U	X	K	W	C	Y	L	D	B	M	V	J	R	Q	N	Z	T	I
R	J	T	B	G	I	Q	H	P	F	V	Y	L	X	D	Z	M	E	C	N	W	K	S	R	O	A	U
S	V	K	U	C	H	J	R	I	Q	G	W	Z	M	Y	E	A	N	F	D	O	X	L	T	S	P	B
T	C	W	L	V	D	I	K	S	J	R	H	X	A	N	Z	F	B	O	G	E	P	Y	M	U	T	Q
U	R	D	X	M	W	E	J	L	T	K	S	I	Y	B	O	A	G	C	P	H	F	Q	Z	N	V	U
V	V	S	E	Y	N	X	F	K	M	U	L	T	J	Z	C	P	B	H	D	Q	I	G	R	A	O	W
W	X	W	T	F	Z	O	Y	G	L	N	V	M	U	K	A	D	Q	C	I	E	R	J	H	S	B	P
X	Q	Y	X	U	G	A	P	Z	H	M	O	W	N	V	L	B	E	R	D	J	F	S	K	I	T	C
Y	D	R	Z	Y	V	H	B	Q	A	I	N	P	X	O	W	M	C	F	S	E	K	G	T	L	J	U
Z	V	E	S	A	Z	W	I	C	R	B	J	O	Q	Y	P	X	N	D	G	T	F	L	H	U	M	K

FIGURE 4. ROTOR 2.

To demonstrate, if the rotor position was A-B then the rotor 2 table must have the same letter under plaintext H in position A that it has under plaintext D in position B. This is because the letter Z occurs in both these positions in the above tables. This condition is not satisfied since the corresponding characters from the rotor 2 table are J (under H) and G (under D). The next sequence, positions B-C, is seen to be correct. Extracting from the above tables, we have

Plain:	A B C D E F G H I J K L M N O P Q R S T U V W X Y Z
Tab. 1,B	D L V S G U Y N J Z F
Tab. 2,C	S R C V L A H Y O B T

while, from the rotor 2 table, we find

Plain:	A B C D E F G H I J K L M N O P Q R S T U V W X Y Z
B	G U C Y D L S Z F N J
C	Y H V C U E R S Q I O

The table entries are isomorphic and thus we have found the correct rotor position. At this point, the positions and identities of the first and second rotors are known. The mapping *V* can be found, in part at least, and the rest of the message deciphered with great probability if the third rotor does not move during the message text so that *V* remains constant. Of course the same procedure outlined previously would recover the position of the third rotor if plaintext and corresponding ciphertext could be found for which rotor 3 had occupied two different positions.

In practice, it is easier to catalog all of the permutations generated using a third rotor and the reflecting rotor Z. For three rotors there are only $26^2 \cdot 3 = 2028$ such permutations to index for look-up. The partial knowledge of *V* would allow one to determine the setting of the third and reversing rotors quite rapidly using such a table. It is also practicable to catalog by hand permutations corresponding to the second, third, and reversing rotor combinations. There are 35,153 of these. In that case, only the first rotor need be discovered.

REFERENCES

1. Kahn, D. (1967), *The Codebreakers*. New York: Macmillan.
2. Rohrbach, H. (1978), Mathematical and Mechanical Methods in Cryptology II. (Bradford Hardie, translator.) *Cryptologia*. 2: 20–37.
3. Clark, R. (1977), *The Man Who Broke Purple*. Boston: Little, Brown.

The Black Chamber: How the British Broke Enigma by Cipher A. Deavours

This column begins what is planned as a regular feature of *Cryptologia*— a series of articles dealing with classical machine and computer cryptology. In spite of the plethora of public cryptographic literature appearing in technical journals these days, the machine period, 1925–1965, remains in darkness. We hope to shed light upon the cryptologic path. The design of high speed encryption algorithms for computers, especially microprocessors, is another of our concerns. Generally, explanations will be kept at as low a technical level as possible consistent with conciseness and clarity, but we will employ mathematics freely when it seems called for. The reader is assumed to be familiar with the subject of cryptology in general. Comments and additional information from readers are always welcome.

While the Engima story has been unraveling through books and papers too numerous to mention during the last few years, technical information about just how the Allied penetrations of the system were attained has not been forthcoming. The viewpoints of both the British and American Governments are that the *results* of wartime cryptanalysis will now be made public, but the *methods* whereby they were obtained will remain secret.

The cryptanalytic history of the Enigma systems can be viewed in four time periods:

1. *Polish Period:* 1928–40. Message indicator dependent methods. Plugboard model.

   A. Six letter indicators (1928–38). Two methods employed based on the same cryptologic attack—cycle factorization and table lookup using tabulation tables prepared by the cyclometer.

From *Cryptologia*, Vol. 4, No. 3, July 1980.

B. Nine letter indicators (1938–40). Two methods. Mechanical plugboard-dependent solution using the "bomby" and hand method using canvases.

2. *Spanish Civil War:* 1936–39. Probable plaintext method called the "baton method" by the French, "casting the rods" by the British, and the "strip" method by the Americans. Commercial Enigmas with variants used by German, Italian, and Spanish Nationalist forces.

3. *British Period:* 1940–45. Probable plaintext method for plugboard models. Polish methods employed to some extent. Construction of high speed "bombes" for mechanical solution—cryptanalytic methods employed, dissimilar from Polish "bomba."

4. *Postwar Period:* 1945–? Solutions using general purpose computers.

Polish work has been analyzed in a lengthy unpublished work by this author. The "baton method" will be the subject of our next column. [See preceding article by C. Deavours (Oct. 1980).] It was this method which was discovered by everybody and was a major impetus for the original German Enigma modifications made in the 1920's. It is interesting to note that even trivial problems often seemed to reproduce themselves among cryptanalysts of different nations. As an example, Polish mathematicians were held up for several months in their work trying to discover the wiring between the keyboard and the input contact board. On the earlier commercial version of the Enigma, this permutation had been based on the standard typewriter keyboard: QWERT . . . On the Army model of the machine the wiring was altered to the normal alphabetic sequence ABCDEFG . . . The same problem repeated itself later in the British camp when Dilwyn Knox agonized over the identical problem for some time before seeing the light through the trees.

If p denotes a plaintext character and c the corresponding ciphertext character, then, at a fixed rotor position, the equation for encipherment is

$$P^{-1} E^{-1} R_1^{-1} R_2^{-1} R_3^{-1} RR_3 R_2 R_1 EP (p) = c \tag{1}$$

where

P is the plugboard permutation—a reciprocal interchange of letters. Varying number of plugs were used, 10 being the most common number in later years. The permutation P is self-reciprocal so that $P^{-1} = P$.

E is the aforementioned keyboard-to-input wiring, which, for the Army model, is the identity transformation, so $E = I$.

R_i is the permutation generated by the ith rotor at the position in question. If we know a rotor permutation at any position, say Q, then the other rotated positions are generated by the group $C^{-i}QC^i$, where i is an integer and C^i is a Caesar shift of i letters in the normal alphabetic sequence.

R is the reflecting rotor wiring permutation; self-reciprocal of 26 letters (. . . comprised of 13 cycles of length 2).

Due to the nine-letter indicators used by the German Army and Air Force, one could often deduce the partial rotor order and rotor stepping positions after a number of messages in the same key (but different rotor starting positions) had been intercepted. The British bombes could then be set up using this information. Probable plaintext in one of the messages was required for the solution process. This never proved to be much of a problem since the Germans sent very stereotyped messages and the redundant nature of the language itself helped. For example, one cryptographer connected with the Rommel circuit between Germany and North Africa began every message exactly the same! The reciprocal nature of Enigma encipherment where no letter could represent itself was, of course, another great aid to Allied cryptanalysts.

The British bombes performed the task of determining the rotor positions and plugboard wiring for the probable plaintext. The calculation had two parts:

1. Step through allowable rotor positions.

2. At each rotor position determine its feasibility by applying the constraints imposed by the plugboard wiring.

The British machine could examine about five rotor positions per second. The Polish bomba, which employed another method but also did a rotor search, had a speed of about 2.7 rotor positions per second. Thus, if the identity of two of the three rotors could be determined and those three rotors had been chosen from the usual five, the other rotor is one of the three remaining ones. Three bombes could be employed, if available, to examine the three possible rotor orders with the entire operation requiring a maximum of about one hour.

To illustrate the computation which the bombe carried out, let us suppose that we have identified the plaintext OBERKOMMANDO to be JMFLYWASOCBD in cipher. (This plaintext is too short for good results, but is used as an illustration only.) Further suppose equation (1) is rewritten as $PZP(p) = c$, where the product of all rotor permutations is represented by Z at a fixed rotor position. By stepping through the possible rotor positions we are trying to determine if the equation $PZP(p) = c$ holds at a successive set of Z's. Since OBERKOMMANDO has 11 characters, we want to know if the equations:

$$PZ_iP(p_i) = c_i, \ i=1,2, \ldots ,11$$

hold, or equivalently, since $P = P^{-1}$,

$$Z_iP(p_i) = P(c_i), \ i=1,2, \ldots ,11 \qquad (2)$$

In equation (2), the p_i's, c_i's and set of permutations Z_i are assumed known. (It should be clear that trying all rotor positions is the same thing as testing all possible sets of Z_i's.) Since the patchpanel wiring, P, is unknown, we cannot check the equation directly, but only determine if a set of data is consistent with the existence of such a permutation P at the assumed rotor positions.

Let us assume that at a rotor position to be tested, the 12 successive permutations Z_i generated by the rotors during the encipherment of OB-ERKOMMANDO are those given in the Appendix to this paper. We have to test the assumption:

	1 1 1
Rotor Positions	1 2 3 4 5 6 7 8 9 0 1 2
Plaintext	O B E R K O M M A N D O
Ciphertext	J M F L Y W A S O C B D

In the plain-cipher pairs, we select a frequently occurring character—the letter "O" is an obvious choice in this example. The panel wiring P is unknown, but it must map the letter O into one of the letters of the alphabet A,B, . . . ,Z. We can test each assumption. If the permutation P contains the cycle (O,A), then we must have

	1
Rotor Position	1 6 9 0
Plain-Cipher	0 0 0 0 $\rceil P$
P Output	A A A A $\rfloor$
Z Output	E O J B $\rceil P$
P Output = Ciphertext	J W A C $\rfloor$

Note that in the plain-cipher pairs, either letter can be considered plaintext because the encipherment is reciprocal. In passing from *Z Output* to the final text the mapping P is encountered, thus the assumption that P contains (O,A) means that P also contains the pairs: (*EJ*), (*OW*), (*JA*), (*BC*). This cannot be, since P could not contain both the cycles

(*OA*) and (*OW*), or the same letter, *O*, would be mapped to two different characters, A and W.

Similarly, if *P* contains the cycle (*OB*), then it must also contain the cycles (*OJ*), (*NW*), (*VA*), and (*AC*). The cycles (*OB*) and (*OJ*) contradict one another, as do (*VA*) and (*AC*).

Assuming that the plaintext has been correctly placed, a contradiction such as the above indicates that either the rotor position being tested is wrong, or else the wrong *P* has been encountered.

Using the assumption that *P* contains (*OF*) implies that it also contains the pairs (*TJ*), (*EW*), (*NA*), (*PC*)—none of which pose a contradiction. Further consideration reveals the falsity of this assumption, since rotor position 7 contains the plaintext-ciphertext pair (*MA*). If *P* contained (*NA*), then, since Z_7 takes *N* into *W*, *P* must also contain the cycle (*MW*), which is impossible since it must also contain (*EW*) as derived previously. Thus, contradictions are sometimes secondary implications in the chain of reasoning.

Note that in the plain-cipher pairs, either letter can be considered plaintext because the encipherment is reciprocal. In passing from *Z Output* to the final text the mapping *P* is encountered, thus the assumption that *P* contains (O,A) means that *P* also contains the pairs: (*EJ*), (*OW*), (*JA*), (*BC*). This cannot be, since *P* could not contain both the cycles (*OA*) and (*OW*), or the same letter, *O*, would be mapped to two different characters, A and W.

Similarly, if *P* contains the cycle (*OB*), then it must also contain the cycles (*OJ*), (*NW*), (*VA*), and (*AC*). The cycles (*OB*) and (*OJ*) contradict one another, as do (*VA*) and (*AC*).

Assuming that the plaintext has been correctly placed, a contradiction such as the above indicates that either the rotor position being tested is wrong, or else the wrong *P* has been encountered.

Using the assumption that *P* contains (*OF*) implies that it also contains the pairs (*TJ*), (*EW*), (*NA*), (*PC*)—none of which pose a contradiction. Further consideration reveals the falsity of this assumption, since rotor position 7 contains the plaintext-ciphertext pair (*MA*). If *P* contained (*NA*), then, since Z_7 takes *N* into *W*, *P* must also contain the cycle (*MW*), which is impossible since it must also contain (*EW*) as derived previously. Thus, contradictions are sometimes secondary implications in the chain of reasoning.

While the above type of approach may seem reasonable enough, the reader may wonder how it could be carried out, even by a machine, within reasonable time. At each rotor position we must rule out all mappings of a given character to any of the 26 letters of the alphabet in order to discard that rotor position as possible. The British found the solution to the time problem by applying all possible mappings for a given character, e.g. (OA), (OB), (OC), . . . ,(OZ), *in parallel* for each of the plain-cipher pairs. A complicated system of relays then keeps track of results. The machine circuitry was designed so that impossible values of the permutation P were not tried. Thus, if the cycle (OA) is ruled out, no permutation P containing the cycle (OA) need be pursued. Two crucial ideas are involved in the bombe's success:

Parallel computation;
Reduction of key space by rejecting blocks of impossible P values.

Without trying to assign specific credit, Gordon Welchman and Alan Turing are the architects of the bombe's design. In a very real sense, the computational procedure used was a natural adaptation of the earlier strip methods used by hand to solve the commercial Enigma. No cryptanalytic debt is owed to the Poles since it is clear that the British bombes were not technological descendants of the Polish bomba, although the psychological impetus the Poles gave the British by their solutions must have been immense.

Note: The solution of the Naval (4 rotor) Enigma was achieved in the same manner as noted previously, the obstacle to success in that case being the message indicator system employed by the Germans.

APPENDIX

Z Permutations

Input		A B C D E F G H I J K L M N O P Q R S T U V W X Y Z
	1	E O I V A T J Z C G R U Y X B Q P K W F L D S N M H
	2	Z J X T S H N F M B U W I G V Q P Y E D K O L C R A
	3	J I L O G M E N B A P C F H D K X T V R Y S Z Q U W
	4	G V E M C Q A U R O N T D K J W F I Z L H B P Y X S
	5	T V Z F H D E N X O L K U H J S Y W P A M B R I Q C
Rotor	6	O N G W F E C M R L U J H B A Y Z I V X K S D T P Q
Position	7	U L H Y M K V C R O F B E W J S T I P Q A G N Z D X
	8	Q X H T K Z C O P N E Y S J H I A W M D V U R B L F
	9	J V U L T N K Z Y A G D P F S M X W O E C B R Q I H
	10	B A Y N L P S J K H I E O D M F R Q G U T Z X W C V
	11	R J U I Y W Z K D B H P O V M L T A X Q C N F S E G
	12	W U Z T P N J V G R Y O X F L E T J Q D B H A M K C

P: (AE) (BI) (CV) (FJ)
(HR) (KQ) (LU) (NZ)
(OT) (WX) (D) (G)
(M) (P) (S) (Y)

										1	1	1
Rotor Positions	1	2	3	4	5	6	7	8	9	0	1	2
Plaintext	O	B	E	R	K	O	M	M	A	N	D	O
P Output	T	I	A	H	Q	T	M	M	E	Z	D	T
Z Output	F	M	J	U	Y	X	E	S	T	V	I	D
P Output=Cipher	J	M	F	L	Y	W	A	S	O	C	B	D

Decrypting a Stream Cipher Based on J-K Flip-Flops*
by Frank Rubin

ABSTRACT: Pless has proposed a stream cipher based on J-K flip-flops that uses eight linear shift registers with feedback, having a combined length of 97 bits, four J-K flip-flops, and a four-stage cycling counter. The cipher has 2.54×10^{51} initial states (keys), and generates a presumably pseudorandom stream whose period is 1.52×10^{29} bits. Despite these impressive statistics, it is computationally feasible to solve such a cipher with a known-plaintext attack, using as few as 15 characters.

Index Terms: Cryptography, J-K flip-flop, linear shift register, stream cipher, Boolean equations, code breaking.

1. INTRODUCTION

In a previous issue of [*IEEE Transactions on Computers*], Vera Pless [2] published a correspondence that proposes several schemes for generating pseudorandom streams of bits, based on J-K flip-flops. These bit streams are then added (modulo 2) to a binary message to produce an enciphered message.

Pless' arrangements A and B are for illustrative purposes. They are not claimed to be cryptographically secure. Arrangement C is proposed as secure, but has the disadvantage that it must generate four output bits for each bit used. Therefore this arrangement would have to operate at four times the data rate of the communications channel. Finally, Pless proposes arrangement D, which is intended to have all of the security of arrangement C, but which runs at the same rate as the data channel. This last arrangement possesses some very impressive properties that suggest

From *Cryptologia*, Vol. 5, No. 1, Jan. 1981.

extreme security, yet it will be shown here that a known-plaintext attack on this cipher is computationally feasible with today's computers.

Before proceeding to the analysis, there are three items that must be explained in some detail.

1.1 Feedback Register

A general n-stage feedback register (FR), or more precisely, a linear shift register with feedback, consists of n binary storage elements (register positions) and n gates. Let $x(s,i)$ represent the state of register position i, $1 \leq i \leq n$, at stage s, and $c(j)$ be 0 or 1, according to whether gate j, $1 \leq j \leq n$, is closed or open. Then the contents of register position i at stage $s+1$ is given by

$$x(s + 1,i) = x(s,i + 1), \quad \text{for } 1 \leq i \leq n \tag{1a}$$

$$x(s + 1,n) = c(1)x(s,1) \oplus...\oplus c(n)x(s,n), \tag{1b}$$
$$\text{where } \oplus \text{ indicates addition modulo 2.}$$

The output bit at stage s, for $s + 1, 2, \ldots$, is $x(s) = x(s - 1,1)$, where $x(0,i)$ represents the initial contents of the register. The sequence of output bits repeats with a period that depends upon the values of the coefficients $c(j)$. When these are properly chosen, the period of the output sequence achieves its maximum value, $P = 2^{n-1}$, provided that the $x(0,i)$ are not all 0. Such a choice of the $c(j)$ is called *primitive*.

It can be seen that when the coefficients $c(j)$ are all known, equation (1b) is linear. Therefore, knowing any n output bits $x(s)$ of the register will result in n linear Boolean equations in the variables $x(0,1)$ through $x(0,n)$. Thus, the initial contents of the register can easily be found.

Conversely, if $x(s,i)$ for $1 \leq i \leq n$ are known, equation (1b) is linear in the n variables $c(1)$ through $c(n)$. Thus, if $x(s)$ and $x(s,i)$ $1 \leq i \leq n$ are known for n distinct values of s, n linear equations result that will determine the coefficients $c(j)$. (These equations will be linearly independent, unless two of the values of s differ by a multiple of p, the period of the register. In practical cases, p will be so large that this is very unlikely.)

A special case of particular interest [1] occurs when $2n$ consecutive output bits, $x(s + 1)$ through $x(s + 2n)$, of the register are known. This allows simultaneous solution for $x(s,i)$ and $c(j)$. This requirement can be reduced to $2n - 1$ bits when the coefficients are known to be primitive, since then $c(1)$ must be 1.

1.2 J-K Flip-flop

A J-K flip-flop is a two-state device with two binary inputs, denoted *J* and *K,* and one binary output. The state *S* of the device is equal to the previous output bit. The output bit and next state of the device depend upon inputs and current state *S* as follows:

J	K	Output
0	0	S
0	1	0
1	0	1
1	1	$S \oplus 1$

Given one output bit of the J-K flip-flop, it is impossible to determine either input uniquely; however, the two inputs are restricted to three of their four possible values. If the previous output bit is also known, then one of the input bits is uniquely determined. For example, if a 0 is emitted following a 1, then the *K* input must be 1.

1.3 Cryptographic Complexity

The cryptographic complexity of a decryption method means the number of random or exhaustive trials that must be made. Each trial may involve the solution of a set of linear equations, or it may require some statistical test, such as testing the frequency distribution of the characters in a supposed solution. Therefore, the cryptographic complexity may, in general, be several orders of magnitude smaller than the computational complexity.

Most of the trials [presented here] will involve solution of linear Boolean equations. These can be solved by the familiar Gauss-Seidel elimination method, but, because only binary operations are involved, and because the size of the equations is small enough to allow all coefficients to be kept in a single 32-bit word, solution is much faster than for conventional linear equations with real-valued coefficients.

To illustrate the concept of cryptographic complexity, suppose that every fourth output bit from a feedback register were known. We will compare the cryptographic complexity of three methods of solution.

Suppose the FR had *n* stages. If we knew $2n - 1$ consecutive output bits, the register could be completely solved. Of the first $2n - 1$ output bits, we already know $(2n - 1 + 3)/4$ or $(n + 1)/2$ bits. (Integer division is assumed, so 7/2 yields 3.) We could attempt to guess the remaining

$2n - 1 - (n + 1)/2$ bits. The cryptographic complexity of this method is then $2^{(2n-1-(n+1)/2)}$, or $2^{((3n-3)/2)}$.

A second method would be to guess the $n - 1$ coefficients. This will result in n linear equations for the first n known output bits. The cryptographic complexity of this method is 2^n.

A third method involves examining the first four iterations of equation (1). After four iterations, the expressions for $x(4,1)$ through $x(4,n - 4)$ do not involve any of the coefficients $c(j)$. The expression for $x(4,n - 3)$ involves products $c(1)x(1,i)$. The expression for $x(4,n - 2)$ involves products $c(i)x(1,i + 1)$ and $c(n)c(i)c(1,i)$. The expressions for $x(4,n - 1)$ and $x(4,n)$ involve higher-order products, involving $c(n - 2)$, $c(n - 1)$, and $c(n)$. If we guessed the values of these last three coefficients, we would be left with terms involving only the original $c(1,i)$ and products of the form $c(j)x(1,i)$. By using a sufficient number of known output bits, there would be enough linear equations in these $n(n + 1)$ variables to solve for all of them. The cryptographic complexity of this method is 2^3.

2. SOLVING THE PLESS STREAM CIPHER

Pless' arrangement D consists of eight feedback registers X_1, through X_8, four J-K flip-flops, F_1 through F_4, and a cycling counter C. The output of registers X_1 and X_2 are connected to the J and K inputs of the flip-flop F_1. This portion of the arrangement will be called register pair 1. Similarly, X_3 and X_4 are connected to the J and K inputs of F_2, X_5 and X_6 to F_3, and X_7 and X_8 to F_4.

The outputs of F_1, F_2, F_3, and F_4 are connected, respectively to inputs 4, 3, 2, and 1 of the cycling counter. This device simply transmits one of its inputs to its output, input $i + 1$ following input i (modulo 4).

Let the number of stages of the FR's X_1 through X_8 be R_1 through R_8. Let the number of primitive sets of coefficients for the FR's be P_1 through P_8. There are four unknown initial states for F_1 through F_4. The cycling counter could emit its first output from any of its four inputs. Therefore, the total possible number of initial states for such a system is

$$4 \times P_1 \times P_2 \times \ldots \times P_8 \times 2^{(R1+R2+\ldots+R8+4)}.$$

Pless gives a specific set of values for R_1 through R_8 such that the periods of the eight FR's are pairwise mutually prime. With these values, the entire arrangement of eight registers will have a maximum period equal to the product of the periods of the eight FR's. While this is only an example, and many other combinatioins are possible, Pless explicitly states that she believes this to be a highly secure arrangement. For these particular values, arrangement D has a period of $1.52E^{29}$ (that is, 1.52×10^{29}) bits, and $2.54E^{51}$ distinct initial states (keys). These values will therefore be used so that actual numeric estimates of the cryptographic complexity of this cipher can be obtained.

An exhaustive solution for this encryption scheme would involve testing the entire set of $2.54E^{51}$ keys. Even using one billion parallel processors, each testing one key per nanosecond, the sun would burn out before that many keys could be tested.

The weakness of the scheme is that each of the four register pairs can be considered separately. Two methods for solving a register pair, each using a moderate amount of known plaintext, will be shown. Both methods are computationally feasible on today's large computers.

Consider the first register pair, X_1 and X_2 connected to F_1. For simplicity, assume that the case where the cycling counter C transmits intput 1 in the first cycle is being tested. Then C transmits output bits 4,8,12,... from F_1. For this pair, $R_1 = 5$, $R_2 = 19$, $P_1 = 6$, and $P_2 = 27594$, thus there are $5.38E^{12}$ distinct initial states for this register pair. Without special-purpose hardware for testing these possibilities, even this number cannot be tested exhaustively. Therefore, two methods for reducing the number of combinations that must be tested will be described. The first method is particularly applicable when the number of known plaintext characters is small, say five.

2.1 Method 1

There are only $P_1 \times 2^{R_1} = 186$ distinct choices for the initial state of register X_1. After F_1 emits its fourth output bit, which is transmitted by C, there are 256 total choices for the next four J and K inputs to F_1. Of these, exactly 128 will produce the next known output bit $F_1(8)$. Since the complete state of X_1 is assumed to be known, all of the J inputs to F_1 are known. Then there are a variable number of K inputs that will combine with these known J inputs to produce the known output bit. This number varies from 0 to 16, and averages 8.

Here is an example. Suppose U_0, U_1, and U_2 are given by

```
   A B C D E F G H I  J K L M N O P Q R S T U V W X Y Z
0  K G O R Y L T C V E N B H W U J I D G Z M S F P A X
1  B D V P S E R N A M X G F C J I L Q W H Z K Y O T U
2  F L D K O B E A S Y I M C P H N J W X U R Q T G Z V
```

so that, for example, U_0 maps "C" to "O," U_1 maps "I" to "A," and U_2 maps "K" to "I," etc. (From now on, we will drop the quote marks from letters of the alphabet.)

We want an X such that (with $Y = U_0$) we have $U_1 = XU_0X^{-1}$ and $U_2 = X^2U_0X^{-2} = XU_1X^{-1}$.

The first step is to write out the U_i as products of disjoint cycles to "chain" them. We get

$$U_0 = \text{(AKNWFLBGTZXPJEY)} \quad \text{(COUMH) (DR)} \quad \text{(IVSQ)},$$
$$U_1 = \text{(ABDPI)} \quad \text{(CVKXOJMFESWYTHN) (GRQL)} \quad \text{(UZ)},$$
$$U_2 = \text{(AFBLMCDKISXGEOH)} \quad \text{(JYZVQ) (PN)} \quad \text{(RWTU)}.$$

By the general theory of permutations, we know that the cycle diagram of $U_1 = XU_0X^{-1}$ must also be

$$U_1 = (X(A), X(K), X(N),...) (X(C), X(O),...) (X(D), X(R)) (X(I),...).$$

In particular, the cycle $(X(\text{D}), X(\text{R}))$ must equal the cycle (U,Z). Thus X either maps D to U or it maps D to Z.

Case 1: $X(D) = U$. Then $X(R) = Z$, and on conjugating U_1 by X, we see that $U_2 = XU_1X^{-1}$ must have the four-cycle $(X(G), X(R), X(Q), X(L)) = (X(G), Z, X(Q), X(L))$. But we know that the Z in the cycle diagram of U_2 is in a five-cycle, and hence cannot be in this four-cycle. Thus, case 1 is impossible.

Case 2: $X(D) = Z$. Then, (ABDPI) in U_1 gets mapped to $(X(A), X(B), X(D), X(P), X(I)) = (X(A), X(B), Z, X(P), X(I))$ in U_2. This can only happen if (ABDPI) gets mapped to (JYZVQ), so $X(A) = J$, $X(B) = Y$, $X(P) = V$, and $X(I) = Q$. Now we go back to U_0. The big cycle begins $(A, K, N,...)$ and X maps it to $(X(A), X(K),...)$, that is, to $(J, X(K),...)$. Rotating the big cycle in U_1 to align the J's, we get $X(K) = M$, $X(N) = F$, etc.

So far, we have the following alignments and rotations:

$$U_0 = \text{(DR)} \qquad\qquad \text{(AKNWFLBGTZXPJEY)},$$
$$U_1 = \text{(ZU) (ABDPI)} \qquad \text{(JMFESUYTHNCVKXO)},$$
$$U_2 = \qquad\quad \text{(JYZVQ)}.$$

By reading down the columns we have the following fragments of the cycle diagram of X: (DZNFS...), (RU...), (AJKM...), (BYO...), (PV...), (IQ...), (WEXC...), and (GTH...).

Continuing, we soon get the rest of X. When correctly aligned, the cycle diagrams of U_0, U_1, and U_2 are seen to be

$$U_0 = \text{(AKNWFLBGTZXPJEY)} \quad \text{(COUMH)} \quad \text{(DR) (IVSQ)},$$
$$U_1 = \text{(JMFESWYTHNCVKXO)} \quad \text{(BDPIA)} \quad \text{(ZU) (QLGR)},$$
$$U_2 = \text{(KISXGEOHAFBLMCD)} \quad \text{(YZVQJ)} \quad \text{(NP) (RWTU)},$$

and the cycle diagram of X is

$X = $ (AJKMIQRUPVLWEXCBYODZNFSGTH).

Note that this calculation is aided by the very uneven cycle structures of the U_i. When the U_i have several cycles of the same size, there are typically many more cases to consider, and the wrong cases do not run into self-contradictions as quickly as case 1 did above.

If the U_i have a very even cycle structure, the following trick sometimes helps. Since $U_1 = XU_0X^{-1}$ and $U_2 = XU_1X^{-1}$, we have $U_1U_2 = X(U_0U_1)X^{-1}$ and $U_1U_2^{-1} = X(U_0U_1^{-1})X^{-1}$. It can often happen that the cycle structures of U_1U_2, U_0U_1, $U_1U_2^{-1}$, and $U_0U_1^{-1}$ are more uneven than those of the U_i; in this case, by working with the new equations the cryptanalyst can save a lot of checking.

Since the solution set is a coset of the centralizer subgroup T, to know one solution and to know T is to know all solutions. This means, you only need to explore all the way through *one* self-consistent case. Note in our example, T is trivial.

An example may clarify this. Suppose the 4th and 8th output bits are known to be 0 and 1. If the output bit sequence $X_1(5)$ through $X_1(8)$ for this choice of the initial state of X_1 is 0000, then there is no possible sequence of $X_2(5)$ through $X_2(8)$ that will produce $F_1(8) = 1$. This would eliminate this choice for the initial state of X_1. But if the J input sequence $X_1(5)$ through $X_1(8)$ were 1111, then any of the following K input sequences would produce $F_1(8) = 1$:

$$
\begin{array}{lll}
0000 & 1000 & 0011 \\
0010 & 1010 & 1011 \\
0100 & 1100 & \\
0110 & 1110 & \\
\end{array}
$$

Given 37 consecutive output bits of X_2, we can determine its initial state. This is nine groups of four bits, and one extra bit. So, given 10 output bits of F_1, there would be about 2×8^9 possible K input sequences that could produce these 10 bits. Since there were 186 choices for the initial state of X_1, the cryptographic complexity of this method is about $5E^{10}$.

The effect of method 1, then, is to use 10 known plaintext bits to reduce the number of trials to solve the first FR pair from $5.38E^{12}$ to about $5E^{10}$. Many of these will yield values for the coefficients $c(j)$ that are not primitive, so that the number of possible initial states that must be tested further will be about $5.25E^9$. The method for such further testing will be described in Section 3.

Any additional known output bits of F_1 can be used to reduce the number of initial states that must be tested by about half. Thus, if 20 more output bits of F_1 were known, the number of initial states that required further testing would be reduced by a factor of about 2^{20}, or $1.05E^6$. By judiciously choosing the nine consecutive groups of K inputs among the 30 known groups, it may also be possible to substantially reduce the number of trials needed to solve the register pair from the expected number, $5E^{10}$.

2.2 Method 2

Suppose that we have guessed the intial state of X_1 and the primitive coefficients for X_2. There are a total of $5.13E^6$ choices for these. Then determining any 19 output bits of X_2 will determine its initial state.

Consider any known output bit of F_1, say $F_1(4s)$. There are three combinations of the J and K input bits that could produce this output bit. One of the two possible values of the J input will uniquely determine the value of the K input bit. This should happen about half of the time. Now all of the output bits of X_1, which are the J inputs to F_1, are assumed to be known. Therefore, to determine 19 values of the K input, we would expect to need to know 38 ouptut bits of F_1.

The cryptographic complexity of this method is $5.13E^6$. Once both X_1 and X_2 are known, we would use the entire set of 38 known output bits to reduce the number of possible initial states to about 20. These would then be tested, as described in the next section.

3. EXTENSION OF KNOWN PLAINTEXT

Suppose that the message is known to consist of standard English in mixed upper and lower case, with blanks and punctuation normally placed, all represented in EBCDIC. For simplicity, assume that one choice for the state of the cycling counter has been made. Now consider the situation where 20 characters (160 bits) of plaintext are known.

There are 40 known output bits for each of the four FR pairs. This should be sufficient to solve each pair by method 2 (Section 2.2). Table 1 shows I, the number of initial states for each pair; T, the number of trials needed to solve each pair by method 2; and P, the number of initial states that could be expected to produce the given 40 output bits. The total number of trials needed to solve all four FR pairs is $3.00E^8$.

TABLE 1. THE CRYPTOGRAPHIC COMPLEXITY OF SOLUTIONS USING 20 CHARACTERS OF KNOWN PLAINTEXT.

	I	T	P
Pair 1	5.38E12	5.13E6	5
Pair 2	4.62E12	1.76E7	5
Pair 3	6.58E12	5.02E7	6
Pair 4	3.72E12	2.27E8	4

I = the number of initial states possible;
T = the number of trials required for solution;
P = the number of possible input states that could produce the known output bits.

After solving all of the FR pairs, there are an expected $5 \times 5 \times 6 \times 4 = 600$ possible initial states that could have produced the 160 known output bits. Allowing for the four possible initial states of C, there are a total of 2400 possibilities to be tested. Exhaustive testing is quite feasible. An elementary method would be to print out the next 20 characters of the enciphered message that would have been produced by each of the 2400 choices. Then a human operator could choose the one that was normal English.

Next, consider the case where only 15 characters of plaintext are known. This provides 120 known output bits, 30 for each FR pair. This is sufficient to solve FR pair 4 by method 2. For the other three FR pairs, it is more efficient to use method 2 and guess the unknown bits than to use method 1. For example, in FR pair 1, 30 known output bits can be expected to determine 15 output bits of X_2. To solve X_2, 19 output bits must be known. There are 16 possibilities for the next four output bits of X_2. It is more efficient to try 16 solutions by method 2, using $8.21E^7$ trials, then to use method 1, using $5E^{10}$ trials.

Table 2 shows the complexity of the solution using 15 known-plaintext characters. The columns I, T, and P are the same as in Table 1. A total of $4.80E^8$ trials are required to solve the four FR pairs. The number of possible initial states for the four FR pairs that would produce the 120 known output bits is the product of the figures in column P, about $4.6E^{14}$.

TABLE 2. THE CRYPTOGRAPHIC COMPLEXITY OF SOLUTIONS USING 15 CHARACTERS OF KNOWN PLAINTEXT.

	I	T	P
Pair 1	5.38E12	8.21E7	5000
Pair 2	4.62E12	7.05E7	4300
Pair 3	6.58E12	1.00E8	6100
Pair 4	3.72E12	2.27E8	3500

I = the number of initial states possible;
T = the number of trials required for solution;
P = the number of possible input states that could produce the known output bits.

It is infeasible to test this number of initial states exhaustively without the use of special-purpose hardware. Using currently available general-purpose computers, the alternative is to test the outputs from the four FR pairs independently. This process will be sketched briefly.

Consider FR pair 4, consisting of registers X_7 and X_8 connected to J-K flip-flop F_4. Let us assume we are testing the choice of C in which outputs 1,5,9,... of F_4 are transmitted. If we extend the output string from F_4 beyond the 15 known-plaintext characters, this will determine the first and fifth bit in each subsequent message character. This is done for each of the 3500 possible choices.

These two bits divide the message characters into 4 classes:

00 blank, minus, slash;
01 all other punctuation;
10 upper and lower-case letters a–g, j–p, s–x, and digits 0–7;
11 all other letters, digits 8 and 9.

Each of the 3500 possible sequences is tested statistically against the known distribution for these four groups of characters, and against the known distribution of word lengths in English.

Now the next FR pair X_5 and X_6 connected to F_3 is tested. These determine bits 2 and 6 of each character. Since bits 1 and 5 are now known, this divides the character set into 16 classes. The 6100 choices for this FR pair are tested against the frequencies and distributions for these 16 classes.

The same procedure is applied for the remaining two FR pairs. All of this testing requires only about 19,000 trials, and thus can be considered negligible. If fewer than 15 plaintext characters are known, this number of trials increases by a factor of 4 for each character.

4. CONCLUSIONS

Allowing for the four possible states of the cycling counter, the Pless stream cipher can be solved with about $1.2E^9$ trials using 20 characters of known plaintext, or about $1.9E^9$ trials using 15 characters of known plaintext. With today's largest computers, such trials can be made in less than 10 microseconds, so this many trials could be made in about three to five hours. Using special hardware for the solution of linear Boolean equations, these times could likely be improved by a factor of 10 or more.

Pless' scheme already has the disadvantage that about 38,000 sets of primitive coefficients must be stored in order to obtain the full set of initial states. An attempt to improve the security of the cipher by increasing the size of the FR's would greatly increase this storage requirement.

REFERENCES

1. Meyer, C. H., and W. L. Tuchman (1972), Pseudorandom Codes can be Cracked. *Electronic Design*. 23:74–76.
2. Pless, V. S. (1977), Encryption Schemes for Computer Confidentiality. *IEEE Transactions on Computers*. 26:1133–1136.

Rotor Algebra
by James Reeds

In many cipher systems, the Hebern rotor machine included, a relatively small number of primary cryptographic elements interact to produce a large number of secondary enciphering alphabets. These secondary alphabets are all interrelated and by studying them in combination the cryptanalyst can often recover (or partially recover) the primary elements. This is well known in the case of sliding alphabet ciphers, where the various enciphering alphabets are said to display "symmetry of position," and where the usual techniques of sequence reconstruction skeletons, alphabet chaining, etc. are used to recover the primary alphabets. A similar situation holds in the case of rotor machines, but the details of "rotor symmetry of position" are a bit more complicated than those of "alphabet slide symmetry of position." A knowledge of rotor symmetry of position is just as essential for the cryptanalysis of rotor machines as ordinary alphabetic slide symmetry of position is for the analysis of the classical cipher systems.

This note explains elementary rotor symmetry of position in terms of a certain algebraic notation. We have found this system of notation (inspired by a formula in Hans Rohrbach's splendid paper "Mathematische und maschinelle Methoden beim chiffrieren und dechiffrieren," *FIAT Review of German Science,* 1948 [3]) to be very useful in the study of a variety of rotor machines and of proposals for their solution. We also find it to be much simpler and more useful than the notation for rotors described in the appendix of General [Luigi] Sacco's *Manuel de Cryptographie* (French translation of 3rd Ed., Paris, 1951 [4]).

In Section 1 we define the notation. Section 2 gives examples of familiar cipher systems in this notation. Section 3 states the basic computational problems involved in this kind of algebra, and gives a detailed

From *Cryptologia*, Vol. 1, No. 2, April 1977.

example of a new type of problem. Section 4 applies these ideas to the four different rotor machine cases relevant to the paper, "Analysis of the Hebern Cryptograph Using Isomorphs," [1]. A diagram at the end of the section summarizes these Hebern applications.

1. DEFINING THE NOTATION

Let $A = \{$"A," "B," ..., "Z"$\}$ be the 26-letter alphabet. Lower-case Greek letters denote elements of $A : \alpha \in A$, etc. Capital Roman letters denote permutations of A, acting on the left: $X : A \rightarrow A$ is one-to-one onto, and $X\alpha$ denotes the X-transform of the letter α. We will also write $X(\text{"A"}) = \text{"C"}$ etc., meaning that X transforms the letter "A" to "C." Lower-case Roman letters are exponents, subscripts, etc.

We will typically let μ denote a plaintext letter, and λ a ciphertext letter. In a cryptogram, the tth plaintext and ciphertext letters are μ_t and λ_t. Thus, monoalphabetic substitution is denoted by

$$\lambda_t = X\mu_t$$

for all t, for some X.

Let C denote the Caesar substitution $C(\text{"A"}) = \text{"B"}$, $C(\text{"B"}) = \text{"C,"}$ ..., $C(\text{"Z"}) = \text{"A."}$ The permutation C written out in cycle form is $C = (\text{"A," "B," "C," ..., "Z"})$.

2. EXAMPLES

1. We saw $\lambda_t = X\mu_t$ is monoalphabetic substitution.
2. $\lambda_t = C^i \mu_t$ with fixed i is monoalphabetic substitution with a Caesar alphabet.
3. $\lambda_t = C^{p(t)} \mu_t$, where $p(t)$ is a periodic function, is Vigenère encipherment.
4. $\lambda_t = C^t \mu_t$ is the simplest Vigenère key progression.
5. $\lambda_t = XC^{p(t)}Y\mu_t$ is periodic-polyalphabetic encipherment with two (different) mixed alphabets sliding against each other.
6. $\lambda_t = XC^{p(t)}X^{-1}\mu_t$ is the same, but with identical mixed components sliding against each other.
7. $\lambda_t = C^t RC^{-t}\mu_t$ is the simplest possible one-rotor machine. We now introduce some more notation. For given R, let $R[t]$ denote $C^t RC^{-t}$. Then, example 7 is $\lambda_t = R[t]\mu_t$.
8. A one-rotor machine with irregular progression: $\lambda_t = R[p(t)]\mu_t$.

9. A "straight-through" rotor machine with five rotors:

$$\lambda_t = R_5[p_5(t)]R_4[p_4(t)] \ldots R_1[p_1(t)]\mu_t.$$

10. Deavours' idealized Hebern machine [1]: same as example 9, but with special choice $p_1(t) = t$, $p_2(t) = [t/26]$, $p_3(t) = [t/676]$, etc. (Here $[x]$ is the ceiling of x: the least integer $\geq x$.)

11. The actual Hebern machine: same as example 9, but with special choices $p_1(t) = t + a$, $p_5(t) = [(t + a/26]$, $p_3(t) = [(t + a)/676]$, and $p_2(t) = p_4(t) = 0$, so that rotors 2 and 4 are actually "stators." Here a is an arbitrary constant (the starting position).

12. Idealized Hebern machine for first 676 encipherments is effectively

$$\lambda_t = XS[(t/26)]R[t]\mu_t.$$

13. Actual Hebern machine for first 676 encipherments is effectively $\lambda_t = S[(t/26)]XR[t]\mu_t$ (assuming $a = 0$). In these two examples, the combined effect of the slowest rotors, X, is effectively a stator.

14. Enigma machine, pre-war model, as described in S. Türkel, *Chiffrieren mit Geräten und Maschinen,* Graz, 1927 [5], and in André Müller, *Les écritures secrètes,* Paris, 1971 [2]: Let

$$B(t) = R[p_1(t)]S[p_2(t)]T[p_3(t)].$$

Then, $\lambda_t = B(t)UB(t)^{-1}\mu_t$, where U is a "reflecting rotor" with cycle structure of product of 13 disjoint 2-cycles. Here $p_1(t) = t + a$, $p_2(t) = $ a certain function of $p_1(t)$ which is too complicated to explain here, and $p_3(t) = [p_2(t)/26]$.

15. War-time Enigma: $\lambda_t = PB(t)UB(t)^{-1}p^{-1}\mu_t$. Here, P is the "plugboard" and $B(t)$ is as in example 14, although the p_i functions might be different.

3. COMPUTATIONS

If we know several (that is, at least one) values of α_i and β_i such that $\alpha_i = X\beta_i$, we say we have *partial knowledge* of X. There are a number of problems (equations) having solutions that are needed in cryptanalysis. For example:

Problem 1. Given permutations T_i, for $i = 1,\ldots,26$, find X such that $T_i = XC^iX^{-1}$, for all i.

Problem 2. Given permutations S_i, $i = 1,\ldots,26$, find X and Y such that $S_i = XC^iY$.

Problem 3. Given permutations U_i, $i = 0,1,\ldots,26$ (or even higher), find X and Y such that $U_i = X^iYX^{-i}$.

A special modification of problem 3 is:

Problem 3'. Given U_0, U_1, ... , find X and Y with $U_i = X^i Y X^{-i}$, where X has the cycle type of C, that is, where $X = ZCZ^{-1}$ for some Z.

To each of these problems there is the corresponding partial knowledge problem:

Problem 1'. Given partial knowledge of T_i for some values of i, find X so that $T_i = XC^i X^{-1}$.

Problem 2'. Same as problem 2, but have partial knowledge of the S_i.

Problem 3''. Same as problem 3', but only have partial knowledge of the U_i.

The solutions to these problems are not unique. If X solves problem 1, the solution set is $\{XC^i\colon i = 1,\ldots,26\}$. If (X, Y) solves problem 2, the solution set is $\{(XC^i, C^{-i}Y)\}$. And if (X, Y) solves problem 3, the solution set is $\{(XT, Y)\colon T \in \mathrm{T}\}$, where T is the centralizer subgroup of the group generated by the U_i: $\mathrm{T} = \{T\colon TU_i = U_iT \text{ for all } i\}$.

The computation of solutions to problems 1 and 1' is called "chaining," and is a standard, well known procedure in cryptanalysis. Problems 2 and 2' may be reduced to problems 1 and 1' by setting $T_i = S_{i+j}S_j^{-1}$ and $T_i = S_j^{-1}S_{i+j}$, for arbitrary j. The study of problems 1, 1', 2, and 2' is central to the classical (alphabet slide) symmetry of position.

The computation of solutions to problems 3, 3', and 3'' is important in the cryptanalysis of rotors, and has not been described in the open cryptanalysis literature. We explain problem 3. Knowledge of U_i for three values of i typically suffices.

4. APPLICATIONS TO ROTOR CASES

With these notations we formulate (and solve) four rotor problems discussed or implied in the paper.

A. Idealized Model of Hebern Machine

Known data: λ_{ij}, μ_{ij}, R, for various values of i and j.

Unknown: X and S.

Problem: Find X and S so that $\lambda_{ij} = XC^jSC^{-j}C^iRC^{-i}\mu_{ij}$.

Solution: Data is equivalent to partial knowledge of $T_{ij} = XC^jSC^{-j}C^iRC^{-i}$, which is equivalent to partial knowledge of $U_{ij} = T_{ij}C^iR^{-1}C^{-i}C^j$. But this is equal to $U_{ij} = XC^jS$. Thus, recovery of X and S is reduced to a type 2' problem.

B. Actual Hebern Machine

Known data: R, and various values of λ_{ij} and μ_{ij}.

Unknown: Y and T.

Problem: Find Y and T such that $\lambda_{ij} = C^j T C^{-j} Y C^i R C^{-i} \mu_{ij}$.

Solution: Data equivalent to partial knowledge of $T_{ij} = C^j T C^{-j} Y C^i R C^{-i}$, which is equivalent to partial knowledge of $U_{ij} = C^{-j} T_{ij} C^i R^{-1} C^{-i}$, which equals $TC^{-j}Y$. Here again we get a problem of type 2′.

C. Idealized Hebern Machine

Known data: Values of λ_{ij}.

Unknown: X, R, and S; μ_i. Note that μ_i is independent of j.

Problem: Find X, R, and S so that $\lambda_{ij} = XC^j SC^{-j} C^i R C^{-i} \mu_i$.

Partial Solution: Consider the permutations $T_{kj} = (XC^k SC^{-k})(XC^j SC^{-j})^{-1}$ $= XC^k SC^{j-k} S^{-1} C^{-j} X^{-1}$. They obey $T_{kj}\lambda_{ij} = \lambda_{ik}$, so we have partial knowledge of the T_{kj}. Consider in particular $U_k = T_{k,k+1}$. We have

$$U_k = XC^k X^{-1} XSCS^{-1} C^{-1} X^{-1} XC^k X^{-1}$$
$$= (XCX^{-1})^k (XSCS^{-1} C^{-1} X^{-1})(XCX^{-1})^{-k}$$
$$= Z^k YZ^{-k}$$

where $Z = XCX^{-1}$ and $Y = XSCS^{-1} C^{-1} X^{-1}$. Thus getting Z and Y from several instances of U_k is a problem of type 3″. Once we have Z, we get X by solving a problem of type 1; finally, we can get S by solving another type 1 problem for $X^{-1}YXC = SCS^{-1}$. This all means we have X and S, so we can now reduce the cryptogram to

$$\tilde{\lambda}_t = C^t R C^{-t} \mu_t$$

terms; that is, to a one-rotor machine, which is easily solvable.

D. Actual Hebern Machine

Known data: Values of λ_{ij}.

Unknown: Y, R, T, and μ_i. Note that μ_i is independent of j.

Problem: Find Y, R, and T so that $\lambda_{ij} = C^j T C^{-j} Y C^i R C^{-i} \mu_i$.

Partial Solution: Consider $T_{kj} = (C^k TC^{-k} Y)(C^j TC^{-j} Y)^{-1}$; it obeys $\lambda_{ik} = T_{kj} \lambda_{ij}$, so we have partial knowledge of T_{kj}, and hence of $C^{-k} T_{kj} C^j = TC^{j-k} T^{-1}$. Recovery of T is a type 1' problem; the machine is now reduced to

$$\bar{\lambda}_t = YC^t RC^{-t} \mu_t$$

terms; that is, to an idealized Hebern machine with fewer rotors.

Summarizing, we have the following diagram:

	Actual Hebern	Idealized Hebern
Known PT *Known 1st Rotor*	A. Reduced to a type 2' problem	B. Reduced to a type 2' problem
	←(same)→	
Unknown PT *Unknown Rotors* *Known Isomorphs*	C. Reduced to Type 3"	D. Reduced to Type 1'
	←(different)→	

REFERENCES

1. C. A. Deavours, Analysis of the Hebern Cryptograph Using Isomorphs, *Cryptologia,* 2 (1977), 167–185.

2. André Müller, *Les écritures secretès,* Presses Universitaires de Fance, Paris, 1971.

3. Hans Rohrbach, *Mathematische und maschinelle Methoden bei chiffrieren und dechiffrieren, FIAT Review of German Science,* 1939–1946, Applied Mathematics, Office of Military Government for Germany. Field Information Agencies, Technical, Weisbaden, 1948, Part I, 233–257. (Also available in English translation [Tr. Bradford Hardie (1963)] from the New York City Public Library, mimeographed pages.)

4. General Luigi Sacco, *Manuel de Cryptographie,* 3rd Edition, Payot, Paris, 1951. (Also available in English translation [Tr. Capt. J. Bres] from Aegean Park Press, Laguna Hills, CA.)

5. Siegfried Türkel, *Chiffrieren mit Geräten und Maschinen. Eine Einführung in die Kryptographie,* Graz, Verlag von U. Mosers Buchhandlung, 1927.

The Siemens and Halske T52e Cipher Machine
by Donald W. Davies

THE SIEMENS AND HALSKE T52e CIPHER MACHINE.
(Photograph courtesy of Siemens Institute, Munich.)

A series of cipher machines designated T52 was manufactured by Siemens and Halske between 1934 and 1944. They were built around a teleprinter, by adding encipherment and decipherment mechanisms. The machine could be used like a teleprinter, enciphering its output to the telegraph line and, when it was receiving from the telegraph line, deciphering the message before printing it. So the T52 machines operated on-line and when two machines were connected by a telegraph line (or equivalent communications path) they could be used like standard teleprinters, sending messages in cipher from one to the other. As with

From *Cryptologia*, Vol. 6, No. 4, Oct. 1982.

teleprinters, only one direction of transmission could be used at a time but the operator did not have to switch from send to receive, or from encipher to decipher. The use of the keyboard established the sending and enciphering mode.

The teleprinter used was the T-type-25, named T29 by the Deutshe Reichpost. When the T36 became available in 1932, this was used instead, allowing a tape transmitter and perforator to be connected.

A patent for a "secret telegraph system" was filed in Germany on 18 July 1930 by Jipp, Rossberg and Hettler, and assigned by Siemens and Halske. The patent was granted as DR Pat. Nr. 615016 on May 29th, 1935. This became US patent 1,912,983 dated 6 June, 1933. The basic principles of the T52 machines can be found here. Other German patents were numbered 547360 and 641560.

The design of the T52 machines was continually improved, particularly under the stimulus of the 1939–45 war. Models a, b, c, d, e and f have been reported. It is said that a model known as a/b was in use at the beginning of the war and that model T52f was never put into production because the factory was bombed in October 1944.

This report is based on a close examination of two T52e machines, one in Munich at the Werner von Siemens Institute for the History of the House of Siemens and the other in the Science Museum, London. Both machines came from Norway and were probably part of a group of machines in use in Oslo at the end of the war. The assistance of the Siemens Institute and the Science Museum is gratefully acknowledged, and so is the help of the Norwegian Technical Museum in Oslo.

Mr. W. Mache and Mr. W. Reichert gave considerable help concerning the sequence of development of T52 cipher machine. A further article will deal with this question [*Cryptologia*, Vol. 7, No. 1, 1983; see below].

PHYSICAL LAYOUT

Figure 1 shows the plan view of the machine. It contains six subunits which are attached to a heavy base.

The base contains, at its back, sockets for the tape-reader and punch and large resistors for the motor ac supplies. At the front it has two control knobs operating large multi-contact switches. One of these connects the input of the machine either to the tape-reader or the keyboard. The other switch sets the machine in one of the three conditions T52d, clear, or T52e.

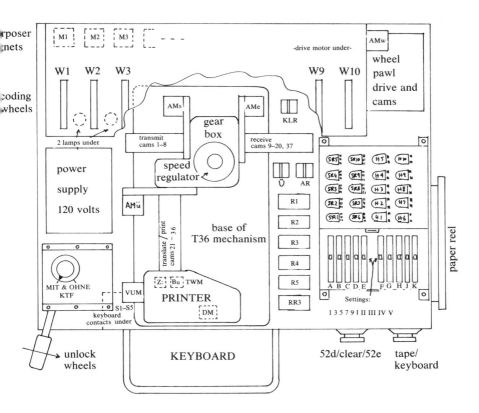

FIGURE 1. PLAN VIEW OF T52e.

The various sub-units except the keyboard connect electrically to the base through jack points. Within the base is a mass of wiring connecting the jack points and also the control switches mentioned above and a set of capacitors. The six sub-units will next be described, followed by a description of the function as a whole.

Wherever possible in this report the names used for the parts are those originally used or have been taken from documentation. Where the correct name is not known our invented name will be marked in the report by the symbol (*) where it is first used.

1. The Teleprinter Mechanism

The center of the machine contains the teleprinter mechanism on its own base, which can be detached by removing two bolts. This mechanism has a drive motor with a speed regulator, driving three camshafts through a gearbox. We have called these the transmit, receive, and translate/print camshafts, respectively. Each camshaft rotates when a clutch is released by a magnet (AMs, AMe, AMue) shown in the diagram. The translate/print camshaft has, attached to its front end, a type wheel containing raised letters and figures. A magnet DM hits the paper tape against the inked type wheel, on-the-fly.

2. Keyboard

The keyboard fits into the base and, unlike the other sub-units, is connected by wires to terminal points, not by jacks. It operates five changeover contacts S1–S5 and a trip contact. Its mechanism is linked by a lever and a wire linkage to a cam on the transmit camshaft.

3. Coding Wheels and Cams

At the back of the machine is a large frame containing, at the top, 10 independently moving wheels which are stepped on by pawl mechanisms. Each wheel has a different number of steps for a complete rotation. For wheels W1–W10 (*) the number of steps is 47, 53, 59, 61, 64, 65, 67, 69, 71 and 73, respectively.

Each wheel has a cam which operates two sets of changeover contacts shown in Figure 2, which we have called A and B (*). The cam profiles generate a pseudorandom binary sequence. The same sequences were found in all model e machines we examined. The positions of the wheels can be set by releasing the pawls using the large lever shown at the front of the machine.

Wheel positions can be read from numbers as shown at the right of Figure 2 where the indicator, the thumb wheel used for setting, the ratchet wheel and the cam are shown. Note that there would be room for additional cam wheels to the right of the existing one. Modes a, b and d had four cams in each position.

As shown in Figure 2, the contact sets A and B are spaced about $\frac{1}{3}$ revolution apart on the cam. Reading from contact sets A, Figure 3 shows the pseudorandom cam sequences as taken from the Munich machine. In the figures which follow, contacts A and B are shown in their unoperated or zero position, i.e., the low condition of the cam surface.

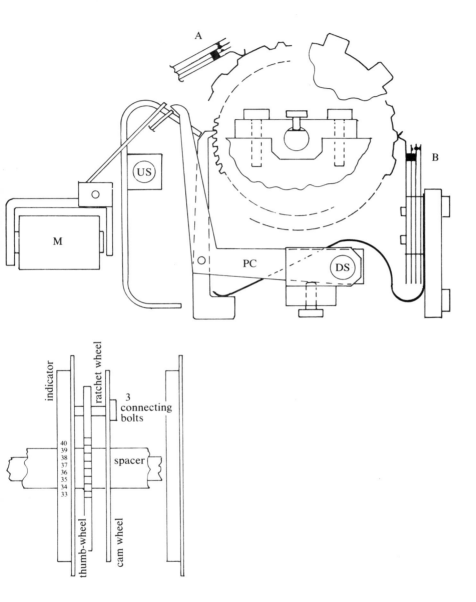

FIGURE 2. INTERPRETER MECHANISM, CAM-WHEELS AND CONTACTS.

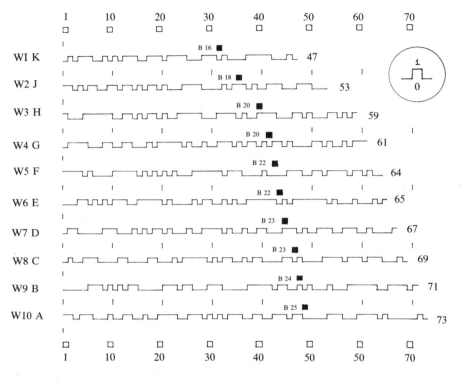

FIGURE 3. CODING CAM OUTPUTS.

The separation between the A and B contacts is indicated in Figure 3. When the wheels are set at position 1, the A contacts read the state 1 of this figure and the B contacts read the state at the black square. The spacing between A and B contacts is given. Note that the output sequence at contact B is delayed by approximately ⅓ revolution compared with that at contact A.

In the Science Museum model, the pattern of coding on the cams is the same, but the wheel numbering does not agree.

Figure 2 shows the interposer mechanism operated by a magnet M (*) which can inhibit the motion of a cam. Normally, all the pawl carriers PC (*) are dropped by the rotation of the drive shaft DS (*) allowing the pawls to fall and then positively rotate the coding wheels when they return. When M is operated an interposer prevents the pawl carrier from dropping and the wheel does not rotate. Each wheel has such a magnet.

For setting the wheels, the unlocking shaft US (*) rotates anticlockwise lifting the pawl from the ratchet wheel. A sprung roller pressing on this wheel locates and holds the wheel during setting. In the Munich machine, but not the Science Museum machine, there is an additional pawl which prevents counter-rotation. This makes the mechanism more reliable but allows the wheels to be manually set only in the forward direction, which is inconvenient.

The movement of the pawl carriers by shaft DS is derived from a cam driven by a motor through a one-cycle clutch which is released by magnet AMC (*).

The frame containing the motor, drive mechanism and coding wheels can be tilted backwards against stops when two bolts are removed from the front feet, the link to the unlocking lever is lifted off and a safety latch on the left of the machine is released. This gives access to the rear of the teleprinter mechanism. By removing a clip and a shaft, the coding wheel mechanism can be detached for maintenance or replacement.

4. The Relay and Key-Setting Box

On the right of the machine there is a black box with a lockable lid containing 20 relays and 10 rotary switches, shown in Figure 1.

The switches are used to set the "basic key" of the machine. The 10 switches are labelled, A, B, C, D, E, F, G, H, J, and K. They correspond to reverse sequence of the wheels W10 to W1, respectively. Each switch has 10 positions which are labelled 1, 3, 5, 7, 9, followed by the Roman numerals I, II, III, IV, V.

5. KTF Unit

At the front left of the machine is a small box containing a switch with 10 changeover contacts KT1–KT10. It can be removed by releasing four bolts. The switch is labelled "with" and "without" KTF. The meaning of "KTF" is unknown but its function will be described later. Only contacts KT1, KT3, KT5 and KT7 of the switch are in use but the others have been used at one time then disconnected. The precise way in which the KTF switch is included in the machine's circuits was probably changed from time to time as an additional security feature. This is the reason why all the connections via the KTF jack are shown in the circuit diagram of Figure 10, where the KTF contacts appear.

6. Power Supplies

The machine appears to require three dc power supplies as well as 220 Vac. Two of the dc supplies come from outside the machine and one is internal. This internal supply was measured as 150 volts in the Munich machine and 120 volts in the Science Museum machine. It provides the source of power for the 20 relays in the black box.

THE CONNECTING PLUG, EXTERNAL SUPPLIES AND CIRCUIT NOTATION

From the back of the base of the machine a flexible cable is joined to a 13-pin plug. In operation, this was attached to a line-connection unit to which were attached power units and the telegraph line. This line-connection unit contains additional relays U, ER, V, D and Th for which we have obtained the circuit from the documentation of the teleprinter.

LOGICAL PLAN OF THE MACHINE

Figure 4 shows, in schematic form, the plan of operation of the machine.

Encipherment and decipherment take place in the contacts of relays SR1–SR10. The keyboard contacts (or tape-reader contacts if this is switched in) generate five signals which after encipherment are sampled by cam contacts F2–F6 on the transmit camshaft. When transmitting, the real U (which is in the line-connection unit) is operated so that the telegraph signal leaves on "line a." At the same time the signal operates the polarized relay ER which generates the copy of the telegraph signal which enters the "receive" section of the T52 machine. Here, it is sampled by the receive cam contacts F10–F14 and, passing through the "decipher" contacts of SR1–SR10, the five samples operate the relays R1–R5 (*) which then store the plaintext character. The outputs of these relays operate the translate and print unit.

When receiving, the U relay is released, the ER relay operates from "line a," and a repeated signal enters the receive cams. During transmission, the transmitted ciphertext is received and deciphered to generate the local printout.

Printing locally from a deciphered character checks the correct operation of the contacts of relays SR1–SR10 but does not verify that the correct SR relays are operated.

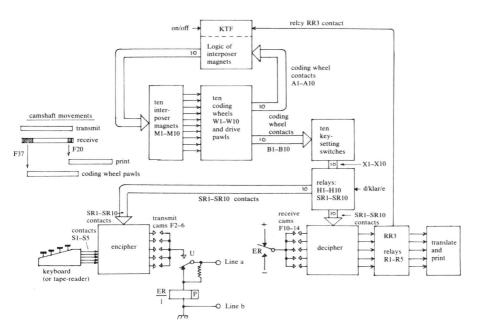

FIGURE 4. LOGICAL DESIGN OF THE T52e.

Details of the encipherment and decipherment method will be given later. The remainder of the system is concerned with generating pseudorandom binary sequences for the 10 channels SR1–SR10.

The sources of the pseudorandomness are the B contact outputs of the 10 coding wheels W1–W10 shown in the figure. The movement of these coding wheels is controlled by the interposer magnets M1–M10 which are operated by logical functions of the outputs from coding wheel contacts A1–A10. This feedback mechanism generates a long sequence of pseudorandom data from the wheels. Part of the logic of the interposer magnets is provided by the KTF circuits using a relay contact RR3 (*) derived from the third telegraph element of the plaintext as stored on relay R3. Thus, when KTF is switched on, the motion of the coding wheels depends on an earlier plaintext character. In such an operation, errors on the line will affect the wheel motion at the receiver and put the two machines out of synchronism. If the line is bad, KTF can be switched off. Without KTF, the synchronism of wheel positions at the sender and the receiver is dependent on having the same initial setting and then stepping both sets of wheels whenever any character is sent.

The B contacts from the coding wheels (at a different place on their circumference) provide the signals which, after transformation, operate the relays SR1–SR10. The B outputs are first transposed by the key-setting switches according to the setting of the basic key. The transposed channels are called X1–X10 (*). The H relays are logical functions of these channels, and the SR relays are logical functions of the H relays, when the machine is operating as a T52e. In the clear position, the relays SR are set so that the characters are not transformed. In the T52d setting, the SR1–SR10 relays are operated directly by the channels X1–X10.

Figure 4 also shows the relative timing of the camshaft movements. When transmitting, the receive camshaft operates very soon after the transmit camshaft. (When the machine is receiving, the transmit camshaft does not turn at all.) Near the start of the motion of the receive camshaft, cam F37 operates the magnet (AMC) which releases the coding wheel pawl mechanism. Near the end of the receive camshaft motion, cam F20 operates the magnet AMu which releases the translate/print camshaft. At the end of these cycles, the motion of the camshafts can be repeated almost at once. Experimentally, it was found that about six characters could be sent per second. The relays R1–R5 hold the character to be printed during the delayed motion of the print camshaft.

To summarize, the 10 coding wheels control their own motion by feedback from contacts A through the logic of the interposer magnets. From their contacts B, they produce signals which, after transposition by the key-setting switches and logical operations due to the H relays, generate the 10 pseudorandom binary sequences of the SR relays which carry out the encipherment and decipherment functions. Receiving a character involves the receive camshaft and decipher logic, the relays R1–R5 and the translate and print logic. When a character is transmitted, it is at the same time received, deciphered and printed in clear form.

ENCIPHER-TRANSMIT CIRCUIT

Figure 5 shows the circuit used to transmit an enciphered character. The plaintext character is generated by the keyboard contacts S1–S5 or by the tape-reader if this is used. The circuits involving the tape-reader are not shown. With the voltages shown on the contacts of S1–S5, if they were connected directly through to the contacts F2–F6 they would generate the five information-carrying elements of the telegraph signal on the transmit circuit, which leaves the machine on pin P9 (*) of the connection plug.

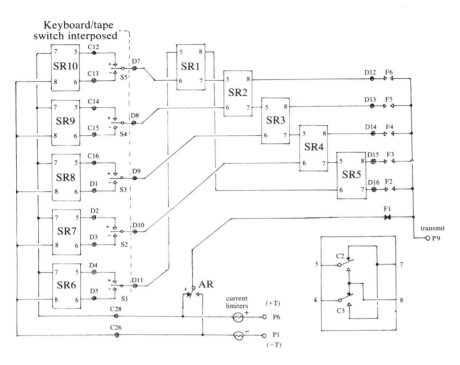

FIGURE 5. ENCIPHER-TRANSMIT.

In the rest state, relay AR is off and a positive signal appears on the transmit circuit. The telegraph signals are derived from a power supply T (*) through current limiters. When any key is depressed, relay AR operates and places the negative or "start" element on the transmit line through contact F1. At the same time, current goes to the release magnet AMs, starting the transmit cycle. Relay AR is soon released so that at the end of the cycle cam F1 again transmits the stop signal of positive polarity.

Encipherment is carried out by the changeover contacts shown in our diagram in the rectangular boxes associated with each of the 10 relays SR1–SR10. The contents of one box are shown and the particular contacts used can be identified in the plan of the SR relays shown in Figure 6. Each box either transposes two lines or connects them straight through. In the nonenciphering or "clear" condition, SR6–SR10 are released, but SR1–SR5 are operated and, for this reason, the connection points of the latter relays are located differently in our diagram so that the "clear" connection is straight through.

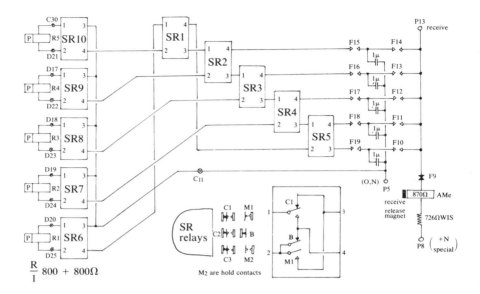

FIGURE 6. RECEIVE-DECIPHER.

The operation of individual relays of the set SR6–SR10 reverses the positive and negative connections to the corresponding send contacts S1–S5. This effect can be expressed as a modulo 2 addition (or exclusive-or [X-OR]) of the five encipherment channels with the five elements of the telegraph code. This is a typical Vernam cipher operation.

The relays SR1–SR5 carry out transpositions of the five telegraph elements. The 32 different settings of these five channels produce 32 different transpositions out of the 120 possible.

The combination of Vernam addition with transposition of the signal elements is the principle described in the early patent of Jipp and others. However, in that patent there were 10 binary channels generating transpositions. (This was unnecessary, since eight channels can easily be made to generate the complete set of 120 transpositions.) In the T52e machine, with five transposition channels, the full set of transpositions is not employed.

RECEIVE-DECIPHER CIRCUIT

In Figure 6, the received signals pass from right to left so that the SR contacts can be shown in the same relative positions as in Figure 5.

The first negative-going signal on the receive line from P13 operates the receive release magnet AMe through F9 and the camshaft then turns.

The five information-bearing elements of the signal are sampled by the short operations of cam contacts F10–F14. These signals are stored as charges on the five capacitors shown. The capacitors are in the base of the machine, towards the back.

Near the end of the cycle, five simultaneously closing F15–F19 contacts connect the stored charges on the capacitors through the decipherment circuit to the polarized relays R1–R5 shown on the left of the figure. These are bistable relays which hold the value of the received character until the next one is received. The circuits of the relays SR1–SR10 used in this decipher circuit, being identical to the encipher circuit, ensure that a true plaintext character is stored on the polarized relays. The current pulse to set these relays lasts 2–3 ms only.

LOGIC OF THE INTERPOSER MAGNETS

Figure 7 shows the circuits of the interposer magnets M1–M10. These magnets are operated by relay logic from the cam contacts A1–A10 together with the KTF switch. Contacts KT1, KT3, KT5 and KT7 belong to the KTF switch and are shown in the circuit in the "without KTF" position. Figure 8 shows the logic of the magnet circuits in each setting of the KTF switch.

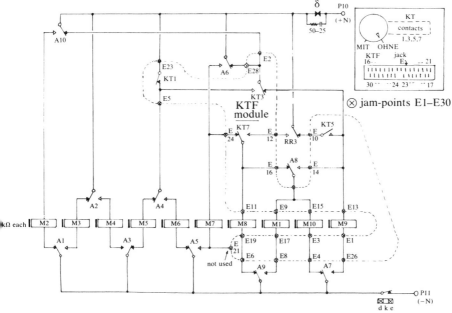

FIGURE 7. INTERPOSER MAGNETS.

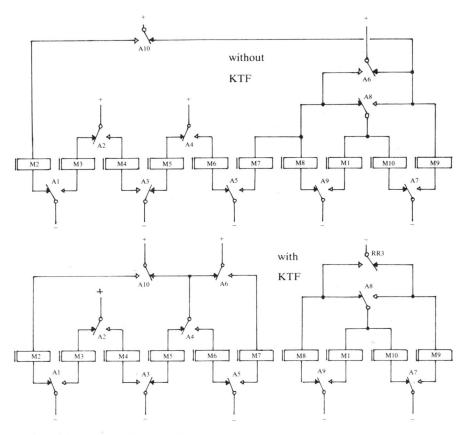

FIGURE 8. LOGIC OF MAGNET CIRCUITS.

With the KTF switch on, the operation of magnets M1, M8, M9 and M10 is dependent on element 3 of the coded plaintext character which was last received. This is the character stored on relays R1–R5 from the previous cycle. If there has been a long pause, the character will have been printed but the setting of the relays R1–R5 is not changed until late in the receive cycle so the old setting is effective in the interposer logic circuit. With KTF, a plaintext character has no effect on encipherment in the cycle in which it has been sent. In the next cycle, it can alter the wheel movements at both sender and receiver. The effect on encipherment and decipherment takes place for the next character, two characters later than the one causing the change. The contact RR3 belongs to an extra relay which enslaves the R3 relay.

We remarked earlier that the wiring of the KTF switch had been altered. All 10 contacts have been in use at some time. Some may have been used in the negative supply circuits of M1, M7, M8, M9 and M10 where there are now fixed connections in the KTF box.

Figure 9 gives an example of the wheel motion produced by the action of the interposers. In this example, KTF is off and the starting position has all the wheels set at "1." The M magnet operations are shown, and the consequent output from the A contacts. In all, 25 successive states of the wheels and 24 operations of the pawl-drive mechanism are shown. When an M magnet is operated, the corresponding wheel does not move and, in the next state, the A contact holds its previous position. These wheel positions (which are identical with the previous positions) are shown by broken lines in the figure. This sequence was verified by experiment on both machines examined, though the numbering difference meant that the Science Museum machine did not start at all ones.

The logic of the M magnets can be verified. For example, M4 operates whenever A2 and A3 are operated, as in phases 1, 7, 8, 9, 10, etc., in the figure. At the right of the figure, the final positions of the wheels in the Munich machine, after the 24 operations, are listed.

Because of this feedback from the A contacts to the interposer magnets, the motion of the cams is complex and will not repeat for a very long time. A choice of relatively prime numbers for the numbers of steps in the coding wheels is not significant when a complex sequence of movements like this is employed. This "relatively prime" feature is perhaps left over from an early version in which the stopping of the coding wheel movements by an interposer was not employed.

The signals which operate relays H and SR are derived from the B contacts on the coding wheels, after transposition by the key-setting switches. Each switch takes the output of one wheel:

Wheel Number: 1 2 3 4 5 6 7 8 9 10
Switch letter: K J H G F E D C B A

The switch outputs are labelled 1, 3, 5, 7, 9, I, II, III, IV, V. The reason for the notation appears when the development through models a, b, c and d is examined, and this will be the subject of a later article. For the machine to operate correctly each switch must be set to a different position. An error in this respect short circuits the on-board power supply, causing relay Ue to release and prevent operation. It is important not to move the switches with power on them.

Each H relay operates as an X-OR function of two of these outputs, called X1–X10 in Figure 4. The SR relays are X-OR functions of two of the H relays. The resultant functions SR(X) are shown in Figure 10.

316

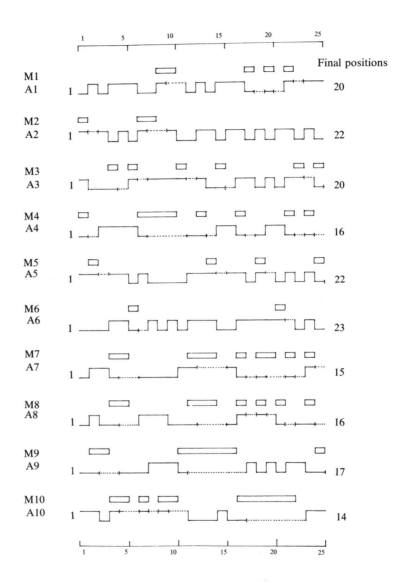

FIGURE 9. EXAMPLE OF WHEEL MOVEMENT, WITHOUT KTF, STARTING ALL ONES.

1	3	5	7	9	I	II	III	IV	V

Logical relations X → SR

Two independent Linear

relationships between SR1–SR10

	X1	X2	X3	X4	X5	X6	X7	X8	X9	X10
SR1	X	X						X		X
SR2						X	X	X	X	
SR3			X	X				X		X
SR4	X	X	X				X			
SR5	X			X	X		X			
SR6			X	X			X		X	
SR7		X	X		X					X
SR8	X	X				X			X	
SR9				X	X		X			X
SR10				X	X	X			X	

X		X
	X	X
	X	X
X		X
	X	X
X		X
	X	X
	X	X
X		X
X		X

SR-encoding relays

$$\sum_{i=1}^{10} {}^{\uparrow} SR_i = 0$$

FIGURE 10. KEY-SETTING SWITCH POSITIONS.

In the model d setting of the machine, this logic is absent. Outputs X1–X10 of the key-setting switches operate SR1–SR10 directly. In the "clear" position, SR1–SR5 are operated and SR6–SR10 are released.

The logical relations which make each SR relay depend on four X outputs are a feature of the T52e. The purpose of the relations is easily deduced. Even though the coding cam sequences are reasonably random, the outputs on contacts B are not, because the stopping of the wheels makes it more likely that 0 will be followed by 0 than by 1. Such strong statistical properties in the sequences controlling Vernam addition and element transposition are a weakness in the cipher. It is easily seen that the modulo 2 sum of four of those channels has a much better statistical distribution. Evidently the H and SR relays and the logical relations summarized in Figure 10 increased the strength of the cipher.

CONCLUSION

We have described the principle of operation of the T52e cipher machine. The machines we examined had not been maintained as they would be for practical use, but were easy to adjust and could be made to run properly. The modular construction helped to make adjustment and repair easy. In this paper we have not given details of the timing relationships or the operation of the printer head. These are contained in a fuller report which is available from the author.

In its early form, as shown in the 1930 patent, the combination of Vernam addition with transposition of the signal elements produced a cipher of only moderate strength since the wheel cycles were fixed. The two additional features found in the T52e are the stopping of wheels and the logic provided by the H and SR relays. The way in which the wheel-stopping logic (Figure 8) uses the same 10 cams, but with displaced contacts is ingenious and seems to make a very effective cipher.

The H relay logic helps to make the operation of the SR relays more random and spreads the effect of any one cam profile.

The KTF feature uses the middle element of the cleartext character to affect the control of wheel movement. A line error would cause a cleartext error at the receiver and have a moderate probability of affecting the wheel movement. If this happened, the synchronization would very probably be lost. KTF could therefore be used only if there were very few line errors.

Part of the sequence of development of the T52 series of machines has been discovered with the help of W. Mache and W. Reichart. This will be described in a further paper [see next article].

ACKNOWLEDGEMENTS

Dr. Goetzeler of the Werner von Siemens Institute for the History of the House of Siemens in Munich provided the facilities for examining the T52e machine in their collection. Dr. Schoen and Mr. Bayer of that Institute also gave useful help. Dr. Pramm of the Norsk Technisk Museum in Oslo allowed the examination of their machine. Dr. Strimpel of the Science Museum provided the opportunity to examine their machine at length, enabling much of the detail to be filled in.

Prof. Randell of Newcastle University provided notes of a conversation with Mr. Fricke on the manufacture of these machines and Dr. Huttenhain of Bonn provided useful information about the T52 and a photograph of an early model. The help of all these people is gratefully acknowledged.

The Early Models of the Siemens and Halske T52 Cipher Machine
by Donald W. Davies

INTRODUCTION

Seimens and Halske designed and built an important cipher machine of World War II, the machine designated T52 and sometimes known as the Geheimschreiber. The machine was manufactured in five models, labelled from a to e. Surviving T52e machines are in the Science Museum, London, the Norsk Teknisk Museum, Oslo, the Siemens Museum, Munich, and the collection of Crypto AG, Zug. A T52d is in the Musée Militaire, Dieppe. The article by David Kahn [2, p. 210] contains a picture of T52 model d shown in Bonn in 1978, but we have not been able to find where that machine is kept.

Some of the people who helped design, build and use these machines have given information from their memory, but these events took place from 40–50 years ago and firm facts are not easily obtained. Nevertheless it has been possible to reconstruct the operating principles of these machines. A paper [1] described in detail the last manufactured model, called T52e. A full description was possible because many examples of this model exist, having been preserved in Oslo when the rest were destroyed.

In this paper we describe the operating principles of the earlier models designated T52a, b, c, and d. It is known that a model f was ready at the end of the war, but the scale of destruction by bombing prevented its manufacture and no information about T52f appears to have survived.

From *Cryptologia*, Vol. 7, No. 3, July 1983.

The development from models a to e was probably motivated by the need to improve its cryptographic strength, and also by the desire of different sections of the German armed forces to have machines which could not interwork, in order to preserve their autonomy. It seems that models a and b were used by the Kriegsmarine for communication with naval ships in port. It is also reported that the T52e was specified by the Luftwaffe. The T52 machine was used mainly for fixed circuits and employed the five-unit telegraph code. Near the end of the war it is reported that its signals were sometimes sent by radio because of the mobility then needed.

FIGURE 1. EARLY DEVELOPMENT MODEL FOR T52 SERIES.

The origin can be traced to German patent 615016 by August Jipp and Erhard Rossberg filed on 18 July 1930. The US patent, which comes closer to the eventual T52 series, is number 1,912,983, dated June 6, 1933, by Jipp, Rossberg and Hettler. This describes a machine with 15 wheels. A photograph from the Siemens archives (Figure 1) shows, on the left of the picture, an early development model with 20 wheels. The keyboard machine on the right is a standard teleprinter with which it worked.

It seems that Rossberg began to work on the principle of the T52 on his own initiative, then the company took up the project. The T52 was at first a commercial product and machines were supplied to Hungary in 1932. The first customer was the Kriegsmarine in 1931. The machine was demonstrated to a Russian military delegation after the Germany-USSR agreement of 1939.

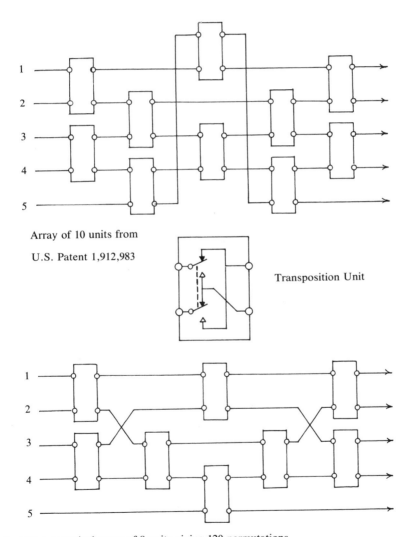

Array of 10 units from U.S. Patent 1,912,983

Transposition Unit

A more economical array of 8 units giving 120 permutations

FIGURE 2. PERMUTATION ARRAYS.

THE PRINCIPLE OF THE T52 CLASS OF MACHINES

As in the more famous Enigma cipher, the principle is to carry out a substitution cipher on each alphabetic character, changing the substitution for each character in a message by the movement of a number of wheels (rotors in Enigma). The wheels in the T52 each carried a cam (or cams) which operated contacts to change the encipherment. The cam profiles represented pseudorandom binary digits but repeated, of course, when the wheel had done a revolution. The wheels generated 10 binary sequences which were used to determine the substitution cipher. The earlier paper gave the cam profiles of the 10 wheels.

If the five-unit telegraph code is regarded as a five-bit number, there, are two obvious transformations that can be made to it, modulo 2 addition of another five-bit number and permutation of bits. Thus,

plaintext	1 0 1 1 0	
add	0 1 0 1 0	modulo 2
gives	1 1 1 0 0	
permute		
gives ciphertext	0 1 0 1 1	

These were the operations used in the T52. The added bits were derived from five of the channels and the permutation derived from the remaining channels. Figure 2 shows, at the top of the figure, how one version of the permutation is proposed in the US patent, using 10 channels from the cam contacts to operate "transposition units" shown schematically by the rectangular boxes. All 120 different permutations are achievable with this circuit. It is interesting to note that this is not an economical circuit. Eight channels allow all the permutations to be built out of transpositions, as shown at the bottom of the figure, but seven channels do not. In the patent, particular cams are associated with fixed functions, whether addition modulo 2 or transpositions, and there is no provision for a cryptographic key. The way in which the 20 wheels of the prototype were used is unknown.

All the manufactured machines of the T52 series had 10 wheels and an integral teleprinter. The output channels of these wheels were permuted to operate the encipherment and decipherment processes. Thus the five bits that were added to the telegraph code might be derived from any of the 10 wheels. This channel permutation formed the main key (*grundschlussel*) of the cipher. In order to prevent early repetition of the cipher as the wheels revolve, each at one step per character, the numbers of positions of the wheels were relatively prime. The numbers:

47, 53, 59, 61, 64, 65, 67, 69, 71, 73,

were used on all the models we have examined and we believe they were used from the beginning.

The details of the operation of the T52e were described in the earlier paper [see preceding article]. A schematic is shown in Figure 3 (which includes all the variations used in models a–e). The components of this schematic will be described below. For the present, notice that encipherment and decipherment both took place during any sending operation of the machine, making it necessary to have separate circuits for these two functions. In this paper we will not give all the details again but describe mainly those features which are different in the various models.

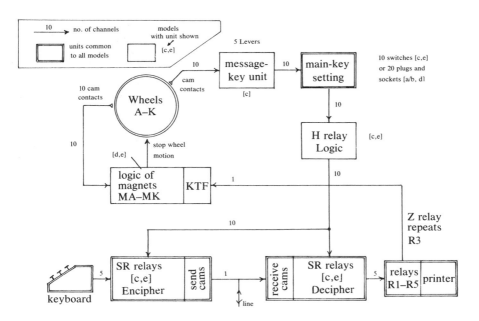

FIGURE 3. SCHEMATIC OF ALL MODELS.

It will help the comparison with the earlier paper if some notation is clarified, since we did not have the authentic notation at the time that the earlier paper was written. We labelled the wheels W1, W2, . . . , W10, from left to right as the operator views the machine. The correct designation of these units is by letters A–K in the opposite direction, i.e., from left to right the wheels were designated by the letters:

K J H G F E D C B A.

Correspondingly, the magnets which stop wheel rotation in some models were designated MA/MB, . . . The relay which we called RR3 was in fact named Z.

Model T52a was found to interfere with reception of short wave radio, so an interference suppressor was fitted and this became model T52b. There was no change in the cipher so the model is referred to in what follows as model a/b.

ADDITIONAL FEATURES

In addition to the main components of the machine, there were five features which appeared in different models. The presence of these features in models a–e is indicated in the table below. It is evident that models c and d were derived separately from the first model a/b, then their features (except 1 and 5) were combined in model e. The features will be described briefly and then in more detail subsequently.

	Model Designation			
Features	a/b	c	d	e
1. Wheel resetting	x	x		
2. Main key on switches		x		x
3. Relays H and SR		x		x
4. Wheel stopping			x	x
5. Message key unit	1	x		

1. Wheel Resetting Mechanism

This can be recognised by the handle or crank on the right front of the machine. See Figure 4 which shows a model c. The feature was present only in models a/b and c. It is not known why it was dropped. Figure 4 also shows, though not clearly, a special "cursor" by the left side of each of the 10 windows where the numbers of the wheels appear. The mechanism is described in detail below. Briefly, it enabled a standard "initial setting" of the wheels to be entered into the machine. Using the crank, all the wheels could be reset conveniently to this standard initial setting.

FIGURE 4. MODEL C MACHINE.

2. Main Key on a Plug Field or on Switches

The main key or *grundschlussel* consisted of a permutation to the 10 binary channels leading from the cam contacts on the wheels to the encipher/decipher logic. Thus any wheel could be plugged to any of the 10 encipherment channels. At first the permutation was set on a plug field. In models c and e, this arrangement was replaced by a set of 10 rotary switches which were described in the paper on the T52e. Each switch carried only one circuit because relays H and SR (10 of each) were introduced and these could be operated by a single circuit. The four cams of models a/b were replaced by a single cam in models c and e.

3. Relays H and SR

In models c and e there were 10 H relays, which performed logical functions on the ten channels leading from the cam contacts via the main key permutation to the encipherment channels. The outputs operated ten SR relays which performed the modulo 2 additions and permutations used in encipherment and decipherment. For the other models a/b and d, the additions and permutations were carried out by multiple cam contacts instead of relays.

4. Wheel Stopping

In models a/b and c, each wheel moved one step after a character had been sent. Since the numbers of positions of the various wheels were relatively prime, the whole wheel position did not repeat until about 8.9×10^{17} characters had been sent. In later models, logic based on outputs from displaced cam contacts on each wheel was used to determine the pattern of wheel movement. Each wheel did not move on approximately one quarter of occasions. A detailed description was contained in the earlier paper. This complex movement made it unnecessary to retain different and relatively prime wheel sizes, but the original wheel sizes were kept. The stopping logic differed between the models d and e.

5. Message Key Unit

This unit can be seen in Figure 4 on the left side. It was used only in model c. The name message key or *spruchschlussel* implies that the setting is changed for each message. The unit had five levers that were accessible from outside the machine cover, whereas the main key was in a locked box under the main cover. Each lever could be set into one of eight positions labelled by letters P, S, T, U, W, X, Y, Z. The unit produced a permutation in the ten binary channels between the cam contacts and the encipherment. Its place in the circuit is shown in Figure 3.

WHEEL RESETTING MECHANISM

A schematic of the wheel resetting mechanism is shown in Figure 5, as it applies to model a/b. Model c differs only in having a single cam in place of the four cams shown here. One wheel only is shown in the

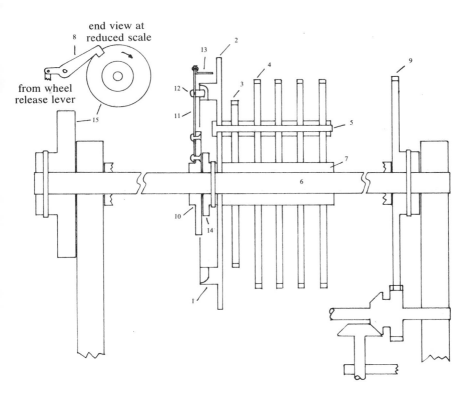

FIGURE 5. WHEEL RESETTING MECHANISM.

figure, together with the mechanism at each end of the main shaft which performs the resetting. Since no machine with this mechanism has been examined, the figure may not be exact, but the principle is correctly described.

The wheel, as in all T52 models, comprises a number ring (1), a finger wheel (2), a ratchet wheel (3) and one or four cams (4), all connected firmly by three pillars of which one (5) is shown in the figure. The wheel rotates freely about the main shaft (6), being located by spacing pieces (7). In normal operation, its rotary position is maintained by a spring roller and it is moved by a pawl as shown in the earlier paper [see Fig. 2, preceding article].

The main shaft (6) is normally locked in a fixed position by a locking plate (15) into which the head of the locking arm (8) is pressed by a spring. In order to reset the wheels, this shaft slowly makes one full turn, the top of the shaft moving towards the keyboard of the machine. The locking plate is on the extreme left of the machine as seen by the operator at the keyboard. The view from the left of the machine shows the resetting motion of the shaft as clockwise—the same direction as the normal motion of the wheels.

In order to reset the wheels, the operator first pulls to the right the wheel release lever (on the left of the machine) and latches it. This releases the pawls and frees the wheels. Next, he turns a small crank at the right side of the machine, which is visible in Figure 4, slowly clockwise and when it has moved two turns, unlatches the wheel release lever. He continues turning until the wheel release lever falls back into place. The effect of the crank movement is transmitted through two shafts and 1:1 bevel gears to spur gears which turn the main shaft via the gear wheel (9). The overall gear ratio is an integer, allowing the crank to end in the down position. The wheel release lever is rigidly coupled to the locking arm (8) and raises it when the lever is pulled right.

After the main shaft has begun to move, the locking wheel prevents the wheel release lever from returning, so the unlatching of the lever after two turns allows the arm to ride on the surface of the locking plate (7) until the main shaft (6) has returned to its rest position. Then the arm drops and the pawls are relocked, fixing the wheels again. The number of crank revolutions needed is not known, but it seems likely to be three, since the wheel locking lever is unlatched after two turns.

The means by which the revolution of the main shaft resets the wheels are the small collar (10), the leaf spring (11) with its locating pin (12), cursor (13) and a pawl, which is not shown. This assembly can rotate on the shaft, but normally it is locked to its wheel by the pin (12) falling into a slot on the left side of the number ring.

Each number on the number ring has a corresponding slot, thus the 47 position wheel has 47 slots, for example. By flexing the leaf spring (11) to the left, the pin (12) can be located at any number position and stays there. The number chosen is indicated by a short red line on the cursor and this is the number to which the wheel will be reset by the turning of the crank.

The resetting is performed by the small cam (14) fixed to the main shaft, containing one slot which engages with a pawl (not shown) on the collar (10). As the small cam rotates clockwise, seen from the left, it picks up the pawl and moves the collar and spring with it to a standard position, at which point the cursor on the number wheel coincides with the reading window and the wheel (and all other wheels) has returned to the initial position determined by the location of the pin (12) in the slots of the number ring. Normal movement of the wheel is clockwise so the pawl does not hinder wheel movement relative to the small cam (14).

When the operator wishes to alter the initial wheel positions, he first resets all the wheels, so that all the cursors (13) are aligned at the windows. Then he releases the wheels, again using the locking lever. It is possible that there is an intermediate position of this lever, allowing the wheels to be moved but still holding the main shaft fixed. An alternative would be a ratchet to prevent anticlockwise movement of the main shaft (as seen from the left). Then each cursor (13) on its leaf spring could safely be pushed backwards against the restraint of its pawl. In either case, the operator sets each wheel in turn to its new initial position by pulling the cursor and spring to the left, thus removing the pin (12) from its slot, then setting the wheel by the motion of the finger wheel (2) towards him. When the new position is reached, the leaf spring is released and the pin located in a new slot.

THE USE OF WHEEL RESETTING

No operating instructions have been found, so the use of the resetting is conjectural. We assume that each message has a different initial setting, otherwise messages would be sent "in depth." The initial setting can be encoded as two decimal digits per wheel, 20 digits in all, and this setting must be transmitted to the receiving station. To do this, a standard initial wheel setting is needed. This is the initial wheel position which is set into the machine.

According to this hypothesis, the operator would establish the initial setting using the leaf springs as described above. The setting would be obtained from a table of daily values, for example, in the same way as the main key. For each message, a message key would be chosen, consisting of 20 decimal digits representing its own initial setting. The procedure according to this theory was:

(1) Reset the wheels using the crank.
(2) Transmit the message key (20 digits), perhaps repeated for certainty.
(3) Set the wheels individually to the values shown in the message key.
(4) Begin transmitting the message.

The message key may also have contained the wheel letters, A–K, to identify the settings.

MAIN KEY SETTING BY PLUG FILED OR SWITCHES

The earlier paper described the setting of the main key or *grundschlussel* by 10 rotary switches in the T52e. Only one connection was made by each switch. The only problem with this method was to ensure that a true permutation was set, because if any two switches had the same setting the connection of two input wires together produced a short circuit of the power supply.

Models a/b and d had a set of 20 plugs attached to cables and connected to the cam contacts. These were plugged into 20 sockets or jacks to connect the transposition circuits into the encipher and decipher circuits. The absence of relays in these models required the whole encipherment and decipherment circuit to be constructed from cam contacts, with four changeover contacts per wheel. Consequently each of the 10 channels needed eight wires in the plug-jack connection. These were contained in a red and a black plug for each wheel, which were plugged into a corresponding pair of jacks. The plugs were labelled A–K, red and black.

Figure 6 shows the circuit. Each wheel had four cam contacts (on different cams) called I, II, III and IV. These were connected to make two transposition circuits, one each for encipherment and decipherment.

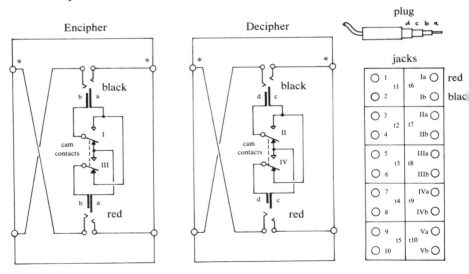

FIGURE 6. CIRCUIT OF PLUGS AND JACKS FOR MAIN KEY SETTING.

Via the red and black plugs, these were joined to sockets labelled 1–10 and I–V, a and b, which allowed them to operate in the encipher and decipher circuits for modulo 2 addition (I–V) and permutation (1–10). The layout of jacks is shown in the figure. Our notation t1–t10 refers to their function in the encipher/decipher circuits. Neither circuit was complete until both red and black plugs were inserted. Accidental interchange of red and black plugs would not have affected operation.

Figure 7 shows the enciphering circuit. Each of the enclosed boxes contained a transposition circuit which was derived from one of the SR relays in models c and e. In models a/b and d, these boxes were replaced by the direct connection to the cam contacts shown in Figure 6. Only 30 of the 120 possible permutations were used in the T52 machines.

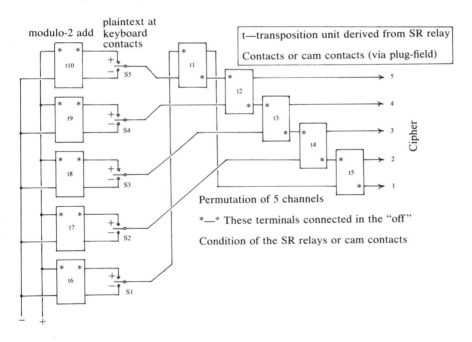

FIGURE 7. ENCIPHERMENT CIRCUIT—ALL MODELS.

The four cams on each wheel in models a/b and d each operated one changeover contact in the cipher circuits. If the circuits were to work correctly, with encipherment and decipherment complementary, these contacts must have operated simultaneously, although they were positioned at different places on the periphery of their respective cams. A fifth contact was placed to give the same bit sequence but displaced about ⅓ of a cam revolution and this provided the input to the wheel stopping logic.

The designation of the 20 jacks is strange. It may be derived in some way from the 15-wheel version described in the patent or the 20-wheel early development model, but there is no way of telling. This curious notation explains the strange numbering of the settings of the main key switches in models c and e, namely 1, 3, 5, 7, 9, I, II, III, IV, V, which must have caused some operator errors.

RELAYS H AND SR

Kahn's article ([2], Fig. 10) showed how the SR relays depended on the outputs from the key setting switches for the model e machine which had been examined. The documentation for model c shows the same circuit principles but different logic, which is summarized in Figure 8. A cross (x) in the table indicates that the corresponding SR relay depends (by modulo-2 addition) on the corresponding key switch output. This arrangement is more degenerate than that of model e, having two linear relations and a surprising identity in the operation of relays SR4 and SR10. Model c generates only 120 alphabets, whereas model e generates 240.

Models c and e, which used these relays, also provided a switch that allowed reversion to an earlier model. Whereas models a/b and d had a clear/secret lever, the later models had a three position switch:

a/b enciphered / clear / c enciphered (in model c)
and
d enciphered / clear / e enciphered (in model e)

When this switch was set in the "reversion" position, the H and SR relays were bypassed. In the case of model c, the effect of the message key unit (to be described) was also bypassed to produce a copy of the operation of the T52 a/b.

Since this switch was included to allow the new model to interwork with the old, it follows that the cam pattern must have been unchanged. This argument does not tell whether models d and e had the same pattern as models a/b and c.

Outputs of main-key switches

Model T52c

Logic due to H relays

Note that SR4 = SR10

$$\sum_{i=1}^{5} \mathrm{SR}\, i = 0 \quad \sum_{i=6}^{10} \mathrm{SR}\, i = 0$$

(modulo-2 addition)

	1	3	5	7	9	I	II	III	IV	V
SR1	x	x				x		x		
SR2		x	x				x		x	
SR3			x	x				x		x
SR4				x	x	x		x		
SR5	x				x		x			x
SR6			x	x			x		x	
SR7		x	x					x		x
SR8	x	x					x			x
SR9	x				x	x		x		
SR10				x	x	x			x	

FIGURE 8. CIRCUIT LOGIC FOR MODEL C.

WHEEL STOPPING

The circuit used for wheel stopping in model e was described in detail in the earlier paper. For model d, a different circuit was used, which is shown in Figure 9. KT1–KT10 are contacts of the KTF switch. According to the setting of the KTF switch, this produces one of the two circuits shown in Figure 10. In the unit containing the KTF switch of model e there was evidence of changes to the wiring which had been carried out without removing the ends of old wires.

MESSAGE KEY UNIT

This feature produced a permutation of the 10 channels between the cam contacts and the main key switch, as shown in Figure 3. The circuit employed is given in Figure 11 and used 15 transposition circuits. These were operated by the five levers in a pattern derived (we assume)

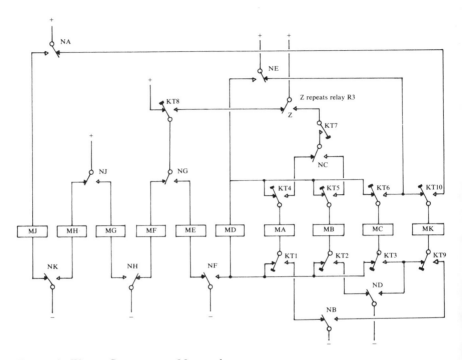

FIGURE 9. WHEEL STOPPING ON MODEL d.

from cams. The setting PZXUS produced a straight-through connection with all the transposition units unoperated. The result of the message key and main key permutations was another permutation of the channels from the cam contacts to the encipher/decipher circuits. The permutation varied from message to message because of the message key unit.

THE USE OF THE MESSAGE KEY

If this key was changed for each message, there must have been some way to inform the receiver of the message about the key setting—a group of five characters giving the lever positions. Since model c had wheel resetting, we can guess the following:

(1) Reset the wheels using the crank.
(2) Set message key to PPPPP.
(3) Send initial data in the form of 20 digits for initial wheel settings and five characters for message key.

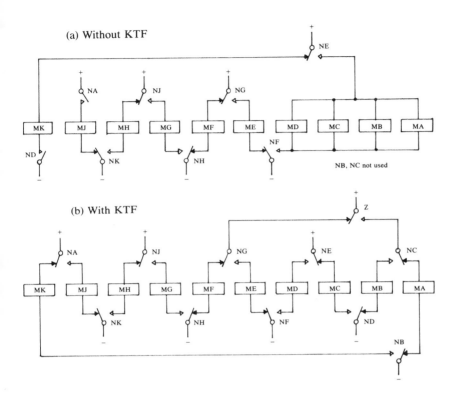

FIGURE 10. WHEEL STOPPING ON MODEL d—WITH AND WITHOUT KTF.

(4)   Set the wheels to the chosen initial settings.
(5)   Set the levers to the chosen message key.
(6)   Begin transmitting the message.

CONCLUSION

In an early form, the cipher was broken in Sweden by Arne Beurling (see [3]). Introduction of the message key in model c together with the relays H and SR made it more secure. The wheel stopping feature was an improvement introduced independently in model d. When this was combined with the H and SR relays in model e, a formidable cipher was produced. It would be very interesting indeed to find what new features were planned for model f.

Lever		Lever position: P	S	T	U	W	X	Y	Z
1	t1	·	·	·	X	X	X	·	X
	t6	·	X	·	·	X	·	X	X
	t11	·	·	X	·	·	X	X	X
2	t2	·	·	X	X	X	·	X	·
	t7	X	·	·	X	·	X	X	·
	t12	·	X	·	·	X	X	X	·
3	t3	X	X	X	·	X	·	·	·
	t8	·	X	·	X	X	·	X	·
	t13	·	·	X	X	X	·	·	X
4	t4	X	·	X	·	·	·	X	X
	t9	·	X	X	·	X	·	·	X
	t14	X	X	X	·	·	X	·	·
5	t5	X	·	·	·	X	X	X	·
	t10	X	·	X	·	·	X	·	X
	t15	X	·	·	X	·	·	X	X

X—transpose

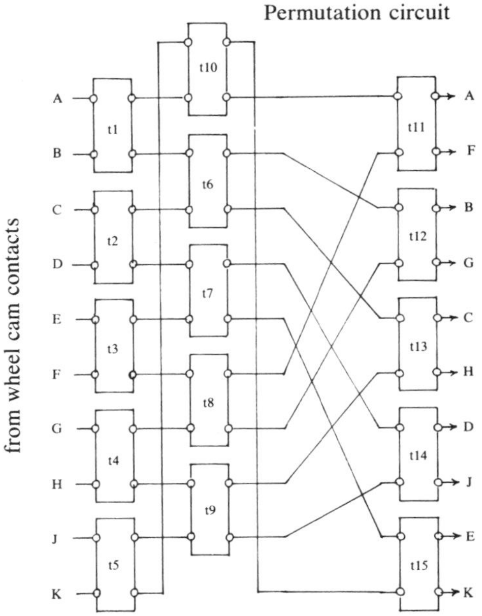

FIGURE 11. MESSAGE-KEY UNIT FOR MODEL C.

If the cam profiles were never changed, as we believe, this was a weakness. The replacement of wheels could have been carried out without special tools, though some skill would be needed to readjust the machine. Probably the reason for this omission was the difficulty of making a simultaneous change on all the machines in a given network.

The author would be very pleased to learn of any documents or further surviving machines, especially machines other than T52e.

ACKNOWLEDGEMENTS

Many people provided information and help in the investigation of the T52 machine and its development. I am particularly indebted to Mr. W. Reichert and to Mr. W. Mache for their help and to the Siemens Museum, the Norsk Teknisk Museum, and the Science Museum. Mr. W. Mache gave invaluable help by searching for documents and photographs, and speaking to those involved in the early history of the machines.

REFERENCES

1.   Davies, D. W. (1982), The Siemens and Halske T52e Cipher Machine. *Cryptologia*. 6:289–308.

2.   Kahn, D. (1979), The Geheimschreiber. *Cryptologia*. 3:210–214.

3.   Kahn, D. (1967), *The Codebreakers*. New York: Macmillan.

Geheimschreiber
by Wolfgang Mache

ABSTRACT: World War II's *"Fish"* cipher was a British cover word for all kinds of encrypted German radio *teleprinter* messages. The GC&CS at Bletchley, Buckinghamshire, did not only attack successfully Enigma traffic (Morse signals on radio links) by the electromechanical deciphering machines called *bombes*. In addition, Bletchley's electronic text processor *Colossus* broke the German *"Tunny"* ciphers, generated by *teleprinter attachments* "SZ," employed by the "Heer" (Army) on HF radio links.

FOREWORD BY LOUIS KRUH

On March 4th, 1985, a traveler called me at my office from the Drake Hotel, New York City, befoe he left for Kennedy Airport and then Munich. He referred to *Cryptologia* 4 (1984) and Prof. Hinsley's newest Vol. 3, Part 1 of *British Intelligence in the Second World War.* He expressed his regret that some authors had led to confusion about the Siemens Geheimschreiber (SFM T52) by stating that the objective of the *Colossus* was to attack the Siemens & Halske (S&H) Geheimschreiber cipher (British codeword "Sturgeon"). Instead we know *now* about the true working and objectives of *Colossus*: the successful attack on the Tunny cipher, which originated from the C. Lorenz *Schlüsselzusätze* (SZ 40, 42). He mentioned also that it is better not to equate Geheimschreiber with "Fish," in order to avoid misleading or false information in the future, because "Fish" meant the whole family of German five-unit-code (teleprinter) cipher machines of different manufacturers. My instant answer came up very briefly: "Write an article!" Now, here is the response of the traveler, a contribution to *Cryptologia.*

From *Cryptologia*, Vol. 10, No. 4, Oct. 1986.

* * *

I would first refer to what Donald W. Davies wrote in *Cryptologia* [Vol. 6, No. 4 (1982) and Vol. 7, No. 3 (1983)], i.e., that Siemens & Halske (S&H) designed and built one of the important cipher machines of WW II, designated SFM T-type-52 and often called "The Geheimschreiber . . ." The author of both studies had already given a deeper insight into the Geheimschreiber system family, developed after the year 1928 in response to a request of the Reichsmarine, predecessor of the Kriegsmarine.

Telecommunications exposition of the Dieppe Pourville Military Museum (Musée Militaire, Route de Pourville) Sept., 1984, France.
The Geheimschreiber S&T52d is in the center. A frame was delivered containing 3 pages of information about the T52's, sponsored by Siemens, Munich. [Photograph courtesy of W. Mache.]

Originally, Marinedienstvorschrift "M.Dv. Nr. 35," issued in Oct. 1937 in Berlin by the "Oberkommando der Kriegsmarine" (German navy's supreme command or *OKM*), referred to the machine as "Geheimfernschreibmaschine" (cryptoteletypewriter), built around a *KFM* (Klartextfernschreibmaschine, plaintext teletypewriter) "T-type-36," an electric-tape teleprinter which had been in production since 1934 and from which the Calcutta version, which was supplied for the Indian telegraph network in the '30s, had been derived.

Until the second half of 1942, the first three S&H Geheimschreiber models (a/b/c) were officially called "Geheimzusatz der Siemens Fernschreibmaschine" (T-type-52a/b) by the Kriegsmarine, and "Schlüsselzusatz der Siemens-Fernschreibmaschine" (T-type-52c) by the Luftwaffe. Then, on July 20th, 1942, all the machines existing within the 3 arms of the "Wehrmacht," received a uniform designation by a secret order of the OKM: "*Schlüsselfernschreibmaschine T52*," abbreviated *SFM T52*. This change was, for instance, mentioned in the "Geh. N.T.B. Nr. 42" (*Geh*eimer *N*ordsee-*T*ages-*B*efehl = secret North Sea order of the day), issued at Wilhelmshaven on July 31st, 1942. The new designation "SFM" (key-teleprinter machine) came into use before the improved T52d version appeared (1943), and the T52e was, in 1944, also called the SFM T52e (Geheimschreiber).

SEPT. 1984. DIEPPE-POURVILLE (FRANCE), NORMANDY RADAR-BUNKER (1942 RADAR STATION) CASEMATE, SERVING THE MILITARY MUSEUM, TELECOMMUNICATIONS EQUIPMENT.
Center: Siemens and Halske Geheimschreiber SFM T52d (1943).
Right: Creed teleprinter (Telex USA).
Left: Siemens and Halske teleprinter T-type-37 (page printer).
Person: Deborah Mache. [Photograph courtesy of W. Mache.]

All these on-line cipher machines belong to the group of "Fernschreib-Schlüsselmaschinen" (teleprinter cipher machines) that include other models as well, among them machines of other manufacturers (Dr.-Ing. R. Hell, Olivetti). Recently, documents have appeared which refer to an "Olivetti-Geheimschreiber" and a "Hell-Geheimschreiber," but no further details are available for the moment. Dr.-Ing. Herbert Wüsteney, born on July 6th, 1899 (living near Lake Starnberg, southern Bavaria), the "father of the Siemens teletypewriters," responsible for the development of the electric-tape teletypewriter T-type-25, which was introduced in January 1928, and of the mechanical-page teletypewriter "T-type-24" a few months later, used the abbreviation "G-Schreiber" (G-writer) instead of Geheimschreiber. In 1938, the German Railways (Deutsche Reichsbahn) began testing a species of "teleprinters" intended to replace 30,000 Morse recorders. The smaller teleprinter was called K-Schreiber (K = *klein,* English: small), in order to prevent its being confused with the larger, heavy-duty, standard 50-Bd teleprinter (e.g., the Siemens T-type-26, starting in 1929). The latter machines were called "G-Schreiber" by the railways (G = *gross,* English: large). As far as we know, they were not teamed up with cipher devices [and] neither was the K-Schreiber, for which specfications were issued by the railways in 1934, and which was designed in 1936 by S&H. These examples of abbreviations used for a crypto device should help to understand what happened to the Siemens-Geheimschreiber. This machine was not *the* source of the Fish cipher. Instead, it might be considered *one* possible source. "Geheimschreiben" (crypto messages) were enciphered and transmitted messages. "Geheimschreiber" was also the name of a cipher machine operator or of a person writing private or secret messages. The word "secret(ary)" or "private secretary" is, in German, closely related to "secret writer."

SCHLÜSSEL-ZUSÄTZE (CIPHER ATTACHMENTS) INSTEAD OF THE GEHEIMSCHREIBER MACHINE (SECRET WRITER)

The German Luftwaffe (Air Force) and Kriegsmarine (Navy) used, besides the famous Enigma supplied by the Heimsoeth & Rinke Company, the S&H Geheimschreiber SFM T52, while the much larger Heer (Army) employed, in addition to a few T52's, attachments "Schlüssel-zusätze" (SZ) for their Lorenz teletypewriters. These German Army devices were also called G-Zusätze (Geheim-Zusätze) "SZ 40" and SZ 42 a, b, c [etc.], designed and manufactured by the C.Lorenz Company. All three above-mentioned suppliers were independent of each other; they were competitors and had their respective seats in Berlin. Their facilities were damaged or totally destroyed under RAF and USAF bombing, particularly in the autumn of 1944.

Siemens & Halske "Geheimschreiber" SFM T52b, ready for shipment, door opened, total weight 180 kg.
[Photograph courtesy of Siemens Museum (SIM), Munich/City Center.]

Professor F. H. Hinsley *et al.*—Prof. Hinsley is now President of St. John's College, Cambridge, England, and was a Bletchley (GC&CS) staff member during WW II—made it quite clear that the early British electronic computer *Colossus* successfully attacked enciphered teleprinter messages transmitted over the German Army's (Heer) key radio links by means of SZ 40/42 cipher attachments, which the British interceptors called "*Tunny*" ciphers. The Siemens Geheimschreiber with the British code name "*Sturgeon*" has not been confirmed as having been penetrated by the *Colossus* computer. According to one source, this cipher was "never routinely broken." A German "*Thrasher*" machine, too, was—unsuccessfully—attacked, but this source of a Fish cipher has not yet been identified.

The SZ-equipped Army (Heer) teleprinter links were observed or intercepted in England from 1940 on. In 1944, the contents of the messages obtained from these communications links may have reached or exceeded the importance of the intelligence gained from the Enigmas. Their influence on the strategy and operations of the Allies before D-day (June 6th, 1944) or during Operation Overlord (Normandy landing) has remained incalculable up to this day. This gain in intelligence obtained started with the *Colossus I* electronic codebreaking machine in March 1944 and, thanks to the improved *Colossus II,* was accelerated after June 1st, 1944. This success against Tunny ciphers (each German Army link got its own fish-name) probably was the most significant cryptanalytic event for Bletchley in that crucial year 1944.

T52d, Manufactured 1943, Picture taken 1985.

The British code word "Fish" referred to all the German five-unit-code teleprinter traffic that was enciphered, but not all the cipher machine models were identified until the end of the war. The official history of British Intelligence in WW II has not yet described or confirmed decrypts obtained from the Geheimschreiber *SFM T52d* or from the *SFM T52e*. The T52a/b and T52c machines were designed for wired connections and hardly ever used on wireless links. Only some vague information exists on the probable penetration into Sturgeon's. Best known is one case of tapping the German teleprinter channel on Swedish territory over an extended period of time, starting early in 1940 (David Kahn, *The Code-breakers,* pp. 482–483). The earlier T52 models were not used over wireless links, but we know that a few links made occasional use also of T52d machines, although these were not equipped with a synchronization device as were the SZ's approved for radio application.

"Die SFM T52 wird für die Verschlüsselung von Geheimen Kommandosachen und für den Einsatz auf Funkfernschreiblinien als *ausreichend sicher* angesehen. Die Vorschrift zur Verwendung von Wahlwörtern muss beibehalten werden, die Beschränkung der Spruchlänge auf 20,000 Zeichen kann jedoch fortfallen. Da die jetzige (feste) KT-Funktion (KTF) Einbruchsmöglichkeiten über Kompromisse begünstigt, wird sie nicht eingeschaltet. Für den Grundschlüssel dürfen nur nicht zerfallende Pyramiden benutzt werden."

Report 5 Sept 1944

"Ein zusammenhängender Geheimtext von 30,000–40,000 Buchstaben ist lösbar. Phasengleiche Sprüche können gelöst werden, ebenso Sammelsprüche von 1000 Buchstaben an. Aus einem Kompromiss (Zuordnung von Klar- und Geheimtext) von ca. 500 Buchstaben ist die Nockenbestückung rekonstruierbar."

"Die SZ 40 und SZ 42 dürfen daher nur im Linienverkehr eingesetzt werden, weil hier phasengleiche Sprüche, Sammelsprüche und Kompromisse vermieden werden können . . ."

"Die Untersuchung der SZ 42c ist noch nicht abgeschlossen. Bis jetzt wird keine Möglichkeit gesehen, aus reinem Schlüsseltext die Maschineneinstellung zu rekonstruieren . . ."

Report 26 Sept 1944

EXCERPTS, TAKEN FROM DOCUMENTS, ISSUED AT BERLIN, 1944, BY A TEAM, WORKING ON GERMAN CIPHER EQUIPMENT SECURITY; E.G., ANSWERING QUESTIONS ON THE ENIGMA, THE "GEHEIMSCHREIBER" T52 AND "SCHLÜSSELZUSÄTZE" SZ 40, 42.

SCHLÜSSELZUSÄTZE SZ 40/42.
[Photograph courtesy of C. Lorenz, Berlin.]

T52 AND SZ 40, 42 SECURITY IN 1944

In 1944 a special German committee was set up in Berlin to verify the security of the Wehrmacht's own cipher machines, e.g., the *Geheimschreiber* (SFM) and the *Schlüsselzusätze* (SZ). On August 25th, 1944, the working party held a meeting on all the T52 models, and on September 5th declared, under the seal "Geheime Kommandosache" (G. Kdos), among other things, the following with regard to the SFM T52d:

The SFM T52 is considered sufficiently secure for the encryption of secret command matters (G. Kdos) and for operation over radio teleprinter links. The instructions concerning the use of *Wahlwörter* [option words?/optional terms?] remain in force, but the limitation of the message length to 20,000 characters may be abandoned. Since the present (fixed) KT function (KTF) increases the possibility of solution by "compromises," it will not be activated. For the *Grundschlüssel* [basic key, a permutation by 10 Stecker cables], only "*nicht zerfallende Pyramiden*" (nondissociating permutations?/continuous key patterns?) ought to be used.

The special committee on cipher security (Wehrmacht, Berlin) also scrutinized the Schlüsselzusätze SZ 40 and SZ 42 on September 11th 1944. The relevant part of the report, dated 26 September 1944, can also be quoted today:

A coherent cryptogram of 30,000 to 40,000 characters is solvable. *"Phasengleiche Sprüche"* (in-phase messages) can easily be solved, as can *"Sammelsprüche"* (collective messages?/collected messages?) of more than 1,000 characters. The cam setting is reconstructable from a compromise (matching clear and cipher text) of approx. 500 characters . . .

The SZ 40 and SZ 42 may consequently be put into operation only on wire links, because *"Phasengleiche Sprüche"* (in-phase messages), *"Sammelsprüche"* and *"Kompromisse"* (compromises) can then be avoided.

The investigation of the SZ 42c has not been concluded yet. Until now, no possibility of reconstructing the machine setting from pure coded text is seen . . .

The SZ (Schlüsselzusätze) attachments for the Lorenz teleprinters were used on dozens of text communication radio links between Heeres (Army) headquarters in Europe. They were mainly attached to *"Sägefisch"* (sawfish) radio stations consisting of Telefunken receivers-transmitters and S&H radio telegraph systems *WTZ* or *WTK* (double-tone multiplex channels).

CONCLUSION

As far as the five-unit code is concerned, the observation of the Sägefisch traffic by the British intercept stations and the Secret Service in the '40s probably fathered the codeword *Fish,* derived from the "sawfish" patterns common to all recorded teleprinter start-stop signals. Consequently, the automated solution of "Fish ciphers" at Bletchley does not necessarily refer to the S&H Geheimschreiber T-type-52, models a, b, c, d, e, manufactured between 1932 and 1944. Instead, the success of *Colossus* was from the solution of the Tunny cipher generated by the SZ attachments employed on the upper-command communications level by the German Army's High Command (OKH).

Colossus 1944.

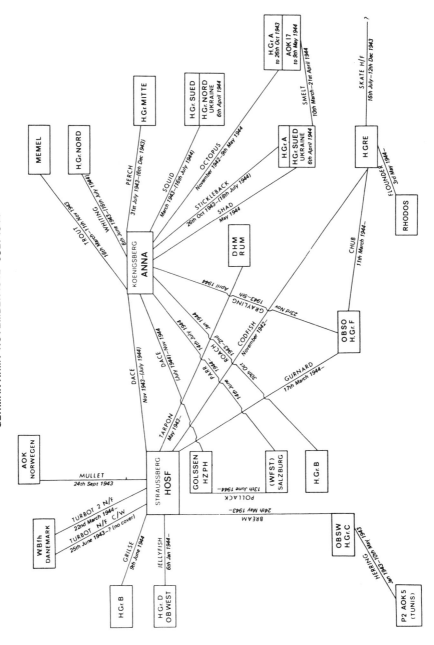

Tunny Cross Country Links German Army, November 1942–July 1944.

ACKNOWLEDGMENT

The author wishes to acknowledge gratefully the support of those who have provided specific and authentic information for this contribution, e.g., Mr. Willy Reichert (Mils, Tyrol), Mr. Fritz Trenkle (Fürstenfeldbruck), and Mr. Joachim Timm (Flensburg).

REFERENCES

1. Kahn, D. (1979), The Geheimschreiber. *Cryptologia*. 3:210–214.

2. Davies, D. W. (1982), The Siemens and Halske T52e Cipher Machine. *Cryptologia*. 6:289–308.

3. Davies, D. W. (1983), The early models of the Siemens & Halske T52 cipher machine. *Cryptologia*. 7:235–253.

4. Hinsley, F. H., *et al*. (1984), *History of the Second World War: British Intelligence in the Second World War*. 3:447 (Her Majesty's Stationery Office, 49 High Holborn, London WC1V 6HB).

5. Maas, F. J. (1946), *Der Stand der Funkfernschreibtechnik in Deutschland bis 1944*. 15.2.1946.

6. Mache, W. Referring to the codeless "K-Schreiber," see *"Lexikon der Textund Datenkommunikation"* (1980), Oldenbourg), pp. 175 (text), 355 (diagrams).

Mechanics of the German Telecipher Machine by Cipher A. Deavours and Louis Kruth

The following appendix [to Geheimschreiber by W. Mache (Oct. 1986)] is offered to the reader as a description of the mechanics of the T52 series of telecipher machines as well as the SZ machines [1]. As can be readily seen, a machine like the T52e is every bit as complex as many of today's electronic "black boxes."

The Siemens and Halske T52 series of machines included some of the most complicated telecipher machines of their day. The original models (a and b) were fairly simple in operation. Model a bore 10 pinwheels of relatively prime sizes 47, 53, 59, 61, 64, 65, 67, 69, 71, 73. These wheels were also denoted 1, 3, 5, 7, 9, I, II, III, IV, V, respectively (after the 10 enciphering relays they controlled). With each character enciphered all wheels advanced one step. The second five wheels I,II,III,IV,V) each enciphered one of the plaintext (Murray code) bits by the usual XOR operation while the first set of wheels (1,2,3,4,5) transposed the result of the previous XOR operation. Each of the five transposition wheels controlled a relay which either switched two bits of neighboring channels or passed them straight through. The relay transpositions were applied in series with a binary "1" on a pinwheel yielding the "untransposed" relay state. The 32 possible transpositions were:

Pinwheels	Transposition	Pinwheels	Transposition
11111	12345	01111	52341
11110	21345	01110	25341
11101	13245	01101	53241
11100	31245	01100	35241
11011	12435	01011	52431
11010	21435	01010	25431
11001	14325	01001	54231

From *Cryptologia*, Vol. 10, No. 4, Oct. 1986.

Pinwheels	Transposition	Pinwheels	Transposition
11000	41235	01000	45231
10111	12354	00111	52314
10110	21354	00110	25314
10101	13254	00101	53214
10100	31254	00100	35214
10011	12534	00011	52134
10010	21534	00010	25134
10001	15234*	00001	51234*
10000	51234*	00000	15234*

It should be noted that two transpositions are repeated twice (indicated by *) so that only 30 of the 32 possible pinwheel combinations result in distinct bit permutations.

The resultant T52a cipher was of moderate strength and was not fully trusted by the Germans to be insolvable. Swedish mathematician Arne Beurling was, in fact, able to solve intercepted traffic on an early machine by hand methods. Bletchley Park did the same.

Model a of the T52 also contained a small 10-position plugboard which had been incorporated into the T52 so that the choice of the XORing and transposing wheels became part of the cipher key. This plugboard was replaced in later models by a set of 10 rotary switches, each bearing the letters A, B, C, D, E, F, G, H, J, K (corresponding to the 10 pinwheels in descending size order) which performed the same function as the earlier plugboard. Each switch had to be set to a different setting (1,2,3,4,5,I,II,III,IV,V) to generate the wheel control permutation.

Model b of the T52 (circa 1936) differed from model a only in the fact that it had better radio interference suppression.

The modified Model c = model e and the modified model a/b = model d of the T52 series introduced irregular wheel motion present in later models. There were two types of irregular pinwheel motion: Ohne ("without") Klartextfunktion and Mit ("with") Klartextfunktion, which are described below:

OHNE KLARTEXTFUNKTION

Wheel	Condition for Stepping
73	0 on 65 or 64 wheel
71	" "
69	" "

Wheel	Condition for Stepping
67	" "
65	1 on 64 *or* 0 on 61
64	1 on 61 *or* 59
61	0 on 59 *or* 53
59	1 on 53 *or* 0 on 47
53	1 on 47 *or* 0 on 73
47	0 on 67 *or* 1 on 65

MIT KLARTEXTFUNKTION
(Model d)

Wheel	Condition for Stepping
73	(1 on 71 *and* 1 on 69) *or* 1 in P3
71	(0 on 69 *and* 1 on 67) *or* " "
69	0 on 67 *or* 1 on 65
67	0 on 65 *or* 0 on 64
65	(1 on 64 *and* 0 on 61) *or* 0 in P3
64	(1 on 61 *and* 1 on 59) *or* " "
61	0 on 59 *or* 0 on 53
59	1 on 53 *or* 0 on 47
53	1 on 47 *or* 0 on 73
47	1 on 73 *or* 0 on 71

In the second motion, P3 denotes the middle bit on the *preceeding* plaintext character. Thus, the *Mit* motion has a plaintext autokey feature. Transmission garbles can cause out of phase keys between two teleprinters in the *Mit* mode of operation so it would seem, considering all conditions, that this cipher mode would be seldom used. The "reading station" on each of the wheels which controlled the above stepping functions was not the same position as that from which pulses which controlled the encipherment were derived, but was delayed about ⅓ revolution on each wheel.

Added complexity was achieved in Model e of the T52 by not only permuting the outputs of the 10 pinwheels, but deriving from these 10 combinations of the outputs, each depending on the XOR of four of the 10 permuted wheel outputs and using these resulting bits to operate the 10 XOR and transposition relays. If the switch-permuted outputs are labeled X1, X2, . . . , X10, then the combinations were as follows for Models d and e (some Model c machines also contained relay logic but different from that given):

Cipher Relay Controlled	XOR Combination
1	1 2 8 10
3	6 7 8 9
5	3 4 8 10
7	1 2 3 7
9	1 4 5 7
I	3 4 7 9
II	2 3 5 10
III	1 2 6 9
IV	5 6 8 10
V	4 5 6 9

The Lorenz firm, which also manufactured teletype equipment, built a comparable machine, the Schlüsselzusatz (SZ). While the T52 series of cipher teleprinters incorporated a standard teletype unit as part of the machine's design, the Lorenz machine was a separate entity designed to be plugged into a teletype unit. The SZ 40 contained 12 pinwheels of relatively prime sizes: 23, 26, 29, 31, 37, 41, 43, 47, 51, 53, 59, and 61 pins. The wheels may be divided into three classes:

SPRI (fast) Wheels: 23 26 29 31 41
SPA (slow) Wheels: 59 53 51 47 43
SPA Drive Wheels: 37 61

Machine Simulation

PL	BAUDOT	SPRI	DRIVE	SPA	RSULT	CPHR
E	10000	00000	00	00000	10000	E
N	00110	01111	00	00000	01001	L
E	10000	11111	00	00000	01111	V
M	00111	01100	10	00000	01011	G
Y	10101	11010	10	00000	01111	V
	00100	01001	11	*11001	10100	S
A	11000	10111	01	*10001	11110	K
I	01100	00100	10	10001	11001	W
R	01010	10101	00	10001	01110	C
	00100	00000	00	10001	10101	Y
S	10100	10011	00	10001	10110	F
T	00001	01010	11	*11011	10000	E
R	01010	00010	10	11011	10011	B
I	01100	01000	11	*10011	10111	X
K	11110	00111	10	10011	01010	R
E	10000	11001	00	10011	11010	J
	00100	10111	00	10011	00000	7

Machine Simulation

PL	BAUDOT	SPRI	DRIVE	SPA	RSULT	CPHR
H	00101	10001	00	10011	00111	M
A	11000	01111	00	10011	00100	9
S	10100	10000	10	10011	10111	X

LORENZ SCHLÜSSELZUSATZ 40.
* Indicates motion of SPA wheels.

Plaintext (Murray code characters) are XORed first with the character formed by the SPRI wheels and then the character formed by the SPA wheels. The SPRI wheels move regularly with each wheel advancing for each character enciphered. The SPA wheels also step together, but in this case the movement is irregular and controlled by the two drive wheels. The 37-pin drive wheel moves with each character enciphered. When an active pin comes up on the 37 pin wheel, the 61 pin-wheel steps. When the 61-pin wheel has an active pin at the sensing station, the SPA wheels step. It should be noted here that the authors' information in this regard is somewhat uncertain. The role of the 37- and 61-pin wheels may have been reversed, but this fact is of small consequence (unless one is engaged in solving the machine's ciphers). The above simulation should make the operation clear.

NOTES

1. Much of the material on the T52 machines found in this [article] is due to Donald Davies of the National Physical Laboratory, Teddington, Middlesex. Davies has carefully examined and reported on several World War II machines. It is due to his work that much has been learned about this vital period in the history of machine cryptography. His excellent article on the Siemens and Halske machine may be found in *Cryptologia,* October 1982, pp. 289–308.

Part III

Mathematics and Cryptanalysis

Unicity Points in Cryptanalysis
by Cipher A. Deavours

Claude Shannon, the father of information theory, also laid the foundations of mathematical cryptanalysis in 1945 with his publication, "A Mathematical Theory of Cryptology" (reprinted later under the less descriptive title, "Communication Theory of Secrecy Systems" [1]). Shannon sets forth in this paper, using characteristically clear and direct prose, the essence of cryptography and cryptanalysis. The paper can be read with profit by anyone interested in the foundations of the cryptographic science and requires a minimal degree of mathematical maturity in most parts.

An interesting section of the paper deals with the concept of *unicity point*. The unicity point of a cipher is the message length beyond which decipherment using a known system becomes a unique process. For messages shorter than the unicity point distance, plural decipherments are the rule and the would-be cryptanalyst has no possible method of selecting the correct decipherment from the many available ones. Thus, even assuming the intercepter of the cryptogram to have complete knowledge of the system of encipherment used (excluding the particular key), no unambiguous solution is possible if the amount of text intercepted is less than the required amount set by the unicity point.

For a *random cipher,* the unicity point can be estimated using the simple formula:

$$U = H(K)/D.$$

$H(K)$ is the logarithm of the number of possible keys in the given system and D is the redundancy per letter of the source messages. English has a redundancy of about 1.11 digits or 78%. The formula is simple enough but its accuracy rises or falls to the extent that the encipherment system

From *Cryptologia,* Vol. 1, No. 1, Jan. 1977.

is random in Shannon's sense. A complete discussion of just what constitutes a random cipher would require too much space here. But the two most stringent requirements are that each encipherment key be equiprobable in use and that decipherment of a message using a randomly selected key be equally likely to produce any possible source message. (For our purposes, a *source message* means any arbitrary string of plaintext characters, meaningful or not, which has the same length as the cryptogram.) A related cipher model is discussed in Appendix A of this paper. Monoalphabetic substitution and transpositions are not good examples of random ciphers, but even in these cases, the unicity point formula serves as a lower bound for the actual unicity point [2]. More intricate ciphers such as the Playfair, trifid, N-gram substitutions, and polyalphabetics of fairly long key usually approximate random ciphers to a satisfactory degree. An index of coincidence near the random value of .038 is an appropriate statistical test in many cases.

Shannon's derivation of the unicity point formula is couched in information theoretic terms, but a simpler approach is possible [2]. Suppose the plaintext message consists of alphabetic characters. There are 26^N possible source messages of length N. It is usual to write this number in exponential form:

$$26^N = 10^{(\log 26)N} = 10^{1.41N}.$$

Most of the N-character strings will be meaningless jumbles of letters, but some strings will constitute valid English plaintext segments. For fairly long character strings, the number of valid English plaintext segments has been found to be approximately $10^{.30N}$. By analogy with classical statistical mechanics, the constant .30 is called the *entropy* per letter of the language. If we randomly pick a cipher key and decipher an N-character cryptogram, we may get a recognizable English message or a collection of N disconnected letters. Even if the message is valid English, we cannot assume it to be the intended one, since we might have chosen the wrong key. The chance, i.e., p, the probability of getting a meaningful message should be, on the average, the number of meaningful messages divided by the total number of possible source messages, so

$$p = 10^{.30N} / 10^{1.41N} = 10^{-1.11N}.$$

In general, this last term is written 10^{-DN}, where D is termed the *redundancy in digits* of the language in question. A D value of 1.11 for English means that English is about $1.11/\log 26 = .78 = 78\%$ redundant.

If there are 10^H keys for the cipher and if we try all of them, how many meaningful messages should we recover? There will be at least one meaningful message (the correct one); using the other $10^H - 1$ keys should give about $10^H \cdot p$ more meaningful messages. Thus, the expected number of "spurious" decipherments is given by:

$$E = 10^{-1.11N}(10^H - 1) = 10^{-1.11N+H} - 10^{-1.11N}.$$

For N even modestly large, the second term on the right is negligible and can generally be neglected. E is large if the exponent $-1.11N+H \gg 0$ and is small if $-1.11+H \ll 0$. The point where $-1.11N+H = 0$ or $N=H/1.11$ divides the region of few solutions from the region of many solutions and thus appropriately termed the unicity point. Figure I shows the unicity point line $\log E = -DN+H$ for a Vigenere cipher of period 5 assuming 26^5 possible keys and differing redundancies for the message source. The less redundancy the message source has, the farther out is the unicity distance ($\log E = 0$).

In practice, the redundancy of the message source can be lowered by coding before applying the cipher. Simple abbreviations can be used for this purpose, e.g., REPORT RECEIVED might become RPRT RCVD.

To illustrate Shannon's result, we shall calculate some sample unicity points applied to several classical ciphers assuming English to be the language of the message source. For a Vigenere cipher which uses an alphabetic key of length P the key can be chosen 26^P ways. Since the alphabetic sequence is normal, no freedom of choice exists in that direction. Thus,

$$H(K) = \log 26^P = P \log 26 = 1.41P,$$

and so,

$$U = 1.41P/1.11 = 1.27P \text{ letters.}$$

We interpret this result as follows. Suppose a cryptogram known to be in Vigenere is intercepted. A proposed solution is offered which results in valid text. If the proposed period is P, then more than $1.27P$ characters present in the original cryptogram indicates that the solution offered is probably unique. Less than $1.27P$ characters present in the cryptogram forces us to reject the proposed solution as only one of a set of possible ones.

If we mix the cipher alphabets in the above system, the number of keys increases to $26! \cdot 26^P$, since the alphabet can be disarranged in 26! ways (26 possible substitutes for "A," 25 for "B," etc.) and with each of these permutations any one of the 26^P possible key phrases of length P can be used. The unicity point now shifts out to

$$U = \log (26! \cdot 26^P) = 23.97 + 1.27P \text{ letters.}$$

Note that mixing the alphabetic sequence extends the unicity point by a distance which is *independent* of the key phrase length and contributes negligible security to the system for long key phrases or ciphertext. Some other sample unicity point data are given below.

Type of Cipher	Unicity Point in Number of Letters
Vigenere, key of length P	$1.27P$
Vigenere, mixed cipher alphabet, key length P (Quagmire II)	$23.97 + 1.27P$
Vigenere, mixed cipher alphabet and mixed plain alphabet	$47.94 + 1.27P$
Sequence, key length P (Quagmire IV)	$23.97N$
N independently mixed alphabets used successively	$23.97N + 1.27P$
N independently mixed alphabets, key of length P, key composed of M distinct characters	$.90 \log M + 23.97N$
Random digraphic substitution	1460.61
Playfair	22.69
Foursquare (two mixed alphabets)	45.38
Random N-gram substitution	$.90 \log (26^N)!$
Homophonic substitution with N substitutes per letter	$(\log (26N!/N!^{26}))/1.11$

The number of keys used in this last result can be found as follows. Since there are N substitutes per letter, there are $26N$ substitutes in all. The N substitutes for "A" can be chosen $26N!/N!25N!$ ways (combinations of $26N$ things taken N at a time). The N substitutes for "B" can then be chosen $25N!/N!24N!$ ways, etc. Thus, the total number of keying choices in deciphering is

$$\frac{26N!}{N!25N!} \cdot \frac{25N!}{N!24N!} \cdots \frac{N!}{N!0!} = \frac{26N!}{(N!)^{26}} .$$

Homophonic substitutions are interesting in that one needs to know not only the substitution key, but the order of use of the substitutes to encipher and to produce a unique cryptogram, whereas, to decipher, one only needs to know the substitution table. The above result is based on the assumption that the key is not further restricted such as using the same substitute for every letter and producing a monoalphabetic substitution. For N large enough that the Stirling factorial approximation may be used, the unicity point value is found to be approximately $U = 33.14N$. In effect, this result tells us how to design a homophonic substitution cipher whose unicity point is always longer than the message length. For example, to encipher a 500-letter message, we need $U = 33.14N > 500$ or $N > 15$ to avoid unique solution. For homophonics using proportional representation of the cipher substitutes, the corresponding calculation of the number of keys yields a multinomial coefficient.

The unicity point for the Playfair cipher seems too short to most people. Who can solve a Playfair only 23 letters long? The beginner's method of solving such ciphers using only digraphic frequency tables without subsequent buildup of the keysquare is seen to be futile, since this method would require about 1400 characters, which is far longer than the usual message length.

An interesting example of such a near unicity point solution is to be found in the Nov.–Dec. 1936 edition of the *Signal Corps Bulletin*. An American Army private, A. Monge, solved the following 30-letter challenge Playfair cryptogram offered by a British general:

BUFDA GNPOX IHOQY TKVQM PMBYD AAEQZ.

The plaintext which Monge obtained makes it clear that he had the intended message. Although the cryptogram is near the unicity point in length, Monge assumed, correctly, that the keysquare was of the keyword mixed variety. Restricting oneself to such incomplete mixings of the alphabet reduces the unicity point even farther. For instance, if the last row of the keysquare can be assumed to be V W X Y Z, the unicity point falls to no more than 16.56 letters. Hence, Monge was in better shape than might first appear. (There seems to be no record pertaining to a transfer of funds upon Monge's solution.)

As anybody knows, showing that a solution is unique (which is what the unicity point does) and actually finding the solution (solving the cryptogram) are two different things. Unicity point studies only indicate the amount of similarly keyed text which can fall into enemy hands without compromising the plaintext.

As an example, consider the Allied World War II SYKO field cipher described in David Kahn's masterwork *The Codebreakers* [3]. One version of the SYKO system consisted of 32 independently mixed cipher alphabets of 37 characters each (26 letters, 10 digits, and a "-" for word divisions). The alphabets were used in sequence to produce a polyalphabetic cipher of period 32. We have,

$$U = \log (37)!^{32}/1.11 = 1244 \text{ characters.}$$

This is about 39 characters per alphabet. Solution of this system based on a Kerckhoff's superimposition would require a similar number of characters per alphabet. In this case, the unicity point and the actual amount of text needed for a working solution are very close.

A further example of the usefulness of unicity point studies is provided in the study of ciphers with compound or *Vernam* keys. A progressive key Vigenere cipher is a very simple example of such a system. If the primary key has length 7 and the index of progression is 1, then the total period is $7 \times 26 = 182$ characters before keying repetition. The unicity point for this cipher is *not* $1.27P = 1.27(182) = 231.14$ characters as might be supposed from the foregoing table. Because the key is a compound one, the primary key can be chosen 26^7 ways and the index of progression 26 ways $(1,2,3,...,26)$ making a total of $26^7 \cdot 26$ possible keys. This yields a unicity point of $\log 26^7 \cdot 26 / 1.11 = 10.20$ characters. A drastic reduction!

In general, if a primary key is alphabetic of p_1 characters and is followed progressively by a secondary key of p_2 alphabetic characters then the number of key choices is $26^{p_1} \cdot 26^{p_2} = 26^{p_1+p_2}$. The unicity point for the compound system is then

$$U = \log 26^{p_1+p_2} / 1.11 = 1.27 (p_1 + p_2).$$

This interesting result shows that a compound key of the Vernam type increases the unicity point by a length which depends on the *sum* of the separate keys although the key length depends on their *product*. Vernam keying is seen to be very inefficient in improving the security of a cipher system. Bryant Tuckerman, in a computer investigation of Vernam-Vigenere ciphers [4], uncovered the same disagreeable property of Vernam keying. Shannon's work makes it plain just why Tuckerman got the result he did.

Turning back to our previous formula for E, the expected number of spurious decipherments, we can extract some interesting information.

Consider a running key Vigenere cipher which uses normal English plaintext as a key. Experience has shown that almost all cryptograms using this system are solvable provided only that they are long enough. From this observation alone, one can estimate the redundancy of English. The approximate number of coherent English plaintext strings of length N characters is

$$10^{RN}$$

where R is the redundancy of English and N is the number of characters present in the string. This formula holds well only if N is in excess of 15 or so characters. For a running key cipher, the above number is also the number of keys of length N. The formula for E becomes, in general,

$$E = 10^{-DN+RN} + 10^{-DN} \doteq 10^{(-D+R)N}.$$

If the cipher is uniquely solvable for large enough N, then E must approach zero as N increases. This can only happen if the exponent $-D+R$ is less than zero. Since $D = \log 26 - R$, we have

$$-D+R = -D+\log 26 - D = -2D+\log 26 < 0$$

or

$$D > \log 26/2 = .71.$$

A redundancy of .71 is, in percentage terms, about $.71/\log 26 = 50\%$. We conclude that if the running key cipher of the type described is uniquely solvable then the redundancy of English must be at least 50%.

Returning to our original formula for E and inserting the standard values of $R = .30$ and $D = 1.11$, we find that E is less than 1 for N greater than 1. In other words, the solution to a running key Vigenere is unique if even so much as 1 character is received. This result is obviously false. The problem lies in the original formula which was calculated using the redundancy of English as 1.11. In actuality this value is not reached until more than $N=20$ letter groups are used in the entropy calculation for English. D and R are functions of N. A better procedure in the formula for E would be to use values of D and R based on the entropy of English calculated for the appropriate value of N. Appendix B shows how an approximate formula of this type may be derived. Using this approximate formula in the equation for E results in the unicity point curve shown in

Figure II. The curve shows the unicity point for a running key Vigenere cipher to lie at about eight characters. This result seems to the author in accord with experience.

Most persons acquainted with unicity point theory feel that its results are usually too severe and that, in reality, much more than the minimum number of specified characters are needed to affect solution of a given cryptogram. This feeling arises, no doubt, from experience gained by applying a certain method to cryptanalyze a particular type of cipher. Redundancy of the message source which is carried over into the cipher text is the basis of most cryptanalytic methods. The less a given method makes use of the redundancies present in a cryptogram, the more text will be required for a solution. One can define an *effective unicity point* based on these ideas.

As an illustration, consider monoalphabetic substitution. (Not a good example of a random cipher, but an easy one with which to demonstrate our method.) The unicity point for monoalphabetic substitution is approximately

$$U = \log 26!/\ 1.11 = 24 \text{ characters.}$$

(This is a remarkably good estimate in view of William F. Friedman's corresponding estimate of 25 characters.) If one attempts to solve a monoalphabetically enciphered message using *only* letter frequencies, then the effective redundancy which should be used in calculating the unicity point is 0.20 digits. This is because the entropy of English calculated on the basis of single letter frequencies is about 1.21; hence, the redundancy is $\log 26 - 1.21 = .20$ (14%). Thus,

$$U_{\text{eff}} = \log 26!/.20 = 133 \text{ characters.}$$

Correspondingly, using only digraphic frequency data $U_{\text{eff}} = 65$ characters; and, with trigraphic data, $U_{\text{eff}} = 55$ characters. When we consider 8-grams about 38 letters are required to effect solution. What actually happens in the solution process is that one uses first-order entropy knowledge to gain a foothold and then rapidly expands to use of higher order relations as entire patches of plaintext are revealed. This explains why only 25 letters are needed. It also explains why more than the minimum number of characters are usually needed to achieve a solution in a reasonable amount of time.

In general, the effect of encipherment is to spread out, "diffuse." Such a diffusion process forces the would-be penetrator of a message to intercept a relatively large amount of encrypted material before he can rederive the redundancy present in the source messages. A simple heuristic argument will demonstrate the point. Consider a Vigenere encipherment of the phrase "ofthe" using the key word KING. The entropy of English plaintext is defined as

$$R = \lim_{N\to\infty} - \sum_{i=1}^{26^N} p_i^N \log p_i^N/N$$

where the p_i^N are the probabilities of occurence of English N-grams. In the cipher, the phrase "ofthe" may appear as either YNGNO, WSZRM, BLDPR, or UPBVK, depending on how the phrase straddles the key word KING. These four 5-grams will each occur in the cryptograms received with approximate probability $p/4$ if p is the probability with which "ofthe" occurs in the plaintext messages. Furthermore, we can assume that the ciphertext phrase OFTHE occurs with probability zero, and the plaintext phrases "yngno," "wszrm," "bldpr," and "upbvk" occur with probability zero also, since they are not pieces of coherent English text.

With a polyalphabetic cipher of period p, a given N-gram which occurs with probability p_i^N in plaintext gives rise to p cipher N-grams, which each occur with probabilities p_i^N/p. The original plaintext N-gram will be expected to occur with probability zero in the cipher text if N is very large and the cipher N-grams will occur with zero probability in plaintext.

Therefore, if we compute the entropy of the message source, a series term of the form:

$$-p_i^N \log p_i^N/N$$

is replaced, if the entropy calculation is done on the ciphertext, by p terms of the form

$$-(p_i^N/p) \log (p_i^N/p)/N$$

totaling

$$-(p_i^N/p) \log (p_i^N/p)/N$$

The termwise difference between these two values is

$$-p_i^N \log p/N.$$

The total of all such differences is

$$\left(\sum_i p_i^N \log p\right) /N = (\log p/N) \left(\sum_i p_i^N\right) = \log p/N.$$

This last term can be thought of as an "entropy diffusion factor" for polyalphabetic ciphers. Since $\log p/N \to 0$ for $N \to \infty$ and p fixed, we see that if enough text is intercepted the entire redundancy calculation can be done using cryptograms instead of plaintext. This is important because most statistics used to cryptanalyze messages are based ultimately upon redundancy present in the cryptograms.

Since redundancy in the source messages which is carried over into cryptograms provides the cryptanalyst with his primary means of attack, then any method of reducing the redundancy present in the source messages will ultimately complicate the would-be penetrator's problem. English has an estimated redundancy of 78%; this means that up to 78% of most English text could be deleted and that text could be unambiguously reconstructed. (Not *any* 78% can be deleted, of course, some parts of the text carry more of the meaning than others.) This process, if fully utilized, would reduce the redundancy of English to zero and therefore extend the unicity point out to infinity. No message having zero redundancy could, when encrypted, ever be uniquely solved, no matter what amount of text is intercepted. One can calculate the percentage reduction in redundancy which will occur when different percentages of text are deleted.

Let p represent the fraction of text deleted. The total number of English messages which are of length N *after* the deletion equals the total number of messages which were, *before* deletion, of length N', where N and N' are related by the equation $N' - pN' = N$. Since the original number of messages was $10^{RN'}$ (R = entropy of English = .30), the new number of messages of length N is

$$10^{(R/(1-p))N}.$$

The effective entropy after deletion is changed from R to $R/(1-p)$. The new percentage of redundancy can be found from computing

$$(\log 26 - (R/(1-p))/\log 26.$$

Figure III shows a plot of percentage deletion *versus* remaining percent redundancy.

As an example, all vowels A,E,I,O,U and Y (when occuring as a vowel) can usually be deleted from English without risking loss of meaning; this deletion shortens the average text by about 40%. The effective entropy after deletion is therefore .30/.6 = .5 or about 65% in terms of redundancy.

An interesting question which Figure III answers is the following. How much text must be deleted from the key and plaintext of a running key Vigenere cipher in order to render unique solution impossible? Deletion of vowels is not enough, since our previous results have indicated that a redundancy of less than 50% is necessary. Referring to the figure, we see that to lower the percentage redundancy to 50% or less we must delete about 58% of both key and plaintext.

If the reader desires to test his skill on a redundancy reduced cipher, below is given a running key Vigenere cryptogram in which all vowels have been deleted from key and plaintext. Persons shown the deleted key and plaintext were able in a matter of minutes to reconstruct both.

AAETU GPDLZ MOEEK KOKAA PXFIE PZFP

The remaining topic to be considered is application of our methods to the study of ciphers with purely random keys. Such keying sequences cannot be generated by mathematical formulas but can be constructed by using physically random phenomena such as radioactive decay to activate recording devices. Suppose each character of plaintext is encrypted using one character, either numeric or alphabetic, chosen randomly from a set of L possible ones. To encrypt a string of N characters the number of random keys possible is L^N. Our previous expression for the number of spurious decipherments becomes

$$E = 10^{-1.11N + N \log L} - 10^{-1.11N},$$

since $H(K) = L^N = 10^{N \log L}$.

Unique decipherability implies

$$-1.11N + N \log L < 0$$

or,

$$L > 10^{1.11} = 13.$$

If fewer than 13 choices are available at each encryption step, the cryptogram is uniquely solvable given enough text *even if the keying sequence is completely random.* To illustrate, suppose we are given a one-time pad composed of the random digits 0,1,...,9, and we use the pad as a random key for a Vigenere cipher. This amounts to using 10 of the 26 possible Vigenere alphabets randomly. The number of possible keying sequences which can be used to encipher N letters is 10^{26}, so $L = 10$ and the cipher is solvable uniquely by writing down all possible decipherments and picking out the (unique) one which is coherent English. As one can see, the result is theoretical and not particularly practical in most cases.

To an extent, the result shown above is obvious. If all 26 Vigenere alphabets were used in the preceeding example [5] randomly, then $L=26$ and no unique solution can be found. This is because any letter is equilikely to replace any other letter in the encipherment making all texts equilikely. If, on the other hand, only two or so cipher alphabets were used, a unique reconstruction of the text is usually possible. The reader can verify this by solving the message below, which is Vigenere enciphered using a randomly chosen key consisting of B's and C's. In this case, one can go through the cipher, writing down the two substitutes for each letter. By choosing the more probable of the two based on English letter frequencies, enough plaintext will emerge to complete the solution. The random use of the key does not prevent decipherment.

TPOGD JRJFS UBSFC SQLGP COFUQ NFDSF CLVIF TONWG T

A favorite "spy" cipher of the fifties and sixties was a straddling checkerboard encipherment followed by addition modulo-10 of a series of random numbers to the enciphered text. For example, if the checkerboard is taken to be

```
  0 1 2 3 4 5 6 7 8 9
  E T N R I   O A S
8 B C D F G H J K L M
9 P Q U V W X Y Z
```

and we have a random one-time pad which begins

03948 23348 78539 55683 ...

We encipher as follows:

Plaintext:	A	R	S	E	S	T	C	E	L	A	R	E	A	R	T	E	M
Numeric Encipherment:	6	3	7	0	7	1	81	0	88	6	3	0	6	3	1	0	89
Random Number Stream:	0	3	9	4	8	2	33	4	87	8	5	3	9	5	5	6	83
Final Cryptogram:	6	6	6	4	5	3	14	4	65	4	8	3	5	8	6	6	62

Transmitted Cryptogram: 66645 31446 54835 86662

The security of the above system is thought to reside in the random key; the straddling feature of the preliminary numeric encipherment is primarily to shorten the message length. We have placed the higher frequency portion of the English letters in the first row of the checkerboard in order to achieve maximum message compression. In our checkerboard, the first row includes about 66% total frequency letters.

The straddling device is a weakness of this cipher, since it reduces the random key consumption per letter. Approximately 66% of an average English text will be represented by one digit with the above checkerboard and will hence require one random digit for encipherment. About 34% of the average text will require two random digits for encipherment. This makes the average key consumption about $.66(8) + .34(20) = 12.08$ digits per letter. We base this on the fact that, if letter divisions were maintained in the final cryptogram, then each one-digit cipher digit is uncertain by eight equilikely digits $0, 1, 2, \ldots, 7$ and each two digit cipher character is uncertain by 20 equilikely digits. (The first digit must be an 8 or 9, the second $0, 1, \ldots, 9$.) This value is lower than the magic number of $L = 13$ derived previously, and so the cipher is solvable uniquely! The first row of the checkerboard could contain letters totaling as low as 58% in frequency for the key consumption to be below 13. All of the above postulates that the checkerboard is known (a reasonable assumption) and that the letter divisions are maintained (an unreasonable assumption).

As we have shown, the security of a cipher system like the one just discussed resides in great part on the fact that letter divisions are destroyed when the final cryptogram is transmitted. We pose the question to the reader: Is this destruction of the letter divisions enough to convey inpenetrability in the theoretical sense? Obviously, ciphers based on one-time pads are not "uncrackable" in the absolute. More needs to be said.

REFERENCES

1. Shannon, C. E., "Communication Theory of Secrecy Systems," *Bell System Technical Journal,* 28, October 1949, pp. 656–715.

2. Hellman, M., "The Shannon Theory Approach to Cryptography," submitted to [IEEE] *Transactions on Information Theory,* Oct. 1975. The author has followed Hellman's approach throughout this paper.

3. Kahn, David, *The Codebreakers,* Macmillian, New York, 1967, pp. 462–464.

4. Tuckerman, Bryant, "A Study of Vigenere-Vernam Single and Multiple Loop Enciphering Systems," RC 2879, IBM, October 1975.

5. Copland, Miles, *Beyond Cloak and Cipher,* Pennacle Books, New York, 1975, pp. 364–466. Vigenere with Random One Time Pad. Accompanying text should be ignored.

372

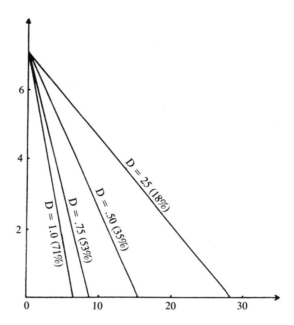

FIGURE I.
Unicity point line $\log E = -D \cdot N + H$ for Vigenere with period 5 and varying source message redundancies. Horizontal axis: $\log E$. Vertical axis: N, number of letters intercepted.

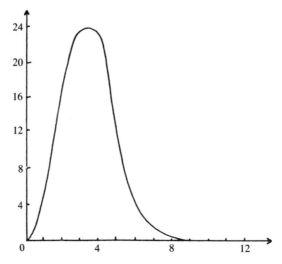

FIGURE II.
Unicity point curve for English running key Vigenere. Horizontal axis: number of letters intercepted. Vertical axis: number of spurious decipherments.

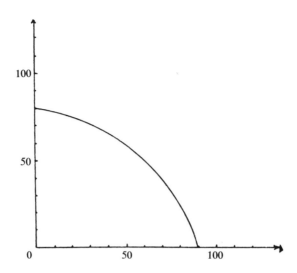

FIGURE III.
Redundancy reduction curve for English. Horizontal axis: percent of plaintext deleted. Vertical axis: percentage redundancy remaining in text.

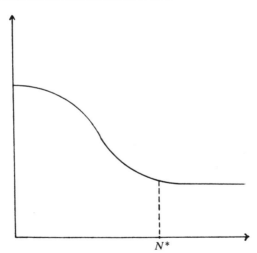

FIGURE IV.
Typical entropy calculation curve. Horizontal axis: log N, where entropy is calculated on basis of N-grams. Vertical axis: entropy.

APPENDIX A

A simple mathematical model of a cipher system can be constructed as follows. Suppose we have M messages $M_1, M_2, \ldots, M_M$ which we might desire to encrypt. To encipher these messages we assume that K keys $K_1, K_2, \ldots, K_K$, all of which may be used to encrypt each message, are available. If we encipher all M messages, each with all K possible keys, we will obtain C cryptograms, $C_1, C_2, \ldots, C_C$. Clearly,

$$C \leqslant MK.$$

The encipherment process can be visualized as shown below [I. Encipherment].

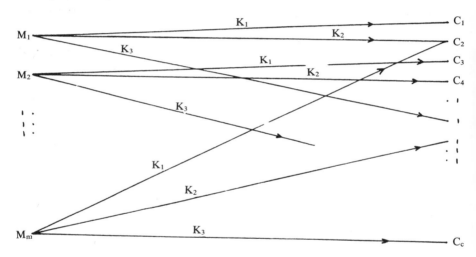

I. Encipherment

In attempting to break a given cryptogram, a penetrator could, we assume, try all possible keys for each possible cryptogram and make a list of cryptograms and corresponding messages. Generally, when all of the keys are tried on a given cryptogram, a number of meaningless decipherments will be produced as well as a number of "spurious" decipherments, which are valid messages, but correspond to the use of the wrong key. The decipherment process can be visualized as follows [II. Decipherment].

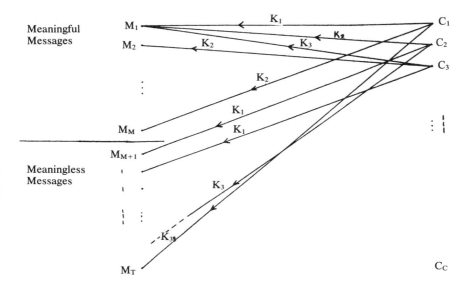

II. Decipherment

We let M_T be the total number of messages, meaningful and meaningless, which are obtained by trying all possible keys on all possible cryptograms.

If we assume that all messages and keys are *equiprobable* in I, then the probability of receiving the ith cryptogram, C_i, is directly proportional to the number of lines ending on C_i in I, thus,

$$p_i = aN_i$$

where

p_i = probability of receiving cryptogram C_i;
a = proportionality constant;
N_i = number of lines ending on C_i in I.

The proportionality constant can be found. Since

$$\sum_{i=1}^{C} p_i = 1 = a \cdot \sum_{i=1}^{C} N_i = a \cdot MK,$$

then, we have

$$a = 1/MK$$

and

$$p_i = N_i/MK.$$

The number of "spurious" decipherments for C_i is the number of lines ending on C_i in I minus 1 (the correct decipherment), if we specify that decipherment using the wrong key does not lead to the correct message. The average number of "spurious" decipherments is, therefore,

$$\overline{N} = \sum_{i=1}^{C} p_i(N_i - 1) = \sum_{i=1}^{C} p_i(p_iMK - 1).$$

It is of particular interest to find out what type of cipher systems are most insecure in the sense that N is a minimum. Mathematically, we seek an extremum of $\overline{N}$ subject to the constraint:

$$\sum_{i=1}^{C} p_i = 1.$$

Introducing the Lagrange multiplier λ, we define

$$\phi = \sum_{i=1}^{C} p_i(p_iMK - 1) + \lambda \sum_{i=1}^{C} (p_i - 1).$$

A necessary condition for an extremum of ϕ is that

$$\partial\phi/\partial p_i = 2p_iMK - 1 + \lambda = 0; \qquad\qquad i=1,2,...,C.$$

Thus,

$$p_i = (1-\lambda)/2MK = \text{constant}.$$

Solving for p_i, we find

$$p_i = 1/C.$$

This extremum is readily seen to be a minimum and so we can conclude that, from this viewpoint, the most insecure cipher systems are those in which all possible cryptograms are equilikely to be received. Note that this result applies to the entire spectrum of cryptograms possible and not to individual cases.

For *any cipher* with equiprobable messages and keys we must have

$$\overline{N} \geqslant \sum_{i=1}^{C} (1/C)(MK/C-1) \qquad = MK/C-1.$$

The unicity point, for this cipher model, may be defined as

$$\overline{N} = MK/C-1 = 0.$$

Comments

(1) It is usual to assume that $C = M_T$. The above formula then becomes

$$\overline{N} \geqslant (M/M_T)K - 1.$$

One can see clearly from this last formula how the unicity point concept arises. If we think of $M, C,$ and M_T as increasing functions of the number of characters intercepted, then the ratio of meaningful messages of a certain length to total messages of the same length would be expected to approach zero rapidly as more characters are intercepted. Thus, the number of spurious decipherments falls rapidly if the number of keys remain fixed. When $\overline{N} = 0$ then only the correct decipherment of the cryptogram remains and this solution is uniquely determined. Two approaches that might prevent $\overline{N}$ from approaching zero immediately suggest themselves. We may attempt to increase the number of keys as the number of characters intercepted increases (e.g., running key ciphers), or we may adjust the cipher generated so that the ratio M/M_T does not tend to zero with the number of intercepted characters. When implemented successfully, either procedure yields a cipher system with unicity point never approaching zero, and hence gives ciphers which are not uniquely solvable, no matter how much text is intercepted.

(2) In Shannon's theory, one can receive "dummy" cryptograms, i.e., $N_i = 0$. In this case, N_i is taken to be a binomially distributed random variable during decipherment using a random key. The binomial p value is taken to be M/M_T. Since there are $K-1$ trials in deciphering, the average of this distribution is

$$\overline{N}_s = (M/M_T)(K-1).$$

The difference between this value and our previous minimum value is

$$\overline{N} - \overline{N}_s = M/M_T - 1$$

indicating that both theories are in good accord.

APPENDIX B

As mentioned in the text, the entropy of a language is calculated from the definition:

$$R = \lim_{N \to \infty} - \sum_{i=1}^{26^N} (p_i^N \log p_i^N)/N$$

where the p_i^N are the probabilities of occurrence of the N-grams of the language. Individual letter frequencies can be used to find the first approximation R_1, digraphic frequencies to find the second approximation R_2, etc. In practice, the curve found by this process has the shape shown in Figure IV. For the first few values of N, the entropy values found decrease in an approximately linear manner as a function of log N. This decrease continues until some value N^* of N is reached (N^* is greater than 20 in English), at which time the entropy values obtained level out. In actuality other methods besides attempting to construct N-gram tables for large N are used to estimate the final limiting value obtained.

In the curve shown in Figure II, the initial decreasing segment of the curve for N less than N^* was approximated by a line of the form:

$$R = R(N) = A \log (N) + B.$$

The constants A and B were found using the known values for entropy when $N = 1$ ($R = 1.24$) and $N = 8$ ($R = .71$). No precise curve fitting was attempted, since the known values themselves are not fully agreed upon and because relatively wide variations of these values yield virtually the same curve as shown in Figure II.

Entropy Calculations and Particular Methods
of Cryptanalysis
by James Reeds

It is well known that the longer a cryptogram is, the easier it is to solve. This fact has two causes. For extremely short cryptograms, cryptanalytic solution is actually impossible: there are several completely different meaningful plaintexts, which, when enciphered by completely different keys, result in the same ciphertext. For cryptograms which are longer than this, solution can be difficult simply because there is not enough data to work on: with the length of text available the cryptanalyst is unable to discern that subtle pattern of regularity by which plaintext and key reveal themselves through the disguise of ciphertext.

We may mark the limits of applicability of these considerations with two theoretical quantities. For a certain given cipher system, let U, the "unicity distance," be that length of text such that cryptograms shorter than U typically do not have unique solutions and those longer than U typically do have unique cryptanalytical solutions; and for the same cipher system, for some given method of analysis, let L denote the length of cryptogram which is typically needed to effect a solution in practice. Thus, messages shorter than U are, in principle, immune to cryptanalysis; those of length between U and L are in principle solvable, but in practice unsolvable; those longer than L are in practice solvable. Of course, these figures are only meant to indicate ranges of values. For instance, when we say $L = 100$ letters, we mean that cryptograms of length 80 cannot typically be solved, and those of length 120 typically can, but we do not mean to imply any drastic difference in kind between messages of length 99 and those of length 101.

Simple formulas for U, and especially for L, would obviously be immensely useful to both cryptographer and cryptanalyst. Such formulas

From *Cryptologia*, Vol. 1, No. 3, July 1977.

are partially available. In [11], Claude Shannon gives a remarkably simple formula for U:

$$U = (\log_2 K)/R,$$

where K is the number of keys the cipher system uses and R is the redundancy, measured in bits per letter, of the plaintext language. Unfortunately, Shannon gives no similar formula for L. Further, we cannot use the formula for U as an approximation to L, because in all but the simplest cipher systems, L is many times larger than U.

In this paper, we show how to write approximations to L, which, although different from Shannon's formula for U, are based on the same kind of reasoning. In essence we propose to underestimate L with U', the Shannon unicity distance figured for a suitably chosen plaintext language and a suitably chosen cipher system, both of which are different from the ones [in which] we are actually interested. Although U', like U, is simply an underestimate of L, it turns out that U' is usually much larger than U, and hence provides a correspondingly better approximation to L. We suspect (on the basis of a limited number of examples) that in many cases our approximations are fairly accurate: that L will lie between U' and 1-1/2 times U'.

Our proposal has two parts: (1) modifying the (plaintext) language and (2) modifying the cipher system. The modification of language aspect of our proposal has undoubtedly occurred to many people before, but we believe that our *justification* of this modification and that our idea of modifying the cipher system are new. In Section 1 below, we review the classical Shannon unicity distance result and show that there are really two related results here. We present their proofs in some detail because in Section 3 we will need to refer back to them. In Section 2 we present our proposal for modifying the language and give numerical examples of its application. In Section 3 we present two arguments for modifying the language that, in effect, put this proposal on the same footing as the classical Shannon result. In Section 4 we give our proposal for modifying the cipher system. The justification of this proposal is based on arguments similar to those given in Section 3, but, because we think the proposal is by then pretty much self-evident, we do not spell out these arguments. In Section 5 we apply both modifications at once to the example of the Hagelin M-209 cipher machine. Finally, in Section 6 we discuss these results in terms of a broader conception of the nature of cryptanalysis.

SECTION 1. SHANNON'S UNICITY DISTANCE RESULT

For simplicity's sake, all our plaintexts and cryptograms are sequences of N letters, written in the ordinary 26-letter alphabet. There are thus 26^N possible plaintexts, 26^N possible ciphertexts, and $(26^N)!$ possible invertible functions from plaintext to ciphertext. A cipher system with K keys is defined by specifying, for each of the K keys, one of these invertible functions.

We denote the entropy of the plaintexts of length N by H_N, so

$$H_N = - \Sigma \, p(X) \, \log_2 p(X)$$

where the summation extends over all 26^N possible sequences of N letters, and where $p(X)$ denotes the probability of the sequence X occurring in the plaintext language. It is known that H_N/N is a decreasing function of N, and hence has a limit H, the "long range" per letter entropy of the plaintext language. If N is large, H_N/N is very close to H. In all cases, $H_N \geqslant NH$. We let $R_N = \log_2 26^N - H_N$ be the redundancy in an N-letter plaintext and we let $R = \log_2 26 - H$ be the long range per letter redundancy. As N increases, R_N/N increases to the limit R.

As we mentioned in the introduction, there are really two unicity distance results. The first is due to Shannon [11], and is slightly reworded in an interesting paper by M. Hellman [5]. We state it informally as:

Shannon's Random Cipher Result: If K is large, then in the typical (or randomly chosen) cipher system with K keys, U is approximately $(\log_2 K)/R$.

The second result is, surprisingly, not to be found in Shannon's paper, even though it follows from his work. It is contained implicitly in a little book by G. Raisbeck [9], and explicitly in Hellman's paper [5]:

Lower Bound for U Result: For any cipher system with K keys, U is at least $(\log_2 K)/R - 1/R$.

We will sketch proofs of both of these results. For simplicity's sake, we suppose we are only interested in solving for the key. (If we make the accurate recovery of the plaintext rather than of the key our criterion of success, the arguments get more complicated but are basically similar to those presented here for the "solving for the key" case.)

Argument for the Random Cipher Result: For a given length of text N and cipher system S, we can (in principle, at least) calculate the probability $p(N,S)$ that the typical cryptogram has a unique, meaningful solution. We prove the claimed result by showing that, if

$$N_1 = (\log_2 K)/R + 20/R$$

and

$$N_2 = (\log_2 K)/R - 4/R,$$

then the following happens for all but (at most) two out of 1000 cipher systems S:

$$p(N_1,S) \geq .999 \tag{1}$$

and

$$p(N_2,S) \leq .001. \tag{2}$$

That is, in the vast majority of cipher systems, cryptograms of length N_2 (or shorter) are just about certain to have more than one valid solution, and cryptograms of length N_1 (or longer) are just about certain to have exactly one valid solution. This essentially identifies U to within a margin of error of $24/R$ letters. For English, $24/R$ works out to about 6-1/2 letters, which "brackets" U to within plus or minus 3-1/4 letters.

Everything hinges on establishing that for the vast majority of cipher systems, inequalities (1) and (2) hold. We see that they do hold by using two ingenious ideas, both due to Shannon.

The first is the *Shannon-McMillan theorem* [3], which essentially counts the number of *meaningful* plaintexts of length N. Specifically, if N is large, there is a special set of plaintexts, the "probable" set (or "typical" set or "meaningful" set), with the following properties:

1. The "probable" set has approximately 2^{NH} texts in it;
2. All the texts in the "probable" set are approximately equally likely, with individual probabilities approximately 2^{-NH}; and
3. The total probability of the "probable" set is approximately 1; that is, the typical, randomly chosen plaintext of length N is most likely in the "probable" set.

(The larger N is, the more exact all these approximations become.)

Now, take a cryptogram and examine all K possible decipherments. The correct decipherment will land in the "probable" set (by property 3); if any spurious decipherment lands in the "probable" set, there is no unique cryptanalytical solution; if no spurious decipherments land in the "probable" set, the correct solution is the unique solution. Thus, $p(N,S)$ is equal to the probability that all $K-1$ spurious decipherments avoid the "probable" set.

Shannon's other ingenious idea is the random cipher system. Here we replace averages of quantities over all cipher systems by mathematical expectations over a randomly chosen cipher system. Remember that a cipher system is specified by choosing K enciphering transformations out of the set of all $(26^N)!$ possible. We define a random cipher by choosing these K transformations at random, independently and uniformly distributed over the set of all possible $(26^N)!$ transformations. Then the *proportion* of all cipher systems that have a given property equals the *probability* that the random cipher has that property.

For given N, we calculate $E[p(N,S)]$, the expectation of the probability that the typical cryptogram in system S has a unique solution, as S varies randomly. This is just the probability that none of the $K-1$ spurious decipherments land in the "probable" set. By the random cipher assumptions, these $K-1$ spurious decipherments are identically and uniformly distributed over the set of all 26^N possible plaintexts; the probability that they all avoid the "probable" set is thus

$$(1 - 2^{NH})^{K-1} = (1 - 2^{-NR})^{K-1}.$$

Hence, $E[p(N,S)] = (1 - 2^{-NR})^{K-1}$.

We now evaluate this for $N = N_1$ and $N = N_2$, using the approximation $(1 - a/K)^{K-1} \approx e^{-a}$, valid for large K:

$$E[p(N_1,S)] = E[p((\log_2 K)/R - 20/R, S)]$$
$$= (1 - 2^{-20}/K)^{K-1} \approx e^{-2^{-20}} > 1 - 10^{-6}$$

and

$$E[p(N_2,S)] = E[p((\log_2 K)/R + 4/R, S)]$$
$$= (1 - 2^4/K)^{K-1} \approx e^{-16} < 10^{-6}.$$

Since the random variables $p(N,S)$—random because S is random—are constrained to lie between 0 and 1, we can deduce $p(N_1,S) \geq .999$ with probability at least .999, and $p(N_2,S) \leq .001$ with probability at least .999.

This completes the proof. Q.E.D.

Argument for the Lower Bound for U Result: Consider the following cryptanalytical procedure (maximum likelihood deciphering): decipher the cryptogram with all K possible keys; choose as solution that one which yields the most likely trial plaintext. If the solution thus calculated is *incorrect*, one of the spurious decipherments has greater likelihood than the correct decipherment, and hence both are cryptanalytically valid solutions. Thus, the probability λ that this maximum likelihood cryptanalytical procedure fails (comes up with the wrong key) is no larger than the probability that a cryptogram has more than one valid solution. For cryptograms longer than the unicity distance, then, this probability λ of cryptanalysis failure must be vanishingly small.

But classical results from information theory allow us to bound λ by a function of K, N, and R. In particular, Wolfowitz [12, Theorem 7.4.2] guarantees that

$$(1-\lambda) \log_2 K \leq R_n + 1 \leq RN+1$$

so $N \geq (1-\lambda)(\log_2 K)/R - 1/R$. Since λ is to be made vanishingly small when N exceeds U, we must have

$$U \geq (\log_2 K)/R - 1/R. \qquad \text{Q.E.D.}$$

Technical Note: We apply Wolfowitz's theorem to the information theoretical channel whose input alphabet is the set of all $(26^N)!$ possible enciphering transformations and whose output alphabet is the set of all 26^N possible ciphertexts. This channel, given a transformation T as input, produces as output the ciphertext $T(X)$, where X is a randomly chosen plaintext sequence of length N. (Thus, we view the cryptogram as a noisy version of the key, the "noise" being the plaintext.) It is easy to see that this channel has capacity R_N; the existence of a cryptanalytical procedure with failure rate λ is equivalent (in Wolfowitz's terminology) to the existence of a (information theoretical) code of type (K,λ).

SECTION 2. MODIFYING THE LANGUAGE

Cryptanalysis is possible only because the plaintext language has certain statistical regularities which distinguish it from purely random text; any successful method of cryptanalysis must exploit some aspect of this regularity. However, the actual structure of natural languages (like English, Russian, etc.) is so complicated that no one actually knows, in detail, the full extent of the statistics of the language. Indeed, natural languages are so complex that no cryptanalytical method (say, no cryptanalytical computer program) can even take advantage of all the *known* aspects of the structure of the plaintext language. Thus, cryptanalysis relies on statistical structure, but in practice it only uses *some* of the statistical structure present.

We propose to take this fact into account in our underestimate U' of the minimum length of text L actually needed by a given cryptanalytical method. We will take $U' = (\log_2 K)/R'$, where R' is an *adjusted* figure for the redundancy of the plaintext language, based only on that *part* of the statistical structure of the plaintext language that our cryptanalytical procedure actually uses. In particular, R' will be the minimum redundancy possible for any language (natural or artificial) which exhibits just those same statistical regularities that our cryptanalytical procedure exploits.

In the examples that follow, S will stand for the statements describing just those statistical regularities of the plaintext language that our procedure exploits. Thus, depending on the particular method of cryptanalysis, S might be "the individual letter frequencies in the plaintext language are such and so," or "the digraph distribution is such and so," or "the index of coincidence of the plaintext language is .067," etc. With this shorthand, we rephrase our definition: R' is the minimal redundancy a language (natural or artificial) can have, as long as it is described by S. Equivalently, $R' = \log_2 26 - H'$, where H' is the maximal entropy a language can have, as long as it is described by S.

As our first example, suppose we are solving Vigenère cryptograms with known periods by frequency count matching. That is, if the period is, say, 17, we make 17 unigraphic frequency counts and we slide the theoretical plaintext distribution against each of these 17 counts. In each count, the relative alignment which gives the closest match (as measured, for example, by the sum of log weights being greatest, or by the chi-squared statistic being smallest) yields a key letter. This method clearly relies only on the single-letter statistics of the language; so in this example S is the theoretical single letter frequency distribution. Now the language with the same S but with maximal entropy (and hence minimal redundancy) is the "urn language" or "Bernoulli shift," in which the individual letters are present in their proper frequencies but where pairs, triplets, etc. of letters have no statistical connection. Ordinary English has an entropy of about one bit per letter; the urn language which has the same single-letter statistics as English has entropy about 4.22 bits per letter. In this example, then, we see L is greater than

$$U' = \log_2 26^{17})/R' = 79.9/(\log_2 26 - 4.22) = 166 \text{ letters}$$

instead of merely greater than

$$U = (\log_2 26^{17})/(\log_2 26 - 1) = 21.6$$

which is predicted by Shannon's theory.

As another example, consider a computer program which solves simple substitution ciphers by matching the observed digraph count to the theoretical digraph count for English. (Such a program might proceed by iteratively shuffling the rows and columns of the observed digraph count by the same permutations so as to bring the row and column permuted count as close as possible to the theoretical English digraph count.) Here the program is only making use of pairs of letter data: S is the theoretical digraphic frequency count of English. It can be shown that of all languages with this same theoretical digraphic count S, the one that maximizes the per letter entropy is the first order Markov chain with transition probabilities:

$$p_{ij} = s_{ij}/(s_{iA} + \cdots + s_{iZ})$$

where s_{ij} is the proportion of digraphs (i,j) in English and p_{ij} is the probability that letter i is followed by letter j. The entropy of this language is 3.57 bits per letter, so we conclude that such computer programs require at least

$$U' = (\log_2 26!)/R' = (\log_2 26!)/(\log_2 26 - 3.57)$$
$$= 88.4/1.13 = 78 \text{ letters.}$$

This example has an obvious generalization to k-gram statistics, where $k \geq 3$.

As a final example, consider a polyalphabetic cipher with unknown primary components sliding against each other one space per letter enciphered, i.e., a progressive cipher with mixed alphabets. The standard method of analysis is to prepare 26 frequency counts, one for each secondary alphabet. Since the primary alphabets are unknown, these counts cannot be slid against a theoretical count; but they can be slid against each other in the manner described in [8, pp. 382–383] and in [4, Vol. 3, pp. 82–89]. The success of this matching procedure depends solely on the value of the index of coincidence (or repeat rate) of the plaintext language: on the fact that $K = p_A^2 + p_B^2 + \ldots + p_Z^2 = .067$. Alternatively, we can describe the matching procedure as attempting to maximize the observed repeat rate (observed phi coefficient) in the reconstructed plaintext. It is easy to see that of all languages with index of coincidence equal to .067 the maximal entropy is achieved by an urn language with all letters equally likely except for one, which is more likely. The probabilities are (choosing "A" to be the more likely letter): $p_A = .201$, $p_B =$

$p_C = \ldots = p_Z = .032$, with per letter entropy $H' = 4.43$ and redundancy $R' = .267$. Thus the alphabet matching part of the cryptanalysis requires at least

$$U' = (\log_2 26!)/.267 \approx 331 \text{ letters.}$$

(We use 26! for K because the alphabet matching recovers only one of the two primary components. When the alphabets are correctly matched we have reduced the cryptogram to monoalphabetic terms; we recover the other primary component by solving the reduced monoalphabetic cipher.)

SECTION 3. JUSTIFICATION OF MODIFYING THE LANGUAGE

So far we have not argued for our proposal to "modify the language," although we hope that the examples in the previous section have some persuasive force. Here we present two approximations to formal mathematical proofs of the proposition that a method of cryptanalysis M which relies entirely on regularity S requires cryptograms of length at least $U' = (\log_2 K)/R'$ letters. We have been able to construe "M relies on S" in two different ways (which give rise to our two different proofs), and we are not completely satisfied with our analysis of this issue. Presumably, a complete understanding of "method M relies on S" would allow us to answer both of the following questions:
1. What does "M relies on S" mean?
2. Given a cryptanalytical method M, how do we discover which S it relies on?

Certainly in any given example we feel more comfortable with question 2 than question 1.

At any rate, we propose two possible "definitions" of "M relies on S," and then we go on to present our two arguments justifying our recipe for U'. Our first definition is based on the internal functioning of the cryptanalytical method M.

Definition 1. M relies on S means that M attempts—either explicitly or implicitly—to make the recovered plaintext exemplify S, that is, make the recovered plaintext "look like" plaintext *with respect to* the features described by S.

By contrast, our second definition is based on the overall performance of the method M.

Definition 2. M relies on S means M works equally well against crypto-grams written in any language, natural or artificial, which has statistical regularities S.

First Argument for Modifying the Language

Suppose M relies on S in the sense of definition 1. Suppose S is couched in terms of theoretical k-gram statistics, so that S takes the form: "The theoretical k-gram distribution has such and such a property." (This includes both possibilities, like "The theoretical pairs of letters distribution is what it is in English" and like "The index of coincidence is .067." We can always reword this second type of statement as "The theoretical single letter distribution p_A, p_B, . . . , p_Z has the property that $p_A^2 + \ldots + p_Z^2 = .067$." If we let the sample k-gram statistics of a message, divided through by the message length N, be denoted by b_N, and if we let its expectation be denoted by β, then β is the theoretical (population) table of k-gram probabilities. Our rewording of S makes S take the form "β is contained in B," where B is some special set of possible theoretical k-gram statistics. Then definition 1 translates into saying that method M tries to make the recovered plaintext have its b_N lie, to within a given statistical tolerance, in the set B. Let the set of all plaintexts whose b_N lies, to within a given tolerance, in B, be known as the "good" set.

The "good" set of plain texts contains the "probable" set guaranteed by the Shannon-McMillan theorem. In the special case where S is the complete statistical description of English, the "good" set and the "probable" set coincide.

Now consider the method of cryptanalysis M^1, which takes a cryptogram, deciphers it with all K possible keys, and randomly chooses as decipherment any of the K recovered plaintexts which lie in the "good" set. The method M cannot perform any better than M^1. For if it did, it could only do so by having some way of automatically ruling out part of the "good" set, i.e., of ruling out some of the trial decipherments which nonetheless exemplify S. M could do this only if it relied on some more detailed description of the language than that provided by S.

Thus, the minimum length of text needed for M is at least equal to that needed by M^1. We now appeal to the *argument* for Shannon's random cipher result given in Section 1. In that argument there was nothing sacred about the genesis of the "probable" set, and the argument works if we replace the "probable" set with the "good" set. The conclusion is that *if* the "good" set has approximately $2^{NH'}$ elements in it, *then* in the vast majority of cipher systems, if $n > U'$, typically only one of the trial decipherments lands in the "good" set; if $N < U'$, typically several land in the good set. (Here $U' = (\log_2 K)/R'$, where $R' = \log_2 26 - H'$.) This in turn means that method M^1 typically picks the correct solution when $N > U'$ and has a high chance of picking an incorrect solution when $N < U'$.

Thus, if we can show that the "good" set has approximately $2^{NH'}$ elements in it, where H' is the maximum entropy that a language described by S can have, the proof is complete. In other words, we need a way to tie up the size of the "good" set with the maximum entropy H', just the way the Shannon-McMillan theorem tied the size of the "probable" set to the actual entropy H.

This connection is provided by a remarkable class of results, known in the theory of probability as "large deviation" or "Sanov" theorems. The original Sanov theorem, which covers the case where only single-letter statistics are of interest, was proved in 1957 [10], [6], [7], [1]. The extension which covers the k-gram statistics case for arbitrary k, is much more recent [2]. Both of these results estimate the probability that a purely random sequence of N letters will have its sample k-gram count land in B; that is, that a purely random sequence of letters lands in the "good" set. We get the size of the "good" set by simply multiplying this probability by the number of sequences of length N, namely, by multiplying by 26^N.

Sanov's Theorem [10]: Let b_N be the sample single-letter frequency count, divided through by N, of a purely random sequence of N letters. Let B be an open set. Then

$$\frac{1}{N} \log_2 [\text{Prob } (b_N \in B)] = -R' + e_N$$

where e_N tends to zero as $N \to \infty$. Here R' is the minimum redundancy an urn language (Markov chain of order 0) can have, whose theoretical single-letter distribution lies in B.

Bahadur's Theorem [2]: Let b_N be the sample k-gram frequency count, divided through by N, of a purely random sequence of N letters. Let B be an open set. Then

$$\frac{1}{N} \log_2 [\text{Prob } (b_N \in B)] = -R' + e_N$$

where e_N tends to zero as $N \to \infty$, and where R' is the minimum redundancy a $(k-1)$st-order Markov chain can have, whose theoretical k-gram distribution lies in B.

These two theorems leave one tiny gap: we want R' to be the minimum redundancy *any* language described by S can have, not just that [which] a Markov chain described by S can have. This gap is closed by the following simple result, whose proof follows from the properties of conditional entropy:

Proposition: Of all languages with given k-gram statistics, the maximal entropy—and hence the minimal redundancy—is attained by a Markov chain of order $k-1$.

This completes our first argument. Q.E.D.

Our second argument is *much* simpler.

Second Argument for Modifying the Language

Assume M relies on S in the sense of definition 2. Consider a new language (possibly artificial) which is described by S with minimum redundancy R'. By definition 2, M works just as well against cryptograms composed in this new language as against those in the old language. By the results of Section 1, applied to the new language, M needs messages of length at least $U' = \log_2 26/R'$ letters. Q.E.D.

SECTION 4. MODIFYING THE CIPHER SYSTEM

As it stands so far, we have proposed using $U' = \log_2 K/R'$ as an estimate of how much text a particular method of cryptanalysis needs. This is, however, only one part of our two part proposal. The *full* proposal is to also replace K by a larger number K', so that $U' = (\log_2 K')/R'$.

Suppose we are using a particular method of cryptanalysis to solve cryptograms composed in some cipher system S with K keys, and suppose there is some other cipher system S' with K' keys, where K' is greater than K. If it happens that our method of cryptanalysis works equally as well against cryptograms composed in S' as it does against those in S, we are entitled to use K' in our formula:

$$U' = (\log_2 K')/R'.$$

This situation occurs, for example, when the enemy's keying discipline is such that he only uses a certain subset of the possible keys available to his general cipher system, and when the method of cryptanalysis does not—either implicitly or explicitly—take advantage of this fact. For instance, the enemy might use a transposition system using a

14-digit key, where the digits are formed in some systematic way from two phone numbers occurring on successive lines of the Manhattan phone directory. Thus the number of keys is approximately equal to the number of phone subscribers in Manhattan, which is of the order of magnitude 10^6; far less than the 10^{14} possible 14-digit keys. If we use the standard techniques for solving transposition ciphers, and pay no attention to the special structure of the key, we have an instance of the type of situation described above. In this case we would have $U' = (\log_2 10^{14})/R'$ instead of $U' = (\log_2 10^6)/R'$.

Another class of examples occurs in cipher machines. Given a particular cryptanalytical technique which succeeds against a given cipher machine, we can often imagine additions and complications to the machine which enlarge the key space but do not affect the success of the technique. Since the structure of a given cipher machine is very often a compromise between cryptographic criteria and mechanical design criteria, we will often find possibilities for this type of addition and complication. We will see an example of this in Section 5 below.

A further type of example concerns product ciphers. Suppose that the enemy first enciphers messages with the Playfair cipher and then subjects them to an irregular columnar transposition. If we are solving these messages by sheer statistical analysis, following a procedure like the general solution for the ADFGVX cipher discussed in [4, Vol. 4], and if we do not take advantage of cryptograms with similar beginnings or endings, the cryptanalysis will be divided into two distinct phases: undoing the transposition and solving the Playfair. Of these, the first is the more difficult, and its difficulty would scarcely be changed if the initial encipherment were done in any digraphic substitution which avoided doubled letters, not just the Playfair. Of course, the second phase is made more difficult than it was by this replacement, but it will not be made more difficult than the first phase. We are thus entitled to replace that part of the key for the Playfair; namely, $K_{\text{Playfair}} = 25!/25$ ($\log_2 K = 79$) by the figure $K' = (25 \cdot 24)! = 600!$ ($\log_2 K' \approx 4678$).

It is clear that to carry out any of these replacements of K by K' we have to have a good knowledge of how our analytical technique works, both against the original system and against the modified system.

SECTION 5. APPLICATION TO M-209

The Hagelin M-209 cipher machine (as described in [8, pp. 427–431]) has three keyed elements: each of 131 pins on the six pin wheels can be set in one of two positions; each of 27 lug bars can be set in any one of 22 cryptographically inequivalent positions; and the six pin wheels can be set in any one of $17 \cdot 19 \cdot 21 \cdot 23 \cdot 25 \cdot 26 = 101,405,850$ starting positions. As far as the encipherment of a single cryptogram is concerned, the wheel starting positions are redundant: all possible encipherments of a single message are produced by varying the pin and lug settings alone. There are clearly 2^{131} different pin settings; we show below that there are $\binom{48}{21}$ cryptographically inequivalent lug bar settings.

Each individual lug bar carries two lugs. Both lugs can be inactive; one lug can be inactive and the other set in any of six active positions; or both may be active, set in two out of the six active positions. This makes

$$\binom{6}{0} + \binom{6}{1} + \binom{6}{2} = 1 + 6 + 15 = 22$$

cryptographically inequivalent ways of setting an individual lug bar. For the lug bar mechanism as a whole, the only thing that matters is how many of the 27 lug bars are set in each of the 22 possible ways. Thus, the overall number of inequivalent lug bar settings is equal to the number of non-negative integer solutions of the equation: $x_1 + x_2 + \ldots + x_{22} = 27$.

Elementary combinatorial analysis gives the number of solutions— and hence of lug bar settings—as

$$\binom{27+21}{21} = \binom{48}{21} .$$

Thus, for the encipherment of a single message, the number of possible keys is

$$K = 2^{131} \binom{48}{21} \approx 6.07 \times 10^{52} \text{ and } \log_2 K \approx 175.3.$$

Taking the redundancy of English to be about 3.7 bits per letter, the ordinary Shannon unicity distance works out to $U = 47$. We may expect, therefore, that Hagelin messages of length 50 or 60 letters, say, have unique solutions. But nobody believes that a single Hagelin message that short can, in practice, be cryptanalyzed.

There is, however, a method for cryptanalyzing long Hagelin messages by pure frequency analysis. This method first recovers the pin settings, then solves the cryptogram, and finally recovers the lug setting.

The difficult step is the pin setting recovery, which is accomplished by an iterative calculation, each step of which strives to maximize the sample index of coincidence of the recovered plaintext by modifying a trial pin setting. Once the pins are correctly identified, simple alphabet matching is enough to reduce the cryptogram to monoalphabetic terms. The subsequent solution of the cryptogram and recovery of the lug settings is trivial.

Let us see what our proposals for U' imply about the length of text this method needs. Like the final example of Section 2, the method only uses index of coincidence properties of the plaintext language. Since the index of coincidence of the plaintext on the M-209 is .078 (the letter "Z" doubles up as the word space, which inflates the index of coincidence from its usual .067), we are entitled to use for R' the minimum redundancy any language can have, whose index of coincidence is .078. It turns out that the "urn language," where one letter has probability .233 and the other 25 letters each have probability .0307, minimizes the redundancy at $R' = .357$ bits per letter. Thus, our modification of the language proposal yields $U' = (\log_2 K)/R' = 175.3/357 = 491$.

This is just the result of our first proposal. The description of the method of cryptanalysis given above makes it plausible that the lug mechanism could be made more complex without much affecting the ease of solution. This is indeed the case. The cryptographic action of the lug bar mechanism is to convert a sequence of six bits (which are read off of the six pin wheels) into a Beaufort key: to convert an element from a set of 64 elements into one from a set of 26 elements. There are thus

$$26^{64} = 3.617 \times 10^{90}$$

different possible functions like this; the mechanical details of the lug bar mechanism allow only $\binom{48}{21} = 2.231 \times 10^{13}$ of them to be realized. We can thus imagine a "super" M-209, equipped with a more complicated lug mechanism which can realize all possible 26^{64} different functions; this super M-209 has a key size $K' = 2^{131} \cdot 26^{64} = 9.845 \times 10^{129}$; $\log_2 K' = 431.8$. If the method of cryptanalysis works as well against this super M-209 as it does against the actual M-209 (and it does), our second proposal, "modifying the cipher," indicates that the method needs at least $U' = (\log_2 K')/R' = 431.8/.357 \approx 1210$ letters of text. We conclude: both of our proposals together imply that the method of cryptanalysis described here requires on the order of 1200–1300 letters, at least, to effect a solution.

Since first performing these calculations in 1973 we have learned from Mr. Robert Morris that his computer experiments testing this method of cryptanalysis confirm our theoretical calculation: that Hagelin cryptograms shorter than 1200 letters cannot be solved by this method, and that those in the range 1200–1500 can often be solved.

SECTION 6. DISCUSSION

Shannon's paper contains unicity distance calculations for a variety of simple cipher systems. In many of his cases the standard methods of cryptanalysis succeed against cryptograms as short as the unicity distance and are thus unlike all of the examples discussed in this paper. We are able, however, to account for this difference.

We claim that there are really two types of cipher systems, which we call "simple" and "advanced." In the case of simple ciphers, the structure of the enciphering operation is so transparent that our mind comprehends all of its ramifications without any trouble. We are thus able to bring to bear all of our knowledge of the statistical regularities of the plaintext without any conscious effort on our part, and are thus able to solve "simple" ciphers in our heads or with a minimum of paper and pencil work. Chief among these "simple" ciphers is monalphabetic or simple substitution. On the other hand, the "advanced" cipher systems have a more intricate enciphering action, which we can fully understand only by recourse to some branch of mathematics. In these cases, our understanding of exactly how the statistical regularities of the plaintext are deformed and disguised by the enciphering action does not come to us subconsciously without apparent effort, but only after the result of deliberate mathematical investigation. It is this intervening mathematical step which cuts us off from a wealth of statistical structure, present in the language, but not amenable to (easy) mathematical description or treatment.

We can see this as we read through a textbook on cryptanalysis. At the beginning of the book there is an explanation of the solution of monoalphabetic substitution ciphers. The reader learns not only about the unigraphic and digraphic frequency distributions, but also about pattern words, alternation of vowels and consonants, all the two-letter prepositions, orthographic and grammatical oddities, stylistic regularities, and so on. But towards the end of the book, where quite advanced ciphers are discussed, only the unigraphic and digraphic frequency distributions are used. As the mathematical structure of the cipher becomes more complicated, it becomes harder for us to understand what it does to any but the crudest aspects of the statistics of the plaintext.

We can, to some extent, quantify these considerations. For given cipher system and given "standard method" of cryptanalysis, we can compute the Shannon unicity distance U and our modified distance U'. We can also compute (or determine experimentally) L, the minimum length of cryptograms that our method can actually solve. We have the inequalities:

$$U \le U' \le L.$$

If U'/U is close to 1, we conclude the cipher system is "simple"; if U'/U is large, we say the cipher system is "advanced." If L/U' is close to 1, our method of cryptanalysis is efficient in the sense that it is making nearly optimal use of the information available to it. If L/U' is large, we conclude our method is inefficient. In this case, there might be some possible improvement: a different method of analysis, which uses substantially the same data as the original method, but uses [such data] better.

In this essay we have attempted to measure one consequence of the difference between "simple" and "advanced" cipher systems. Our arguments, we realize, are not formulated with any great degree of precision. In particular, our central notion that a given method of cryptanalysis "relies on" some, but not all, statistical features of the plaintext language is unfortunately vague. In spite of this deplorable imprecision, we are convinced that the type of calculation presented in this paper is, in some sense, correct, and can provide valuable information to those interested in the theory of cryptography.

REFERENCES

1. R. R. Bahadur, *Some Limit Theorems in Statistics*. (Philadelphia: Society for Industrial and Applied Mathematics, 1971.)
2. ———— (1977) [n.p.].
3. P. Billingsley, *Ergodic Theory and Information* (New York: John Wiley and Sons, 1965.)
4. W. F. Friedman, *Military Cryptanalysis* (4 vols.) (Washington, D.C.: U.S. Government Printing Office, 1938–1941.)
5. M. Hellman, An Extension of the Shannon Theory Approach to Cryptography. *IEEE Transactions on Information Theory,* May 1977.
6. W. Hoeffding, Asymptotically Optimal Tests for Multinomial Distributions, *Ann. Math. Statist.,* 36 (1965), 369–408.
7. ———— On Probabilities of Large Deviations. *Proc. Fifth Berkeley Symp. Math. Statist. Prob.* (1965), 203–219.

8. D. Kahn, *The Codebreakers*. (New York: Macmillan, 1967.)

9. G. Raisbeck, *Information Theory: An Introduction for Scientists and Engineers*. (Cambridge, MA: MIT Press, 1963.)

10. I. N. Sanov, On the Probability of Large Deviations of Random Variables, *Sel. Trans. Math. Statist. Prob.*, 1 (1957), 213–244.

11. C. Shannon, Communication Theory of Secrecy Systems, *Bell System Technical Journal*, 28 (1949), 656–715.

12. J. Wolfowitz, *Coding Theorems of Information Theory* (Berlin: Springer-Verlag, 1961.)

Automated Analysis of Cryptograms
by Bruce R. Schatz

INTRODUCTION

The solution of simple ciphers has long been a popular activity among amateurs. Many approaches are known and most such problems can be solved in a short period. Although a number of computer programs have been written to assist human cryptanalysts in solving these (by collecting statistics, providing up-to-date accounting, and so on), there have been few attempts to automate this process. And these seem to operate in a very statistical, brute-force fashion. This paper describes a program which attempts to solve a simple class of ciphers, cryptograms, by itself in a more semantic manner. The basic method is to deduce vowels, and then guess other letters by filling in words. The approach throughout was to find a reasonable and somewhat human-like set of methods which seemed to work fairly well.

CRYPTOGRAMS

A cipher is a method for disguising a message by transforming it in some manner. This is typically accomplished by rearranging the letters (transposition) or replacing the letters by a set of symbols (substitution). Cryptanalysis is the process of "breaking" the cipher, i.e., understanding the message by deducing the transformation. The type of ciphers that will be considered are monoalphabetic simple substitution ciphers with word divisions, i.e., the enciphered message is obtained from the original by making a direct substitution for the letters of the original alphabet from a single cipher alphabet (preserving word boundaries). These will

From *Cryptologia*, Vol. 1, No. 2, April 1977.

be called "cryptograms," after their designation in crossword puzzle magazines, their common place of occurrence. (The American Cryptogram Association calls them "Aristocrats.") The messages will be assumed to be in normal English and of reasonable length (say, 100 letters). (Accordingly, the usual letter and word characteristics will not be too maliciously maladjusted.) Cryptograms thus essentially consist of substituting the letters of a permutation of the alphabet for the letters of the alphabet to produce an enciphered message. An example (a Caesar cipher) is

original: a b c . . . x y z
cipher: B C D . . . Y Z A

Then "intelligent" would be represented by "JOUFMMJHFOU" and "SPCPU" would mean "robot." The conventions used here will be used throughout; namely, the original message (the plaintext) will appear in lower case while the enciphered message (the ciphertext) will appear in upper case.

POSSIBLE APPROACHES TO THE SOLUTION PROCESS

Solving a cryptogram is nontrivial, although many people can learn to do it quickly and easily. Only the presence of regularities in the encrypted message makes cryptanalysis possible. Fortunately, for cryptograms the enciphering transformation is simple and does not hide the regularities of the original message much. In addition, there is a large amount of information available on the characteristics of English. (The reference literature on cryptanalysis available and unclassified is somewhat sparse; [10] is the only fairly comprehensive and advanced text in English; [30] is more elementary. There are several good publications sponsored by the American Cryptogram Association, of which [25] and [17] are particularly helpful with cryptograms as defined here. (References [25], [17], and [10] contain much useful data on characteristics of English.) A recent cryptographic series contains a number of useful reprints for more advanced cryptanalysis, e.g., [18] and [8].)

A solution can be conveniently broken into two stages: *entry* and *development* [25]. The first consists of an initial break by guessing what three or four enciphered letters are; the second of filling in the rest by recognizing partially deciphered patterns.

There are a number of known techniques for making an entry. Some of these deal directly with letter frequencies with perhaps some positional constraints (e.g., let the most frequent letter be "e" if it also occurs frequently as a final letter). (See [10, p. 72*ff*], [25], [17].) Others attempt to deduce the transformation (e.g., using specific techniques for special types such as linear transformations [30, Ch. 1] or attempting to deduce the keyword generating the cipher alphabet [10, pp. 70–72]. One can also look for common words, suffixes, and prefixes. Perhaps the most effective technique is trying to determine the vowels. The four common vowels (e, a, i, o) are among the most common letters (a, e, i, o, u, y make up 40% of normal English letters) and every word contains a vowel (except for oddities such as crwth).

Much is known about the characteristics of vowels. Typical facts include: high frequency (for the four), frequent contacting of low-frequency letters, little contact among themselves but a wide variety of contacts, reversals (e.g., re, er) usually are a vowel and consonant, and so on. Possible methods for finding them thus include contact tables (what letter touches what) (see [10, p. 74*ff*]) and use of positional data (e.g., in four-letter words vowels usually occur second) [1, p. 12*ff*]. Another useful technique is Lamb's vowel-line shortcut [10, pp. 88–92], which examines the variety of contacts and attempts to isolate the vowels (which have a wide variety). While all of these are fairly effective, the method used here will be a different one, based on singular value decomposition (a technique of numerical linear algebra), which may be of general interest to cryptanalysts. Although it is extremely unlikely that humans use this, it is quite effective and more human-like techniques could be used instead (as above).

There are also several possible approaches to development. One can attempt to match cipher words against pattern words [13]. These are occurrences of letter sequences in words such as aba for mom, tot; abbc for book, look; and abccbccbddb for Mississippi. Another possibility is nonpattern words [1], where one searches for sequences of consonants (c) and vowels (v). For example, ccvc for bled, drop; ccvcvc for dragon. However, as the author has some interest in investigating human problem-solving, a method most likely used by humans will be used, i.e., guessing words. (Even if one is not interested in how humans "work," mimicking of human behavior is often a helpful heuristic in constructing complicated computer programs (particularly those which do problem-solving where humans provide the only known examples of successful solvers).) The program will attempt to deduce letters by matching partially known words to a vocabulary of common words. For example, if one has QtheT, it is likely that Q=o and W=r (producing "other").

PREVIOUS WORK

There has been little published work on automated cryptanalysis. References [21] and [12] are nice surveys of some of this. There is some general mathematical analysis of the encryption problem [28] and a number of solutions to specialized ciphers [32, 33], [22], [16]. There is also peripheral mention in the growing literature on cryptography (enciphering) for security in operating systems and data banks [6, 7]. Reference [19] is a scholarly, wide-ranging history of cryptanalysis with many technical details.

Silver [29] described a system to solve cryptograms that attempted to find the permutation for which the digram frequencies of the corresponding "deciphered" message most closely matched the normal English frequencies. This made an initial guess of a permutation (e.g., direct match of English to cipher letter frequencies), then successively hill-climbed to more likely neighboring permutations until a peak was reached. A neighboring permutation (i.e., differing by at most two letters) was considered more likely if the standard frequencies of the digrams (considered as probabilities in a Markov process) for its corresponding message was higher. Reference [5] reported on a SNOBOL-like programming language specially designed for cryptanalysis.

Probably the closest approach to the work here is that of Newell and Simon [24], who describe a system for doing *cryptarithmetic* (a simple substitution cipher for the digits 0–9 in an arithmetic problem), based on a detailed model of a human solver. The modeling here was much more intuitive in nature, and as cryptarithmetic is a somewhat easier and different problem than deciphering of a cryptogram, the author's work was essentially independent.

This paper will proceed by explaining the vowel-finding and word-guessing procedures, explaining the program operation (control structure and other pieces), and finally working through an example in detail.

SINGULAR VALUE DECOMPOSITION (SVD)

As mentioned above, the approach of entry chosen is to identify the vowels. Reference [23] [undated] has developed a surprisingly effective method of picking out the vowels using a standard technique of numerical linear algebra, *singular value decomposition* or SVD. (The entire method will be referred to as SVD.)

It is based on the observation that in English (and several other languages, such as Russian), vowels more often follow consonants than other vowels. (In fact, vowels contact consonants some 85% of the time [1, p. 4].) So the following rule usually holds:

$$\frac{\text{Number of vowel-vowel pairs}}{\text{Number of vowels}} < \frac{\text{Number of consonant-vowel pairs}}{\text{Number of consonants}}$$

This essentially says that vowel-vowel pairs should occur less frequently than consonant-vowel pairs. Thus a partition of the alphabet into two classes which satisfied the above rule would likely distinguish between vowels and consonants; [23] gives one such procedure.

First tabulate the digram matrix. (This considers letters two at a time in the cryptogram, i.e., A is a 26 by 26 matrix, where a_{ij} is the number of occurrences of the ith letter followed by the jth letter with blanks and punctuation ignored.) Performing a singular value decomposition finds orthogonal matrices X and Y such that $X^T A Y$ is a diagonal matrix whose diagonal elements are the singular values σ_i. Reference [15] gives a detailed description of singular value decomposition and its computation; [14] gives an algorithm for computing it. For a general exposition, see [31, pp. 317–326].

Now consider a second-order approximation of the digram matrix (the simplest that accounts for correlations between pairs of letters). It can be proved that a partition based on the signs of the elements of the second column vectors of X and Y divides the alphabet into two classes satisfying the above vowel-follows-consonant rule. So, if the classes are labelled vowels and consonants, the vowels have been identified. (One usually also obtains a third class of "neuter" letters, e.g., h.) It should be noted that this is merely another systematic way of finding letters which satisfy vowel characteristics (here, their propensity for contacting mostly consonants). The Appendix contains precise details and a proof of the theorem.

In practice this method works fairly well at identifying the vowels. For example, running it on the titles and first five stanzas of "The Hunting of the Snark" by Lewis Carroll [4] (705 letters) produced:

vowel:	aeijo
consonant:	bcdglmnprstvw
neuter:	fhkquxyz

Running it on a 10-line portioin (448 letters) of a speech on matrix computation by George Forsythe [31], probably much more typical English, produced:

vowel:	aeiou
consonant:	bcfgjlmrst
neuter:	dhkpqvwxyz

OVERVIEW OF THE SOLVER

While the approach used is basically semantic, there will be no use of semantic knowledge beyond words (e.g., of sentences or phrases), nor any knowledge of specialized cipher types (e.g., Caesar ciphers or more general linear transformations). Thus the only attempt is to guess what the cipher letters represent, not to discover the keyword or method generating the transformation.

Essentially, as previously mentioned, the solver consists of an entry and a development. The entry is made by attempting to identify the vowels (in addition to looking for a few special clues). Development continues by a number of routines which communicate in a *heterarchical* fashion (i.e., they exist as coroutines where each calls several others). The major such are the fill-in and the word search. Minor ones include individual letter procedures and frequency playoff.

There is also a data base which contains such empirical data as standard frequencies for letters, initial letters, final letters, and digrams. (See Figures 1 and 2). A word vocabulary and some miscellaneous information (e.g., standard common suffixes and prefixes, contact data) are also available.

e	12.51	c	2.75
t	9.50	m	2.37
a	8.06	w	2.06
o	8.00	p	1.97
n	7.12	g	1.80
i	6.85	y	1.70
r	6.20	b	1.49
s	6.11	v	0.97
h	5.99	k	0.68
d	4.09	x	0.21
l	3.68	j	0.17
f	2.79	q	0.09
u	2.77	z	0.07

FIGURE 1. STANDARD LETTER FREQUENCIES WITH PERCENT OCCURRENCE IN ENGLISH (FROM [25, P. 25]).

Initial	Final	Initial	Final
t	e	d	m
a	s	e	w
s	d	n	k
o	n	l	c
i	t	g	p
c	r	u	i
w	y	y	x
p	o	v	u
b	f	j	b
f	l	k	v
h	a	q	j
m	g	x	z
r	h	z	q

FIGURE 2. STANDARD INITIAL AND FINAL LETTER FREQUENCY ORDERING (FROM [30, PP. 178–179]).

Along the path to solution, a number of "notes" are made. There is one of these for each cipher and plaintext letter. They contain partial possibility information (e.g., e is either Q or Y; W is either a or o) along with a record of which place in which routine provided that information (e.g., word search level one). Thus there is a log of what decisions were made and why; this is often useful in deducing letters by process of elimination (e.g., W is either a or o and o has just been identified, so W = a). The notes are also helpful in choosing alternate paths when backup is necessary.

A description of the program execution follows. (See Figure 3 for a schematic picture of the control flow.)

First, the table generator is called. Various frequency tables from the cryptogram are computed: letter frequency, initial and final letter frequencies, a digram matrix, and a contact count (a list of each letter together with the two letters that flanked it on the left and right each time it was used). These are sorted into descending order for subsequent utilization.

Then, a special clues procedure is used. This tries a few tricks such as looking for single-letter words (which must be a or i) and apostrophes (single letters after apostrophes are s, t; double letters are ll, re, ve).

Next, an entry is attempted by calling SVD to find the vowels. As previously described, this returns several supposed vowels. These are

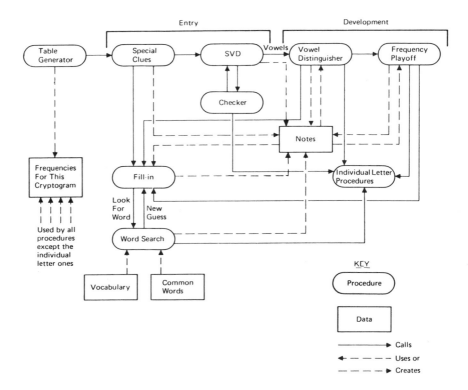

FIGURE 3. SCHEMATIC PICTURE OF THE CRYPTOGRAM SOLVING PROGRAM.

checked against such common vowel characteristics as contact with low-frequency letters, wide variety of contacts, little contact among themselves, and various positional data. Unlikely candidates are removed from the list of vowels. It should be noted that SVD occasionally produces a (mostly) correct partition wrongly labelled, so that supposed vowels are really consonants and *vice versa*. This is accounted for by switching the labels if more than six vowels are found.

A routine which should be mentioned at this point is the fill-in and recording. This is called upon by several others. Whenever a guess of a cipher letter is made, this substitutes the guessed plaintext letter into the cipher message, records the substitution in the list of plaintext and the list of cipher letters, then calls word-search. It also makes a note of which routine called it (made the decision of the letter guess). Each filling in of a guess is made on a different level of a stack so that backtracking is possible. Any words which now have only one or two unknown letters are put onto the appropriate word stack for later viewing by the word search routine. Any just completed words are removed from the word stacks.

Another routine constantly called upon is the individual letter characteristics, [consisting] of a procedure for each English letter that contains basic information about its properties (mostly frequency and position). When a cipher letter is given it, a letter procedure returns an estimate of the probability that the cipher letter is that letter (by summing weighted comparisons of its characteristics). For example, for e—heavily weighted: very high frequency, very frequent final; moderately weighted: often second position, often doubled; lightly weighted: follows bhmw in two-letter words. (References [17] and [25] contain lengthy lists of letter characteristics.)

Continuing the mainstream of execution, SVD has returned several letters now "certified" as vowels, so the vowel distinguishing routine is entered to determine which is which. To make its guesses, the vowel distinguisher goes through a series of standard characteristics such as the following (e.g., [25, pp. 11–13], [10, pp. 78–79]). E is the most frequent (and is a very common final letter). I has high frequency and often occurs as the antepenultimate letter. O and e are often doubled, but rarely touch each other. (O is also frequent and often second or last.) A is frequent and often an initial letter. U and y are infrequent. There are various frequency and positional criteria and the individual letter procedures are used as well.

After a vowel is identified, the fill-in routine is entered. Then, word-search is called to see if any words can now be guessed. If some can, fill-in and word-search are repeated. When no words can be guessed, [the program returns to] the vowel distinguisher. (Note that even deducing one or two vowels will usually enable some short words to be guessed, which in turn enables an entry and a solution.) The program typically identifies a few vowels, then alternates between fill-in and word-search. This process continues until all the vowels are determined as closely as possible (or a solution has been found). Then the frequency playoff routine is entered. If an impasse is reached (no deductions seem reasonable), the program backtracks. (Backtracking involves removing several message development stack levels, leaving the decipherment in some previous state with fewer plaintext letters known. Often, a good strategy is to choose among several possibilities, then backtrack later if incorrect.)

The frequency playoff routine concentrates on trying to deduce what the most frequent cipher letters represent. This is done by using the individual letter procedures and relying on the fact that etaonirsh make up 70% of the letters in normal English. This, interacting with the above routines, executes until the cryptogram is "solved" or the program backs up to the start and fails.

WORD SEARCH

This is probably the most important development routine (for both the program and humans). The objective is to identify unknown cipher letters by guessing at words for which all but a few letters are known. The words thus examined are contained in two stacks, levels 1 and 2, generated by the fill-in routine. Whenever a letter guess is made and fill-in substitutes it into the cryptogram, all of the words which now have only one unknown letter are placed on top of the level 1 stack; those with two unknown on the level 2 stack. (Words are deleted when completely guessed or moved from one stack to another.)

The word-search routine first scans the level 1 stack. For each word in the stack, all possibilities for it are retrieved from a list of the 100 most common words in English [10, p. 226] (simple pattern matching against this list). If there is only one possibility and a brief comparison of the stack word's unknown cipher letter against the usual characteristics of the list's proposed letter is satisfied, the word is removed from the level 1 stack, fill-in is called, and another word-search follows. If there are two or three possibilities, a note is made (of the possibilities for that cipher letter) and the search continues (unless a call to the individual letter procedures or to previous notes can resolve the conflict, e.g., some of the possible English letters have already been guessed). If there are more than three possibilities, it is assumed that nothing can be concluded and the next word in the stack is examined. If no possible words have been found in the common word list, a search through the vocabulary (the 300 most common words, from [3], excluding those in the common word list) is performed. The level 1 search continues through its stack trying each word. When a level 1 search is fruitless (no guessable words in the stack), a search through the level 2 stack is made in a similar manner (first trying common words, then vocabulary for each stack member).

Note that the most recent stack additions are examined before previous ones (i.e., new words are added at the top) and that words not in the vocabulary can still be deduced by guessing all of the letters. No knowledge of English, such as plural, tense, or morphemic knowledge of words is included in the word search. Note there is a tradeoff between too few vocabulary words (providing no help in guessing) and too many (yielding too many possibilities).

The vocabulary lists are stored in the form of a digital tree [20, p. 489]. This has the advantages of facilitating a fast unsuccessful search (necessary as there is often not any such word) and a fairly fast successful search (since the vocabulary is in frequency order). In addition, with encoding five bits per letter (a=00001 . . . z=11010), each search takes at most "five times the word length" comparisons, and this does not depend on the size of the vocabulary.

AN EXAMPLE OF THE PROGRAM'S EXECUTION

A modest implementation in PL/I of the principles outlined above was run on an IBM 370/155 at Rice University, an IBM 360/195 at the IBM San Jose Research Laboratory, and an IBM 370/168 at the IBM T. J. Watson Research Laboratory. (The routines based on characteristics of English, particularly the individual letter procedures, were considered rather perfunctorily. The data base and notes were somewhat incomplete. For facility in stack manipulation and list processing, it would have been preferable to have used LISP or one of the new high-level LISP-like languages [2]. However, the version of LISP available did not have the necessary matrix manipulation and arithmetic capabilities.) A run typically took a few seconds.

XVQIQ HIQ H MIQHX CHSO XVZSMA EY ZCCQSAQ ZSXQIQAX HPEKX LVZJV
AJZQSJQ, HX NIQAQSX, BSELA TZXXTQ. ZX ZA XVQ UEP EY NVZTEAENVO
XE BQQN ANQJKTHXZES HPEKX XVQAQ HTZDQ.

FIGURE 4. THE SAMPLE CRYPTOGRAM.

As an example of what the program can do, a sample cryptogram (Figure 4) will be solved. This is a fairly easy one of reasonable length (132 letters) with word divisions and no special attempt made to distort the normal characteristics of English. Throughout, plaintext will appear in lower case and ciphertext in capitals. The output reproduced is that of an actual program run, slightly abridged and annotated. The name of each routine, its results, and its "reasoning" appear along with comments in parenthesis.

Read-in. (The cryptogram is read in and divided into words.)

Table generator. (Figures 5 and 6 show some of the frequency tables generated.)

408

	High	Middle		Low	
Q	20	I	5	B,L,M,O,Y	2
X	16	N	5	D,U	1
Z	11	T	5	F,G,R,W	0
A	10	J	4		
E	10	C	3		
H	9	K	3		
S	8	P	3		
V	8				

FIGURE 5. LETTER FREQUENCIES IN THE CRYPTOGRAM.

	Initial		Final	
H	5	Q		8
X	5	X		7
Z	4	A		3
A,B,E,N	2	O,Y		2
C,L,M,T,U	1	E,N,P,S,V		1

FIGURE 6. MORE CRYPTOGRAM LETTER FREQUENCIES.

Special clues. A single letter, H, is found. Thus H = a or i. Since H is frequent, a frequent initial, but never final, and not doubled (the a and i procedures were called), and since a is more often used as a single letter in cryptograms, guess:

H = a (This indicated a guess and a call to fill-in.)

Word-search level 1. Looking at aX. Too many possibilities.

Word-search level 2. Looking at aIQ. Too many possibilities.

SVD. The vowels returned and checked are E O Q Z. (Note there are only 4 and that a(=H) was not among them.) Also returned were consonant: ABDIJNPUX and neuter: CFGHKLMRSTVWY. (Here, in fact, x<0 and y>0 for vowels.)

Vowel distinguisher. The frequencies are Q 20, Z 11, E 10, O 2. Q is the most frequent and the most frequent final, so

Q = e

Word-search level 1. Looking at aIe. From common word list, I = r. Had age been on this list, a call to the g and r procedures would have revealed g's favorite position is last while r's favorites are second and next to last. I appears as letter 2 of 3, 2 of 5, 5 of 8, 2 of 7, 4 of 5. Four of these indicate r, none indicate g, so

I = r

Word-search level 1. aX still unresolved.

Word-search level 2. Looking at MreaX. Since great is on the common word list and X is very frequent (overall, initially, and finally) as is t,

M = g (Letter g is never strongly checked.)

X = t (Important since t is the second most frequent English letter. Note that t could have been guessed from XVere implies there if great was not known.)

Fill-in. New word generated. at.

(At this point an entry has certainly been made since 5 letters, including 3 of the most frequent (e t a), have been guessed. Figure 7 gives the progress so far. Note the control still remains in the vowel distinguisher.)

```
 t  ere are a grea t    a    t    g         e   e   tere  t a     t
XVQIQ HIQ H MIQHX CHSO XVZSMA EY ZCCQSAQ ZSXQIQAX HPEKX LVZJV
     e  e
AJZQSJQ,

 at  re  e t         tt e  t    t e                  t    ee
HX NIQAQSX, BSELA TZXXTQ. ZX ZA XVQ UEP EY NVZTEAENVO XE BQQN

    e    at    a    t t  e e a     e
ANQJKTHXZES HPEKX XVQAQ HTZDQ.
```

FIGURE 7. THE CRYPTOGRAM AFTER AN ENTRY HAS BEEN MADE.

Word-search level 1. Looking at tE. From common word list (and since E is frequent vowel),

E = o

Word-search level 1. Looking at oY (twice). From common word list, Y = f n r; r has already been guessed and there is no positive distinction now between f and n so a note of the two possiblities is made. Looking at tVe. From common word list,

V = h

Fill-in. New words generated: there.

Word-search level 1. Looking at theAe. From common word list (r already guessed) and the fact that A is frequent (overall, initially, finally),

A = s

Word-search level 1. Looking at Zs. From common word list, Z = i or u so record for later. Looking at oY (twice) again. Still undecidable. Looking at Zt. From common word list and since Z is a vowel, frequent letter, and frequent initial,

Z = i

Fill-in. New word generated: is.

Word-search level 1. Looking at iSterest. Not in vocabulary. Looking at thiSgs. From vocabulary,

S = n

Fill-in. New word generated: interest. (Note this was not in the vocabulary.)

Word-search level 1. Looking at Nresent. Not in vocabulary. Looking at oY. From common word list (since n and r have now been identified),

Y = f

Word-search level 1. Looking at Nresent. Not in vocabulary.

Word-search level 2. Looking at BnoLs, sJienJe, iCCense, CanO, aTiDe. All of these are not in the vocabulary or have too many possibilities. looking at TittTe. From vocabulary,

T = l

Fill-in. New word generated: little.

Word-search level 1. Looking at aliDe, Nresent. Not in vocabulary.

Word-search level 2. Looking at BnoLs, sJienJe, iCCense. Not in vocabulary. looking at CanO. The deducing of l has enabled a unique match in the vocabulary (previously land also matched). Hence, CanO = many and

C = m

Fill-in. New word generated: immense.

O = y (second part of guessing *many*).

Word-search level 1. Looking at aliDe, Nresent. None in vocabulary.

Word-search level 2. Looking at NhilosoNhy, BnoLs, sJienJe. None in vocabulary. Looking at LhiJh. (Note this was added to word stack 2 some time ago but had not yet been reached, a consequence of adding new words to the top of the stack.) From common word list (there are so many constraints at this stage that letter characteristic checks are not made),

L = w
J = c

Fill-in. Words generated: which, science. (Finally have deduced science despite it not being in the vocabulary, i.e., deduced it letter by letter.)

Word-search level 1. Looking at Bnows, aliDe, Nresent. None in vocabulary.

Word-search level 2. Looking at sNecKlation, NhilosoNhy. None in vocabulary. Looking at aPoKt. (This was also added long ago but never reached.) From common word list,

P = b
K = u

Word-search level 1. Looking at sNeculation, Uob, Bnows, aliDe, Nresent. None in vocabulary.

Word-search level 2. Looking at NhilosoNhy. Looking at BeeN. There are many possibilities for this but only one matching unguessed letters in vocabulary,

B = k

Fill-in. New word generated: knows. (Finally got this. Although "know" is in the vocabulary, the program can't get "knows" from it.)

N = p   (second part of guessing *keep*).

Fill-in. New words generated: present, philosophy, speculation, keep.

```
there are a great many
XVQIQ HIQ H MIQHX CHSO

things of immense
XVZSMA EY ZCCQSAQ

interest about which
ZSXQIQAX HPEKX LVZJV

science at present
AJZQSJQ, HX NIQAQSX,

knows little
BSELA TZXXTQ.

it is the   ob of
ZX ZA XVQ UEP EY

philosophy to keep
NVZTEAENVO XE BQQN

speculation about
ANQJKTHXZES HPEKX

these ali   e
XVQAQ HTZDQ.
```

FIGURE 8. THE CRYPTOGRAM AFTER THE PROGRAM TERMINATES ITS ANALYSIS.

This is as far as the program got. See Figure 8 for its final analysis (the plaintext message was paraphrased from [27]). The complete cryptogram has been deciphered except for two letters (U and D) which only occur once and then in words (job, alive) not in the vocabulary. (Note they also correspond to the low frequency letters j and v, so that the frequency playoff cannot help.) This is true in general—the system deduces nearly all letters except for a few which appear only a few times and then in unknown words. Notice, though, how many of the words in this easy, but not "cooked-up," example were in the vocabulary, and how well the system did at deducing even those that were not. SVD did fairly well with the vowel identification, returning Q Z E D, which turned out to be e i o y.

SUMMARY AND POSSIBLE IMPROVEMENTS

Some techniques for designing a program to solve cryptograms automatically have been described. The program consists of an entry by identifying vowels (using a singular value decomposition method and a vowel distinguisher) and a development by guessing words (pattern matching against a vocabulary) plus referring to individual letter procedures. An implementation of these seemed fairly successful at solving simple examples.

There are a number of possible improvements which could be made. A larger vocabulary would help in guessing words and eliminating impasses caused by being unable to decipher odd letters appearing only in words not in the vocabulary lists. (Perhaps even a third word list to be used only when stuck? See [9] for a good discussion of how to decide when a cipher is solved.) Improving the information on characteristics of English is also important. This includes improving the probability estimation of the individual letter procedures, enhancing vowel distinguishing, taking contact data frequency into account, and perhaps adding such additional characteristics as pattern words or reversal data. Examining even elementary types of syntax or semantics (such as plurals, tenses, and word pieces) would help immensely. (For instance, matching "knows" from "know" or "alive" from "live" in the example worded here.) An easy say to do some of this is to allow partial word matching (e.g., Tnow "matching" knows), but this could lead to sticky probability situations. Providing more informative notes and an evaluation function to determine which word to try to match next would be nice. A periodic examination of the notes to see if anything can be deduced from them yet might speed up the deciphering.

CONCLUSIONS

The current implementation appears to be capable of solving simple cryptograms, and a completion and extension of the ideas outlined above could likely become quite good. It would be interesting to see how much semantic information is needed to write a system which would solve most cryptograms in normal English. The author suspects that not too much would be necessary. The program here did quite well with very little (vowel-identifying and word-guessing, no very sophisticated programming) and probably just automating more of the well known characteristics of English would suffice. Even the present system might be useful for some purposes (e.g., the "learning to problem-solve" system envisioned by [26], which operates at several different levels (mentor, bookkeeper, partner, learner), while utilizing the solution of cryptograms as a basis for computer-assisted instruction).

People can generally learn to solve (easy) cryptograms with logical deduction and only little knowledge of frequency and positional characteristics (but, of course, a large vocabulary). Thus it should not be surprising that the program performs fairly well. (The nonhuman-like vowel identification could be replaced by other methods as mentioned in the section on possible approaches to the solution process. It could even be replaced by a very human-like set of hunt-and-peck procedures which make an entry by trying various tricks such as single letters, quotes, common words, frequency (letter, initial, final), and positional data (see [25], [17]). Another change would be doing the heavy computation like table generation and SVD only when normal solving techniques fail.) It may accordingly be of interest to note that yet another fairly substantial appearing intellectual activity is "easier than first thought" and can be understood by programming a computer to perform it.

ACKNOWLEDGEMENTS

This originated as an independent project at Rice University sponsored by Prof. John Brelsford. Later versions were programmed at the IBM San Jose Research Laboratory and the IBM T.J. Watson Research Laboratory. I thank David Reed and Peter Blatman for comments, and especially Prof. Don Morrison for a copy of his paper on the SVD method. Finally, I would like to express a debt of gratitude to Prof. Joseph Schatz for many stimulating philosophical conversations.

REFERENCES

1. Barker, W. G., *Cryptanalysis of the Simple Substitution Cipher with Word Divisions*. (Laguna Hills, CA: Aegean Park Press, 1975).
2. Bobrow, D. G., and Raphael, B., New Programming Languages for Artificial Intelligence Research. *ACM Computing Surveys*, 6:155–174 (1974).

3. Carroll, J., *et al.* (eds), *The American Heritage Word Frequency Book*. (Boston: Houghton Mifflin, 1971), pp. 565–567.

4. Carroll L., The Hunting of the Snark, in *Alice in Wonderland and Other Favorites*. (New York: Washington Square Press, 1951) (original 1876).

5. Edwards, D. J., OCAS—On-line Cryptanalysis Aid System. MIT Project MAC, TR-27 (May 1966).

6. Feistel, H., Cryptography and Computer Privacy. *Scientific American*, 228:15–23 (May 1973).

7. Feistel, H., Notz, W. A., and Smith, J. A., Some Cryptographic Techniques for Machine-to-Machine Data Communications. *Proc. IEEE*, 63:1545–1554 (1975).

8. Friedman, W. F., *Elementary Military Cryptography*. (Laguna Hills, CA: Aegean Park Press, 1976) (original 1935).

9. Friedman, W. F., and Friedman, E. S., *The Shakespearean Ciphers Examined*. (Cambridge: Cambridge University Press, 1957).

10. Gaines, H. F., *Cryptanalysis: A Study of Ciphers and Their Solutions*. (New York: Dover Publications, 1956) (original 1939).

11. Gantmacher, F. R., *The Theory of Matrices*, Vol. 2 (New York: Chelsea Pub. Co., 1960).

12. Girsdansky, M. B., Cryptology, the Computer, and Data Privacy. *Computers and Automation*, 21:12–19 (April 1972).

13. Goddard, E., and Goddard, T., *Cryptodyct*. (P.O. Box 441, Marion, IA 52302, 1976).

14. Golub, G., Singular Value Decomposition of a Complex Matrix. *Communications ACM*, 12:564–565 (1969), algorithm 358.

15. Golub, G., and Reinsch, C., Singular Value Decomposition and Least Squares Solutions. *Numerische Mathematik*, 14:403–420 (1970).

16. Hammer, C., Signature Simulation and Certain Cryptographic Codes. *Communications ACM*, 14:3–14 (Jan. 1971).

17. Harris, F. A., *Solving Simple Substitution Ciphers*. (Bethesda, MD: American Cryptogram Assn., 1959) (original 1943).

18. Hitt, P., *Manual for the Solution of Military Ciphers*. (Laguna Hills, CA: Aegean Park Press, 1976) (original 1920).

19. Kahn, D., *The Codebreakers: The Story of Secret Writing*. (New York: Macmillan, 1967).

20. Knuth, D. E., *The Art of Computer Programming*, Vol 3: Sorting and Searching. (Reading, MA: Addison-Wesley, 1973), section 6.3.

21. Mellen, G. E., Cryptology, Computers, and Common Sense. *Proc AFIPS Conf.*, 42:569–579 (1973).

22. Meyer, C. H., and Tuchman, W. L., Pseudorandom Codes can be Cracked. *Electronic Design*, 23:74–76 (Nov. 1972).

23. Moler, C. and Morrison, D., Singular Value Analysis of Cryptograms. [n.p., n.d.].

24. Newell, A., and Simon, H., *Human Problem Solving.* (Englewood Cliffs, NJ: Prentice-Hall, 1972), chapters 5–7.

25. Ohaver, M. E., *Cryptogram Solving.* (Columbus, OH: Etcetera Press, 1973) (original 1933).

26. Peelle, H. A., and Riseman, E. M., Four Faces of HAL: A Framework for Using Artificial Intelligence Techniques in Computer-Assisted Instruction. *IEEE Trans. on Systems, Man, and Cybernetics,* SMC-5:375–380 (May 1975).

27. Russell, B., *Bertrand Russell Speaks His Mind.* (New York: World Publishing Co., 1960), pp. 9–10.

28. Shannon, C., Communication Theory of Secrecy Systems, *Bell System Technical Journal,* 28:645–719 (1949).

29. Silver, R., Decryptor, in MIT Lincoln Laboratory Quarterly Progress Report, Division 5 (Information Processing), pp. 57–60, (Dec. 1959).

30. Sinkov, A., *Elementary Cryptanalysis: A Mathematical Approach.* (New York: Random House, 1968).

31. Stewart, G. W., *Introduction to Matrix Computation.* (New York: Academic Press, 1973).

32. Tuckerman, B., A Study of the Vigenere-Vernam Single and Multiple Loop Enciphering Systems. IBM Research Report 2879 (Yorktown Heights, NY, May 1970).

33. Tuckerman, B., Solution of a Substitution-Fractionation-Transposition Cipher. IBM Research Report RC 4531 (Yorktown Heights, NY, Sept. 1973).

APPENDIX: THE MOLER-MORRISON VFC PARTITIONING THEOREM (SVD ALGORITHM)

This appendix proposes a criterion for partitioning the alphabet of a text (cipher or otherwise) into vowels and consonants (based on the signs of the second left and right singular vectors from a singular value decomposition). The criterion is shown to satisfy the *vfc* (vowel follows consonant) rule, i.e., the proportion of vowels following vowels is less than that of vowels following consonants. Many languages, including English, have predominantly *vfc* texts. (The theorem and proof are adapted from [23].

Define n-element column vectors v and c by

$v_i = 1$ if the ith letter of the alphabet is a vowel, 0 otherwise;
$c_i = 1$ if the ith letter of the alphabet is a consonant, 0 otherwise.

Then, the *vfc* rule can be expressed as

$$\frac{v^T A v}{v^T A(v+c)} < \frac{c^T A v}{c^T A(v+c)}$$

where A is the digram matrix of the text. (This is the same rule given earlier in the paper. Note that A is non-negative.) Cross-multiplying and canceling the common term yields

$$(v^T A v)(c^T A c) - (v^T A c)(c^T A v) < 0.$$

The singular value decomposition of A is $X^T A Y = \text{diag}(\sigma_1, \ldots, \sigma_n)$. So $A = \sigma_1 x_1 y_1^T + \sigma_2 x_2 y_2^T + \ldots + \sigma_r x_r y_r^T$, where $r = \text{rank } A$, and x_i and y_i are the ith column vectors of X and Y. The following theorem can now be stated (assuming that the digram matrix A is actually (approximately) of rank 2).

Theorem (Moler-Morrison vfc Partitioning)

Let A be a non-negative matrix of rank 2 with singular value expansion

$\sigma_1 x_1 y_1^T + \sigma_2 x_2 y_2^T$. Use the following to determine v and c:
$v_i = 1$ if $x_{i2} > 0$ and $y_{i2} < 0$, 0 otherwise;
$c_i = 1$ if $x_{i2} < 0$ and $y_{i2} > 0$, 0 otherwise.

Then, the *vfc* rule:

$$D = (v^T A v)(c^T A c) - (v^T A c)(c^T A v) < 0$$

is satisfied.

Remarks

The factor x_{i2} is the second element in the ith column vector. The SVD algorithm is the direct analogue of the theorem, namely the ith letter of the alphabet is a

vowel if $x_{i2} > 0$ and $y_{i2} < 0$
consonant if $x_{i2} < 0$ and $y_{i2} > 0$
neuter if $\text{sign}(x_{i2}) = \text{sign}(y_{i2})$

Proof

Let $z_i = \sigma_i x_i$ and note that sign $(z_i) = $ sign (x_i) since $\sigma_i \geqslant 0$. Now substitute $A = z_1 y_1^T + z_2 y_2^T$ into the expression for D. This yields

$$(v^T z_1 y_1^T v)(c^T z_1 y_1^T c) + (v^T z_2 y_2^T v)(c^T z_1 y_1^T c)$$
$$(v^T z_1 y_1^T v)(c^T z_2 y_2^T c) + (v^T z_2 y_2^T v)(c^T z_2 y_2^T c)$$
$$(c^T z_1 y_1^T c)(c^T z_1 y_1^T v) - (v^T z_2 y_2^T c)(c^T z_1 y_1^T v)$$
$$(v^T z_1 y_1^T c)(c^T z_2 y_2^T v) - (v^T z_2 y_2^T c)(c^T z_2 y_2^T v)$$

Terms 1 and 5 cancel each other, as do terms 4 and 8. (Just calculate the inner products recalling that x_i and y_i are column vectors of X and Y.

e.g., $v^T z_1 y_1^T v = (\Sigma v_i z_{i1})(\Sigma y_{k1} v_k)$.)

Thus,

$$D = (v^T z_2 y_2^T v)(c^T z_1 y_1^T c) + (v^T z_1 y_1^T v)(c^T z_2 y_2^T c)$$
$$- (v^T z_2 y_2^T c)(c^T z_1 y_1^T v) - (v^T z_1 y_1^T c)(c^T z_2 y_2^T v)$$

Label these eight elements $\underline{1} \ldots \underline{8}$. Which of them are negative? By the Perron-Frobenius theorem, z_1 and y have (all) non-negative components (see Lemma); c and v have non-negative components. Thus $\underline{2},\underline{3},\underline{6},\underline{7}, \geqslant 0$.

Now consider the valuations of v_i and c_i as given in the theorem statement. These imply that in $\underline{1},\underline{4},\underline{5}$, and $\underline{8}$, the only negative inner products are $y_2^T v$ (from $\underline{1}$ and $\underline{8}$) and $c^T z_2$ (from $\underline{4}$ and $\underline{8}$). Hence $\underline{1},\underline{4} < 0$ and $\underline{5},\underline{8} \geqslant 0$.

Accordingly, all four terms in D are negative and D is negative, as desired.

Lemma

Show that z and y_1 have (all) non-negative components.

Proof

The Perron-Frobenius theorem (see [11, p. 53, theorem 2]) implies that if M is a non-negative, irreducible matrix, then the eigenvector corresponding to the maximal eigenvalue has positive components. The A here comes from the singular value decomposition $X^T A Y = \text{diag}(\sigma_1, \ldots, \sigma_n)$. So the x_i and y_i are eigenvectors of AA^T and $A^T A$, respectively. In particular, $AA^T x_1 = \lambda_1 x_1$ and $A^T A y_1 = \kappa_1 y_1$ where λ_i and κ_i are the appropriate eigenvalues. Now, A non-negative and irreducible implies that AA^T and $A^T A$ are also. Hence, since σ_1 is maximal, we have $(\sigma_1 \geq \sigma_2 \geq \ldots \geq \sigma_n \geq 0)$ and $\sigma_i = \sqrt{\lambda_i} = \sqrt{\kappa_i}$, λ_1 and κ_1 are maximal eigenvalues. Thus, by the Perron-Frobenius theorem, x_1 and y_1 have positive components. Since $z_1 = \sigma_1 x_1$, both z_1 and y_1 have non-negative components.

Measuring Cryptographic Performance with Production Processes
by Elliot Fischer

ABSTRACT: A measure of complexity based on production processes is presented as a measure of the resistance of a given cipher to cryptanalysis. Complexity calculations for several ciphers are presented and discussed.

I. INTRODUCTION

The purpose of this paper is to present a measure of the resistance to cryptanalysis of the output ciphertext from a given cryptographic algorithm. This is achieved by the use of a complexity measure related to the number and length of repeated substrings in the ciphertext. This measure of complexity is compatible with a measure of cryptographic performance developed in [1] that is related to the size of the encryption algorithm. The measure is shown to yield reasonable results for some well-known ciphers.

In Section II, production processes are discussed and the appropriate complexity measure is defined. In Section III this complexity measure is used to compare the performance of four ciphers: simple substitution, Vigenere of period 3 and 7, and the Hagelin cryptograph.

II. PRODUCTION PROCESSES AND COMPLEXITY

The concept of using properties of production processes to evaluate the complexity of finite sequences has been presented in [2]. Given a finite alphabet A, $\lambda(S)$ denotes the length of a sequence $S \in A^*$, the set

From *Cryptologia*, Vol. 5, No. 3, July 1981.

of all finite length sequences over A. To indicate a substring of S that starts at the ith position and ends at the jth, we write $S(i,j)$. Consider a sequence R formed by the concatenation of two sequences S and Q. We write $R = SQ$ and say R is reproducible from S if Q is a subsequence of S. R is said to be producible from S if the sequence RQ' formed by deleting the last symbol from Q is reproducible from S. Thus reproducibility involves only copying while producibility allows for a single symbol innovation at the end of the copying process.

Given a sequence $S \in A^*$ we can consider it the result of a series of sequence concatenations, or a production process, in which each new sequence is producible from the existing sequence. An example will make this clearer. Consider the English sequence:

$S_1 =$ fourscoreandsevenyearsago

We parse this sequence into phrases according to the following prescription. At position i along S consider $S(1,i-1)$ and $S(i,i+k)$ for $k=1,2,...,$ $\lambda(S)-i$. Find the smallest k for which $S(i,i+k)$ is not a substring of $S(1,i-1)$. This sequence $S(i,i+k)$ is the next phrase in the parsing of S and we next go to the $i+k+1$ position and begin the procedure there. Using this parsing technique, the above sequence S would be parsed into

$S_1 =$ f·o·u·r·s·c·or·e·a·n·d·se·v·en·y·ear·sa·g·o

The dots indicate the individual phrases in the parsing. The first six one-letter phrases result because of the first occurrence of each letter. The seventh phrase, or, results because o had already appeared previously, but or had not. The next four phrases are again due to first occurrences, the next, se, arises because s had already appeared but se had not. The rest of the parsing proceeds similarly.

Any parsing of S into phrases according to the rules of an iterative, self-delimiting vocabulary-building process is called a history of S and one such as the above is termed an exhaustive history in [2]. The complexity $c(S)$ of S is defined as

$c(S) = \min[c_H(S)]$

where $c_H(S)$ is the number of phrases in a history of S and the minimization is over all histories of S. That is, $c(S)$ is the least possible number of steps in which S can be generated according to the rules of a production process. Lempel and Ziv prove in [2] that $c(S) = c_E(S)$, where $c_E(S)$ is the number of components in $E(S)$, the exhaustive history of S.

Such a complexity measure is very natural since redundancy in the sequence leads to much smaller complexity values. Consider the sequence:

S_2=thecatandthedogandthemouse

The exhaustive history of S_2 is

S_2=t·h·e·c·a·ta·n·d·thed·o·g·andthem·ou·s·e

If we normalize the complexity by dividing the number of phrases in the exhaustive history of S by $\lambda(S)$, then the sequence S_1 above has a complexity of 0.76, while the more redundant S_2 has a complexity of 0.577. These numbers may be interpreted as the average number of phrases per letter.

The utility of an algorithm-oriented complexity measure such as defined above, as opposed to measures more statistical in nature, is borne out in cryptanalysis. In many ciphers, it is the existence of repeated sequences that leads to a cryptanalytic wedge that may be used to break the cipher. For example, the Kasiski method [3] for determining the period of a Vigenere cipher consists of noting the intervals at which repeated sequences occur and reasoning that the period is composed of common factors of such intervals. A method for cryptanalyzing the Hebern cryptograph, discussed in [4], relies on finding repeated isomorphs, which are repeated strings that are related to each other by a simple substitution cipher. Thus, the complexity measure described above would be very appropriate in measuring susceptibility to such a cryptanalytic attack, since sequences with relatively few, short repeated subsequences would have a larger complexity than sequences with either relatively many short repeated subsequences or with relatively few long repeated subsequences.

Ultimately, the existence of repeated subsequences is related to the entropy of the sequence. The entropy of the source is related in [2] to the complexity of the source's output strings. However, a calculation of the entropy of a sequence requires frequency calculations over increasingly longer subsequences, whereas the complexity measure described in this section can be easily programmed on a microcomputer using BASIC string functions. Such a computer program can be used to calculate the normalized complexity of a sequence, and we present some results in the next section.

III. COMPLEXITY RESULTS OF SOME SELECTED CIPHERS

In this section we present complexity data from four different ciphers. The ciphers considered are simple substitution, Vigenere of period 3 and period 7, and the Hagelin cryptograph. The simple substitution and Vigenere ciphers are described in [3]. The Hagelin cryptograph is described in [5] and [6]. Unlike the other two ciphers, it is based on the mod-26 addition of plaintext to a pseudorandom key string to produce ciphertext. Since the simple substitution cipher merely substitutes one letter for another throughout the entire cipher, its complexity is the same as plaintext English. The Vigenere, being composed of several simple substitutions repeated periodically, would be expected to be more complex than plaintext, and the complexity would be expected to increase with the length of the period. The Hagelin, being based on a pseudorandom number generator, would be expected to have an even greater complexity than the Vigenere.

It is convenient to have a standard complexity against which the complexity of the ciphers can be compared. We choose to use the maximum complexity for a sequence of given length. For example, the maximum number of phrases in an exhaustive history of a 100-letter sequence can be computed as follows. The first 26 characters are the 26 letters without repetition. The next 74 positions can be filled by 37 pairs of letters chosen so that all of the 99 pairs of adjacent letters in the 100 letter sequence are distinct. (This can be done easily since there are 26^2 or 676 distinct letter pairs available to choose from.) This would result in an exhaustive history containing $26+37=63$ phrases, and a normalized complexity of 0.63. A similar argument for sequences of length 200 would yield an exhaustive history containing 113 phrases and a normalized complexity of 0.565. Different ciphers may be compared on the basis of the percentage of the maximum complexity realized by the cryptogram produced by the given cipher.

Table I presents the results of complexity calculations performed on 20 cryptograms of 100 letters each for each of the four ciphers. Text for English was obtained from various sources. The Vigenere cryptograms were produced by taking English text and enciphering with a keyword of the appropriate length. A different keyword was used for each of the 20 cryptograms. The Hagelin cryptograms were obtained from [6]. The last column indicated that the complexity of the ciphers behaves as expected on intuitive grounds and discussed previously in this section. There is a reasonable separation between the average complexity of each cipher, considering the sample size of 20 cryptograms. It would be of interest to study the behavior of the complexity over longer sequences, and Table II presents results from the same ciphers using 10 cryptograms of 200 letters each. As would be expected, the simple substitution and Vigenere ciphers degrade somewhat in complexity as indicated by the smaller entries in the last column of Table II as compared with Table I. The results indicate that in the second hundred letters, the period 3 Vigenere had only about 40 phrases or an average of 2.5 letters per phrase compared with the minimum possible two letters per phrase. The Vigenere of period 7 had an average of 2.27 letters per phrase in the second 100 letters, while the Hagelin had an average of 2.17 letters per phrase in the second 100 letters. In both cases, the superiority of the Hagelin device, which attained 90% of the maximum complexity is clear. In fact, the Hagelin was the only cipher to show any increase in performance over the longer sequence length. The behavior of the period 7 Vigenere is also interesting since it showed practically no degradation in the second 100 letters, indicating that new sequences were being produced at approximately the same rate as in the first 100 letters. This may be related to the length of the period, which is slightly longer than an average English word and would thus tend to create repeated sequences at a more uniform rate, but this is only speculation.

TABLE I. COMPLEXITY RESULTS FOR SEQUENCES OF LENGTH 100

Cipher	Average Complexity	Standard Deviation	% of Maximum Complexity
Simple Substitution	0.501	0.018	0.795
Vigenere—Period 3	0.537	0.017	0.852
Vigenere—Period 7	0.566	0.018	0.883
Hagelin	0.570	0.013	0.905

TABLE II. COMPLEXITY RESULTS FOR SEQUENCES OF LENGTH 200

Cipher	Average Complexity	Standard Deviation	% of Maximum Complexity
Simple Substitution	0.431	0.012	0.763
Vigenere—Period 3	0.470	0.011	0.834
Vigenere—Period 7	0.498	0.017	0.881
Hagelin	0.515	0.011	0.912

It should be realized that complexity of the output cryptograms alone does not give a complete indication of the susceptibility to cryptanalytic attack, but only a partial indication. Given two ciphers with approximately equal output complexities, the cryptographic strength would be a function of the size of the minimal finite-state machine that describes the cryptographic algorithm, as discussed in [1]. For example, even if a period 10 Vigenere had about the same complexity as the Hagelin, the algorithm that describes the Vigenere is much simpler (and hence its corresponding minimal finite-state machine is much smaller) than the algorithm describing the Hagelin. The Hagelin would still prove the more formidable cipher. This is borne out by the fact that even a Vigenere of period 10 could certainly be broken given a few hundred letters of ciphertext.

In the foregoing we have presented a measure of cryptogram complexity based on the minimum number of steps of a production process required to produce a given cryptogram. It is the author's speculation that minimal algorithm complexity measures such as those discussed here and in [1] can provide new insights into cryptographic processes.

REFERENCES

1.   Fischer, E. (1981), A Theoretical Measure of Cryptographic Performance. *Cryptologia*, 5:59–62.

2.   Lempel, A., and Ziv, J. (1976), On the Complexity of Finite Sequences. *IEEE Transactions on Information Theory*, 22:75–80.

3.   Sinkov, A. (1968), *Elementary Cryptanalysis: A Mathematical Approach*. New York: Random House.

4.   Deavours, C. (1977), Analysis of the Hebern Cryptograph Using Isomorphs. *Cryptologia*, 1:167–185.

5.   Diffie, W., and Hellman, M. (1979), An Introduction to Cryptography. *Proceedings of the IEEE,* 67:397–427.

6.   Barker, W. (1977), *Cryptanalysis of the Hagelin Cryptograph*. Laguna Hills, CA: Aegean Park Press.

A Theoretical Measure of Cryptographic Performance
by Elliott Fischer

ABSTRACT: The concept of the complexity of a sequence is used to develop a measure of cryptographic performance. The discussion is kept for the most part on an intuitive level for the sake of clarity.

Keywords: Complexity, algorithm, finite-state machine.

INTRODUCTION

This paper discusses certain concepts from theoretical computer science and relates them to cryptography, ultimately developing a measure of cryptographic performance. In Section I, the complexity of a sequence is defined and discussed. In Section II, the concept of a finite state machine is introduced and related to cryptographic algorithms, and the definition of complexity is altered to relate to these machines. Section III contains a brief discussion of the apparent complexity of a sequence. This is the complexity of a sequence in which the algorithm used to produce it is not known. Section IV develops a measure of cryptographic performance based on the concepts developed in the previous sections. The discussion as a whole is kept on an intuitive level for the sake of clarity.

I. COMPLEXITY OF A SEQUENCE

In [1], Reeds discusses cryptographic and statistical standards of randomness. In particular, it is shown that the statistical tests (chi-square, autocorrelation functions, and correlation coefficients) do not provide

From *Cryptologia*, Vol. 5, No. 1, Jan. 1981.

any measure of the actual lack of a pattern in a character string, which is the goal of a good cryptographic design. A more appropriate measure was introduced by Chaitin in [2]. Chaitin defined the complexity of a sequence of bits as follows (this definition is taken from [3]):

Let ω be any string of bits. Then ω has complexity n, written $I(\omega) = n$ if:

1. There exists a program P and an input string v for a Turing machine such that the length of P + the length of $v = n$, and P when begun with v will eventually halt with output ω, and

2. There is no smaller n for which this is the case. (A Turing machine is a "universal" computer that can be programmed to carry out any possible computation. An excellent introduction to Turing machines is given in [3].

For example, we can ask how many strings ω of length n are there with $I(\omega) \le n-10$? Each string would have associated with it a program P and input string v such that (length of P) + (length of v) $\le n-10$. There are two programs one digit long that might generate an n-digit string, 2^2 programs two digits long, 2^3 programs three digits long, etc. The sum of this series,

$$2^1 + 2^2 + 2^3 + \ldots + 2^{n-10}$$

is equal to $2^{n-9} - 2$. This is the number of programs of length less than or equal to $n-10$. The randomness concept becomes apparent when the total number of strings of length n is compared to those with complexity less than or equal to $n-10$.

We get

$$\frac{2^{n-9} - 2}{2^n} \approx \frac{1}{2^9} = \frac{1}{512}$$

which means more than 99.8% of all strings of length n have complexity greater than $n-10$. It is important to note that strings produced by a simple algorithm, such as the linear congruential pseudorandom generators discussed in [4] and cryptanalyzed in [1] and [5], will have small complexity, and hence be considered less random, than those produced by a more complicated algorithm. The essential point to be made here is that the size of the smallest algorithm capable of producing a character string is a reasonable measure of the randomness of the string. Basically, a series ω of numbers of length n is considered random if $I(\omega) \approx n$.

II. FINITE-STATE MACHINES

It is convenient to use finite-state machines, as opposed to Turing machines, to describe cryptographic algorithms. A finite-state machine is a 5-tuple $[A,Z,S,\nu,\sigma]$, where

A is a finite list of input symbols,
$A = \{a_0, a_1, \ldots, a_n\}$,
Z is a list of output symbols,
$Z = \{z_0, z_1, \ldots, z_n\}$,
S is a set of *internal states,*
$S = \{s_0, s_1, \ldots, s_n\}$,
ν is a *next-state* function from $S \times A$ into S, and

σ is an *output function* from $S \times A$ into Z.

The above definition appears in [6], which offers an excellent mathematical introduction to finite-state machines. A more descriptive, less mathematical treatment is presented in [7].

Formally, many cryptographic algorithms fit into the formalism of a finite-state machine. Concrete examples of Caesar, Vigenère, autokey, and matrix encipherment are given in [8]. Many classes of cryptanalytic problems can be formulated using a finite-state machine formalism. For example, given the method of encipherment and some intercepted ciphertext, determine the original input. This corresponds to knowing the functions ν and σ and the output from an unknown input string. The problem is to reconstruct the original input. Another such problem would be that of reconstructing the original machine settings of a machine cipher such as the Enigma from matched clear and cipher text. The finite-state machine problem would be to determine the initial internal state given the functions ν and σ and matched input and output.

We introduce finite-state machines because they provide a clearer model of a cryptographic process than the more primitive Turing machines. We now alter Chaitin's definition of complexity by replacing Turing machines by finite-state machines. Thus, the complexity $I(\omega)$ of a string ω of characters is the smallest finite-state machine that will produce ω from a given input. Here, smallest is taken in the sense of the number of internal states and the complexity of the next-state and output functions. That is, the size of a particular finite-state machine is related to the size of the state diagram required to describe the machine. Given a finite-state machine, there exists a procedure (see [6]) to reduce it to an equivalent machine with a minimum number of states called a minimal-state machine. Thus, $I(\omega)$ is the size of the minimal state machine that produces ω from a given output.

III. COMPLEXITY OF A SEQUENCE, REVISITED

Before we discuss cryptographic measures of performance, it is appropriate at this time to consider the problem of defining the randomness, or complexity, of a sequence based only on the sequence itself and not on the algorithm that produced it. Such a definition was given in Lempel and Ziv in [9]. Basically, the complexity of a specific sequence is linked to the gradual buildup of new patterns along the sequence. Without going into details, the complexity of a sequence S is related to the number of distinct patterns, or the vocabulary, and their rate of occurrence along the sequence. We will call this complexity the *apparent complexity* of a string, and denote it by I(apparent)(ω).

IV. CRYPTOGRAPHIC PERFORMANCE

In this section, we apply the development of the previous sections to measuring cryptographic performance. One way of stating the general problem of designing a good cryptographic algorithm would be to design an algorithm that maximizes the apparent complexity of the output string while minimizing the actual complexity, that is, the size of the algorithm. We could state this as maximizing the quantity

$$\frac{I(\text{apparent})(\omega)}{I(\omega)} \tag{1}$$

over a suitable ensemble of strings ω. A better measure might take into account the fact that using some keys and input sequences makes the cipher easy to cryptanalyze. Thus, we might wish to design an algorithm that maximizes (1) with

$$I(\text{apparent})(\omega) > \text{some standard} \tag{2}$$

in order to make the resulting ciphertext sufficiently complex. Those initial states (keys) that do not produce a sufficiently complex cipher text would not be used. For example, users of the DES are instructed not to use certain keys, since the resulting cipher text is easier to cryptanalyze [10].

The measure (1) can be compared with the unicity point derived in [11]. The unicity point, U, is defined as

$$U = \frac{H(k)}{R} \tag{3}$$

where $H(k)$ is the logarithm of the possible number of keys in the cipher and R is the redundancy of the language. U is roughly equal to the number of cipher text characters required for unique decipherment. It has traditionally been used as a measure of cryptographic strength. However, in comparing modern algorithms, (1) with the constraint (2), might be a better indicator of cryptographic performance. For example, in comparing the DES and the Rivest Public Key systems, the complexity of the algorithm becomes important. That is, given that the resulting output sequences from the two ciphers are both sufficiently complex, the question of which algorithm is more efficient reduces to which algorithm is simpler, as in (1), as opposed to which has more keys, as in (3). (Here we do not consider hardware implementation.) Furthermore, the criterion (1) explains why transposition is such an effective enciphering procedure. The resulting cipher text is very complex, since all original sequences of letters have been distributed. This provides a large I(apparent)(ω). At the same time, the actual description of columnar transposition is simple, leading to a small $I(\omega)$. Using (1), this is seen to be the optimal situation for a cryptographic algorithm.

REFERENCES

1. Reeds, J. (1977), "Cracking" a Random Number Generator. *Cryptologia*, 1:20–26.
2. Chaitin, G. (1975), Randomness and Mathematical Proof. *Scientific American*, 232:47–52.
3. Davis, M. (1978), What is a Computation? In *Mathematics Today*, L. A. Steen, ed. New York: Springer-Verlag.
4. Knuth, D. E. (1969), *The Art of Computer Programming,* Vol. 2: Seminumerical Algorithms. Reading, MA: Addison-Wesley.
5. Reeds, J. (1979), Solution of Challenge Cipher. *Cryptologia*, 3:83–95.
6. Birkhoff, G., and Bartee, T. C. (1970), *Modern Applied Algebra.* New York: McGraw-Hill.
7. McNaughton, R. (1961), The Theory of Automata: A Survey. In *Advances in Computer Science,* Vol. 2. F. L. Alt, ed. New York: Academic Press.
8. Halsey, J. C. (1970), Finite Automata Admitting Inverses with Some Application to Cryptography. Ph.D. Thesis. Department of Mathematics. North Carolina State University.
9. Lempel, A., and Ziv, J. (1976), On the Complexity of Finite Sequences. *IEEE Transactions on Information Theory.* 22:75–81.

10. Course notes from Continuing Engineering Education Program Course No. 534. "Computer Cryptography." January 15–17, 1979. George Washington University.

11. Shannon, C. E. (1949), Communication Theory of Secrecy Systems. *Bell System Technical Journal,* 28:656–715.

"Forwards and Backwards" Encryption*
by Ronald L. Rivest

I present here a variation on the use of pseudorandom sequences for encryption which is extremely resistant to probable-word analysis. Decrypting any small fragment of the message does not directly allow the cryptanalyst to read the rest of the message.

The proposed method uses two pseudorandom sequences to encrypt each message. One sequence is generated left-to-right (forwards) in the normal manner, while the other is generated right-to-left (backwards); so that the first message symbol is encrypted using the first generated element of the forwards sequence and the last generated element of the backwards sequence. Each element of the ciphertext is the sum (modulo the alphabet size) of a message element and the corresponding elements of the two pseudorandom sequences.

We observe that this is not a stream cipher, since the entire message must be available before encryption can begin.

The pseudorandom sequences are chosen in such a way that the forwards sequence prevents a cryptanalyst from decrypting the portion of the message that preceded the location of a probable word attack, and the backwards sequence similarly prevents him from decrypting the text after the probable word. Together they make a probable-word attack futile.

We can model the generation of a pseudorandom sequence as follows. An initial state S_1 is chosen for the generator. This "seed" forms the cryptographic key for the sequence, since the entire sequence can be formed from the seed. A "next-state" function f is repeatedly used to form a sequence of states $S_1, S_2, S_3, \ldots$, where $S_{i+1} = f(S_i)$. Finally, the pseudorandom sequence itself is typically not the state sequence but a transformed version of it: an "output function" g is used to transform the ith state S_i into the ith element of the pseudorandom sequence.

From *Cryptologia*, Vol. 4, No. 1, Jan. 1980.
*This research was supported in part by NSF grant number MCS 78-05849.

A probable word attack is often successful in discovering the state of the generator at the location of the attack. We wish to prevent this information from being useful to the cryptanalyst.

Consider the usual situation where only a single (forwards) generator is used. The cryptanalyst presumably knows the next-state and output functions f and g: the cryptographic key is the initial state S_1. Once the cryptanalyst discovers the ith state to be S_i with a probable word attack, he can easily decrypt the ith and all subsequent message elements since he can recreate the pseudorandom sequence from that point forwards. However, a well chosen next-state function f can prevent the cryptanalyst from decrypting the previous $i=1$ message elements.

We will choose the next-state function f to be many-to-one to thwart the cryptanalyst in his efforts to use his knowledge of S_i to determine $S_1, \ldots , S_{i-1}$. If f is many-to-one for each state S_j, there can be many states X such that $f(X) = S_j$; each of these states could have been S_{j-1}. As the cryptanalyst tries to use his determination of S_i to find S_{i-1}, S_{i-2}, etc., more ambiguity is introduced in each backwards step. If the rate at which ambiguity (uncertainty) is introduced exceeds the redundancy rate of the plaintext the cryptanalyst will be unable to decrypt the message prior to the ith element.

If we use a backwards pseudorandom sequence in addition to the forwards one, where both sequences are generated using many-to-one next-state functions, the cryptanalyst will be unable to use a probable word attack to determine *any* portion of the message, since the backwards sequence now prevents him from decrypting the message that follows the probable word.

This completes our description of the basic idea. In what follows, we present examples and suggestions on the choice of suitable many-to-one next-state functions.

There is no reason why the same next-state function f could not be used in the generation of both the forwards and the backwards sequences. The cryptographic key will typically consist of two seeds: one to initialize the generation of each sequence.

One simple choice of the next-state function is to use an f of the form $f(x) \equiv x^2 + a \pmod{p}$. Here p is a randomly chosen large prime number and a is another randomly chosen number $0 < a < p$. For each state S_i, where $i > 1$, of the pseudorandom state sequence $S_1, S_2, \ldots$, there will generally be *two* solutions to the equation $f(X) = S_i$. If the output function g produces one bit of output for each state the ambiguity is introduced at a high rate.

Another technique is to use a nonlinear feedback shift-register of the form [shown below].

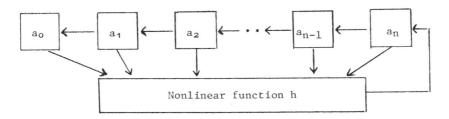

Figure 1

Each register cell holds one bit a_i of information; the next state of the register is $(a_1, a_2, \ldots, a_{n-1}, a_n, h(a_0, \ldots, a_n))$. As long as $h(a_0, \ldots, a_n)$ is not of the form $a_0 \oplus h'(a_1, a_2, \ldots, a_n)$ the next-state function will be many-to-one.

It is important to note that pseudorandom sequences generated using a many-to-one next-state function will not be "maximum period" sequences. If the number of generator states is n, then a maximum period generator will produce a sequence of length n, whereas a pseudorandom sequence produced with a "random" next-state function will have period roughly $\sqrt{n}$. The number n of generator states should be chosen so that $\sqrt{n}$ is much larger than the length of the messages being enciphered.

As an example, consider encrypting the word CRYPTOGRAPHY using the next-state function $f(x) = x^2 + 3 \pmod{1009}$, the forwards seed 919, and the backwards seed 21, and the output function $g(x) = (x \bmod 26)$. The encryption computation is shown in Table 1, the numeric ciphertext 11, 12, 4, . . . , is formed by adding (mod 26) the numeric message codes with the corresponding elements of the forwards and backwards pseudorandom sequences. Our ciphertext is thus LMEDXEIYLBMI.

Even if a cryptanalyst could deduce that the sixth letter of our plaintext was O and that the states of the pseudorandom number generators for that letter were 522 and 248, he would not be able to determine that the next plaintext letter is G, since it equally well could have been F. (Note that $248 \equiv 699^2 + 3 \equiv 310^2 + 3 \pmod{1009}$, so that the next element of the backwards pseudorandom sequence could have been either 23 ($\equiv 699 \pmod{26}$) or 24 ($\equiv 310 \pmod{26}$).) Similarly the previous plaintext letter could be decrypted as either T (which is correct) or W, corresponding to forward states of 103 or 906. Thus a probable-word attack is of no avail to the cryptanalyst.

While the basic principle should now be clear, we leave it to the reader to investigate which many-to-one functions are most suitable for use in our method. The works mentioned in the references describe other pseudorandom sequence generation techniques, or methods for breaking such techniques.

TABLE 1.

Forwards State Sequence	Backwards State Sequence	Forwards Random Sequence	Backwards Random Sequence	Message	Numeric Message	Numeric Ciphertext	Ciphertext
919	130	9	0	C	2	11	L
31	146	5	16	R	17	12	M
964	446	2	4	Y	24	4	E
10	758	10	4	P	15	3	D
103	967	25	5	T	19	23	X
522	248	2	14	O	14	4	E
57	699	5	23	G	6	8	I
225	848	17	16	R	17	24	Y
178	145	22	15	A	0	11	L
408	384	18	20	P	15	1	B
991	444	3	2	H	7	12	M
327	21	15	21	Y	24	8	I

REFERENCES

1.   Gait, J. (1977), A New Nonlinear Pseudorandom Number Generator, *IEEE Trans. on Software Engineering*, 3:359–363.
2.   Kahn, D. (1967), *The Codebreakers*. New York: Macmillan.
3.   Knuth, D. E. 1969. *The Art of Computer Programming*, Vol. 2: Seminumerical Algorithms. Reading, MA: Addison-Wesley.
4.   Meyer, C. H. (1974), Enciphering Data for Secure Transmission. *Computer Design*. April: 129–134.
5.   Meyer, C. H., and Tuchman, W. (1972), Pseudorandom Codes can be Cracked. *Electronic Design*, 23:74–76.
6.   Pless, V. (1977), Encryption schemes for computer confidentiality. *IEEE Trans. on Computers*, 26:1133–1136.
7.   Reeds, J. (1977), "Cracking" a Random Number Generator. *Cryptologia*, 1:20–26.
8.   Reeds, J. (1979), Solution of Challenge Cipher. *Cryptologia*, 3:83–95.

Higher-Order Homophonic Ciphers
by Carl Hammer

ABSTRACT: In a recent paper, James J. Gillogly [1] asserts that Beale Cipher No. 1 is spurious. We take no issue with his statistics but wish to point out that he has missed an important alternative: Higher-Order Homophonics. We provide here an overview of second- and higher-order homophonic enciphering/deciphering principles and apply this concept to a further analysis of the Beale Ciphers. We shall finally suggest that the Beale Ciphers should not readily be dismissed as a hoax, as J. J. Gillogly, Greg Mellen [2,3] and others would have us do.

1. INTRODUCTION

Every cryptogram longer than the unicity distance has but one solution. Simple substitution ciphers may be solved by discovering the key, using trial-and-error methods, or employing formalistic iterative processes and algorithms. An elegant methodology for a computer-aided procedural solution of standard English cryptograms has been published by Shmuel Peleg and Azriel Rosenfeld [4].

But little has been published about ambiguous cryptograms with more than one feasible interpretation, such that the solution can only be inferred from additional "side information."

For example, consider the following excerpt from a simple-substitution cipher: MNOPQRSTUVWXYZ. Unless one has the complete ciphertext, or has the key, the excerpt admits of at least three valid interpretations (ambidextrously, hydropneumatic, and pseudomythical). If one allows hapax legomena, barbarisms and technical words, there are at least 78 interpretations (e.g., unpostmarkedly, unparoxysmlike, and dichlorbutanes). Hence the need for additional information.

From *Cryptologia*, Vol. 5, No. 4, Oct. 1981.

Because of the redundancy of English and other languages, cryptograms longer than the unicity distance do not have more than one (rational) interpretation and are of little practical importance. While it may be feasible to construct short cryptograms with two or perhaps more interpretations, they would be so specialized as to be of no real value to a professional cryptographer. However, such is not the case for homophonic ciphers which possess many degrees of freedom, compared with simple substitution ciphers. But a search of the literature has not revealed examples of higher-order homophonic substitution ciphers.

2. SECOND-ORDER HOMOPHONIC CIPHERS

For an introduction to homophonic and polyphonic ciphers the reader should turn to David Kahn's monumental *Codebreakers* [5]. Further information is found in our study of the Beale Ciphers, the signatures of which we analyzed in 1971 [6]. More recently, we also published [7] a list of "errors" in B2.

During both Beale Cipher Symposia (1971 and 1979), the *existence* of different *solutions* to B1 was mentioned. We also heard that the so-called solution to B2 ("I have deposited . . .") may be an overt cover-up to conceal a second, *covert*, solution. We shall show that it is indeed feasible to construct higher-order homophonics with more than one interpretation or solution. But we shall conclude, from the available evidence, that it is not likely that the three Beale Ciphers have multiple solutions.

We begin with an inductive approach to the construction of second-order homophonics of the Beale type: assume that we want to encipher two messages (of equal length) into one homophonic. The key to the first message might be the sequentially numbered letters of the Declaration of Independence, omitting spaces and punctuations. The key to the second might be sequentially numbered letters of the (English version) Magna Carta [8]. Let $_1M_i$ and $_2M_i$ ($i=1,2,3, \ldots , n$) respectively be the first and second (cleartext) messages, each having n letters. To encipher them into a simple homophonic decipher, we must find a set of n numbers N_i such that they decipher successively into the letters $_1M_i$ if we use the first key document, and into the letters $_2M_i$ if we use the second key document.

To illustrate, we chose two brief messages, the second of which is padded to make them both the same length:

$_1M_i$: DECLARATIONUSEDTOENCODEOTHERMESSAGE

$_2M_i$: MAGNACARTAUSEDTOENCODEOTHERMESSAGEX

We shall encipher these two messages using sequentially numbered letters in two key documents, the DOI and the MC (Declaration of Independence and Magna Carta). Searching for letter concordances between both documents, we find that letter number 656 is a D in the MC, and an M in the DOI. Similarly, E and A coincide at position 27 of these two documents. But within the first 2000 letters, there is no concordance for C and G and we decide to "fudge it" and to use the number 127. It stands for O and G respectively—doesn't "O" look very much like "C"? Continuing, we find that of the $n=35$ letter pairs needed, 9, or about 25 percent, cannot be enciphered without creating additional artificial errors.

Nevertheless, the resultant code 656, 27, 127*, 10, 25, 458, 25, 1189*, 50, 51, 863, 168, 780, 118*, 26, 235, 190, 192*, 667, 132, 63, 244*, 739*, 14, 345, 557*, 248, 1010*, 557, 621*, 62, 147, 276, 89, 70* is quite intelligible, despite the nine arbitrary "errors" indicated by asterisks.

Clearly, the use of any two key documents—numbered letters or words—will lead to the following difficulties:

(i) Some desired letter pairs cannot be enciphered at all as no concordance is achieved, even in two very long documents.
(ii) Other desired letter pairs often occur first only for very large concordance numbers.
(iii) Few desired letter pairs will have small concordance numbers.

Of course, the first of these difficulties can be overcome, albeit rather inadequately, by purposely making erroneous or "punning" entries where required. Thus one might be tempted to explain the known errors in B2 [7] by assuming that it is a second-order homophonic were it not for the fact that 60 percent of the numbers in B2 are below 200—clearly in contradiction of (ii) and (iii) above.

Enciphering second-order homophonics with the help of two key documents is thus not a very satisfying endeavor. The needed letter concordance lead to a sparse 26×26 matrix which is of little practical value. But the use of key texts is readily eliminated if we create a synthetic matrix with 26×26 elements. Such a matrix can be accomplished by manual or computer methods. Its properties are embodied in the following two requirements:

(i) The size of the matrix is 26×26.
(ii) The matrix elements n_{ij} $(i, j=1,2,3, \ldots, 26)$ are a randomly chosen permutation of the set of numbers $(1,2,3, \ldots, 676)$. The numbers thus represent every possible (English) diagram: aa,ab, . . . , zz.

A fortiori this is the smallest set of numbers which can be used for second-order homophonic ciphers.

Obviously this matrix is not sparse as that obtained from letter concordances in two key documents. Since letters used in the written language are not uniformly distributed, letter concordances in second-order homophonics will result in more frequent occurrences of certain a_{ij}'s and in a paucity of others. Linguists have long known of such positional letter probabilities. Empirically obtained autoregressive statistics have been used to advantage in the cryptogram deciphering methodology of Peleg and Rosenfeld.

A typical second-order homophonic enciphering matrix generated by a specially designed computer program is shown in Table 1. We used a specific seed to initiate the random-number generation process. Another seed would, of course, produce another matrix. To illustrate its use, we have prepared the following code: 92, 222, 196, 615, 438, 664, 360, 176, 5, 548, 122, 604, 427, 132, 577, . . .

Horizontal (row) decoding and vertical (column) decoding respectively lead to the following two message fragments:

(H): THEVAULTISFOUND. . .

(V): TJBNEVEREXISTED. . .

Enciphering a second-order homophonic must employ such a matrix from which we select correct letter concordances. To facilitate deciphering, several tools are available. First, we provide two separate, numerically sorted deciphering lists, one each for the horizontal and vertical enciphering entry points: Table 2A and 2B derive readily from the enciphering matrix, Table 1. We observe that the two lists provide capabilities comparable to those embodied in public key cryptosystems [9]. Thus, Table 2A is the nonsecret part of the system which is deposited in a universally accessible place. Table 2B and the enciphering matrix (Table 1) are kept secret, of course.

A second useful deciphering tool is a dual string list of the 676 matrix elements, shown in Tables 3A and 3B, also readily obtained from the enciphering matrix, Table 1. Again, the first of these strings is made public while the second is kept secret. We complete this expository treatment of second-order homophonic ciphers by briefly describing generalized higher-order homophonics. For the sake of simplicity we shall avoid the obviously inferior methodology which results in excessively sparse enciphering and deciphering matrices. Rather we shall deal here only with the more tractable computer-generated matrices.

The extension from second- to higher-order homophonics is both simple and logical. Thus, for third-order enciphering the minimum requirement is a three-dimensional $26 \times 26 \times 26$ matrix with 17,576 random entries. Its four-dimensional cousin has $26^4 = 456,976$ random elements and the general nth order homophonic has 26^n randomly arranged elements ranging from 1 to 26^n. The computer generation of such multidimensional matrices presents no problem, nor does the development of

	A	B	C	D	E	F	G	H	I	J	K	L	M	N	O	P	Q	R	S	T	U	V	W	X	Y	Z	
A	11	614	284	218	202	209	319	290	160	502	288	550	227	476	531	661	58	470	35	289	672	149	491	441	378	527	A
B	205	109	187	587	196	310	444	666	123	18	128	430	331	258	257	216	467	9	493	362	201	296	496	528	557	85	B
C	600	374	504	410	473	241	387	247	453	471	551	616	194	43	643	494	54	652	338	223	351	607	645	142	76	242	C
D	554	597	248	577	393	563	522	593	510	373	565	632	565	379	40	347	211	237	634	93	478	287	656	185	343	181	D
E	438	316	140	279	339	118	219	222	5	629	232	360	446	132	520	345	93	663	66	519	302	233	569	547	390	139	E
F	322	86	583	416	357	152	540	32	324	419	608	10	573	532	432	6	74	154	375	359	156	308	79	60	245	659	F
G	571	114	235	171	141	192	161	567	505	641	369	121	637	423	501	558	183	572	243	156	186	55	596	635	299	584	G
H	537	277	167	447	422	108	147	4	590	479	581	254	12	365	426	177	381	91	51	131	15	23	455	451	143	464	H
I	628	105	429	426	226	122	549	255	271	163	612	262	413	561	263	106	334	306	521	158	358	405	189	391	63	529	I
J	184	150	44	336	269	94	389	162	281	234	146	354	570	217	372	560	101	401	13	454	619	425	116	364	371	648	J
K	291	638	404	34	249	250	377	298	313	214	621	412	130	210	107	31	73	580	585	182	468	509	8	87	297	335	K
L	285	49	526	421	203	450	206	169	420	2	348	647	553	442	588	96	293	37	589	272	646	509	8	111	598	148	L
M	556	669	475	673	536	208	633	361	286	466	48	236	126	402	431	654	440	350	52	575	153	668	340	340	328	320	M
N	483	307	613	333	603	110	657	384	653	115	104	84	303	667	39	511	559	36	62	620	435	615	498	65	225	28	N
O	424	539	305	650	81	380	315	98	518	546	605	83	68	89	151	264	395	662	651	292	472	555	406	498	670	164	O
P	439	578	622	452	400	159	17	418	658	265	503	414	145	574	457	97	610	56	165	477	321	392	649	517	309	594	P
Q	213	616	230	294	579	368	443	524	38	166	576	278	256	300	314	564	252	465	3	366	370	312	624	26	231	178	Q
R	490	514	207	408	675	198	665	1	78	99	492	602	449	495	120	538	77	417	512	176	7	193	33	506	488	168	R
S	283	525	630	676	330	566	21	16	480	274	326	507	396	53	604	552	409	133	448	460	200	244	240	545	113	71	S
T	327	487	437	582	352	644	199	82	636	627	403	266	172	119	75	174	24	138	157	92	427	356	346	352	462	434	T
U	301	671	415	42	363	626	27	129	197	625	188	433	136	280	655	592	508	22	341	246	323	67	337	459	595	127	U
V	259	170	261	562	474	388	386	349	617	135	642	486	318	411	660	20	46	215	72	499	664	534	609	355	500	367	V
W	586	606	41	88	295	179	103	631	189	116	461	329	469	70	112	253	212	376	45	69	383	59	516	50	25	95	W
X	14	497	64	134	80	513	220	482	353	394	137	239	623	436	173	317	484	304	548	456	267	399	481	238	325	342	X
Y	155	117	382	523	591	229	29	485	144	463	195	19	445	311	61	57	542	260	458	221	100	544	530	268	47	191	Y
Z	489	601	124	190	102	30	611	204	251	282	541	407	90	398	228	224	397	180	125	385	543	273	270	640	175	674	Z

TABLE 1. ENCIPHERING/DECIPHERING MATRIX FOR SECOND-ORDER HOMOPHONIC. (USE: ENCIPHERING.)

A : :	11	14	155	205	213	259	285	283	291	301	322	327	424	438	439	483	489	490	537	554	556	571	586	600	628	
B : :	49	86	105	109	114	117	150	170	277	307	316	374	487	497	514	525	539	578	597	601	606	614	618	638	669	671
C : :	41	44	64	124	140	167	187	207	230	248	261	284	305	416	421	426	429	437	475	504	526	583	613	622	630	
D : :	34	42	88	134	171	190	218	279	294	333	336	408	410	447	415	429	437	475	504	526	582	587	650	673	676	
E : :	80	81	102	141	196	202	203	226	249	269	295	330	332	339	357	363	393	400	422	473	474	536	579	591	603	675
F : :	30	94	108	110	118	122	152	159	179	192	198	208	209	229	241	250	310	368	380	388	450	513	563	566	626	644
G : :	17	21	27	29	103	147	161	199	206	219	220	315	319	377	386	387	389	443	444	522	540	549	611	633	657	665
H : :	1	4	16	32	82	98	129	162	169	204	222	247	255	290	298	349	361	384	418	482	485	524	567	593	631	666
I : :	5	38	78	123	144	160	189	197	251	271	281	286	313	324	353	420	453	463	466	471	479	502	510	518	546	590
J : :	2	18	99	115	116	135	163	166	214	234	265	274	282	373	394	419	480	505	541	551	568	576	581	605	608	641
K : :	48	104	128	137	146	188	195	232	288	326	348	369	403	461	492	503	463	466	471	479	502	576	581	605	608	642
L : :	10	19	83	84	121	236	239	254	262	266	278	329	354	360	407	412	414	430	433	486	507	550	565	570	573	647
M : :	12	68	90	126	130	136	145	172	194	227	256	303	318	331	396	398	402	411	413	423	436	442	449	469	476	637
N : :	43	53	70	89	119	132	210	217	258	280	300	311	365	379	398	402	413	423	431	432	442	457	501	520	531	667
O : :	39	40	61	75	107	112	120	151	173	228	257	263	314	372	428	431	457	501	520	531	588	604	643	655	660	
P : :	6	20	31	57	96	97	106	174	177	216	224	253	264	317	345	347	409	440	467	484	508	542	559	592	654	661
Q : :	24	46	54	58	73	74	77	101	183	211	252	293	334	381	395	397	409	440	467	484	508	542	559	610	652	663
R : :	9	22	36	37	56	91	133	138	154	180	215	237	260	304	306	344	350	376	401	417	465	470	472	572	580	662
S : :	3	13	35	45	51	52	62	66	72	125	157	165	243	338	341	375	448	458	493	512	521	548	585	589	634	651
T : :	69	92	93	131	156	158	176	182	221	223	246	272	289	292	359	362	366	385	454	456	460	477	499	519	575	620
U : :	7	15	100	153	186	200	201	267	302	321	323	351	358	370	383	427	435	468	472	478	533	543	619	646	664	672
V : :	23	55	59	67	149	193	233	244	273	276	287	296	308	312	356	392	399	405	425	509	534	544	555	607	615	668
W : :	8	33	79	87	240	270	297	337	346	391	406	455	481	491	496	515	516	530	569	596	609	624	639	645	649	656
X : :	26	50	60	63	65	111	142	185	238	268	340	352	355	364	441	451	459	498	506	517	528	535	545	547	635	640
Y : :	25	47	76	113	143	175	225	231	245	299	309	325	328	343	371	378	390	462	488	500	557	595	598	599	670	
Z : :	28	71	85	95	127	139	148	164	168	178	181	191	242	320	335	342	367	434	464	527	529	584	594	648	659	674

TABLE 2A. MATRIX FOR SECOND-ORDER HOMOPHONIC [ABSCISSA (HORIZONTAL) FIRST].
(USE: DECIPHERING.)

A ::	11	35	58	149	160	202	209	218	227	284	288	289	290	319	378	441	470	476	491	502	527	531	550	614	661	672
B ::	9	18	85	109	123	128	187	196	201	205	216	257	258	296	310	331	362	430	444	467	493	496	528	557	587	566
C ::	43	54	76	142	194	223	241	242	247	338	351	374	387	410	453	471	473	494	504	551	600	607	616	643	645	652
D ::	40	93	181	185	211	237	248	287	343	347	373	379	393	478	510	522	554	563	565	568	577	593	597	632	634	656
E ::	5	66	118	132	139	140	219	222	232	233	279	302	316	339	344	345	360	390	438	446	519	520	547	569	629	663
F ::	6	10	32	60	74	79	86	152	154	245	308	322	324	357	359	375	416	419	432	532	533	540	573	583	608	659
G ::	55	114	121	141	156	161	171	183	186	192	235	243	299	369	423	501	505	558	567	571	572	584	596	635	637	641
H ::	4	12	15	23	51	91	108	131	147	167	177	254	277	365	381	422	428	447	451	455	464	479	537	581	590	599
I ::	63	105	106	122	143	158	163	226	255	262	263	271	306	334	358	391	405	413	426	429	521	529	549	561	612	628
J ::	13	44	87	94	101	146	150	162	184	217	234	269	281	336	354	364	371	372	389	401	425	454	560	570	619	648
K ::	31	34	73	107	130	182	210	214	249	250	275	276	281	296	313	335	377	404	412	468	535	580	585	621	638	
L ::	2	8	37	49	96	111	148	169	203	206	272	285	293	348	420	421	442	450	509	526	553	588	598	646	647	673
M ::	48	52	126	153	208	236	286	320	340	350	361	402	431	440	466	475	536	556	575	603	613	615	639	654	668	669
N ::	28	36	39	62	65	84	104	110	115	225	303	307	333	384	435	483	511	515	559	605	620	650	653	657	662	667
O ::	68	81	83	89	98	151	164	264	292	305	315	380	395	406	424	472	498	518	539	546	555	602	610	622	649	670
P ::	17	56	97	145	159	165	265	309	321	392	400	414	418	439	452	457	477	503	517	524	564	576	578	594	618	658
Q ::	3	26	38	77	78	99	120	168	176	193	198	207	231	252	256	278	294	300	312	314	366	368	370	443	465	624
R ::	1	7	33	53	100	113	133	178	221	240	283	326	330	396	409	448	460	480	492	506	512	514	538	602	630	675
S ::	16	21	53	71	113	133	200	240	244	274	283	326	330	396	409	448	460	480	507	525	545	552	566	604	630	676
T ::	24	75	82	92	119	138	157	172	174	199	246	266	280	301	323	332	341	346	352	356	363	403	427	434	437	462
U ::	22	27	42	67	127	129	136	186	197	259	261	318	355	367	386	388	411	474	486	499	500	508	534	562	609	617
V ::	20	46	72	135	170	215	259	261	318	349	355	367	386	411	461	469	474	486	500	516	534	562	586	606	617	664
W ::	25	41	45	50	59	69	70	88	95	103	112	116	179	189	212	253	295	329	376	383	456	469	481	497	513	631
X ::	14	64	80	134	137	173	220	238	239	267	304	317	325	342	353	394	399	436	445	458	482	484	523	530	548	623
Y ::	19	29	47	57	61	100	117	144	155	191	195	221	229	260	268	311	382	445	458	463	485	542	544	591	640	611
Z ::	30	90	102	124	125	175	180	190	204	224	228	251	270	273	282	385	397	398	407	489	541	543	601	611	640	674

TABLE 2B. DECIPHERING MATRIX FOR SECOND-ORDER HOMOPHONIC [ORDINATE (VERTICAL) FIRST]. (USE: DECIPHERING.)

```
EQUIVALENCES BETWEEN CODE NUMBERS AND FIRST ALPHABETIC SUBSTITUTION
FROM  TO  1234567890 1234567890 1234567890 1234567890 1234567890
   1   50  HJSHIPUWRL AMSAUHGJLP GRVQYXGZGF PHWDSRRIOO CDNCSOYKBX
  51  100  SSNQVRPQVX CSXCXSVMTN ZSQQOYQIWE EHLLZBWDNM RTTFZPPHJU
 101  150  QEGKBPOFBF XOYBJJBFNO LFICSMZKHM TNRDJMKRZC EXYIMKGZVB
 151  200  OFURATSTFI GHJZSJCZHB DMOPYTPZFR ZTQAXUCKID ZFVMKEIFGU
 201  250  UEEHAGCFFN QQAJRPNDGG THTPYEMOFC YKVJCLRXLW FZSVYTHCEF
 251  300  IQPLHMONAR CLOPJLUXEW ITVJYVBLDN IJACAIVKTH ATQDEVUHYN
 301  350  AUMRCRBVYF NVIOGBPMGZ UAUIYKAYLE MEDQZDWSEX SZYRPWPKHR
 351  400  UXILXVEUTL HTEXNTZFKU YOJBSRGYNF QCUHTGGFGY WVEJQMQNVE
 401  450  RNKCVWLDQD NLMLCDRHJI DENAVDUOCL OOLZUNCAAQ XNGGMMDSMF
 451  500  XDITUTOSXT KYJZRJQUMR JUEECNTUJI WHAQHLBYAA WKSPNWBXTY
 501  550  OJKCIXLQVI PSF3WWXITO SGDHBCZXZW ONUVXEAPBG KQUVXJXSGL
 551  600  KPMAVAYPQP NDFPNFHKWM ARMNTKDBER KDCZSADOSI EPHZYWBYYA
 601  650  BLEOKBVKWQ GKCBVLIBUT KCMWJFJAJC HLGSXIMBWX JKOFWULZWD
 651  676  SRIPOWGIZO PRQUGHNVBY BUDZED
```

TABLE 3A. FIRST DECIPHERING TABLEAU FOR SECOND-ORDER HOMOPHONIC.

```
EQUIVALENCES BETWEEN CODE NUMBERS AND SECOND ALPHABETIC SUBSTITUTION
FROM  TO  1234567890 1234567890 1234567890 1234567890 1234567890
   1   50  RLQHEFRLBF AHJXHSPBYV SUHTWQUNYZ KFRKAMLQND WUCJWVYMLW
  51  100  HMSCGPYAWF YNIXNEUOWW SVKFTCRRFX CTONBFJWOZ HTDJWLPORY
 101  150  JZWNIIKHBN LWSGNWYETR GIBZZNUBUK HESXVUXTEE GCIYPJHLAJ
 151  200  OFMFYGTIPA GJIOPQHRLV GTXTZRHQWZ DKGJDGBUWZ YGRCYBURTS
 201  250  BALZBLRMAK DWQKVBJAEX YECZNIAZYQ QEEJGMDXXS CCGSFUCDKK
 251  300  ZQWHIQBBVY VIIOPTXYJZ ILZSKKHQEU JZSALMDAAA KOLOWBKKGC
 301  350  UENXOINFPB YQKQOEXVAM PFUFXSTMWS BTNIKJUCEM UXDEETDLVM
 351  400  CTXJVTFIFE MBUJHQVQGQ JJDCFWKADO HYWNZVCVJE IPDXOSZZXP
 401  450  JMTKIOZRSC VKIPUFRPFL LHGOJITHIB MFUTNXTEPM ALQBYEHSRL
 451  500  HPCJHXPYUS WTYHQMBKWA COCVMAPDHS XXNXYVTRZR ARBCRBXOVV
 501  550  GAPCGRSULD NRXRNWPOEE IDYQSLABIY AFFVKMHROF ZYZYSOEXIA
 551  600  CSLDOMBGNJ IVDQDSGDEJ GGFPMQDPQK HTFGKWBLLH YUDPUGDLHC
 601  650  ZRNSOWCFVP ZINANCVQJN KPXQUUTIES WDMDGTGKMZ GVCTCLLJPO
 651  676  OCNMUDNPFV AOEVRBNMMO UAMZRS
```

TABLE 3B. SECOND DECIPHERING TABLEAU FOR SECOND-ORDER HOMOPHONIC.

computer-assisted enciphering and deciphering processes. But we doubt
whether a human analyst could effectively handle the complex table look-
ups required in higher than second-order homophonics. We also observe

parenthetically that such systems can be made arbitrarily secure, very much like their more elegant counterpart in the binary data communications world. Even second-order homophonics lead the cryptanalyst to search for one among 676! ($\sim 1.88 \times 10^{1621}$) matrices.

3. THE BEALE CIPHERS AND SECOND-ORDER HOMOPHONICS

Using formal logic, it is impossible to prove the negative of a proposition. Thus we will always have to face the hoax alternative as long as the riddle of the Beale ciphers remains unresolved. Some future discovery might lead to a successful decoding of the B1 or B3 codes. Or we might complete a penetrating analysis of their structure, permitting deductively the making of definitive statements about the encoding methodology. We do not concur with Gillogly's observation that the *cleartext* string ABFDEFGHIIJKLMMNOHPP is strong evidence for the hoax theory. On the contrary, we believe it to be a signal, indicating that the (authorized and informed) recipient of the message is on the right track. Although hard evidence is lacking, we explore these conclusions below.

First, let us reject the hypothesis that the Beale ciphers are second-order homophonics. The evidence is against such an assumption. The range of numbers in all three ciphers is far below the level required for a full homophonic encoding of the second or higher order. It is also readily seen that the complexity arising from second-order homophonics must obtain for any other second-order, dual-encoding scheme. Furthermore, the few large numbers occurring in B1 and B3 are in dispute. Many analysts suggest the four-digit numbers are copy errors of pairs of two-digit numbers, or concatenated single and three-digit numbers.

Further, we note once more the matter of errors in the "known" solution to B2. They are all of the clerical type, well-known to accountants and auditors, who have made extensive studies of miscounts-by-one, nine, or eleven, and of transpositions, all resulting from the vagaries of the decimal system. We adhere to our previously stated conviction that TJB was an amateur, unlikely to perform feats of cryptology a hundred years ahead of their time. These errors could be the result of forcefully fitting a second-order encoding scheme with a sparse matrix, resulting from the choice of two texts. Yet on balance the number pattern does not support this hypothesis.

Nevertheless, there is still the matter of Gillogly's string ABFDEF-GHIIJKLMMNOHPP and his assertion that it is evidence for the hoax theory. We believe otherwise. We concur that it is not an accident. But, we suggest that it is a *signal* indicating some relationship between B1 and the DOI. But what might be this relationship? Could it be an attempt, ever so fragile, to confirm something about the construction of the enciphering scheme to the authorized recipient of the message? Might it, in fact, not be a feeble attempt at second-order homophonic encoding, requiring "adjustment" of the alphabetic sequence and make it surface only when one of the two correct documents is used in the decoding process?

We have performed some experiments with this approach to obtain a typical second-order homophonic string from B2. After a few trials, we successfully recoded elements 135, 138, 30, 31, 62, 67, 41, 85, 63, 10, 106 which occupy positions 305 to 315 within the B2 list of 763 numbers. We replaced them by the numbers 490, 79, 304, 263, 71, 793, 521, 7, 464, 566, 57 retaining the *overt* B2 cleartext "DEPOSITEDNO," yet superimposing a second-order solution AACDEFGTIJL upon them with the sequentially numbered letters of the same DOI as key text. Of course, we would have liked to achieve ABCDEFGHIJK but eight out of eleven is not all that bad. Furthermore, the "T" instead of the "H" is a near miss since T=7 is adjacent to H=8. Thus we have only one real "error." With a more sustained effort we could probably achieve even longer and better "signal" strings of this type. But we also note that our replacement elements are much larger than the original numbers by an average of 277. By contrast, the 20 B1 elements which make up the Gillogly string ABFDEFGHIIJKLMMNOHPP are not significantly different from other B1 elements. They have a *local* average of 169 which is practically "on target" for the overall B1 average of 162 shown in Table II of [6]. Nevertheless, we still feel that a superimposed string of this type could be constructed without altering appreciably the characteristic signature of the original B2 code.

Still another explanation, in addition to the doodle hypothesis proffered by Gillogly, is that the author enciphered most of B1 with the help of one document (and methodology), but that he enciphered this signal portion of twenty letters differently, say, with first letters from the numbered words of the DOI, to yield a break in the middle of his B1 message. In that case, perhaps, only a few first and last letters of the signal code are doubly enciphered, leaving a center portion of unknown size (but considerably shorter than 20 letters) to serve no other useful purpose.

In summary, we restate our belief that B1 and B3 are legitimate ciphers and not doodles, or what we shall now call a hoax of the first kind. We believe that they do indeed contain some intelligence and will be deciphered someday, perhaps by a method similar to that developed by Peleg and Rosenfeld. Only then will we know whether they are a hoax of the second kind, containing no information about the treasure. Further, we do not believe that B2 is a higher-order homophonic, nor is it multiply enciphered in any other way. Its only solution, we believe, is "IHAVE-DEPOSITED . . . ."

Finally, we believe that successful deciphering of B1, at least, can only be accomplished in some way with the Declaration of Independence and that the author (TJB?) intended to indicate this fact by a clue which should have been noted long ago. We are grateful to Gillogly for bringing this matter to public attention. We had known about it for some years but had been constrained from discussing it by a promise made to another cryptanalyst. Now, no longer bound by this promise, we asked several experts whether they had spotted this "signal." But none had! Which goes to show something or other about the astuteness of cryptographic analysts . . .

4. SECOND-ORDER HOMOPHONIC EXAMPLE

Finally, we give a complete example of a second-order homophonic. For our enciphering and deciphering matrix we have chosen to use Table 1. As a consequence all the tools shown in Tables 2 and 3 will facilitate efficient deciphering of the second-order homophonic in Table 4. The cipher has 763 elements, some of which are repeated. But even a casual examination shows clearly that its signature differs fundamentally from that of the "real" Beale Ciphers B1, B2 and B3.

Applying the tableau of Table 3A to the data of Table 4, the first cleartext is obtained: "IHAVEDEPOSITED . . . NODIFFICULTY-WILLBEHADINFINDINGIT." See Table 5. The astute reader has probably surmised that a cipher with 763 entries is likely to be the well-known cleartext of the much-maligned Beale Cipher Number Two. We shall leave the deciphering of Table 4 with the second tableau of Table 3B as an "exercise for the readers." We will tell, however, that the plaintext of the second message begins with "THEVAULTISLOCATED . . ." The entirety of this message came to us in the form of a private communication [10].

Because the second message has fewer letters than B2, we padded it in the manner suggested by Gillogly. Our error-free padding string "ABCDE . . . XYZ" was repeatedly added to yield two messages of equal length before we started the second-order homophonic enciphering process.

TABLE 4. SECOND-ORDER HOMOPHONIC MATRIX FOR TWO MESSAGES.

```
IHAVEDEPOS ITEDINTHEC OUNTYOFBED FORDABOUTF OURMILESFR
OMBUFORDSI NANEXCAVAT IONORVAULT SIXFEETBEL OWTHESURFA
CEOFTHEGRO UNDTHEFOLL OWINGARTIC LESBELONGI NGJOINTLYT
OTHEPARTIE SWHOSENAME SAREGIVENI NNUMBERTHR EEHEREWITH
THEFIRSTDE POSITCONSI STEDOFTENH UNDREDANDF OURTEENPOU
NDSCFGOLDA NDTHIRTYEI GHTHUNDRED ANDTWELVEP OUNDSOFSIL
VERDEPOSIT EDNOVEIGHT EENNINETEE NTHESECOND WASMADEDEC
EIGHTEENTW ENTYONEAND CONSISTEDO FNINETEENH UNDREDANDS
EVENPOUNDS OFGOLDANDT WELVEHUNDR EDANDEIGHT YEIGHTOFSI
LVERALSOJE WELSOBTAIN EDINSTLOUI SINEXCHANG ETOSAVETRA
NSPORTATIO NANDVALUED ATTHIRTEEN THOUSANDDO LLARSTHEAB
OVEISSECUR ELYPACKEDI NIRONPOTSW ITHIRONCOV ERSTHEVAUL
TISROUGHLY LINEDWITHS TONEANDTHE VESSELSRES TONSOLIDST
ONEANDAREC OVEREDWITH OTHERSPAPE RNUMBERONE DESCRIBEST
HEEXACTLOC ALITYOFTHE VAULTSOTHA TNODIFFICU LTYWILLBEH
ADINFINDIN GIT
```

Table 5. Message Deciphered with First Tableau.

All work was done most efficiently with the assistance of a FORTRAN program, running flawlessly (?) on our Univac computer system. (Copies of the program will be made available to interested parties, provided we do not receive an avalanche of such requests.) Because of the manner in which FORTRAN operates, leading zeros are suppressed. For convenient operational use, one would make all cipher equivalents of equal length (three digits in this example). So doing has two advantages: the cipher may be transmitted unambiguously in five-digit groups, and the analyst has no way of knowing what order homophonic he is dealing with, assuming that he identifies it as a homophonic cipher in the first place.

REFERENCES

1. Gillogly, James J. (1980), The Beale Cipher: A Dissenting Opinion. *Cryptologia*, 4:116–119.
2. Mellen, Greg (1972), To Hoax or Not to Hoax? Is that the Question? *Proceedings of the (First) Beale Cipher Symposium* (a):77–85.
3. Mellen, Greg (1979), The Beale Cyphers: A Word from the Devil's Advocate. *Proceedings of the Second Beale Cipher Symposium* (a):97–103.
4. Peleg, Shmuel, and Azriel Rosenfeld (1979), Breaking Substitution Ciphers Using a Relaxation Algorithm. *Communications of the ACM*, 22:598–605.
5. Kahn, David (1967), *The Codebreakers*. New York: Macmillan.
6. Hammer, Carl (1971), Signature Simulation and Certain Cryptographic Codes. *Communications of the ACM*, 14:3–14.
7. Hammer, Carl (1979), How Did TJB Encode B2? *Cryptologia*. 3:9–15.

452

8. Swindler, William F. (1900), *Magna Carta—Legend and Legacy.* New York: Bobbs.

9. Diffie, Whitfield, and Martin E. Hellman (1979), Privacy and Authentication: An Introduction to Cryptography. *Proceedings of the IEEE,* 67:397–427.

10. Schoonrok, Peter (1980), Private Communication. Houlton, ME 04730.

(a) Available from the Beale Cypher Association, P.O. Box 216, Medfield, MA 02052.

Graphic Solution of a Linear Transformation Cipher
by Greg Mellen

INTRODUCTION

The linear transformation cipher, known also as the matrix cipher, was first described in 1929 by Lester S. Hill, a mathematician at Hunter College. [1] The system appears to have evolved in conjunction with the development by Hill and Louis Weiner of a mechanical cryptograph based upon modulus arithmetic. [2] Sinkov "popularized" the system in 1968. [3] Prior to that, the cipher was the subject of several articles in the mathematical journals. [4,5,6,7]

Hence, some of the analysis to follow has appeared before in different guise. My present purpose is to present a different perspective of the cipher, one which I think gives a better understanding of the structure of the system than a purely algebraic approach, and one which I think allows faster entry into the system for the cryptanalyst.

MECHANICS OF THE SYSTEM

The linear transformation cipher as described by Sinkov uses two-square matrices for enciphering and deciphering. The enciphering matrix is "valid" if (a) its determinant is an odd number other than 13 or its multiples, and (b) the elements of its inverse are integers. Under these conditions the inverse of the enciphering matrix is the deciphering matrix, serving to undo the work of the first.

If all that sounds very mathematical, it's because I'm paraphrasing

From *Cryptologia*, Vol. 5, No. 1, Jan. 1981.

Sinkov. It is necessary background information. I plan to leave this Algebresian tunnel for the Euclidean fields by the first exit in order to show the different perspective mentioned above.

In his examples, Sinkov observes these conventions:

1. Both plaintext (*pt*) and ciphertext (*ct*) alphabets are straight standard. The letters are given their usual numerical equivalents: A = 1, B = 2, Z = 26 = 0.

2. All arithmetic is performed modulo 26. That is, if any operation results in a number larger than 25 (or less than zero), a suitable multiple of 26 is subtracted from it (or added to it) in order to bring the result within the alphabet range of 0 to 25. Thus, 83 = (83 −78) = 5 = E; −319 = (−319 + 338) = 19 = S.

Changing the conventions (by using mixed *pt* and *ct* alphabets, for example) may strengthen the cipher. But these changes are largely outside the present scope.

To illustrate the system, assume the following enciphering matrix:

$$\begin{bmatrix} 7 & 9 \\ 3 & 12 \end{bmatrix}$$

This two-square matrix enciphers two *pt* characters at a time. (In general, an *n*-square matrix enciphers *n pt* characters at a time.) Using the matrix, P_1-P_2 is converted to its cipher equivalent, C_1-C_2, by the following operations:

$$C_1 = 7P_1 + 9P_2 \text{ (mod-26)};$$
$$C_2 = 3P_1 + 12P_2 \text{ (mod-26)}.$$

To encipher PR_p, then,

$$C_1 = 7(16) + 9(18) = 274 = 14 = N;$$
$$C_2 = 3(16) + 12(18) = 264 = 4 = D.$$

To recover the plaintext, the inverse of the enciphering matrix is used. In this example, the inverse is

$$\begin{bmatrix} 18 & 19 \\ 15 & 17 \end{bmatrix}$$

To decipher ND_c, then,

$$P_1 = 18(14) + 19(4) = 326 = 16 = P;$$
$$P_2 = 15(14) + 17(4) = 278 = 18 = R.$$

I will call this enciphering matrix $|A|$ and its inverse $|A|^{-1}$, and use them for illustrative purposes throughout the next section.

THE IMPLICIT ARRAY

An enciphering matrix with the properties described above is "valid" because it guarantees the existence of a unique C_1-C_2 for every P_1-P_2. There are many invalid matrices, such that C_1-C_2 represents two different P_1-P_2 digrams and *vice versa*.

For each of the 676 possible *pt* digrams, then, matrix $|A|$ implicitly represents an array of 676 *ct* digrams. The abbreviated array is shown in Figure 1. P_1 is the leftmost column and P_2 is the topmost row. For any P_1-P_2, C_1-C_2 is found at their intersection. The array may be used for encipherment, eliminating the need for the equations and calculations involved in the original algorithm.

Similarly, there is an implicit deciphering array for $|A|^{-1}$. Its first few lines appear in Figure 2. C_1 is down the left side and C_2 is across the top.

In general, any valid n-square matrix represents an array of 26^n terms: The three-square matrix represents 26^3 (17,576) trigrams in unique *pt-ct* pairs. The five-square matrix represents 26^5 (11,881,376) pentagrams in unique *pt-ct* pairs. While it is clearly impractical to attempt to reconstruct such large arrays, nevertheless insight into their structure is an aid in the analysis of the system.

PROPERTIES OF THE ARRAY

Examination of the array of Figure 1 reveals a highly regular understructure. Sinkov (*op. cit.*, 117) describes this regularity by means of a set of scales, but I prefer to present it in a different manner.

In Figure 1, the intersections of successive P_1-P_2 points comprise an orderly $X-Y$ grid. The X coordinate of the *pt* increases by one across the rows, and the Y coordinate of the *pt* increases by 1 down the columns. The enciphering matrix, in this case $|A|$, maps *ct* space onto this *pt* space point for point in accordance with the elements of $|A|$. It is worthwhile to study this mapping process in some detail.

The substitute for AA_p is PO_c. P ($= 16$) is the sum of the top row of $|A|$, $7 + 9$. O ($= 15$) is the sum of the second row of $|A|$, $3 + 12$. In

	A	B	C	D	E	F	G	H	I	J	K	L	M	N	O	P	Q	R	S	T	U	V	W	X	Y	Z
A	po	ya	hm	qy	zk	iw	ri	au	gl	ss	be	kq	tc	co	la	um	dy	mk	vw	ei	nu	wg	fs	oe	xq	gc
B	wr	fd	op	xb	qn	pz	yl	hx	qj	zv	ih	rt	af	jr	sd	bp	kb	tn	cz	ll	ux	dj	mv	vh	et	nf
C	du	mg	vs	ee	nq	wc	fo	oa	xm	qy	pk	yw	hi	qu	zq	is	re	aq	jc	so	ba	km	ty	ck	lw	ui
D	kx	tj	cv	lh	ut	df	mr	vd	ep	nb	wn	fz	ol	xx	gj	pv	yh	ht	qf	zr	id	rp	ab	jn	sz	bl
E	ra	am	jy	sk	bw	ki	tu	cq	ls	ue	dq	mc	vo	ea	nm	wy	fk	ow	xi	qu	pa	ys	he	aq	zc	io

FIGURE 1. ENCIPHERING ARRAY.

	A	B	C	D	E	F	G	H	I	J	K	L	M	N	O	P	Q	R	S	T	U	V	W	X	Y
A	kf	dv	vn	pe	iv	bm	ud	nu	gl	zc	st	lk	eb	ws	qj	ja	cr	vi	oz	hq	ah	ty	mp	fg	yw	ro
B	cu	vl	oc	ht	ak	tb	ms	fj	ya	rr	ki	dz	vq	ph	iy	bp	uq	nw	go	zf	sv	ln	ee	wv	qm	jd
C	uj	na	gr	zi	sz	lq	eh	wy	qp	jg	cw	vo	of	hv	an	te	mv	fm	yd	ru	kl	dc	vt	pk	ib	bs
D	my	fp	yg	rw	ko	df	vv	pn	ie	bv	um	nd	gu	zl	sc	lt	ek	wb	qs	jj	ca	vr	oi	hz	aq	th
E	en	we	qv	jm	cd	vu	ol	hc	at	tk	mb	fs	yj	ra	kr	di	vz	pq	ih	by	up	ng	qw	zo	sf	lv

FIGURE 2. DECIPHERING ARRAY.

general, for any enciphering matrix, the *ct* equivalent of $AA \ldots A_p$ is

C_1 = sum of first row;
C_2 = sum of second row;

. . .

C_n = sum of *n*th row.

Again, for any enciphering matrix, the *ct* equivalent of $ZZ \ldots Z_p$ is ZZ $\ldots Z_c$, since in the enciphering equations all terms are multiplied by zero.

For the sake of generalization, replace the elements of $|A|$ with the generic symbols, a_{11}, a_{12}, A_{21}, and A_{22}. Then, for any two-square matrix, the *ct* equivalent of AZ_p is a_{11}, a_{21}—since the second term of the enciphering equations is multiplied by zero in each case. (Thus, in Figure 1, AZ_p is GC_c, or 7,3.) By similar reasoning, the *ct* equivalent for ZA_p is a_{12}, a_{22}.

In the first row of Figure 1, C_1 progresses from left to right by the sequence P-Y-H-Q- . . . , or 16-25-8-17 . . . This is decimation 9 of the alphabet and is determined by element a_{12} of $|A|$. And what is true of the first row is true of all rows: C_1 progresses from left to right by decimation 9.

C_2 progresses from left to right in each row by decimation 12, as determined by element a_{22} of $|A|$.

With respect to the columns, C_1 progresses vertically by decimation 7, as determined by element a_{11}. C_2 progresses vertically by decimation 3, from element a_{21}. The full mapping function of matrix $|A|$ is presented in Table 1.

TABLE 1. MAPPING FUNCTION OF MATRIX $|A|$.

Letter	Direction*	Decimation	Determined by Element
C_1	$+Y$	9	a_{12}
	$+Y$	7	a_{11}
C_2	$+X$	12	a_{22}
	$+Y$	3	a_{21}

*"+" is defined as motion from left to right or from top to bottom of the array.

Inspection of Figure 2 shows that the array for converting ct to pt has the same structure, except that the elements of $|A|^{-1}$ control the decimations. The mapping function is summarized graphically in Figure 3, where it is generalized for all two-square enciphering and deciphering matrices.

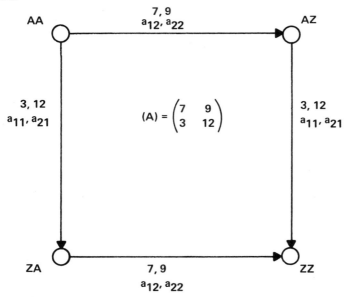

FIGURE 3. STRUCTURE OF THE TWO-SQUARE ARRAY.

APPLICATION TO CRYPTANALYSIS

The parity of the elements of matrix $|A|$ may be represented thus:

$$\begin{bmatrix} O & O \\ O & E \end{bmatrix}$$

where O is odd and E is even. This pattern is reflected in a unique and characteristic parity pattern in the *ct* digram array (Figure 1). The pattern is as follows:

	O	E	O	E	O	E . . .
O	eo	oo	eo	oo	eo	oo . . .
E	oe	ee	oe	ee	oe	ee . . .

This enables one to predict that the *pt* digram *IN*, which has a parity of *OE*, will be reflected in the *ct* by a digram having parity *OO*.

There are 16 possible patterns for a two-square matrix. Of these, however, only six yield valid enciphering matrices: those with integer inverses and odd-integer determinants not equal to 13 or its multiples. Figure 4 shows the six valid patterns and their resulting transformations in the enciphering arrays. (For convenience, I identify the six matrix types as A through F respectively.)

Type A: $\begin{bmatrix} O & O \\ O & E \end{bmatrix}$ Type B: $\begin{bmatrix} O & O \\ E & O \end{bmatrix}$ Type C: $\begin{bmatrix} O & E \\ O & O \end{bmatrix}$

pt	ct		pt	ct		pt	ct
OO >	EO		OO >	EO		OO >	OE
OE	OO		OE	OE		OE	OO
EO	OE		EO	OO		EO	EO
EE	EE		EE	EE		EE	EE

Type D: $\begin{bmatrix} E & O \\ O & O \end{bmatrix}$ Type E: $\begin{bmatrix} E & O \\ O & E \end{bmatrix}$ Type F: $\begin{bmatrix} O & E \\ E & O \end{bmatrix}$

pt	ct		pt	ct		pt	ct
OO >	OE		OO >	OO		OO >	OO
OE	EO		OE	EO		OE	OE
EO	OO		EO	OE		EO	EO
EE	EE		EE	EE		EE	EE

FIGURE 4. VALID MATRICES AND THEIR PARITY TRANSFORMS.

Note that the *EE* digram is invariant under all conditions. Note also that the Type F matrix reproduces the parity of the *pt* in the *ct*; its inverse, the deciphering matrix, must therefore also be Type F. The complete table of correspondence is as follows:

Enciphering Matrix	Deciphering Matrix
A	D
B	B
C	C
D	A
E	E
F	F

Problem 1 of the Cryptanalyst's Corner in the January 1978 *Cryptologia* is a cipher of the kind under discussion. I reproduce it below, and indicate the parity of the *ct* digrams by the numbers 1 *(OO)*, 2 *(OE)*, 3 *(EO)*, and 4 *(EE)*:

2	3	1	1	1	2	4	1	3	1	1	2	2
QH	DI	WQ	QQ	EI	WF	RL	IY	LU	IO	WQ	UV	CN

2	4	2	3	3	4	2	4	2	3	3	1
QD	HV	SN	TQ	VY	RL	EP	RV	MN	DE	RM	OA

2	4	1	1	3	4	3	3	1	2	4	1	2
GT	NF	QQ	GW	BS	TJ	XC	RI	WQ	UH	PB	QM	EX

2	4	2	4	1	1	3	2	1	2	1	2
MT	XH	WF	XJ	SA	CO	ZA	SP	KG	SP	AO	YV

3	3	2	4	3	3	1	1
NS	JQ	KJ	XH	ZU	PA	CA	AI

SUBMARINE and OBSERVING are given as probable words. Table 2 below shows the *ct* appearance of SUBMARINE in its 12 possible *ct* transformations:

TABLE 2. CT PATTERNS OF SUBMARINE.

Matrix Type	SU	BM	AR	IN	E-	-S	UB	MA	RI	NE
A	3	2	1	1		1	3	2	2
B	3	1	2	2		2	3	1	1
C	2	3	1	1		1	2	3	3
D	2	1	3	3		3	2	1	1
E	1	2	3	3		3	1	2	2
F	1	3	2	2		2	1	3	3

If SUBMARINE is, in fact, in the message, one of these 12 parity patterns must appear in the *ct*. Examination shows only 2311, which occurs at the very beginning. The probable word is now placed; the enciphering matrix is Type C, and the deciphering matrix is also Type C.

The following identities are also known: $QH_c = SU_p$; $DI_c = BM_p$; $WQ_c = AR_p$, and $QQ_c = IN_p$. These are entered on the skeleton of a deciphering array (circled entries in Figure 5). C_1 is the left column of the array and C_2 is the top row. The point $ZZ_c = ZZ_p$ may also be entered, always a known point.

In Figure 5, DI_c progresses to WQ_c by decimations 19, 8; at the same time BM_p progresses to AR_p by decimations 25, 5. These two points define a line on the *pt-ct* plane. To discover what other points in the plane are intersected by this line, both *ct* and *pt* are extended by completing their respective decimations as shown below (columns read from top to bottom and left to right):

ct	pt		ct	pt		ct	pt
DI	BM		SC	SF		HW	JY
WQ	AR		LK	RK		AE	ID
PY	ZW		ES	QP		TM	HI
IG	YB		XA	PU		MU	GN
BO	XG		QI	OZ		FC	FS
UW	WL		JQ	NE		YK	EX
NE	VQ		CY	MJ		RS	DC
GM	UV		VG	LO		KA	CH
ZU	TA		OO	KT		DI	BM

These values are added to the deciphering array (underscored in Figure 5). This results in a pair of adjacent *pt* digrams, namely, $QH_c = SU_p$ and $QI_c = OZ_p$. From this pair, one may determine that the *pt* progresses in the $+X$ direction by decimations 22, 5 ($= a_{12}, a_{22}$ of the deciphering matrix). All rows of the array may now be completed, and it will be seen that the *pt* progresses in the $+Y$ direction by decimations 3, 5 ($= a_{11}, a_{21}$ of the deciphering matrix). Obviously, it is not necessary to complete the array; having determined the elements of the deciphering matrix, one may choose to use the algebraic equations to complete the process and read: *SUBMARINERS OFTEN DISPARAGE . . .*

A SECOND EXAMPLE

A probable word is not always available. But since $ZZ_c = ZZ_p$ is a constant, one may run trial "lines" between that point and some assumed point, recover the other *ct-pt* points on the line, and see if acceptable new equivalences emerge in the *ct*.

The identity most likely to suggest itself is the *ct* equivalent for TH_p. TH_p is a Type 4 (*EE*) digram and certain to be represented in the

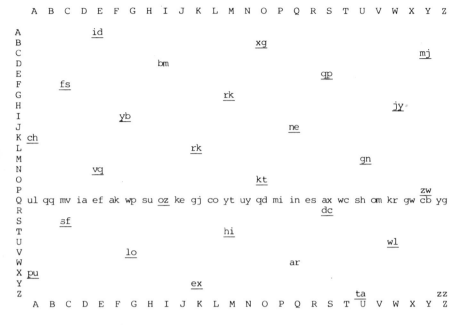

FIGURE 5. DECIPHERING ARRAY FOR CRYPTANALYST'S CORNER PROBLEM.

ct by some other Type 4 digram. But the line between TH_p and ZZ_p connects two Type 4 points by decimations 6, 18. Since both decimations are even, only 11 other *pt* points lie on that line:

TH	RB	PV	NP
ZZ	XT	VN	TH
FR	DL	BF	
LJ	JD	HX	

Except perhaps for *FR*, *RB*, and *DL*, these *pt* digrams are either infrequent or impossible. A better tactic is to assume an identity for IN_p. As will be shown below, this line subsumes all points on the *TH-ZZ* line, but also contains the high-frequency *pt* digrams *IN*, *OF*, and *GH*. (A second line with good cryptanalytic potential is *ER-ZZ*, which in addition to *ER* also intersects *FF*, *AN*, *LL*, *RR*, *NN*, *IV*, and *TT*. Note also that both *IN* and *ER* are Type 2 (*OE*) digrams and will necessarily be represented by the same tpe of *ct* digram, though not necessarily Type 2. If either *ER* or *IN* can be identified, the other may be recovered from a much narrower set of possibilities.)

The following message is available for examination (*ct* parity types above the digrams):

| 1 | 1 | 3 | 1 | 2 | 4 | 4 | 1 | 2 | 1 | 1 | 4 | 2 | 3 | 1 | 1 | 2 |

GM CO BU OW OF YR HNOW AH EKOW DZ OJ XI SC CM UP

| 1 | 2 | 3 | 1 | 1 | 1 | 1 |

WS UT NQ EKOW AK OC

In a longer message, an attack using frequency count by parity type (see Appendix A) might enable us to restore the parity of the *pt*. That would be a substantial help in locating common words. But this tactic is not useful here.

After several false starts, IN_p is tried against GM_c at the start of the message. The *IN-ZZ* line then appears as follows:

ct	pt	ct	pt	ct	pt	ct	pt
GM	IN*	JZ	XT	MM	MZ	PZ	BF
ZZ	ZZ	CM	OF*	FZ	DL	IM	SR
SM	QL	VZ	FR	YM	UX	BZ	JD
LZ	HX	OM	WD	RZ	LJ	UM	AP
EM	YJ	HX	NP	KM	CV	NZ	RB
XZ	PV	AM	FB	DZ	TH*	GM	IN
QM	GH	TZ	VN	WM	KT		

The pairs denoted by asterisks correspond to digrams in the *ct* and are, moreover, very acceptable. Equally important, no "impossible" *pt* has been found. The line is tentatively accepted and its points are entered on a trial deciphering array (circled entries in Figure 6).

Inspection shows that C_2 proceeds in the $+Y$ direction by decimation 13 (note that in the listing above, C_2 alternately equals M and Z). As a result, the partial array contains two half-filled columns which reveal that P_1 proceeds in the $+Y$ direction by either decimation 2 or 15. That is, under C_2, the P_1 sequence is either B-D-F-H-J- ... or B-Q-F-U-J ... Similarly the $+Y$ decimation of P_2 is either 5 (E-J-O-T-Y- ...) or 18 (E-W-O-G-Y ...).

There are thus four potential combinations for the decimations of P_1-P_2. Of these combinatioins, 2, 18 is invalid because it would repeat after 13 steps producing two *ct* digrams for each *pt* digram. The other three possibilities are 2, 15; 15, 5 and 15, 18. In other circumstances, depending upon the cipher in hand, it might be expedient to try all three. In this case, it is impossible to do so because no cipher digram other than the assumed GM_c ends in M or Z.

It is necessary to find a third point in the arrày, not on the *IN-ZZ* line, in order to establish the plane. OW_c occurs three times in the

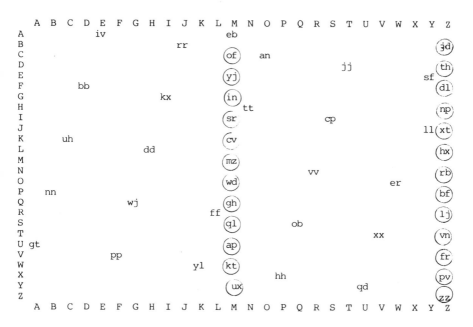

FIGURE 6. DECIPHERING ARRAY FOR SHORT MESSAGE.

message and is likely a high-frequency *pt* digram. It is not TH_p, first because OW_c is not a Type 4 digram and second, TH_p has already tentatively been identified as DZ_c. Nor does OW_c represent RE_p. RE_p is Type 3 (*EO*), whereas OW_c has the same parity as GM_c and therefore represents a Type 2 *pt* digram like *IN*. Hence, $OW_c = ER_p$ is a reasonable assumption. Extending the *ER-ZZ* line, one obtains:

ct	pt	ct	pt	ct	pt	ct	pt
OW	ER*	NR	VV	MM	MZ	LH	DD
ZZ	ZZ	YU	QD	XP	HH	WK	YL
KC	UH	JX	LL	IS	CP	HN	TT*
VF	PP	UA	GT	TV	XX	SQ	OB
GI	KX	FD	BB	EY	SF	DT	JJ
RL	FF	QG	WJ	PB	NN	OW	ER
CO	AN*	BJ	RR	AE	IV		

The pairs marked with asterisks correspond to *ct* digrams in the message, which now appears as follows:

GM CO BU OW OF YR HN OW AH EK OW DZ
i n a n   e r   t t e r   e r   t h

OJ XI SC   CM UP WS UT NQ EK   OW AK OC
        o f   e r

The points of the *ER-ZZ* line are entered on the deciphering array, and it is revealed that the deciphering matrix is $|A|^{-1}$. We then read: IN ANSWER TO LETTER NUMBER THREE SIX OF FOUR DECEMBER STOP.

EXTENSION TO LARGER MATRICES

The principles of graphic solution for the two-square case apply and may be extended to the *n*-square case. An *n*-square matrix enciphers *n* *pt* characters at a time by means of the operations:

$$C_1 = a_{11}(P_1) + a_{12}(P_2) + \dots + a_{1n}(P_n);$$
$$C_2 = a_{21}(P_1) + a_{22}(P_2) + \dots + a_{2n}(P_n);$$
$$\dots$$
$$C_n = a_{n1}(P_1) + a_{n2}(P_2) + \dots + a_{nn}(P_n).$$

The inverse of the matrix is used in parallel computations for decipherment.

THREE-SQUARE CASE

A representative three-square enciphering matrix is

$$|B| = \begin{bmatrix} 7 & 3 & 2 \\ 19 & 11 & 5 \\ 4 & 1 & 15 \end{bmatrix}$$

A portion of its implicit enciphering array is shown in Figure 7. The axes and progressions of Figure 7 should be correlated with the outline of the array in Figure 8. It will be seen that Figure 7 traces three of the six possible paths on the "outside" of the array from point *AAA* to point *ZZZ*. (All arrays are closed; the concept of "outside" is helpful for visualization.)

Figure 8 also indicates the generalized rule for the three-square case. That is, elements a_{11}, a_{21}, a_{31} control the progression of C_1; elements

a_{12}, a_{22}, a_{32} control C_2, and elements a_{13}, a_{23}, a_{33} control C_3. By arbitrary convention, the progression of C_1 is along the Z axis of Figure 8; C_2 along the Y axis, and C_3 along the X axis.

The pt and ct trigrams comprise eight parity types. The following designations are used for purpose of illustration:

Type				_Type_			
1	O	O	O	5	E	O	O
2	O	O	E	6	E	O	E
3	O	E	O	7	E	E	O
4	O	E	E	8	E	E	E

The nature of the algorithm dictates that pt digrams of the same type will be translated to ct digrams of the same type. Hence, the same pattern-matching technique for locating probable words in the two-square cipher may be used for a three-square (and, in fact, for any n-square).

The Type 8 pt trigram (EEE) is invariably transformed to a Type 8 ct trigram. This is a powerful aid, since Type 8 trigrams (such as NTH) are comparatively rare, a result of the six vowels having odd parity. Appendix B shows the parity distribution of the more frequent English trigrams.

$$(B) = \begin{pmatrix} 7 & 3 & 2 \\ 19 & 11 & 5 \\ 4 & 1 & 15 \end{pmatrix}$$

		pt	ct			pt	ct			pt	ct
*+x		AAA	LIT	+y		AAA	LIT	+z		AAA	LIT
		AAB	NNI			ABA	OTU			BAA	SBX
		AAC	PSX			ACA	REV			CAA	ZUB
		...	...			...	...			...	...
		AAX	FTA			AXA	CBQ			XAA	QDH
		AAY	HYP			AYA	FMR			YAA	XWL
		AAZ	JDE			AZA	IXS			ZAA	EPP
+y		ABZ	MOF	+z		BZA	PQW	+x		ZAB	GUE
		ACZ	PZG			CZA	WJA			ZAC	IZT
		...	...			...	...			...	...
		AXZ	AWB			XZA	NSG			ZAX	YAW
		AYZ	DHC			YZA	ULK			ZAY	AFL
		AZZ	GSD			ZZA	BEO			ZAZ	CKA
+z		BZZ	NLH	+x		ZZB	DJD	+y		ZBZ	FVB
		CZZ	UEL			ZZC	FOS			ZCZ	IGC
		...	...			...	...			...	...
		XZZ	MNR			ZZX	VPV			ZXZ	TDX
		YZZ	TGV			ZZY	XUK			ZYZ	WOY
		ZZZ	ZZZ			ZZZ	ZZZ			ZZZ	ZZZ

FIGURE 7. PORTION OF THE ENCIPHERING ARRAY FOR MATRIX |B|.
*Denotes direction of current progression.

Just as three points not on the same line are required to define the two-square array, so four points not in the same plane are needed to define the three-square array. For example, the recovery of *ANA, AND, ATT,* and *ARE* would be insufficient to define the array along the *Z* axis, since these points all lie in the top external plane of Figure 8.

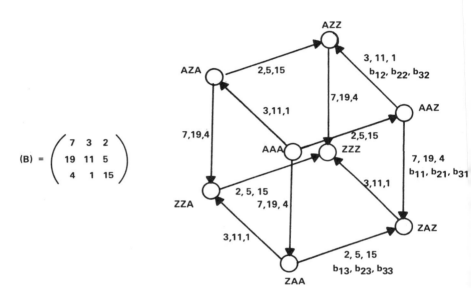

FIGURE 8. STRUCTURE OF THE THREE-SQUARE ARRAY.

A probable word, then, should be at least 11 letters long in order to enable the recovery of three points in addition to *ZZZ* ("11" because of the three possible divisions of the word into trigrams). The following message is available for examination:

```
3    1    3    1    6    6    8    1    1    7    1    1    3
GXM WSO IRQ OWO FAY FKE NJH ESW KIA FPA AKG GIQ ILM
1    2
QIE QKN
```

The message is thought to contain the words: FIFTH BATTALION. There are three possible *pt* parity representations:

```
  6    8    4    3
 FIF  THB  ATT  ALI  ON-

       8    6    6    2
 -FI  FTH  BAT  TAL  ION

       4    7    7    5
 --F  IFT  HBA  TTA  LIO  N--
```

Space prohibits listing the transformations of *pt* parity under the various classes of valid matrices. (Of the 512 possible parity patterns, only 168 may be used to construct valid matrices.) However, the list is not necessary in this instance, for the patterns are sufficiently different from one another to enable them to be distinguished: Two have Type 8 trigrams, which will be Type 8 in the cipher. Of these, one has a doubled parity type. The third pattern lacks Type 8 but also has a double. Isomorphism (or the lack of it) can be used to place the word.

Inspection shows that the words can be in one place only:

```
  6    8    1    1    7
 FKE  NJH  ESW  KIA  FPA
 ?fi  fth  bat  tal  ion
  ?    8    6    6    2
```

From these data it is possible to recover the entire three-square array. (It is, of course, easier simply to recover the elements of the deciphering matrix and to use the equations.)

The array of Figure 8 may be considered as a stack of 26 parallel planes. The top plane contains the 676 points bounded by *pt AAA-AZA-AZZ-AAZ*. The second plane contains the 676 points bounded by *BAA-BZA-BZZ-BAZ*, and so forth.

The deciphering array has exactly the same structure. Four points in the deciphering array can be identified with their *pt* equivalents, as shown above. These points taken three at a time define four nonparallel planes which in turn specify the deciphering array. The same four points taken two at a time define six lines which intersect the 26 parallel planes at various points and at different angles. It is faster to recover the lines than to recover the nonparallel planes. Line recovery is the same as in the two-square case: Both *ct* and *pt* decimations are continued until the line reenters upon itself. The process is shown in abbreviated form in Figure 9.

ct	pt	ct	pt	ct	pt	ct	pt	ct	pt	ct	pt
NJH	FTH	NJH	FTH	NJH	FTH	ESW	BAT	ESW	BAT	KIA	TAL
ESW	BAT	KIA	TAL	FPA	ION	KIA	TAL	FPA	ION	FPA	ION
VBL	XHF	HHT	HHP	XVT	LJT	QYE	LAD	GME	PCH	AWA	XCP
MKA	TOR	EGM	VOT	PBM	OEZ	WOI	DAV	HJI	WQB	VDA	MQR
DTP	PVD	BFF	JVX	HHF	RZF	CEM	VAN	IGM	DEV	QKA	BET
UCE	LCP	YEY	XCB	ZNY	UUL	IUQ	NAF	JDQ	KSP	LRA	QSV
...	...	...	...	...	...	...	...	...	...	...	...
WAS	JMV	QKO	RMD	VDO	CYB	YCS	JAB	DVS	UMZ	PBA	EMJ
NJH	FTH	NJH	FTH	NJH	FTH	ESW	BAT	ESW	BAT	KIA	TAL

FIGURE 9. GENERATION OF TRIGRAM LINES.

From Figure 9: $HHT_c = HHP_p$; $HHF_c = RZF_p$, and $HJI_c = WQB_p$. Using these points, the H plane of the deciphering array, parallel to the Z-axis, can be reconstructed. Reference to an adjacent point on the parallel G or I plane then leads to the recovery of the three orthogonal X-Y-Z decimation sequences. The deciphering matrix is seen to be $|B|^{-1}$, and the message reads: EVENING REPORT FOR FIFTH BATTALION. NOTHING TO REPORT.

FIVE-SQUARE CASE

The five-square case is the largest which can be illustrated easily. The principles, though, apply to any n-square.

Figure 10 represents the "outside" points of the closed array implicit in a five-square matrix. Geometricians may recognize the figure as a five-space hypercube having five orthogonal axes as follows:

AAAAA-AAAAZ
AAAAA-AAAZA
AAAAA-AAZAA
AAAAA-AZAAA
AAAAA-ZAAAA

Arrows and numbers are shown for points $AAAAA$ and $AAAZZ$. The arrow indicates the progression of an axis from A to Z; the number specifies the matrix column which governs that progression. For example, as point $AAAZZ$ progresses to $AABZZ$, $AACZZ$, . . . , $AAZZZ$, the five decimations starting from the left are controlled by c_{13}, c_{23}, c_{33}, c_{43}, and c_{53}, respectively, from any five-square matrix $|c|$. Space on the illustration does not permit showing all arrows and column numbers, but the interested reader may easily derive them. The interested reader may also wish to apply the principles demonstrated in this paper to Problem 4 of Appendix C.

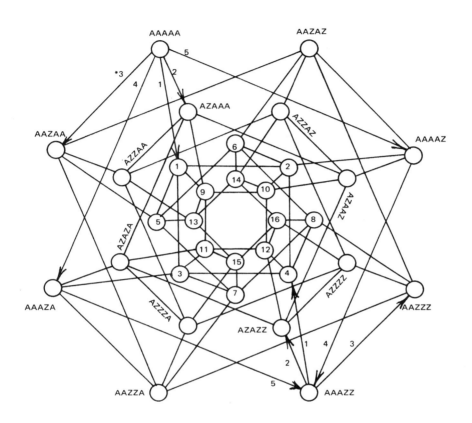

IDENTIFICATION OF NUMBERED POINTS:

1 – ZAAAA	5 – ZAZAA	9 – ZZAAA	13 – ZZZAA
2 – ZAAAZ	6 – ZAZAZ	10 – ZZAAZ	14 – ZZZAZ
3 – ZAAZA	7 – ZAZZA	11 – ZZAZA	15 – ZZZZA
4 – ZAAZZ	8 – ZAZZZ	12 – ZZAZZ	16 – ZZZZZ

*MATRIX COLUMN NUMBER

FIGURE 10. STRUCTURE OF THE FIVE-SQUARE ARRAY.

REFERENCES

1.   L. S. Hill, Cryptography in an Algebraic Alphabet, *American Math. Monthly,* 36 (1929), 306–312.
2.   U.S. Patent 1,845,947.

3.   Abraham Sinkov, *Elementary Cryptanalysis: A Mathematical Approach,* New York: Random House (1968), 115–141.

4.   Jack Levine, Variable Matrix Substitution in Algebraic Cryptography, *American Math. Monthly,* 65 (1958), 170–179.

5.   *Idem,* Some Elementary Cryptanalysis of Algebraic Cryptography, *American Math. Monthly,* 68 (1961), 411–418.

6.   *Idem,* Some Applications of High-Speed Computers to the Case n = 2 of Algebraic Cryptography, *Mathematics of Computation,* 15 (1961), 254–260.

7.   *Idem,* Analysis of the Case n = 3 in Algebraic Cryptography with Involutory Key-Matrix and Known Alphabet, *J. fuer die reine und Angewandte Mathematik,* 213 (1963), 1–30.

APPENDIX A: DIGRAMS BY PARITY TYPE IN ORDER OF FREQUENCY*

1	F	2	F	3	F	4	F
Type:							
ES	108	EN	222	RE	196	NT	164
SE	98	ER	174	TE	142	TH	156
		ON	154	NE	114	ND	104
		IN	150	VE	114		
		AN	128	TO	100		
		OR	128				
		ST	126				
		ED	120				
†	206		1202		666		424
EE	84	AT	94	TI	90	RT	84
CO	82	AR	88	TY	82	HT	56
IO	82	AS	82	FO	80		
OU	74	ET	74	FI	78		
MA	72	AL	64	RA	78		
EA	70	UR	62	LE	74		
IS	70	EL	58	TW	72		
SI	68			DE	66		
CE	64			HI	66		
EC	64			DA	64		
				RS	62		
				NI	60		
				RI	60		
				LA	56		
				RO	56		
				TA	56		

§	936		1724		1766		564
1	F	2	F	3	F	4	F
Type:							
EI	54	AD	54	DI	54	LL	54
ME	52	IR	54	NE	54	TT	38
OM	50	IT	54	NA	52	PR	36
SA	48	SH	52	NS	48	HR	34
IC	44	IV	50	PE	46	RD	34
WE	44	OF	50	HA	40	TR	34
CA	40	OP	50	HE	40	DT	30
SS	38	IL	46	HO	40	PL	26
IG	38	UN	42	LI	40	RP	26
WO	38	EP	40	NC	38		
AI	34	EV	40	TS	38		
QU	30	GH	40	BE	36		
SO	30	OL	38	NO	36		
AC	28	OT	38	PO	34		
AM	28	EF	36	DO	32		
EM	28	IX	30	PA	28		
GE	28	YT	30	DS	26		
OS	28	CH	28	LO	26		
SC	26	CT	28				
WI	26						
MM	26						
AU	26						
IE	26						
¶	1746		2524		2474		876

*Adapted from Solomon Kullback, *Statistical Methods in Cryptanalysis,* Laguna Hills, CA: Aegean Park Press, reprinted 1976. Adjusted to a base of 10,000.

† 25 percent of total.

§ 50 percent of total.

¶ 75 percent of total.

APPENDIX B: 98 ENGLISH TRIGRAMS BY PARITY TYPE IN ORDER OF FREQUENCY*

1	F	2	F	3	F	4	F	5	F	6	F	7	F	8	F
Type:															
ESS	90	ION	252	ING	356	AND	284	TIO	188	FOR	191	THE	1182		
WAS	76	CON	114	ERE	173	ENT	246	HIS	130	HER	170	THA	155		
OUS	70	AIN	108	ATE	165	ILL	118	RES	125	VER	159	THI	100		
AME	61	EST	106	ATI	148	ALL	111	NCE	113	TER	157	PRO	75		
COM	61	MAN	101	ERS	135	ITH	111	REA	95	HAT	138	THO	66		
OME	60	WIT	93	EVE	111	UND	83	HOU	77	ARE	117	NTE	58		
ICA	57	ECT	83	IVE	96	ARD	69	ROM	70	TED	110	NDE	57		
	475	MEN	76	ONS	92	ORT	67	DAY	65	RED	101	PRE	57		
		OUN	75	AVE	84	STR	62	TIC	62	PER	84	TRA	54		
		AST	70	ONE	83	ART	58	LES	59	TIN	71		1804		
		EAR	69	INT	80		1209	HAS	56	DER	70				
		OUT	63	ANT	79				1040	VEN	70				
		OUR	61	STA	75					DIN	68				
		WER	61	INE	73					NOT	67				
		EEN	59	WHI	71					BUT	64				
		SAN	59	OVE	71					LAR	59				
		ICH	57	STI	68					RAT	58				
		WIL	55	ORE	65					TUR	58				
			1562	URE	63					LIN	54				
				STE	59						1738				
				ANY	58										
				ENC	56										
				WHE	55										
				ERA	54										
					2299										

Type: 1—OOO 5—EOO
2—OOE 6—EOE
3—OEO 7—EEO
4—OEE 8—EEE

* Adapted from Helen Fouche Gaines, *Cryptanalysis*, New York: Dover Publications, 1956.

APPENDIX C: PROBLEMS

Of the four problems below, the first three deal generally with cryptology. Problem 1, from a study of previous traffic, is thought to end ER_p SE_p. There is no crib for Problem 2: Solution must be found either through parity analysis or by running trial digram lines through ZZ. Problem 3 is suspected of discussing how cryptanalysts may use statistical analysis. Problem 4 is known to contain the words THE TENTH BRIGADE IS CROSSING.

Problem 1

```
WR OU ZK XI BG JG KC VP UL QW GD MG SU MV OH PL
EW ZH GJ DM UA OM TS QU TC TP KL WA
                                   er  se
```

Problem 2

```
LL HE WN GW GO VI WR RV YD EB UL LL MH IZ MX TC
CT EU YQ LL KN JH LQ UJ NB KD UO XR WN IM WS EU
OD NT FM WG OM VO ZW CK CM XX AY HU AY WU SX CX
SK NA OZ ZS CK IQ NT BM MT QA NT IQ OD TS LQ EM
RV EU ZG WX CR GW XF FM LL WN YQ GL TC VM MZ XK
UE WG JH CW QC MG CE SK GE UD VU GT DX LQ RS QO
PQ WX OZ OD CX DW CC HK EL KN MZ WX FM UH CE GW
NB EU QC UJ QJ ZW PE FM DS KW CK RT YQ QJ KD UO
MK WG GL HJ KX OU IZ HT MV EG IW WG TS EU UD CP
UG PQ OZ EM WK BC ZW DC OB FM YB FN IG KZ QE OU
HI IV MX NX RI SK QA HI SL UH FN KX OU IZ GQ PQ
WX MJ XZ SM UD BM ZS EM FL YQ IM MG OU TC VI QA
NO AZ LA FM WG OM TS ZU
```

Problem 3

```
KTI CNU KUD HZQ CGZ NZB MNG AWQ GJZ HSL  UYC ENW
PIF MFI VPU HOM GPO WCJ UWP ALG UGD KWY  MLF NXG
WQL NTA ZDN PYX SUU EHX CDA ALG OMH WRW  ODH UFS
ERC OTP YVG YTU BOL HOM NRS GXM SUS NUM  VFW OJT
DEC YVF XTU WGP EZW PXW MOU GOK ZOZ AIS  MJA LAU
YGH FVI ETU QVR BVY TPL VUN OUW VST RET  HOM JOI
HSL MOU RDU SNL XDY MHE HKY WDY WGE EVN  QUE ECS
OJQ RQJ BHS AXP PHA KQE GRL KTJ IBG UTM  UAX UCJ
```

```
IVV  WAK MXD PCK  MHO EZJ  UWP FQQ THS  UFS   UTM AUG
UFS  FFK  PEQ WBF  KNK WRG NDQ JVI  WKX BUJ   VNO PYX
CGZ  UKV  UXU ZXC  JMM UJL  YYO WKK JMM UYC   FYZ FID
ILI  OZI  SEW RSF  ESN WCJ  NYF VVR CLK  HWG  KNQ CVB
EHX  YVN  KLU RRG  HOA LOB  KER MLH ZMG UFI   SYZ ZDN
FCD  MED  TND VTR  XZK MZG  BLM UQK GFK  LGH  ZIL  OUJ
JDY  AGW ZWX GPB  UBA ATW  UCJ HPJ  SBO KAJ   CUU UWP
NEZ  UGN RIO
```

Problem 4

```
KHSJY  KVBXX BWRFK UVWIT FABMV MHZVJ WWHCZ   RJFZP
JDQEL  ZFWKZ NJUED RWATZ XMIYA HOVCA FQQBT   GBLKS
AFQJG  AZRBR YIQXI  FGYNH PKKWB PQBGT OETBE   EFCJH
```

The Automated Cryptanalysis of
Substitution Ciphers
by John M. Carroll and Steve Martin

ABSTRACT: Expert systems programmed in artificial intelligence languages can break simple substitution ciphers by capturing and employing knowledge about the relative frequencies of single letters and certain combinations of letters in certain positions. These techniques can be extended to fixed-key polyalphabetic ciphers after using regression analysis to separate out the segments of text enciphered in each component alphabet.

INTRODUCTION

Our interest in machine cryptanalysis arose out of a graduate course in Cryptography and Data Security taught by Helmut Jurgensen and J. M. Carroll in Spring 1985.

One student project involved computer aided analysis of simple substitution ciphers; that is, making and displaying frequency counts and implementing trial substitutions. Another group implemented the Peleg and Rosenfeld [7] relaxation algorithm on a VAX 11-780. This group achieved qualified success but tied up the machine for a weekend to do so.

FIRST ATTEMPT

Our first program ran on a Texas Instruments professional computer in MS/BASIC. Its objective was to disambiguate automatically the letters E, T, A, N, O, S, I, and R in cryptograms in English having 50 or more letters, using only the 26 alphabetic characters with spaces left in, incorporating no proper names or initials, and enciphered in a fixed, single-alphabet, random key (i.e., not a Caesar, etc.).

Our program is shown by a structure chart in Figure 1. In Figure 2, the steps included in each symbol box are expanded. The fourteen tests were derived from occurrence frequency characteristics summarized by Caxton Foster [4].

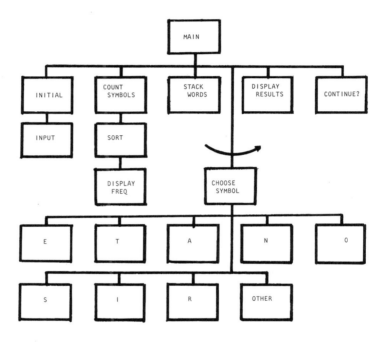

FIGURE 1. STRUCTURE CHART OF A SEMI-AUTOMATED CRYPTANALYSIS PROGRAM.

KEY:
1. Number of symbol occurrences.
2. Number of occurrences as a one-letter word.
3. Number of occurrences as the initial character of a word.
4. Occurrences as the second character.
5. Occurrences as the third character.
6. Occurrences as the fifth character.
7. Occurrences as the sixth character.
8. Occurrences as the terminal character.
9. Next to last.
10. Third from end.
11. Fourth from end.
12. Fifth from end.
13. Sixth from end.
14. Occurrences as a member of a pair of doubled characters.

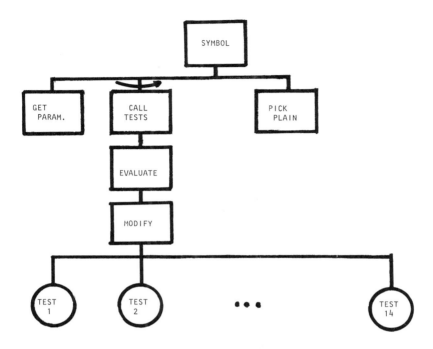

FIGURE 2. STRUCTURE CHART EXPANDING THE PROGRAM ELEMENTS INDICATED BY BOXES LABELED E, T, A, N, O, S, I, AND R.

The program had limited success. We could always disambiguate E and usually T, then solve the crypt manually. Sometimes we solved four or five letters automatically. Running time was on the order of five minutes or less.

EXPERT SYSTEM

Next we tried to automate the process. The data flow diagram (Figure 3) shows main parts of the program. The program was written in the artificial intelligence language MICROPROLOG. It runs on an IBM-PC/AT. The program DECODE sets up a 26-by-26 matrix that encapsulates all the knowledge about the crypt we can acquire from statistical analysis. The program RESTORE-CHOOSE then starts making guesses as to the plain text equivalents of crypt symbols while testing them against *impossible* digraph combinations on one hand (removing bad guesses) and *common* digraph and trigraph combinations on the other (reinforcing good guesses). RESTORE-CHOOSE also allows the user to intervene when the program runs out of guesses (although by that time the content and meaning of the cryptogram are usually evident).

478

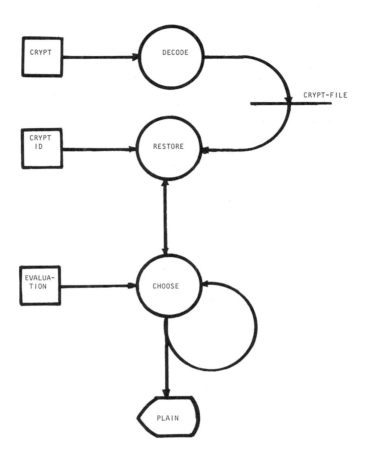

FIGURE 3. DATA FLOW DIAGRAM OF THE AUTOMATED CRYPTANALYSIS SYSTEM.

Figure 4 is a structure chart of the DECODE and RESTORE-CHOOSE programs. Figure 5 expands the IMPOSSIBLE and ADJUST-COUNTS modules of the DECODE program. However, the heart of the DECODE program is the GET-FREQUENCY module.

"GET-FREQUENCY" MODULE

Let X stand for any crypt symbol, there are 26 of them; and let y stand for any of the 26 plaintext symbols. Let L stand for the number of symbols in the cryptogram; $F(X)$ is the number of times a particular crypt symbol appears in the cryptogram; $F(y)$ is the number of times a particular

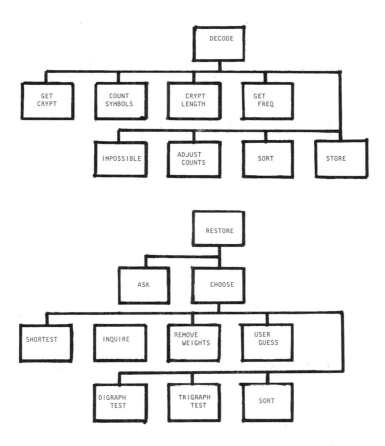

FIGURE 4. STRUCTURE CHARTS OF THE DECODE AND RESTORE-CHOOSE PROGRAMS.

plaintext symbol appears in 1000 words of plaintext (according to Fletcher Pratt [8]). Then $W(X,y)$ is the weight of crypt symbol X evaluated as plaintext symbol y. It is found from

$$W(X,y) = (F(X) \times 1000 - F(y) \times L)/100$$

If $L = 50$, $F(X) = 7$, and $y = e$, then

$$W(X,e) = (7 \times 1000 - 131 \times 50)/100 = 61$$

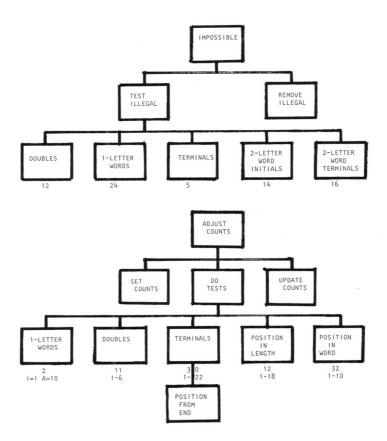

FIGURE 5. STRUCTURE CHARTS EXPANDING THE IMPOSSIBLE AND ADJUST-COUNTS MODULES OF THE DECODE PROGRAM.

Here is a sample list; there are initially 26 of them, one for every crypt symbol:

y	$F(y)$	$W(X,y)$
e	131	61
t	105	34
o	80	10
z	1	−60

The program suggests to the user a plaintext equivalent for the crypt symbol having the shortest list (i.e., the one from which the greatest number of "impossible" equivalences have been removed); on this list the plaintext equivalent is taken as the one with the highest $W(X,y)$ value. In this case, the program would suggest that X equals e.

Figure 6 expands four key modules of the RESTORE-CHOOSE program: INQUIRE, USER-GUESS, DIGRAPH-TEST, and TRI-GRAPH-TEST.

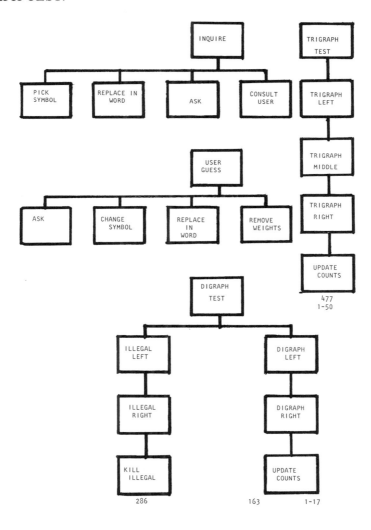

FIGURE 6. STRUCTURE CHARTS EXPANDING THE INQUIRE, USER-GUESS, DIGRAPH-TEST, AND TRIGRAPH MODULES OF THE RESTORE-CHOOSE PROGRAM.

In our expert system we made use of character-occurrence statistics from both Pratt [8] and Gaines [5].

We regarded 12 alphabetic characters as being "impossible" doubles; 24 as "impossible" one-letter words; 5 as "impossible" terminals; 14 as "never" occurring as initial characters of two-letter words; and 16 as "never" occurring as terminal characters of two-letter words.

A crypt character appearing as a one-letter word was given one added weight count for being an "i" and 10 added weight counts for being an "a." Eleven plaintext equivalents were given added weight counts when crypt characters appeared doubled; counts ranged from 1 to 6.

Added counts for terminals and initials were assigned to 30 plaintext characters (some got points in both cases); counts ranged from 1 to 22. There were 12 cases of positions from the front of a word with counts ranging from 1 to 18; and 32 cases of positions from the end, with counts ranging from 1 to 10.

We regarded 286 digraphs as "illegal" combinations and 163 as "common" digraphs, there were awarded from 1 to 17 bonus points. We regarded 477 trigraphs as "common" and awarded from 1 to 50 bonus points.

The weakest part of this procedure is the selection of weights to assign to symbol occurrences and co-occurrences. No set of tables is reliable for all languages, nor even for all variants of one language. However, the cryptanalyst can usually rely on exogenous information to suggest what kind of plaintext went into the cryptogram (military, telegraphic, literary, computer programs, etc.); then acquire a corpus of corresponding text and run statistical programs to particularize the schedule of weights.

PROGRAM DETAILS

Decode is a PROLOG program that tries to incorporate the knowledge of a cryptanalyst in breaking simple substitution ciphers. This program uses traditional methods of decryption such as frequency counts, double letters, and letter position. As well, it employs some newer tactics such as common digraphs and trigraphs, and illegal character positions, doubles, and digraphs. The process of decryption is broken into two parts, a static part in which evaluation of the encrypted text occurs, and an interactive part where guesses are made as to the plaintext substitutions. In the static part of the decryption process, frequency counts are made and probabilities are calculated as to the likely plaintext identity of each cipher letter. These probabilities are based on the positions in which the cipher letters are found in the crypt text and whether they are found doubled. The interactive part of the program determines the most likely substitutions and presents these to the user. Here the user may either accept them, reject them, or substitute on his own. As each substitution is made, the system determines what new information it has gained in the areas of possible trigraphs and digraphs, and updates its probabilities.

PROLOG is well suited for implementing a system such as this. It provides features that allow the easy manipulation of strings (lists) and the representation of knowledge about the decryption problem. On the other hand it has the drawback of being relatively inefficient. Because of limitations imposed by the system that was used, we had to simplify the program at the cost of some useful features.

DECRYPTION METHOD

The usual method of solving a simple substitution cipher is based on frequency counts and a visual analysis of the crypt text. The cryptanalyst pays special attention to letters that appear doubled or frequently as initial or terminal letters of words. He will proceed by trying to find letters that are easy to identify and will thereby lead to the identification of more obscure letters.

Two easy plaintext letters are "e" and "t" as they both appear with high frequency as terminal and initial letters respectively. (Note that plaintext letters or substitutions will always be shown in lower case, while the crypt letters will be shown in upper case.) Once some easy letters have been identified it may become easier to find other letters that appear in some combination with them. Examples are "h" and "r" which form the common digraphs "th" and "er." Other letters are sometimes found by examining other positions of letters, for example the letter "s" is found commonly as the second last letter of a word. This can be seen in the word endings "st," "se," and "sh." As well, a common second letter is "h" which is found in words starting with "th," "sh," and "ch." Thus the position of letters in words can give a lot of information as to their identities. A final common clue that is useful in this type of decryption is the occurrence of double letters. A letter doubled in the middle of a four letter word is almost always either an "o," as in the word "look," or an "e" as in "keep." This information along with that obtained from the analysis of frequencies and letter positions can usually lead to the identification of at least one or two of the more common letters. Once the cryptanalyst has determined a couple of letters using these methods, it becomes easier to find the identities of the less common ones. This is done by observing that certain letters appear commonly in digraphs or trigraphs.

PROGRAM IMPLEMENTATION

The decryption program tries to accurately represent the process performed by the cryptanalyst. For each crypt letter, it maintains a list of all plaintext letters that it may represent. Paired with each plaintext letter is a value proportional to the probability that it is the proper substitution for the crypt letter. These *probabilities* will be referred to as weights from here on. The weights are initially obtained by counting the frequency of the crypt letter in the crypt text and comparing it to observed frequencies of letters in plaintext. Each crypt letter and its frequency are brought to a common denominator and compared with the observed frequency of every plaintext letter in a string of one thousand characters. A formula involving the relative frequency of the plaintext letter and the frequency of the crypt-text letter and the difference between the two is used to determine the initial value of the weight. At the end of the frequency counting portion of the program, there is a list for each crypt-letter type in the crypt text. These lists contain 26 entries, one for each plaintext letter of the alphabet. Each entry consists of the plaintext letter and its weight, which is indicative of the probability that it is the proper substitution for the crypt-text letter based on frequency-count evidence alone.

The next part of the process is to remove entries from the weight lists that can not possibly be proper substitutions for the crypt letters. Entries can be removed for three reasons. The first of these is the most useful; it involves crypt letters that are doubled. Less than half of the letters in the alphabet ever appear doubled. Thus if a crypt letter appears in the crypt text as a double, we can remove all the entries in its weight list that never are doubled in plaintext. The second reason that an entry can be removed from the weight list is similar and involves terminal letters. There are several letters in English that seldom or never appear as terminals and thus may be removed from the weights of some crypt letters. The final case involves letters that appear as single-letter words, of which there are two, "a" and "i." Thus if a crypt letter appears as a single-letter word, all the entries except those for "a" and "i" are removed from its weight list.

Once the impossible letters are removed from the weight lists, the next step is to use more information about the English language that may help in the decryption. This process involves adding weight to some of the entries in the lists to show that one substitution may be more likely than another. The weights are altered according to statistics obtained from studies of English text. These statistics show that certain letters appear in certain places in words with a certain frequency. Thus if a crypt letter is found to occur at the beginning of a word, the weights of each of the plaintext letters are increased by a value that represents the number of times the letter appears as an initial character in English. Thus, for example, if the crypt letter "B" appears as the first letter in a word of cipher text, the weight for the plain letter "t" will be incremented by a substantial amount reflecting the fact that "t" occurs often as an initial letter. On the other hand, the weight for the plaintext letter "x" will hardly be increased at all because "x" is almost never an initial character. All the other weights in the list will also be increased accordingly. The weight lists will also be adjusted in the same manner for crypt letters that appear as terminals, doubles, and at other key locations in words.

Once the static analysis of the crypt text has been performed, the program begins to make suggestions. These suggestions are based on a simple algorithm that tries to determine the most likely substitution. The algorithm defines the best possible guess to be the plaintext letter with the highest weight in the shortest weight list. The reason for this choice is based on the premise that if a substitution is made from the shortest list, it has a greater probability of being correct. Therefore the choice with the greatest weight in the shortest list is the most likely substitution. When the program suggests a substitution to the user, he has the option to either accept it, reject it, or make a substitution of his own. If the suggestion is rejected, the system will try to make the next-best suggestion. The process in which the program produces suggestions is part of the PROLOG backtracking procedure. This causes it to produce alternative suggestions and to also possibly repeat previous guesses. This is actually a desirable attribute because it allows the user to review different alternatives while not totally discarding a rejected suggestion.

When the user accepts a guess or makes his own, a number of functions are performed by the system. The first is to remove the weight list for the substituted crypt letter from its database. This has the effect of preventing any further action regarding that guess. In addition, all plaintext weight pairs are removed from the rest of the weight lists for the plaintext letter involved in the substitution. Again this stops the program from suggesting the plaintext letter in any further guesses. At this point the system assumes that a correct substitution has been made and goes on to analyze the new information that it has gained from it. This new information deals with how the guessed plaintext letter effects the weight lists of the crypt letters that are found in proximity to it in the text. This is where the digraphs and trigraphs come into play. If, for example, we have just guessed the plaintext letter "t" and it is found to precede the crypt letter "X" in the text. We can increase the weight for the plain letter "h" in the weight list for "X." This is done because "th" is a very common digraph. The amount that the weight for "h" is increased by is based on the frequency of "th" in the English language. The process of updating weights for digraphs and trigraphs is similar to the process used in the static analysis of the text. Another and possibly more important function that is performed here is the removal of plaintext letters from weight lists for crypt letters that would form an illegal digraph with a guessed plaintext letter. This is done because some letters never appear together, such as "tk." Therefore in our previous example the plaintext letter "k" and it's corresponding weight can be removed from the weight list of the crypt letter "X." This is done because "X" was found to follow the plain letter "t" in the text. Removing entries from weight lists in this fashion has the effect of increasing the probability that one of the remaining letters in the list is the correct guess and reduces the amount of work that must be done by the system. The process of making suggestions and substitutions continues until either all of the crypt suggestions have been substituted, or all possible suggestions have been rejected.

LIMITATIONS

The PROLOG system depends extensively on a run-time stack. This allows it to do one of its major features called backtracking. Backtracking happens when the PROLOG system attempts to prove a clause and fails. The system starts to "undo" work that it has already accomplished and "redo" it in an effort to solve the problem in a different way. This can be seen using an analogy of a maze. A person attempting to find his way through a maze will follow an arbitrary path until he finds his way out or he is blocked. If the person is blocked, he must backtrack or retrace his steps until he returns to an intersection. At the intersection, he will take an alternative path and continue until he is again blocked or he is successful. The PROLOG system works much like a person finding his way through a maze. A problem, in this case decryption, is like the maze and the steps or clauses that must be proven are the paths and intersections. As the PROLOG interpreter attempts to solve the problem, it must solve the clauses or follow the paths. When it fails to prove one of the clauses, it must backtrack and follow a different path by proving a clause differently. In order for the system to remember where it has been, it must save a map of the paths that it has followed. This is done by pushing clauses onto the stack as it proceeds. Thus, as the system gets deeper and deeper into a problem, the stack grows very large.

In the PROLOG system that this program was implemented on, the stack size was limited to 64,000 bytes of memory. Since the program must continually pass on a large amount of information as it solves a cipher, this amount of space is not nearly enough. Fortunately, PROLOG provides a feature, called a *cut*, which allows the programmer to keep the stack usage at a minimum. This cut has the effect of committing the search to the path it has followed to that point. This can be thought of as putting a sign at a point on the path that says "NO RETURN BEYOND THIS POINT." Thus if we try to backtrack past the sign, we have failed in our search. In the PROLOG system this has the effect of reducing the stack back to the start of the current search. In the decryption program a cut was executed every time a guess was accepted. Thus once we have guessed a letter, we are stuck with it. In general this is not much of an obstacle, and even when a wrong guess has been made, it is usually still possible to solve the cipher.

The other major problem that we encountered was that the PROLOG system is very inefficient and time consuming. This is evident in the fact that the static part of the process usually takes about one hour to run for a cipher of about 50 characters. The interactive part can take up to 10 minutes between guesses. Unfortunately it is not possible to improve the performance of the system to any great extent due to the amount of work it must perform to complete the task. However, we are happy to report that although the program is slow, it has been very successful at breaking the ciphers that it was designed to do.

POLYALPHABETIC CIPHERS

The first step in cryptanalysis of a polyalphabetic cipher is determining the number of crypto alphabets or length of key. We felt the classical Kasiski analysis as described in Denning [3] was too difficult to program and tended to be indecisive in many instances. Instead we opted to use an adaptation of the log-sort-fit technique that Kahn [6] describes as being used to differentiate between transposition and substitution ciphers.

We assumed one, two, three, four, five, etc. alphabets. For all text enciphered in a given alphabet, we performed a symbol frequency count and arranged the counts in order of decreasing value. Then we took the natural logarithm of each value; where the count was zero we left it alone. Next we performed a simple linear Gaussian regression [1], where the X values were the numbers 1–26 and the Y values were the logarithms of the sorted symbol frequency counts.

The analysis program is written in MS/BASIC. It is shown in Figure 7. We calculated all the usual regression parameters: *mean Y* (EXY), *standard deviation Y* (SDY), *covariance XY* (COVXY), *regression coefficient* (R(I)), *intercept* (A(I)), and the *standard deviation of the estimate of Y* (SY(I)). The *slope* and *covariance* proved to be the most interesting.

Given a four-alphabet substitution cipher, we obtained the following results:

Alphabet #	Guess = 4	
	Slope	Covariance
1	−.1380	−7.7646
2	−.1383	−7.7796
3	−.1255	−7.0604
4	−.1364	−7.6718
Alphabet #	Guess = 3	
	Slope	Covariance
1	−.1071	−6.0224
2	−.0931	−5.2359
3	−.0771	−4.3386
Alphabet #	Guess = 5	
	Slope	Covariance
1	−.0747	−4.2015
2	−.0908	−5.1103
3	−.1018	−5.7288
4	−.0882	−4.9630
5	−.0844	−4.7500

These results suggest that, given a large amount of crypto text, the slope and covariance will attain minima and exhibit their greatest uniformity (except for guesses 1 and 2) when the cryptanalyst guesses the actual number of cipher alphabets.

Another way to determine the number of cipher alphabets is to use the *index of coincidence* (IC). (See reference [3].) The IC is calculated over the total crypto text so it is more economical to compute than the regression covariance (RC). The IC varies from 0.66 (one cipher alphabet)

```
1520 '
1530 ' LINEAR REGRESSION/CORRELATION SUBROUTINE
1540 '
1550 ' Y = RESULT(I,J): X = J
1560 SUMX = 0: SUMY = 0: SUMSQX = 0: SUMSQY = 0: SUMXY = 0
1570 FOR J = 1 TO 26
1580 IF RESULT(I,J) > 0 THEN RESULT(I,J) = LOG(RESULT(I,J))
1590 SUMY = SUMY + RESULT(I,J)
1600 SUMX = SUMX + J
1610 SUMSQY = SUMSQY + RESULT(I,J)*RESULT(I,J)
1620 SUMSQX = SUMSQX + J*J
1630 SUMXY = SUMXY + RESULT(I,J)*J
1640 NEXT J
1650 EXX = SUMX/26: EXY = SUMY/26
1660 SDX = SQR((1/26)*(SUMSQX - 26*EXX*EXX))
1670 SDY = SQR((1/26)*(SUMSQY - 26*EXY*EXY))
1680 COVXY = (1/26)*(SUMXY - 26*EXX*EXY)
1690 R(I) = COVXY/(SDX*SDY)
1700 B(I) = (R(I)*SDY)/SDX
1710 A(I) = EXY - B(I)*EXX
1720 SY(I) = SQR(SDY*SDY*(1 - R(I)*R(I)))
1730 RETURN
```

FIGURE 7. BASIC CODE OF THE LINEAR REGRESSION/CORRELATION SUBROUTINE OF THE POLYALPHABETIC ANALYSIS PROGRAM.

to 0.38 (infinite key). The plot of the cipher alphabet is roughly a negative exponential. While it is easy to discriminate among 1, 2, or 3 alphabets, this indicator becomes ambiguous for 4 (IC = 0.45), 5 (IC = 0.44) or more alphabets (IC = .041 for 10 alphabets). In such cases, cryptanalysts must rely on Kasiski analysis to resolve doubt.

In a way, this is fortuitous because the IC and RC can work together. The IC can easily resolve the 1 and 2 alphabet cases, in which the RC behaves poorly.

One can postulate another area of cooperation: breaking product ciphers. Suppose a message is enciphered first by substitution using N alphabets then by one of the 32 regular two-dimensional route transposition ciphers (24 matrix, eight-rail fence; neglecting the constants for length and width of matrix and depth of fence). One can use the IC on the total crypto text to estimate the number of cipher alphabets. Then one can reverse each regular transformation and test using the RC to determine which is correct. After that, the cryptogram can be solved using forked processes—possibly incorporating fuzzy digraph analysis.

Solutions can also be achieved for product, ciphers using pre-substitution transposition or both pre- and post-substitution transpositions, but each of these embellishments presents a quantitative leap in difficulty with a consequent requirement for a larger quantity of encrypted text on which to work.

CONCLUSION

Given a sufficiently large amount of text it should be possible to reduce any fixed-key polyalphabetic cipher to a finite number of simple substitution ciphers. Then, given sufficiently prodigious computational capability, it should be possible to use a modification of our expert system to solve enough of these simple substitution ciphers to infer the content and meaning of the text and, over time, determine the cipher mechanism and keying schedules.

For this reason, any fixed-key substitution cipher should be regarded as potentially breakable by a ciphertext-only attack. We have had no direct experience with running-key polyalphabetic ciphers, but we tend to distrust them as well. For critical applications, it would seem prudent to rely only on Vernam [3], multiple key ciphers [2], or product ciphers with randomly selectable transpositions, substitutions, and key progressions.

ACKNOWLEDGMENT

This research was supported by the National Scientific and Engineering Research Council (Canada) under grant #A-7132. Their support is gratefully acknowledged.

REFERENCES

1. Burington, R. S., and D. C. May (1958), *Handbook of Probability and Statistics with Tables*. Sanduksy, OH: Handbook Publishers.

2. Carroll, J. M. (1984), The Resurrection of Multiple-Key Ciphers. *Cryptologia*, 8:262–265.

3. Denning, D. E. R. (1982), *Cryptography and Data Security*. Reading, MA: Addison-Wesley.

4. Foster, C. C. (1982), *Cryptanalysis for Microcomputers*. Rochelle Park, NJ: Hayden.

5. Gaines, H. F. (1956), *Cryptanalysis*. New York: Dover Publications.

6. Kahn, D. (1967), *The Codebreakers*. New York: Macmillan.

7. Peleg, S. and A. Rosenfeld (1979), Breaking Substitution Ciphers Using a Relaxation Algorithm. *Communications of the ACM*, 22:598–605.

8. Pratt, F. (1938), *Secret and Urgent*. Garden City, NY: Blue Ribbon Books.

Computer Methods for Decrypting
Random Stream Ciphers
by Frank Rubin

1. INTRODUCTION

One of the simplest types of stream ciphers consists of XORing (adding modulo 2) a random sequence of key bits to a binary representation of the message. Although the key may have been generated by some mathematical algorithm, it will be assumed that the decryptor is, thus far, unable to determine this algorithm, so that the key will be treated as a true random sequence of bits.

If the user of the cipher can arrange that the random sequence used for each message is never reused, then this cipher is believed to be totally secure from analytic attack. The only possible solution is to obtain the keys. However, this ideal situation is hard to achieve in practical situations, since there are difficulties in generating, transmitting, storing, and synchronizing so many random keys.

One likely retreat from this optimum situation is to have a very long random key, and to use different segments of the key for different messages. In effect, each message has two keys: the random sequence itself, and the number specifying the starting position in the sequence.

This article explores the security of this type of encipherment. We shall show how such ciphers can be decrypted, using computers, without any knowledge other than the language of the plaintext. The methods exploit certain characteristics of some binary character representations commonly used in today's computers and communications networks.

From *Cryptologia*, Vol. 2, No. 3, July 1978.

2. TERMINOLOGY

A message of length L is a sequence M of characters $m(i)$ for $1 \leqslant i \leqslant L$ in an alphabet consisting of groups of b bits (binary digits) each. A random key K is a fixed sequence of b bit groups $k(j)$ for $1 \leqslant j \leqslant N$. A position key is an integer p with $0 \leqslant p < N$.

The encipherment of the message M with the random key K and position key p is the sequence of characters C, with $c(i) = m(i) \oplus k(i + p)$, where $\oplus$ indicates XORing (addition modulo 2) performed on b bit quantities.

Decipherment is identical to encipherment, and is given by

$$m(i) = c(i) \oplus k(i + p).$$

It is understood that when $i + p$ exceeds N, selection of the random key characters resumes once again at 1. That is, $k(aN + i) = k(i)$ for any integer a.

3. DECRYPTION

The term *decryption* refers to any analytical procedure by which an outside individual, having obtained the enciphered message and without initial possession of the key [or keys], determines the plaintext message. Several assumptions may be made about the amount of information that the decryptor may possess about the messages and keys. These are arranged from best (from the decryptor's point of view) to worst. It is assumed that the method of encipherment is known.

A1. The decryptor is able to have any messages desired enciphered with the same key, and can obtain both the plaintext and ciphertext.

A2. The decryptor has lengthy messages in both the plaintext and the ciphertext.

A3. The decryptor has some probable words or phrases the message may contain, or knows the general subject matter or the format of the message (e.g., it is a FORTRAN program).

A4. The decryptor knows the language of the message.

A5. The decryptor knows nothing whatever about the plaintext content of the message.

Case A5 is beyond the scope of this article. In [subsections 3.1–3.6], we shall discuss the security of the random stream cipher under the assumptions A1 to A4.

3.1 Arbitrary Messages can be Sent

Assume that the decryptor can have any desired message enciphered and can obtain the resultant ciphertext. Both the random key and the positional key are unknown. Let the decryptor choose any message of length N, the length of the key. Then, by XORing the message with the ciphertext, the random key will be recovered. Thus:

$$x(i) = m(i) \oplus c(i) = [m(i) \oplus m(i)] \oplus k(i + p) = k(i + p).$$

The value of N is presumably unknown to the decryptor, but can be determined by using successively longer messages until a repetition of the key has been obtained, that is $k(i) = k(i + N)$.

Although the key has been shifted, this poses no problem. Suppose a new unknown enciphered message A has been received. By sliding this message against the shifted key X, the plaintext is recovered. If message A has been enciphered with the positional key q, and it is matched against position r of X, then the recovered text will be

$$s(i) = a(i) \oplus x(i+r) = [t(i) \oplus k(i+q)] \oplus k(i+p+r)$$
$$= t(i) \oplus [k(i+q) \oplus k(i+p+r)] = t(i)$$

where $r = q-p$ (or $r = N+q-p$ if $q<p$). Here $t(i)$ is the assumed plaintext of message A.

To decrypt the new message, then, one needs only to try all possible shifts r until plaintext emerges.

3.2 Known Plaintext/Ciphertext Pairs

Assume that the decryptor has obtained both the plaintext and the ciphertext for one or more messages. As before, the plaintext and ciphertext may be xored to obtain a segment of the random key. The positions of these key segments within the full key are unknown.

Suppose that a number of other ciphertext messages are available, for which the plaintexts are unknown. By sliding these messages against the recovered segments of the key, the decryptor may find that some of the messages are enciphered by overlapping segments of the random key.

When such an overlap is found, the opportunity to extend the recovered segment of key is created. The decrypted segment of the new message will usually suggest several characters which might follow or precede the segment. These, in turn, will determine several additional key groups. The extension process is greatly aided when other segments of the same message are recovered, or when additional overlapping messages are identified [see Sec. 5].

Finally, as the recovered segments of the random key become larger, they may begin to overlap. Two or more segments may then be combined to produce a much larger segment of the random key, and eventually the entire random key [see Sec. 6].

3.3 Probable Words

Assume that the decryptor has a list of probable words [or] phrases which might appear in the messages [for which we have obtained] ciphertexts. The problem then becomes one of identifying the correct placements of the words in the message.

Let the probable word [or words] be tried in all possible positions in a given message. Each placement provides possible recovered segments of the random key. Now consider each such segment in all possible positions in other available messages: if a key segment results in recognizable plaintext in one of these other messages, the placement of the probable word [or words] in the given message is verified, and two messages enciphered with overlapping segments of the random key will have been identified.

Once such a placement has been made, the two recovered plaintext segments can be expanded to recover the entire segment of the key for the overlapping segment of the two messages. Separate segments of random key may be combined into longer segments [see Sec. 6 below].

A disadvantage of the method described is that the number of possible placements of probable words and the number of possible placements of corresponding segments of the random key increases rapidly as T, the total length of all ciphertext messages, grows larger. Thus, the total number of placements for each probable word is on the order of T^2. Since $T > 2N$ will be required to recover the entire random key, the method described is prohibitive for large N. Therefore, it is preferable to use the method outlined [Sec. 4] when possible.

3.4 Known Language

Assume that the decryptor knows only the language in which the messages are written. For simplicity, it will be assumed that the language is based on the Roman alphabet. The decryption can still be performed as a three-stage process:

1. Identify segments of the ciphertext which have been enciphered with the same part of the random key.
2. Determine the plaintext equivalents, and recover the overlapping segment of the key.
3. Combine recovered segments of the random key.

[Sections 4, 5, and 6] deal with these three steps individually. It will be shown how certain regular features of common character representations can be exploited in a computationally feasible manner.

4. IDENTIFYING OVERLAPS

Suppose that a large number of enciphered messages have been obtained. Let us consider the problem of identifying segments of these messages that might have been enciphered with the same segments of the random key.

One technique, developed by William F. Friedman, is the coincidence method. Its principle is as follows: samples or segments of, say, 100 characters from each of two messages are compared. If these two segments of ciphertext have been enciphered with different keys, the chance of any two ciphertext letters being the same is about one in 26. But, if the two segments have been enciphered with the same random key, the chance of two ciphertext letters matching is about doubled. So, for 100 characters, about four would be equal if the keys are different and eight if the keys are the same.

To detect whether any two messages have been enciphered by the same segment of the random key, one might take samples from each character position in each message and match them. The more letters that match between the two messages, the more likely it is that the messages have been enciphered with the same segment of random key. [Editor's note: Cryptanalysts in using the coincidence test often refer to the matches as "hits." Thus, the more hits between messages, the more likely it is that they have been enciphered with the same key. But it should be mentioned that what the cryptanalyst is perhaps most interested in is to find numerous *successive* hits between messages, i.e., to find long common sequences of letters between messages! A long sequence of ciphertext letters that repeats itself in another message, indicating that a common phrase has been enciphered with the same key, is a better indicator of messages being enciphered with the same segment of random key, than a tabulation of widely scattered hits. Messages enciphered with the same segment of the random key are said to be "in depth."] But there are many problems in using the coincidence method. Where there is a long random key involved, the amount of ciphertext required to find ciphertexts enciphered with the same segment of key might be too large to be practical. And, too, as the amount of ciphertext grows, the number of possible matchings grow: the number of possible matchings is proportional to the square of the number of samples being matched! Indeed, the probability of false matches (for example, eight equal characters out of 100 happening by accident) becomes so large that far more false than valid matches will be obtained.

The next three subsections [4.1–4.3] discuss feasible computational methods for detecting reuse of random key segments. Specifically, these methods will exploit certain regularities in three of the binary character representations commonly used in current computers and communications networks.

4.1 Eight-Bit ASCII

Eight-bit ASCII has a characteristic ideal for identification of overlaps. In each character, the first (high-order) bit always equals the third bit. This happens because the eight-bit code was developed as an extension of the older seven-bit ASCII representation.

If the first and third bits of a ciphertext character are XORed, the result bit will be 0 if the first and third bits of the key group are equal, and 1 if unequal. It follows, therefore, that if two sequences of ciphertext characters are enciphered with the same segment of random key, the two sequences of bits thus formed—one for each ciphertext sequence—will be equal.

From each message, select such sequences of n bits each, starting at each position in the ciphertext. With each sequence include the message number and starting position. Sort these records on the sequence field. Equal sequence fields will indicate likely key overlaps.

Let T be the total length of the ciphertext messages obtained. By choosing n larger than log T (all logarithms are understood to be binary or base-2 logarithms) the probability of a false match is reduced. However, if n is chosen too large, valid key overlaps of fewer than n characters will not be detected. Matching sequences can be checked by considering the next or the preceding several ciphertext characters.

4.2 EBCDIC

EBCDIC has the characteristic that the two high-order bits of each eight-bit character is 01 for all punctuation characters, 10 for all lower-case letters, and 11 for all digits and upper-case letters.

Suppose that the plaintext is enciphered with blanks and (possibly) other punctuation characters deleted. Then, long sequences consisting solely of lower-case letters would be expected in all messages. If two such sequences are enciphered with the same segment of the random key, then the two high-order bits of corresponding ciphertext characters would be equal. Such sequences might then be sorted, as described [subsection 4.1 above], to detect the overlaps.

If blanks are present—as we should normally expect—sufficiently long sequences of lower-case or upper-case letters would be rare. But sequences of characters in which the blanks aligned would not be uncommon, as in [the following]:

 . . . TOLD <u>THE SOVIET REPRESENTATIVE</u> . . .
 . . . BUILD<u>ING PLANES WITH</u> GROUND . . .

When two such sequences are aligned, that is, enciphered with the same segment of the random key, the two high-order bits of corresponding characters will again be equal.

The approach is again to take sequences of the two high-order bits from each character, starting at each position in each message. The length, n, of these sequences is more critical in these cases. If n is taken to be small, so that $2n$ is not significantly larger than $\log T$, the number of false matches will be large; however, if n is taken much larger than 10, the likelihood of finding sequences of n characters with blanks aligned decreases, so that many valid key overlaps will not be detected.

To overcome this problem, a two-stage process is used. Choose sequences of n bit pairs so that $2n$ is significantly larger than $\log T$. Refine the set of all such sequences so that the first 10 pairs must be equal. Since normal English text has one blank for every five nonblank characters (and similarly for other languages using the Roman alphabet), about four of every six pairs of characters in a pair of texts should both be lower-case letters. Therefore, if both texts are enciphered by the same segment of the random key, about four of every six pairs of two high-order ciphertext bits should be equal. If the same messages are enciphered with different segments of the random key, only one of every four bit pairs would be equal. This provides a test for verifying the matches found in the first refinement step.

An example may help clarify the importance of the choice of n. Suppose the random key has length $N = 1,000,000$; and $T = 5,000,000$ characters of ciphertext have been obtained. If n is taken as 12, the chance of finding a legitimate match in correctly aligned ciphertexts is about one in 300. There will be about 10,000,000 pairs of correctly aligned ciphertext, so that about 33,000 valid matches wil be found. Since the chance of a false match is about one in 16,000,000, and since there are about 12,500,000,000,000 pairs of 12 character samples, there may be about 780,000 false matches.

If, however, $n = 10$ be chosen, this will divide the 5,000,000 samples into about 1,000,000 lists averaging five samples each. These represent some 10,000,000 matching pairs, with perhaps 100,000 of them being valid. We might use the next 15 characters in each message to validate these matches by rejecting any pair with fewer than 10 high-order bit pairs equal. Perhaps 50,000 of the valid matches would then remain; and fewer than 5000 false matches would pass this screening.

4.3 Seven-Bit ASCII

In seven-bit ASCII, as in seven-bit paper-tape code, there is only one bit which is common to all lower-case letters of the alphabet. To keep the probability of false matches low, it will be necessary, therefore, to have $n > \log T$. When messages have been enciphered with blanks and punctuation removed, a large n is workable, but when blanks are retained, as in normal text, for T greater than 1000 this would require $n > 10$, so that most legitimate matches would be overlooked. Consequently, a two-stage process must be used.

As an example, suppose the random key has a length $N = 1,000,000$, and the combined length of the intercepted messages is $T = 5,000,000$. Here, there will be somewhat less than 5,000,000 starting positions for sequences of 10 single bits taken from each character of ciphertext. To be exact, if there are m messages, all at least 10 characters long, there will be $T - 9m$ such sequences. If these are matched for equality, there will be about 1000 lists with about 5000 matching sequences in each.

As before, the problem is to eliminate the false matches in each such list. In English we would expect about four of every six character pairs in a pair of matched plaintexts to consist of two lower-case letters, and about two of six to match a letter against a blank. This fact can be exploited to give a number of criteria for rejecting possible pairs of matching sequences:

C1. Reject any pair in which fewer than three of each six bits are equal.

C2. Reject any pair in which fewer than seven of each twelve bits are equal.

C3. Reject any pair in which fewer than 18 of each 30 bits are equal.

C4. Reject any pair in which more than 10 of each 12 bits are equal.

C5. Reject any pair in which more than 25 of each 30 bits are equal.

Again, let $N = 1,000,000$ and $T = 5,000,000$. Choose samples of 40 characters starting at each position in each ciphertext, and form 40-bit sequences from their high-order bits. After sorting and matching on the 10 leading bits, there would be 1000 lists of 5000 elements each. It would be possible to examine all of the pairs using the rejection criteria C1–C5 above on the remaining 30 bits, but this would require on the order of $1000 \times 5000^2/2 > 10^{13}$ such tests.

Instead, a process of successive refinements can be used. First, consider only the first bit in the 30-bit test field, which is the eleventh bit in each 40-bit sequence. The list of fields whose first bit is 0 can be paired with itself to give a pair of lists. Every field in the first list matches every field in the second (identical) list on the first bit. Likewise, the list of fields whose first bit is 1 can be paired with itself to give another pair of lists matching on the first bit. The list of sequences whose first bit is 0 can be paired with the list whose first bit is 1 to give a pair of lists which do not match on the first bit. The pair of lists for the combination 1 and 0 need not be kept, since it is identical.

The result is three pairs of lists refined on the first bit. Now take each of these three pairs and refine them on the second bit. This will result in 10 pairs of lists, four of which will match on both bits, four on just one bit, and two on neither bit.

The process continues. When refinement reaches the fourth stage, there will be 136 pairs of lists. Of these, eight will not match on any of the four bit positions. These eight pairs can be eliminated immediately, since it will not be possible for sequences in these pairs to meet criterion C1. Thus, only 128 pairs of lists will be considered at stage 5. These produce 496 refined pairs of lists, 64 of which can be eliminated by criterion C1.

When refinement reaches the seventh stage, criterion C1 will be applied directly to bit positions 2 to 7 of the 30-bit fields, and predictively to bit positions 3 to 8 and 4 to 9. When the ninth stage is reached, criterion C2 can be applied; and at the eleventh stage, criterion C4 can be used.

As the successive refinements continue, the sizes of the lists in each pair will decrease. When these sizes become adequately small, the remaining criteria can be applied to all pairs of individual sequences. That is, if the two lists in the pair contain p and q bit sequences, respectively, then the criteria C1 to C5 can be applied to the pq pairs of sequences. Of course, when any list becomes empty, the pair will be eliminated.

It might seem that a great deal of moving and copying of lists will be done. Actually, no movement of lists is required at all. Since the entire 40-bit samples were sorted, each list of 5000 of the 30-bit sequences will already be sorted. So, a list at any level of refinement can be represented by just two integers, representing the starting position and length of the list in the full list of 5000 elements.

It also might seem that the storage requirements for the method might be very high, since the number of possible pairs at the rth stage of refinement is on the order of 2^{2r}, while the length of each list is on the order of $5000/2^r$. Thus, it might seem that the number of lists would become very large before each list becomes small enough to begin pairwise comparisons. For example, with $r = 10$, there would be 2^{20} (about 1,000,000) pairs of lists averaging about five elements each. Since many lists would be much longer than five, full pairwise comparison might not begin until the eleventh stage.

This problem can be eliminated by performing the refinement process in a depth-first rather than a breadth-first manner. At the first stage, three pairs of lists are generated. Instead of refining all three of these pairs of lists simultaneously, choose one of them to refine; for example, the third. Replace the third pair of lists by its three refinements, thereby creating five pairs of lists, two at stage 1, and three at stage 2. Choose the last of these to refine, replacing it with its three refined pairs of lists.

The depth-first expansion continues until the last pair of lists is deemed small enough for exhaustive pairwise comparisons. This point must be determined empirically; it is the point at which exhaustive pairwise comparison requires less computer time than continuing the refinement process down to lists of length one. After the last pair of lists has been exhaustively compared, it is eliminated, and refinement continues with the penultimate pair of lists.

It is also possible to adopt a mixed approach to the refinement process. Refinement could be carried out in parallel to some fixed depth;

for example, six or eight stages. Then further refinement would be carried out in the depth-first manner just described.

During the refinement process, a very large number of searches will be made for the limits of the lists. For example, when refining a list of sequences starting with 00110, it is necessary to determine how many of the elements start with 001100, and how many with 001101. Rather than perform searches for all of these refinements, an index might be built showing the starting point for all sequences starting with each of the possible 10 or 12 bit combinations. This index can be built in a single pass over the list of 5000 sequences. For any refinements beyond these 10 or 12 levels, the limits could be found by binary searching, or the index could have a pointer to a detailed subindex for those 10 or 12 bit initial sequences which started many of the 30-bit sequences.

The refinement process can only be performed efficiently if the list of fields being tested is small enough to fit into primary storage. In the above example, if the $T = 5,000,000$ test fields fit conveniently into primary storage, then the initial matching on 10 bits could have been eliminated. This would greatly improve the chances of finding most of the key overlaps. Otherwise, the number b of bits involved in the initial exact matching should be kept as small as possible, subject to the ability to keep $T/2^b$ test fields in primary storage.

5. RECOVERING KEY SEGMENTS

Let us now suppose that two or more segments of the ciphertext have been identified as being enciphered with the same segment of the random key. The next step is to recover this segment of the random key, together with segments of plaintext. This process is described as a computer-aided manual process, but it is feasible as a wholly computerized process.

The case for EBCDIC is considered here, but the principles are the same for all character representations.

If the messages have been enciphered with blanks and punctuation intact, then the recovery is particularly easy. First XOR the high order two bits for each pair of corresponding ciphertext characters. When the result is 01, this indicates a lower-case character in one message, and an upper-case letter or digit in the other. A result of 10 indicates a punctuation mark in one message opposite an upper-case character. A result of 11 indicates a lower-case character opposite a punctuation character. A result of 00 indicates that both characters are of the same type.

A sequence of 01's may indicate an uppercase acronym or a decimal number in one message. A sequence of 11's suggests a sequence of punctuation marks, possibly the end of a sentence, with a period and two blanks, to be followed by a capital letter.

These considerations allow the detection of most blanks or punctuation characters. It is then necessary to determine which of the messages contains the punctuation. This can often be done by elementary logic when three or more key overlaps are available. For example, if the XOR of a and b has high-order bits 01, a and c give 10, and b and c give 11, then a must be an upper-case letter, b a lower-case letter, and c a punctuation character.

For two messages, an assumed plaintext character in one message determines the plaintext character in the other message. When one placement gives a common character, and the other a rare or unused character, then the first choice is presumably correct. If both choices give rare characters, then the punctuation mark was probably not a blank. Other logical choices for a single isolated punctuation character are hyphen and apostrophe. Pairs of punctuation characters are often comma followed by blank.

Proceeding in this manner, a potential placement of blanks and other punctuation can be made. The final check is to see whether the distribution of blanks in both messages follows normal patterns. The next step in this case would be to examine the one-, two-, and three-character words in the messages. By trying the most common choices for these words, various characters in the opposite message will be found. The remainder of the decipherment consists of bridging the spaces between these characters to form words, phrases, and finally sentences, a procedure familiar to every cryptanalyst.

Now consider the case where the messages have been enciphered without blanks, punctuation, or capitalization. This will be evident because the XOR of the two high-order bits of corresponding characters will consist mainly of long sequences of 00's. It is not known whether the plaintext is in lower case or upper case, but this does not affect the decryption process. The decryption can proceed as though all plaintext were in upper case, and the necessary clues will be provided later by the identity of those characters found to be in the opposite case.

Examine one matching character position in the ciphertexts. Call the ciphertext characters a and b. Since the plaintext characters are presumably upper-case letters, the two high-order bits of the key are determined. There are 64 choices for the six low-order key bits, 26 given valid letters. So about 10 choices may be expected to give valid letters for both a and b.

Sort the 10 or so pairs of reconstructed letters in decreasing order by joint probability. Write each pair vertically, and place the entire set of pairs in a vertical column. This is done for each position in the overlapping message segments. The result might resemble the following partial reconstructions:

```
E T S E O A
R A E I I N

R E O A R O
H D N N N I

T N H T H E
C F S L E G

L A T I S U
S M G S L H

A M L R E W
G C D F V T
```

FIGURE 1. PARTIAL RECONSTRUCTION OF PAIRS IN MESSAGE TEXT.

Now the message texts may be recovered by matching pairs in consecutive columns. For example, the pairs in Figure 1 lead to such plausible reconstruction as:

ETTERE or TTHERE or LASTSO
RAGING   CASING   SMELLI

It is assumed that this tabulation is carried out by computer, but that the extraction of the plaintext is a human operation. However, with a little more sophistication, the extraction may also be done by computer using first letter pair frequencies, and then dictionaries of common words.

6. RECOVERING THE RANDOM KEY

When the message characters have been recovered for a large number of overlapping message segments, many separate segments of the random key will be recovered. These segments may be combined into longer segments, and ultimately into the full random key by a fairly straightforward method.

From each recovered segment take every four consecutive key characters. Sort these four character segments. Each occurrence of equal segments indicates a probable overlap of two of the recovered segments of the random key. Test such potential overlaps by comparing the preceding or following characters in the recovered key segments.

The recovery of longer random key segments permits further decipherment. For any message partially recovered by discovery of a partially overlapping message, the extension of the recovered key segment will allow recovery of more of that message. In overlapping message pairs where some of the recovery was tentative, the discovery of third or fourth overlapping messages will help to verify or to correct the tentative solutions. And in cases where overlaps have not been discovered, sliding the message against the recovered long random-key segments may divulge the plaintext.

These processes have a snowball effect. The more messages recovered, the more key segments can be recovered and then combined. And the longer the recovered key segments, the more chance of recovering still more of the plaintexts. Likewise, discovery of the subject matter and examination of the terminology will speed recovery of further plaintexts in overlapping messages.

When new messages are received, they should first be slid against the recovered segments of the key. If plaintext appears, the message can then be solved immediately. If plaintext appears, but the message only overlaps part of the recovered key segment, this will help extend that key segment. But if no such recovery is possible, then the high order two bits of consecutive ciphertext characters will be formed into sequences [as in Sec. 4]. These are added incrementally to the sorted list of such sequences formed during the original overlap detection phase. Thus new message overlaps may be discovered.

Although the random key has been treated as though it were truly random throughout this paper, it may, in fact, have been derived from some mathematical algorithm. As soon as significant segments of the key have been recovered, a search for this algorithm can begin. This would include chained addition, chained XOR, linear congruential recurrences, and feedback register techniques. The subject of inverting such an algorithm is a large one, and is not treated here.

The decryptor should also look for regularity in the positional keys. These are likely to depend on the time and date of the transmission, the sequence of the transmission, or even the message length.

7. OTHER STREAM CIPHERS

So far this paper has dealt only with stream ciphers formed by XORing the random key to the plaintext. Many seemingly more complex stream ciphers can be reduced to this simple case. For example, suppose that eight-bit plaintext characters were being enciphered by 16-bit random key groups by

1. XOR the character with the first eight bits of the key, K_1.
2. Permute the bits in a known fashion, or, in general, apply a known nonsingular linear transformation L.
3. XOR the result with the second eight bits of the key, K_2.

If the resulting ciphertext character is transformed by the inverse linear transformation L', then the result is the same as if the original character had been XORed with the random key character $K1 \oplus L'$ (K_2).

The methods of this paper also apply where the random key is added rather than XORed to the plaintext. In EBCDIC, all lower-case characters have numeric values between 129 and 169. Therefore, subtracting two such characters enciphered by the same key character must give a signed result between -40 and $+40$. This provides a method for detecting key overlaps by the refinement process of subsection 4.3.

8. COUNTERMEASURES

Having discussed methods for decrypting random stream ciphers at some length, it is appropriate to point out some countermeasures the informed user could take to defy these methods.

The most obvious method would be to increase the key length. Throughout this paper, the example of key length $N = 1,000,000$ has been used. It is clear that with enough ciphertext, such a cipher would be decrypted at very little computer cost. As N was increased to 10 or 100 million, the solution would become infeasible for EBCDIC or seven-bit ASCII, and expensive for eight-bit ASCII. The problem with this idea is that storage for such a large key becomes expensive. It is difficult to store, transmit, and access such a key.

Another idea is to generate a key to enormous length by some mathematical algorithm. Unfortunately, this is likely to produce a regularity in the key which could be exploited to lead directly to a solution.

The present attack is based on the idea that there is a certain regularity in the bit representations for the message characters. One direct countermeasure is to destroy this regularity. This might be done with a well chosen simple substitution applied before the XOR with the random key. The simple substitution must be chosen so that in each bit position a 0 or 1 is about equally likely. Further, in each pair, or generally n-tuple, of bit positions, each of the bit combinations is about equally likely. And, finally, no bit position should be a linear combination of the other bit positions, or even approximately so. In particular, no bit should act as a parity or check bit. Assuring that all of these conditions are met may not be easy.

The present attack assumes that consecutive groups are taken from the key. Suppose, instead, that every qth key group were taken, with $1 \leq q < N$, and q relatively prime to N. If q as well as the positional key p varied from message to message, much more intercepted text would be required to recover the random key. The problem with this idea is that if the random key were stored on secondary storage, the cost of accessing the key in this manner might be very high.

Instead of an integer q, let an r-bit quantity R be associated with each message. With the ith character of the message, use the ith bit of R, taken modulo r. If $R(i) = 0$, use the next sequential character of K. But if $R(i) = 1$, skip this character, and use the following random key character. So, if R has about $r/2$ zeros and $r/2$ ones, then about $1.5r$ key characters would be needed to encipher every r characters of the message. This would not significantly increase the cost of retrieving the key.

The effect of this technique would be that the amount of text needed to recover the random key would be increased by a factor of 2^r.

"Cracking" a Random Number Generator
by James Reeds

The purpose of this note is to illustrate how the ordinary standards of randomness have little to do with the type of randomness required for cryptographic purposes. That is, there are really two standards of randomness.

I. Consider the usual standards for random number generators. Here the general idea is that standard techniques of statistical analysis are not able to discriminate between the sequence of numbers generated and a sequence of independent uniform deviates from the unit interval. Thus, χ^2 tests, autocorrelation functions, and correlation coefficients are used to judge the random number generator in question. These are discussed at length in [1]. The point of this standard is that acceptable random number generators should be suitable for *Monte Carlo* applications.

II. On the other hand we have the standards of cryptography. For cryptographic purposes the matter of predictability is exceedingly important. If, after examining, say, a sequence of four random numbers, one is able to predict the fifth (and all subsequent) numbers, then that generator is useless for cryptographic purposes. In predicting the next number we are allowed to examine the low-order bits (or digits) as well as the high-order bits. As a result, the "rule" which predicts the next number may be *discontinuous*, and thus not be discovered by the standard statistical methods used to evaluate *randomness I* properties of a random number generator.

As an illustration of what I mean, let us examine a "typical" cryptographic example. Let us say that a secret message has been prepared by converting the letters into digits, following the rule A=01, B=02, etc., to Z=26. Then the successive digits are added, modulo 10, to the successive digits of the output of a *linear congruential* random number

From *Cryptologia*, Vol. 1, No. 1, Jan. 1977.

generator. The correspondents have previously agreed upon a *modulus* $M = 8397$, a *multiplier* $a = 4381$, and a constant term $b = 7364$. That is, if x_n is the nth random number, the next is given by the rule:

$$x_{n+1} \equiv 4381 \, x_n + 7364 \text{ (modulo 8397)}.$$

(I chose these three numbers entirely at random, insisting only that they have four digits. The reader will see how the analysis given below is general and will apply to other choices of M, a, and b.)

Let us assume further that the correspondents have agreed (ahead of time) to encipher this message by starting up the random number generator with the *initial key* of $x_0 = 2134$. With the generator given above, we get

$x_0 = 2134$	$x_4 = 8295$	$x_8 = 7907$	$x_{12} = 7648$	$x_{16} = 6636$
$x_1 = 2160$	$x_5 = 5543$	$x_9 = 0766$	$x_{13} = 0825$	$x_{17} = 0869$
$x_2 = 6905$	$x_6 = 7213$	$x_{10} = 3231$	$x_{14} = 2582$	$x_{18} = 2215$
$x_3 = 3778$	$x_7 = 1578$	$x_{11} = 1865$	$x_{15} = 8347$	$x_{19} = 4347$

These successive digits (starting with $x_1 = 2160$, 6905, etc.) are added (modulo 10) to the message digits to get the cryptogram:

Plaintext	S	E	C	R	E	T	T	R	E	A	T	Y
Plaintext digits	19	05	03	18	05	20	20	18	05	01	20	25
Key digits	21	60	69	05	37	78	82	95	55	43	71	23

Ciphertext	30	65	62	13	32	98	02	03	50	44	91	48

S	I	G	N	E	D	B	Y	P	A	K	I	S	T	A	N	A	N	D
19	09	07	14	05	04	02	25	16	01	11	09	19	20	01	14	01	14	04
15	78	79	07	07	66	32	31	18	65	76	48	08	25	25	82	83	47	66

24 77 76 11 02 60 34 56 24 66 87 47 17 45 26 96 84 51 60

I	S	R	A	E	L
09	19	18	01	05	12
36	08	69	22	15	43

35 17 77 23 10 55

Now, it is not suggested that the preceding cipher system is a good system, or an especially practical one, or a widely used one. I show below why it is not a good system, and I doubt if it is widely used. The point is that very similar systems might well be in use in computers. The "linear congruential" random number generator is by far and away the most popular generator in the computer world, and similar cipher systems (based on bits, not digits) might well be used with computers. In such a computer system, the correspondence between letters and bits is provided by one of the standard codes: Baudot, ASCII, or EBCDIC.

Let us now assume that this message is intercepted by a cryptanalyst. He does not know the starting random number x_0, nor the modulus, nor the multiplier, nor constant terms M, a, and b. What he does know (from the study of similar messages) is that the numbers are four digits long. Further, he suspects that the word "Pakistan" occurs in the messages. He uses the *probable word method* to recover the key digits, and mathematical analysis to reconstruct the generator. He tries to fit the word "Pakistan" in at the beginning of the message, gets *false* key digits, and hence the wrong generator. This wrong generator does not yield any intelligible text, so the cryptanalyst tries another place to fit "Pakistan" in. Place by place the analysis is followed, and time after time no intelligible text is produced. Finally, however, "Pakistan" is fitted into the correct place, and at last the *true* key digits are produced. The analysis is as follows:

The cipher text has been lined up with the digits for "Pakistan", and the probable word has been subtracted out, modulo 10:

Ciphertext:	24 66 87 47 17 45 26 96 84 51 60 etc.
Probable word:	16 01 11 09 19 20 01 14

Key:	18 65 76 48 08 25 25 82

By blocking off digits by fours from the beginning of the message, we get four consecutive four-digit numbers: 1865, 7648, 0825, 2582. The cryptanalyst tries to recover the entire random number generator from these data.

It is clear that the modulus M is at least as large as 7649 (and, by the rules of this cipher system, no greater than 10,000). Referring back to the equation defining the "linear congruential" system, we get

$$7648 \equiv 1865\,a + b \quad (\text{modulo } M) \tag{I}$$

$$825 \equiv 7648\,a + b \quad (\text{modulo } M) \tag{II}$$

$$2582 \equiv 825\,a + b \quad (\text{modulo } M) \tag{III}$$

Take equation (I) and subtract it from (II) and (III), to get

$$-6823 \equiv 5783\,a \quad (\text{modulo } M) \tag{IV}$$

$$-5066 \equiv 1040\,a \quad (\text{modulo } M) \tag{V}$$

Thus, b is eliminated from these equations. Now we try to eliminate a. We can find no common factor (other than 1 and -1) of the two numbers 5783 and -1040, so in order to eliminate a from (IV) and (V) we have to multiply (IV) by 1040 and (V) by 5783 and add the two together. Thus, we get

$$-36,392,598 \equiv 0 \quad (\text{modulo } M) \tag{VI}$$

This lets us say that M divides 36,392,598, and, if we list all the divisors of this large number, M will be found among them. So we must factorize the number $N = 36,392,598$. (This can be done automatically on a computer, but it is fun to do by hand.) First off, it ends in an even digit, so we can divide out 2:

$$N = 36,392,598 = 2 \cdot 18,196,299.$$

The sum of the digits is 45, so 3 divides N:

$$N = 2 \cdot 3 \cdot 6,065,433.$$

Again, 3 divides 6,065,433:

$$N = 2 \cdot 3 \cdot 3 \cdot 2,021,811,$$

and again:

$$N = 2 \cdot 3 \cdot 3 \cdot 3 \cdot 673,937.$$

Now we try trial divisors of primes higher than 2 and 3: 5, 7, 11 etc. We find 5 and 7 don't divide 673,937, but 11 does:

$$N = 2 \cdot 3^3 \cdot 11 \cdot 61,267.$$

We try 11 again, and all of the primes lower than the square root of 61,267, i.e., less than 247. We find that the lowest prime divisor of 61,267 is 197, which goes in 311 times. This last number is (by reference to a table of primes) seen to be a prime, and so we have

$$N = 2 \cdot 3^3 \cdot 11 \cdot 197 \cdot 311,$$

as the complete factorization of N. There are 64 possible divisors, but many are too big (i.e., larger than 10,000), and others are smaller than 7649.

Look at Figure 1, a table of size 8×8, showing all the possible divisors of N.

		1	2	3	$2 \cdot 3 = 6$	$3 \cdot 3 = 9$	$2 \cdot 3 \cdot 3 = 18$	$3 \cdot 3 \cdot 3 = 27$	$2 \cdot 3 \cdot 3 \cdot 3 = 54$
Values of A	1								
	11								
	197								
	311								
$11 \cdot 197 = 2,167$									
$11 \cdot 311 = 3,421$									
$197 \cdot 311 = 61,267$									
$11 \cdot 197 \cdot 311 = 673,937$									

(Values of B)

FIGURE 1.

A possible divisor is formed by picking a cell, and multiplying the numbers A and B standing at the ends of the row and column that meet at the cell in question. This product may be entered in the cell.

Before we begin, we see that we may rule out many entries in the last two rows in the table, because these products will be greater than 10,000.

We similarly rule out the ▨▨▨ cross-hatched regions ($A \cdot B$ is too big) and the ⸬⸬⸬ stippled regions ($A \cdot B$ is too small). In fact, there is

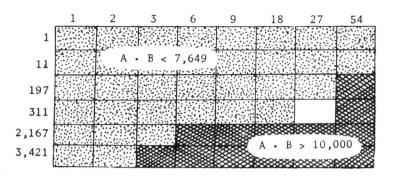

Figure 2.

only one divisor of N left (in the range 7649 through 10,000), and it is $27 \cdot 311 = 8,397$. This is thus the only candidate for M.

Referring back to the original generator, we see that this is indeed correct. We can now try to solve equation (IV) for a:

$$-6823 \equiv 5783\, a \quad \text{(modulo 8397)}$$

Without going through the calculation, we can check to see if this is in fact solvable. If 5,783 has no common factor with 8,397, there is a unique solution. Well, 3 doesn't divide 5,783, and neither does the prime 311, so they are in fact relatively prime, and thus a unique solution exists. [It can be found by application of Euclid's algorithm for finding the greatest common divisor of two numbers.]

Once a is found, the cryptanalyst can solve equation I for b:

$$b \equiv 7648 - 1865\, a \quad \text{(modulo 8397)}.$$

At this point, the cryptanalyst has recovered the generator, and he can crank out the next several numbers to decipher the words following "Pakistan." He finds, of course, "and Israel." This makes sense (linguistically, if not politically!) and the cryptanalyst knows he has the right key. Since $a = 4381$ is relatively prime to $M = 8397$, the random number generator may be "cranked" backwards to yield the previous parts of the keying sequence, and the whole message may be read.

This may all, of course, be done automatically on a computer. The computer will try a probable word in each of the possible places it could fit in the message, go through the calculations outlined above very rapidly, and then print out a portion of the resulting supposed plaintexts.

The cryptanalyst could quickly scan the list of trial decipherments and pick out the correct one. Of course, if such a method of encipherment were ever to be used, it would be based on much larger numbers: of 10 instead of four digits, and its decipherment would be a bit more difficult, especially at the factorization step. But this is nothing a good computer could not handle.

Thus, we've seen how *linear congruential* random number generators are unsuitable for cryptographic applications. The method presented above is applicable against any linear congruential generator, and is not affected in the least by whether or not the generator is judged highly random or not by *standard I* criteria mentioned at the beginning [of this article]. Moreover, the general idea of the analysis presented in this note may be carried over to other random number generators, including the "squaring the middle half" and "shift register sequence" generators, for instance. That is to say, cryptography has its own standards of randomness, which do not necessarily coincide with the more usual standards.

REFERENCE

1. Knuth, Donald E., *The Art of Computer Programming*, Vol. 2, Seminumerical Algorithms, Addison-Wesley, Reading, MA, 1969, pp. 1–99.

The Editors

Cipher Deavours is co-author of *Machine Cryptography and Modern Cryptanalysis* (Artech House, 1985) with Louis Kruh. Dr. Deavours is a founder and co-editor of *Cryptologia*, and is currently a professor of mathematics at Kean College of New Jersey. He received his Sc.M. and Sc.D. in applied mathematics from Brown University and the University of Virginia, respectively. Dr. Deavours lives in Montclair, NJ.

David Kahn is the author of *The Codebreakers*, *Hitler's Spies*, *Kahn on Codes*, and numerous articles on cryptology and military intelligence. Dr. Kahn is a founder and co-editor of *Cryptologia* and has taught military and political intelligence at Yale and Columbia. He received his Ph.D. in modern history from Oxford University and serves on the boards of the American Committee for the History of the Second World War and the International Association for Cryptologic Research. Kahn is Assistant Editor of "Viewpoints" at *Newsday*, the Long Island daily. He lives in Great Neck, NY, with his wife, Susanne, and their sons, Oliver and Michael.

Louis Kruh holds B.B.A., M.B.A., and J.D. degrees and is co-author of *Machine Cryptography and Modern Cryptanalysis* (Artech House, 1985) with Cipher Deavours. His interest in cryptology started as a teenager before WW II when he read Edgar Allan Poe's *The Gold Bug*. In addition to reviewing all literature related to cryptology for *Cryptologia* Mr. Kruh writes extensively on cipher equipment and historical events. He has one of the largest private collections of cryptologic related books, manuals, articles, cipher devices, and machines, and continually seeks additional memorabilia. Kruh is past president of the American Cryptogram Association and the New York Cipher Society. He lives in Merrick, NY, and is an advertising director for the New York Telephone Company.

Greg Mellen studied electrical engineering at Columbia University and graduated from Fordham University with a B.A. in classical languages. Mr. Mellen recently retired from Sperry UNIVAC (now UNISYS) after 30 years. His work with several communication systems, as well as early trials of machine translation, stimulated his interest in cryptography and cryptanalysis. Mellen also participated in the design of several large computers, terminal air traffic systems, and digitized speech systems. He holds a basic patent for multiprocessors.

Brian Winkel holds a Ph.D. in mathematics (algebra) and has work experience at the National Security Agency. His reading of David Kahn's book, *The Codebreakers*, rekindled an interest in cryptology. Dr. Winkel is a professor of mathematics at the Rose-Hulman Institute of Technology in Terre Haute, IN, where he regularly teaches seminars on cryptology. He has been the managing editor of *Cryptologia* since its inception and has very much appreciated the writing and editing efforts of his editorial colleagues, Messrs. Deavours, Kahn, Kruh, and Mellen.

The Artech House Communication and Electronic Defense Library

Principles of Secure Communication Systems by Don J. Torrieri

Introduction to Electronic Warfare by D. Curtis Schleher

Electronic Intelligence: The Analysis of Radar Signals by Richard G. Wiley

Electronic Intelligence: The Interception of Radar Signals by Richard G. Wiley

Signal Theory and Random Processes by Harry Urkowitz

Signal Theory and Processing by Frederic de Coulon

Digital Signal Processing by Murat Kunt

Analysis and Synthesis of Logic Systems by Daniel Mange

The Design of Automatic Control Systems by Olis Rubin

Advanced Mathematics for Practicing Engineers by Kurt Arbenz and Alfred Wohlhauser

Mathematical Methods of Information Transmission by Kurt Arbenz and Jean-Claude Martin

Codes for Error-Control and Synchronization by Djimitri Wiggert

Machine Cryptography and Modern Cryptanalysis by Cipher A. Deavours and Louis Kruh

Cryptology Yesterday, Today, and Tomorrow, Cipher A. Deavours et al., eds.

Microcomputer Tools for Communication Engineering by S.T. Li, J.C. Logan, J.W. Rockway, and D.W.S. Tam